NARRATIVE

OF THE

OPERATIONS AND RECENT DISCOVERIES

IN

EGYPT AND NUBIA.

LONDON:
PRINTED BY THOMAS DAVISON, WHITEFRIARS.

G. BELZONI.
Printed by C. Hullmandel. Drawn from life.

NARRATIVE

OF THE

OPERATIONS AND RECENT DISCOVERIES

WITHIN THE

PYRAMIDS, TEMPLES, TOMBS, AND EXCAVATIONS,

IN

EGYPT AND NUBIA;

AND OF A

JOURNEY TO THE COAST OF THE RED SEA, IN SEARCH OF
THE ANCIENT BERENICE;

AND ANOTHER TO

THE OASIS OF JUPITER AMMON.

BY G. BELZONI.

———

LONDON:

PREFACE.

As I made my discoveries alone, I have been anxious to write my book by myself, though in so doing, the reader will consider me, and with great propriety, guilty of temerity; but the public will perhaps gain in the fidelity of my narrative, what it loses in elegance. I am not an Englishman, but I prefer that my readers should receive from myself, as well as I am able to describe them, an account of my proceedings in Egypt, in Nubia, on the coast of the Red Sea, and in the Oasis; rather than run the risk of having my meaning misrepresented by another. If I am intelligible, it is all that I can expect. I shall state nothing but the plain matters of fact, as they occurred to me in these countries, in 1815-16-17-18 and 19. A description of the means I took in making my researches, the difficulties I had to encounter, and how I overcame them, will give a tolerably correct idea of the manners and customs of the people I had to deal with. Perhaps I have spoken too much of the obstacles thrown in my way, by the jealousy and intriguing spirit of my adversaries, without considering that the public will care little about my private quarrels, which to me, of course, appeared of the greatest consequence on the spot, in these countries. But I hope that a little indulgence may be allowed to my mortified feelings, particularly when I reflect that it was through them that I was compelled to leave Egypt before I had completed my plans.

I must apologise also for the few humble observations I have ventured to give on some historical points; but I had become so familiar with the sight of temples, tombs, and pyramids, that I could not help forming some speculation on their origin and construction. The scholar and learned traveller will smile at my presumption, but do they always agree themselves in their opinions on matters of this sort, or even on those of much less difficulty? Much has been written on Egypt and Nubia by the travellers of the last century, by Denon, and the French sçavans, whose general account of these countries has scarcely left any thing unnoticed; and by Mr. Hamilton, to the accuracy of the latter of whom I can bear the most ample testimony. But what can I say of the late Sheik Burckhardt, who was so well acquainted with the language and manners of these people, that none of them suspected him to be an European? His account of the tribes in these countries is so minutely correct, that little or nothing remains for observation in modern Egypt and Nubia.

I have, however, one more remark to make on myself, which I am afraid the reader will think very vain: it is this, that no traveller had ever such opportunities of studying the customs of the natives as were afforded to me, for none had ever to deal with them in so peculiar a manner. My constant occupation was searching after antiquities, and this led me in the various transactions I had with them, to observe the real character of the Turks, Arabs, Nubians, Bedoweens, and Ababdy tribes. Thus I was very differently circumstanced from a common traveller, who goes merely to make his remarks on the country and its antiquities, instead of having to persuade these ignorant and superstitious people to undertake a hard task, in labours, with which they were previously totally unacquainted.

My native place is the city of Padua: I am of a Roman family, which had resided there for many years. The state and troubles of Italy in 1800, which are too well known to require any comment from me, compelled me to leave it, and from that time I have visited different parts of Europe, and suffered many vicissitudes. The greater part of my younger days I passed in Rome, the former abode of my ancestors, where I was preparing myself to become a monk; but the sudden entry of the French army into that city altered the course of my education, and being destined to travel, I have been a wanderer ever since. My family supplied me occasionally with remittances; but as they were not rich, I did not choose to be a burthen to them, and contrived to live on my own industry, and the little knowledge I had acquired in various branches. I turned my chief attention to hydraulics, a science that I had learned in Rome, which I found much to my advantage, and which was ultimately the very cause of my going to Egypt. For I had good information, that a hydraulic machine would be of great service in that country, to irrigate the fields, which want water only, to make them produce at any time of the year. But I am rather anticipating. In 1803 I arrived in England, soon after which I married, and, after residing in it nine years, I formed the resolution of going to the south of Europe. Taking Mrs. Belzoni with me, I visited Portugal, Spain, and Malta, from which latter place we embarked for Egypt, where we remained from 1815 to 1819. Here I had the good fortune to be the discoverer of many remains of antiquity of that primitive nation. I succeeded in opening one of the two famous Pyramids of Ghizeh, as well as several of the tombs of the Kings at Thebes. Among the latter, that which has been pronounced by one of the most distinguished scholars of the age to be the tomb of Psammuthis, is at this moment the principal, the most perfect and splendid monument in that country. The celebrated bust of young Memnon, which I brought from Thebes, is now in the British Museum; and the alabaster sarcophagus, found in the tombs of the kings, is on its way to England.

Near the second cataract of the Nile, I opened the temple of Ybsambul; then made a journey to the coast of the Red Sea, to the city of Berenice, and afterwards an excursion in the western Elloah, or Oasis. I now embarked for Europe, and after an absence of twenty years, returned to my native land, and to the bosom of my family; from whence I proceeded to England.

On my arrival in Europe, I found so many erroneous accounts had been given to the public of my operations and discoveries in Egypt, that it appeared to be my duty to publish a plain statement of facts; and should any one call its correctness in question, I hope they will do it openly, that I may be able to prove the truth of my assertions.

CONTENTS.

FIRST JOURNEY.

Arrive at Alexandria, 1.
Description of the plague, 2.
Departure for and arrival at Cairo, 3.
Visit the Pyramids—view from the top, 4.
Excursion to the Pyramid of Dajior—return to Cairo, 5.
Become acquainted with Mr. Burckhardt, 6.
Wounded by a Turk on horseback—observations on the Moors from Mecca during my confinement, 7.
Presented to the Bashaw—rebellion of part of his army, 8.
Danger in proceeding to Cairo—confined to the house in consequence of the revolution—description of it, 11.
Commenced hydraulic operations, 12.
Soubra, chief residence of the Bashaw, 13.
His manner of living, 14.
He is electrified—description of Zulfur Carcaja, governor of Soubra, 16.
His mode of curing diseases—marriage ceremonies and festivals of the Arabs in Soubra, 17.
Arabian play and farce, 19.
Shot at by a soldier, 20.
A young lady shot by a soldier, 21.
Complete the water machine, 22.
The English consul arrives in Cairo, 22.
Decision of the Bashaw on the hydraulic machine—his frolic with it—the Irish lad's thigh broke in consequence, 23.
Decided on ascending the Nile, 24.
Undertaking to remove the colossal bust, and received instruction, 26.
Left Boolak for Thebes—saw Hermopolis—arrived at Monfaluth, 29.
Siout, description of it, 31.
Saw Gow—a curious interview with the Cacheff of Acmin, 32.
Arrival at and description of Dendera, 33.
Arrival at Kenneh—arrival at and description of Thebes, 37.
Begin operations for removing the bust of young Memnon, 40.
First interview with the Cacheff of Erments—his objection against the removal, 41.
Farther difficulties encountered, 42.
Begin the operation of removing it, 43.
Removed from its original place and put upon a car, 44.
Removed out of the ruins of the Memnonium—delay in consequence of indisposition—works resumed, 45.
The Fellahs prevented from working by order of the Cacheff, 46.

b 2

CONTENTS.

Insolence and duplicity of the Caimakan, 47.

Account of a Turkish dinner in Ramadan time, 48.

Obtain a firman and again proceed in the works, 49.

Arrival of the great Colossus on the banks of the Nile, 50.

First visit to a Mummy Cave, 51.

Preparations for departing to the first Cataract of the Nile, 54.

Visit to Khalil Bey at Esné, 55.

Arrival at and description of the ruins of Edfu, 56.

Distant view of Assouan—tradition relating to an ancient King, 59.

Arrive at Assouan, or first Cataract, 60.

Description of the Aga of Assouan—description of the island of Elephantine, 61.

Difficulties in obtaining a boat to proceed to the second Cataract, 63.

Set off for the isle of Philœ, 65.

Continue the voyage—alarmed by the natives, 66. Continuation of the voyage, and arrival at El Kalabshé, 67.

Description of it, 68. Arrive at Garba Dandour—proceed to Garba Merieh—arrival at Garba Gyrshé, and description of it, 71.

Arrival at and description of Dakke—Greek inscription, 72.

Arrive at Meharraka, or Offelina—Greek inscription—curious figures on an ancient wall, 73.

Arrival at and description of Seboua—arrival at and account of Korosko, 74.

Arrival at Deir—interview with the Hassan Cacheff, 75.

Leave Deir—arrive at Ibrim, 77.

Continuation of the voyage, and description of the country, 78.

Arrive at and description of Faras, and the temple of Ybsambul, 79.

Arrival at the village of Ybsambul—interview with the Davoud Cacheff—description of the natives, 81.

First introduce money into the country, 83.

Further description of the natives, 84.

Proceed towards the second Cataract, 85.

Arrive at Wady Halfa, 86.

Excursion by land on camels up the Cataract—view of it—visit to the isle of Mainarty, 87.

Frighten away the natives, 88.

Ascend the Nile against the eddies and current—visit the Rock of Apsir, 89.

View of the Cataract from it—go on to the island of Gulgé, 90.

Foundation of a Greek church on the island—return to Mainarty—leave it and descend the Nile—arrive at Iskus, 91.

Interview with the Osseyn Cacheff, 92.

Leave Iskus—return to the village of Ybsambul—description of a small temple opposite it—endeavour to persuade the natives to open the temple, 93.

Begin operations at the temple, 94.

Difficulties encountered from the natives, 95.

Embarrassment of the Cacheff in fixing the price of a sheep, 97.

He drinks wine for the first time, 98.

The natives come to work in great numbers—their ideas on the treasure to be found, 99.

Attempt to rob the boat, 100.

Causes for quitting the works at the temple, and leave Ybsambul, 101.

CONTENTS.

Hailed and received letters sent by a soldier from Deraou, 102.

Proceed to Cardassy—return to the first Cataract—take possession of a small obelisk and various other blocks of stone in the island of Philœ, 103.

Return to Assouan — visit the granite quarries in the mountains, 105.

Discover a Latin inscription on a column in the quarry—the little knowledge they have of diamonds, 106.

Prepare to depart, 107.

Observation on the manners of the Arabs, 108.

Leave Assouan and arrive at Luxor—proceedings taken to obtain a boat to convey the bust of Memnon to Alexandria, 109.

Works recommenced in Carnak, 111.

Secure a boat—beginning of discoveries, 112.

Count de Forbin, 114.

Description of the place where I first discovered the lion-headed statues, 115.

Further proceedings in Carnak, 116.

Meet Khalil Bey on the Nile, 117.

Conversazione with the Bey and his court, 118.

Account of a dinner with him, 119.

Description of the sepulchres in Gournou and Medinet Aboo, 120.

First excursion in the valley of Beban el Malook—first discover the tomb of a king, 123.

Description of the mountains round the valley—water descends from the desert, 124.

Further difficulties in obtaining a boat, 125.

Curious incident by which the boat was obtained, 126.

Trial respecting the boat, and decision in favour of the author, 129.

Works recommenced in Gournou—embark the colossal bust of Memnon, 131.

Preparations for departing to Cairo—Ophthalmia—leave Thebes for Cairo, 133.

Arrival in Cairo—leave Cairo for Alexandria, 134.

Arrive in Rosetta—Bogase—and in Alexandria—landed and lodged the colossal head in the Bashaw's magazine ready to be embarked for England—farther proposal to ascend the Nile, 135.

Return to Cairo—account of Captain Cabillia's operations at the Pyramids, 136.

SECOND JOURNEY.

Left Cairo for Thebes, 141.

Stopped at Tabeen and Boorumbol, 142.

Description of an Arabian dance—arrival at Minieh, 143.

Arrival at Eshmounein, and sudden departure for Luxor, 144.

A forced march to Thebes, 145.

Account of Bedoween horsemen and their tents, 146.

Disagreeable consequences occasioned by the interpreter omitting to send a letter to the Defterdar Bey, 148.

CONTENTS.

Another interview with the Cacheff of Erments—miracles performed by a Santon, 150.
Further proceedings in Luxor, 151.
Description of the temple of Carnak, 152.
Further proceedings in Thebes, 154.
Description of the natives, and tombs of Gournou, 155.
Observations on the mode of discovery of the tombs, 158.
Further account of the natives—manner of the Fellahs making their researches, 159.
Purchase two metal vases from a chief of the Fellahs, 160.
Further operations and discovery of lion-headed sphinxes in Carnak, 162.
Iron sickle discovered under one of the sphinxes, 163.
Further knowledge acquired on the discovery of tombs—Herodotus's description of mummies, 165.
Observations on the various classes and descriptions of mummies, 167.
Of animal mummies, 168.
Of mummy priests, 170.
Mummies discovered in their original position, 171.
Farther account of mummies, 172.
Their decorations—linen manufactures—enamelling, gilding and other arts, 173.
Art of painting, 174.
Sculpture, 175.
Architecture, and knowledge of arches with a key-stone, 176.
Sculpture, 179.
Uncover the foundation of a temple in the waste of Gournou—curious manner in discovering a tomb, 180.
Description of a night's lodging in the tomb, 181.
Happiness of the natives of Gournou, 182.
Their preparations for a wedding, 183.
Proceedings in Carnak—discovery of a colossal head—accumulate various articles, 184.
Arrival of the Defterdar Bey at Gamola, and his orders—receive information from the Sheik of Gournou, 185.
Present a letter from the Bashaw to the Defterdar Bey, 186.
The Bey visits Thebes, 187.
He visits Medinet Aboo, 188.
His barbarous conduct towards the Sheik of Gournou, 189.
He ascends the Nile, and returns to Thebes, 191.
Interview with the Bey on his return from Deraou, 192.
Arrival of two of the fathers of the Propaganda at Thebes, 192.
Description of a whirlwind, 195.
Mirage, 196.
Locusts—deception of Defterdar Bey in issuing a firman for men to work, 197.
Preparations for and departure to the island of Philœ—further account of its monuments, 199.
Preparations for Ybsambul—arrival of Captains Irby and Mangles, 202.
Celebration of the birth-day of his Majesty George III.—leave Philœ, and arrive at Ybsambul, 203.
Proceed to the second Cataract—combination of the natives and boatmen to extort money, 204.
Return to Ybsambul—arrival of the Cacheffs, Daoud and Khalil—displeasure of Khalil—preparations for opening the temple, 205.
Commence opening the temple, 206.

CONTENTS.

Works stopped by the Ramadan—resolve to work ourselves, 207.
Visits from strange Cacheffs, said to be from Ibrim, 208.
Their conduct, 209.
Works continued—entry into the temple—description of the interior, 211.
Description of the exterior, 213.
Leave Ybsambul, 214.
Arrive at Tomas—return to Deir, 215.
Arrive at Almeida—return to Kalabshe—opposition of the natives to our entering the temple, 216.
Arrival at Hindau, 217.
Arrival at Debod, and return to Philœ—descend the cataract to Assouan—visit the granite quarries and the Latin inscription, 218.
Departure from Assouan—pass Edfu—landed at Elethias—description of it, 219.
Return to Luxor, 220.
Return to Erments to obtain a firman for labourers to work at Gournou—the Cacheff is displaced by the Bey, 221.
Commence searching for the kings' tombs, 222.
Description of the valley of Beban el Malook, 224.
Number and description of the tombs, 225.
Further discovery of tombs, 227.
Arrival of travellers, 228.
Their visit to a newly discovered tomb, 229.
Recommence operations, and point out the spot where the great tomb is found, 230.
Further proceedings, 231.
Enter the tomb, 232.
Further entrance, and description of its various apartments, 234.
Discovery of the sarcophagus of alabaster, 236.

Description of the entrance into the tomb of Psammuthis, 237.
Description of the various representations in the tomb, and figures in sculpture on the walls, 238.
Painting—method taken for procuring a *fac simile* of the tomb, 239.
Description of the various figures, 240.
Dr. Young's discovery of the name of the tomb, 242.
Continuation of the description of the figures, 243.
Mahomet Aga visits the tomb, 246.
Unfortunate fate of the stones prepared to be taken from the isle of Philœ, 248.
Arrival of a noble family and the consul at Thebes—set off for and arrive at Boolak, 250.
Meet with Count de Forbin, 251.
Despatches arrive from India, 252.
Farther account of Count de Forbin, 253.
Transmit to Europe, by the Count, an account of his proceedings, 254.
Visit the Pyramids—reflection on the possibility of penetrating that of Cephrenes, and motive which induced the author to undertake it, 255.
Difficulties encountered, 256.
Observations on the Pyramids, 257.
Mode of obtaining permission for the operation, 258.
Caution observed not to let the proceedings be known, 259.
Begin the undertaking, 260.
Foundation of a large temple discovered, 261.
Tedious operations without any prospect of success—first discovery of an entrance, 262.
Disappointment, and determination still to persevere, 265.

Calculation by which the true entrance was discovered, 266.

Again resume the work—Arrival of Chevalier Frediani, 267.

Discovery of the blocks of granite belonging to the true entrance—discovery of the true entrance, 268.

Difficulties in entering—description of the portcullis, 270.

Description of the interior—the sarcophagus found in the great chamber, 271.

Arabic inscription observed on the wall of the chamber—translation of it, 272.

Bones found in the sarcophagus—place from whence the stones have been taken for building the Pyramids, 275.

Accounts of the Pyramids, 276.

The supposed purpose for which they were erected, 277.

Their dimensions, 278.

Opinion on there not being hieroglyphics on the Pyramids, 279.

Their coating—on their being surrounded by the Nile—operation on the third Pyramid, 280.

Preparations for a third journey to Thebes, 282.

Set off for Thebes, 283.

THIRD JOURNEY.

Visit the Defterdar Bey of Siout—his amusements in military exercise and observations on fire-arms, 283.

Mode of trying capital crimes, 284.

The Bey's knowledge on architecture, 286.

Proceed towards Thebes—visit my old friend Soliman, Cacheff of Erments, at Tacta, 288.

Eclipse of the sun—arrival and proceedings at Thebes, 289.

Discover a fine colossal statue—opinion on the right site of the temple of Memnon, 291.

Hints to travellers where to dig for antiquities, 292.

Take models of the tombs in wax, 294.

The author's motives for undertaking a journey to the Red Sea, 295.

Preparations for departure, 296.

JOURNEY TO THE RED SEA.

Set sail—extraordinary inundation of the Nile, 299.

Arrive at Esne, and visit Ibrahim Bey—arrive at the island of Hovassee, 302.

Preparations for entering the desert, 303.

Set off for the desert towards the Red Sea—arrive at the first well in the desert, 304.

Approach towards Wady el Meeah—its temple, 305.

Continuation of journey, 307.

Observe several hills of granite, 308.

Description of the Ababdy tribes, 309.

Continuation of the journey—sight of the Red Sea, 313.

CONTENTS.   xvii

Sight of the Zubara or Emerald Mountains—description of the miners, 314.
And of the mines, 315.
Preparations for journey to Sakiet, 316.
Description of the road towards it—searches for Sakiet in consequence of Mr. Caliud's erroneous information, 317.
View the Red Sea from the top of a mountain, 321.
Continue our journey towards the Red Sea, 323.
Arrival at the Red Sea, 324.
Description of the coast, 325.
Correctness of Mr. Bruce's account of that coast—sulphur mines, 326.
Fishermen—their mode of fishing, 327.
Island of Gambe—its situation with the Wady el Gemal, 328.
Sulphur mines—effects of the south-east wind—arrive at Cape Golahen, or Lept Estrama, 329.
Arrive at the ruins of an ancient town—its situation, bay and harbour, 330.
Dimensions of the town, 331.
Farther account of the town and lands round it—proved to be the Berenice described by D'Anville, 332.
Its supposed ancient population, &c. 334.
Left Berenice on return to the Nile—arrived at the first well, 335.
Arrive at Haboo Grey, station of the ancient caravan passing to and from Berenice, Coptos, and Amusue—a spring of running water, 336.
Arrive at Sakiet—returned to the Red Sea—observations on the coast, 337.
Return to Sakiet, 338.
Greek inscription found there, 339.
Arrive at Kafafeet, another caravan station—arrive at Habookroog—description of a desert, 341.
Arrive at Hamesh—arrive at Samout, another caravan station—arrive at Dangos, 344.
Returned to Wady el Meeah—return to the Nile—interview with the Sheik of the Ababdy, 345.
Voyage from Elethias to Gournou, 346.

ACCOUNT OF THE TAKING THE OBELISK FROM THE ISLAND OF PHILŒ TO ALEXANDRIA.

Arrival of various persons in Thebes, 347.
Account of their proceedings, 348.
Set off for the first Cataract—arrive at Elethias and Edfu, 351.
Account of Silsili, 352.
Arrive at Assouan, 353.
Proceedings of the agents of Mr. Drouetti at Philœ, 355.
Commencement of operations for removing the obelisk—difficulties encountered, 356.
It falls into the Nile, 357.
Preparations for taking it out—description of the operation, 358.
Again embarked—preparations for launching it down the Cataract—observations on the various colours of the cut granite, 360.
Launch the obelisk, 361.
Arrive at Assouan, and voyage to Thebes, 363.

Account of a stranger, 364.
Visit Carnak, 365.
Assaulted by a band of Arabs, led on by two Piedmontese in Mr. Drouetti's employ, 366.
Preparations for returning to Europe, 370.
Reflections on the climate under the tropic of Cancer on the Nile, 371.
Left Thebes—arrive at Benisouef, and met with Mr. Pearce, the Abyssinian traveller, 373.
Difficulties and delay in embarking for Europe, 375.
Form a resolution of making a journey into the Oasis, 376.

JOURNEY TO THE OASIS OF AMMON.

Arrive at Benisouef—entrance into the Faioum, 377.
Description of the first pyramid of bricks, 378.
Visit to the second pyramid of bricks—arrive at Medinet el Faioum—set off for the lake Mœris, 379.
Arrive at the lake—description of the fishermen and their boat—embark for the town of Haron, 380.
Reflections on the shore, 381.
Visit to and description of the town and temple of Haron, 382.
Surprised by a hyæna—further account of the town, 383.
Opinion on the Labyrinth—re-embarked for the north side of the lake, 384.
Visit and description of the ancient town of Denay, the ancient Bacchus, 385.
Visit the island of El Hear, and return to the east of the lake—make a tour in various places in the neighbourhood—reflection and opinion on the situation of the Labyrinth, 387.
Account of Fedmin el Kunois, 389.
Arrive at the ruins of ancient Arsinoe, 390.
Description of it—preparations for a journey into the Oasis, 391.
Visit Khalil Bey at Benisouef, 393.
Obtain a guide for the desert, 394.
Residence at the Bedoweens' camp, 395.
Description of it, 396.
Set off for the desert—arrive at El Kharah—continue the journey, 397.
Arrive at Rejen el Cassar—proceed on, and discover various tumuli, 398.
Opinion on them, 399.
Arrive at Bahar Bela Me, 401.
Arrive in sight of the Elloah—description of it, 402.
Approach the village of Zaboo—introduction to the natives, 404.
Their reception, 405.
Excursion round the country in search of antiquities, 408.
Curious mineral fountain—their worship—mode of living, 410.
Information received respecting the village of El Cassar, 411.
Interview with the great Sheiks of El Cassar, 412.
Quit Zaboo for El Cassar—prevented from entering the village, 415.

CONTENTS.

Enter the village, 416.
Visit the ruins at El Cassar, 418.
Go to see the tombs, and the noted fountain mentioned by Herodotus, 421.
Set off for El Haix, 424.
Return to El Cassar, 429.
Return to Zaboo, 430.
Proceeding there, 431.
Left the Oasis for Moele, 432.
Arrival at that place—description of it—continuation of the journey towards the Nile—arrival at Benisouef, 433.
Return to Cairo—leave Cairo—return to Rosetta—proceeding and conclusion of the action carried on against the two Piedmontese in Mr. Drouetti's service, 434.
Return to Europe, 437.

ERRATA.

Page 24, line 21, *for* Memnion, *read* Memnonium.
— 62, line 1, *for* El Shal, *read* El Shag.
— 102, line 32, *for* Todfa, *read* Taffa.
— 103, line 20, *for* large, *read* small.
— 168, line 15, referrence omitted to Plate 44.
— 208, line 28, *for* opposite Deir, we found that the Cacheffs were not there but at Tomas, *read* we found that the Cacheffs were not there, but at Tomas opposite Deir.
— 338, line 20, *for* six hours, *read* twelve.
— 389, line 29, *for* Fedmin el Hanaiser, *read* Fedmin el Kunois.

RESEARCHES AND OPERATIONS

IN

EGYPT, NUBIA, &c.

FIRST JOURNEY.

We sailed from Malta on the 19th of May, 1815, and arrived at Alexandria on the 9th of June following. Mrs. Belzoni, myself, and James Curtain, a lad, whom I brought with me from Ireland, formed our party. The principal cause of my going to Egypt was the project of constructing hydraulic machines, to irrigate the fields, by a system much easier and more economical than what is in use in that country. On entering the harbour of Alexandria, the pilot informed us, that the plague was in the town. To a European, who had never been in that country, this was alarming intelligence. As I wished to have some information concerning the state of the disease, we did not land till the next day, when two European gentlemen came alongside in a boat, and informed us, that it was rapidly diminishing. We accordingly landed, but with much caution, as, in our way to the French Occale, where we were to perform quarantine, we had to pass through the town. Fortunately, St. John's day, which is the 24th of June, was not far off; and on that day the plague is supposed to cease. Some superstitious persons attribute this to the power of the saint himself; but it is too well known, that extreme heat checks the plague in the same manner as the cold season;

B

and I observed myself, that when the heat of summer was not so great as usual, the plague lasted longer; while, on the other hand, when the cold season lasted longer, the plague came later.

The necessity of putting ourselves into a voluntary prison; the caution we were obliged to take, not to touch any person, or suffer any one to touch us; the strict order to be observed in receiving any thing that came from out of doors; and the continual perfumes with which we were regaled, to prevent the plague, as they say, were extremely strange to a novice in the customs of the country. We were confined to our apartment, and for three or four days no one came near us. We were really sick, but I took the caution not to let it be known; for the plague is so dreadful a scourge, and operates so powerfully on human fears and human prejudices, that, during its prevalence, if a man be ill, he must be ill of the plague, and if he die, he must have died of the plague: no inquiry is made, no examination takes place. Accordingly, had the people of the Occale come to the knowledge of our being indisposed, and particularly that we vomited, they would have concluded, though it was merely the effect of a new climate, that we had caught the pestilence in passing through the town; and the whole Occale would have been struck with terror, thinking the enemy was within the gate.

The Occale is an enclosure of several houses, so disposed as to form a square. There is no entrance to the area of the square but by the great gate, leading to a common staircase, above which a gallery takes you to every house. In plague time, the people of these habitations must communicate with each other without touching: no provision can enter without being passed through water, nor must bread be touched whilst warm. The disease is so easily caught, that a piece of thread blown by the wind is quite sufficient to infect the whole country. Had it been known that we were ill, no one would have come near us, except the Arabs, who go in case of sickness indiscriminately to every one; and are thus likely to spread the plague, by giving it to those who had it not. Many die the victims of neglect, merely because every disease is taken for the plague: others are victims of a different kind, of the atrocious, interested views of their relatives, who, profiting by their death, may take what advantage they please, even by poison, as no investigation takes place in any instance. "He died of the plague," is the general cry, whatever may be the disease; and as several hundreds perish daily, they are all carried away without distinction.

After the 24th June, called the great St. John, the plague nearly ceased; and as my principal view was to reach Cairo, we hired a boat, in company with Mr. Turner, an English gentleman, who was going up the Nile. We sailed on the 1st of July, but, owing to contrary winds, were brought back the same evening. The next day we re-embarked, and were then obliged to land at Aboukir, in consequence of high winds. We visited the place, where many a brave fellow had fallen a sacrifice to the war, and to the glory of his country. Human bones were scattered here and there.

Continuing our voyage the same day, we entered the mouth of the Nile, and landed at Rosetta; four days more brought us to Boolak, within a mile of Cairo. Though our eyes began to be accustomed to the sight of the Arabs in Alexandria, the bustling scene here was still more striking. The majestic appearance of Turkish soldiers in various costumes, without regularity or discipline, Arabs of many tribes, boats, canjeas, camels, horses, and asses, all in motion, presented a striking picture. I landed, and went immediately to Cairo; and as the holy fathers of the convent of Terrasanta could not receive women within their walls, we were accommodated in an old house in Boolak, belonging to Mr. Baghos, to whom I was recommended. He was the principal interpreter of Mahomed Ali, and director of all foreign affairs: a man of great acuteness of understanding, and so well disposed towards strangers, particularly Europeans, that it was soon arranged, that on such a day I was to be presented to his highness the Bashaw, to make my proposal. The house we inhabited was so old and out of repair, that I expected every moment it would fall on our heads; all the windows were shut up with broken wooden rails; the staircase was in so wretched a condition, that scarcely a step was left entire; the door was fastened simply by a pole placed against it, having neither lock nor any thing else to secure the entrance. There were many rooms in it, but the ceiling in all of them was in a most threatening state. The whole furniture consisted of a single mat in one of the best rooms, which we considered as our drawing-room. We had mattresses and linen with us, otherwise we must have adopted the Arab method of sleeping: as no chairs are to be had in this country, we sat on the ground; a box and a trunk served as a table: fortunately, we had a few plates, as well as knives and forks, which we had provided to use in the boat; and James, our Irish lad, bought us a set of culinary utensils, of pottery. Such were our accommodations.

Though my principal object was not antiquities at that time, I could not restrain myself from going to see the wonder of the world, the pyramids. I took an opportunity of going with Mr. Turner, who obtained an escort of soldiers from the Bashaw, to accompany us. We went there to sleep, that we might ascend the first pyramid early enough in the morning, to see the rising of the sun; and accordingly we were on the top of it long before the dawn of day. The scene here is majestic and grand, far beyond description: a mist over the plains of Egypt formed a veil, which ascended and vanished gradually as the sun rose and unveiled to the view that beautiful land, once the site of Memphis. The distant view of the smaller pyramids on the south marked the extension of that vast capital; while the solemn, endless spectacle of the desert on the west inspired us with reverence for the all-powerful Creator. The fertile lands on the north, with the serpentine course of the Nile, descending towards the sea; the rich appearance of Cairo, and its numerous minarets, at the foot of the Mokatam mountain on the east; the beautiful plain which extends from the pyramids to that city; the Nile, which flows magnificently through the centre of the sacred valley, and the thick groves of palm trees under our eyes; all together formed a scene, of which very imperfect ideas can be given by the most elaborate description. We descended to admire at some distance the astonishing pile that stood before us, composed of such an accumulation of enormous blocks of stones, that I was at a loss to conjecture how they could be brought thither; and presently we entered the pyramid: but I must reserve for some other time the more minute account of this wonderful work. We went round the second pyramid, examined several of these mausoleums, and returned to Cairo with the satisfaction of having seen a wonder, which I had long desired, but never supposed I should have the happiness to behold.

A few days after we made a party of Europeans, to go as far as Sacara by water, and after visiting the pyramids of that place, the party returned to Cairo, except Mr. Turner and myself, who went to see the pyramids of Dajior. These are considerably smaller than the large ones, I believe in the proportion of about one to six. One of them is of a different form, as it has a curve in the angles, which brings it to a perpendicular near the ground. This, and those at Sacara, which appear like hanging galleries, differ from the generality in point of shape; but the two of Dajior are in better preservation than any of the rest. I observed also near Sacara and Betracina, which I believe to be the central part of Memphis, the remains of other pyramids, which, by their dilapidated state, induced me to suppose, that they are of an earlier date than any of the rest. At this time I had no opportunity of visiting the pits of the embalmed mummies, and birds; but a Fellah brought us one of the earthen vases that contained a bird, which I believed to be a hawk by the shape of the bones. The vase was so perfect, that we laughed at the Arab for his attempting to impose on us. Seeing that he could not sell his piece of antiquity, and that he was laughed at besides, he broke the vase before us, to show what connoisseurs we were of antiques. We overshot the mark this time; for the caution that had been given us, never to credit what an Arab says, made us disbelieve the truth. On our returning towards the Nile, we passed by the broken pyramid of sun-baked bricks; and it appeared to me, on examining it afterwards, that it did not decay gradually, like the other pyramids, but by large masses of the bricks separating at a time from the rest.

On our arrival at the Nile it was quite night, and we had to pass several villages to come to a place where we could embark for old Cairo. Our road was through a cluster of palm trees, which by moonlight had a most solemn effect. Some of the Arabs were dancing to the usual tunes on the tambourines; and, forgetting perhaps the slavish condition in which they are held by the Turks, were happy for a while. We took a small boat, and arrived in old Cairo before day. Two days after I was to be presented to the Bashaw on the subject of my hydraulic project; and accordingly I went to the house of Mr. Baghos, where I first became acquainted with the late Mr. Burckhardt. This acquaintance was a fortunate circumstance for me, as the various and important information I acquired from him proved to be of the greatest service to me in that country, and I shall ever remember it with the deepest gratitude. Going to the citadel with Mr. Baghos, we had to pass through several of the principal streets, which are always crowded with people, and for this reason a stranger supposes the capital to be very populous; but except these streets and the bazars, the rest of the town is quite deserted, and a great number of falling houses and much rubbish are to be seen every where. We were mounted on our asses, the most convenient and only mode of travelling for Franks in that city. We met a soldier on horseback, who, when he came near, gave me such a blow with his staff upon my right leg, that I thought he had cut it in two. The staves of the Turks, which are like shovels, cut very sharp; and one of the corners, catching the calf of my leg, tore off a piece of flesh in a triangular form, two inches broad, and pretty deep. After this he swore two or three oaths at me, and went on as if nothing had happened. The blood ran out copiously; and, instead of seeing the Bashaw, I was taken to the convent of Terasanta, as the nearest Christian place I could go to. It is to be remarked, that, at this time, there was a great discontent among the soldiers against the Bashaw, for having given orders, that they should learn the European military evolutions; and, as I was in a Frank's dress, I suppose the fellow paid me for what he had learned of European fighting. From the convent I was taken home to my house in Boolak, where I remained under cure for thirty days, before I could stand on my legs.

During my confinement in this house, I had an opportunity of observing at some distance the manners of the Arabs, who passed under our window. Our house stood in a good situation, where we could observe all the landing from the boats that came from Alexandria and Rosetta. All the goods which went or came passed our residence; and the caravans of the Moors from Mecca halted for several days in this place. It was a strange sight for us, to observe these people in their tents, living in separate families, while their chief occupation was sitting on the ground, smoking, singing, and saying prayers, which I observed lasted sometimes three or four hours, besides the ceremonial prayers, repeated standing and kneeling. I did not make any minute observations, for, as I have said, my first occupation was with a different view; nor did I expect at that period, that I should ever have any thing to do with these people, as a traveller.

When I recovered, I was presented to Mahomet Ali Bashaw, who received me very civilly. Seeing that I walked lamely, and being told the cause, he said, such accidents could not be avoided where there were troops. I made an arrangement with him, and undertook to erect a machine, which would raise as much water with one ox, as the machines of the country with four. He was much pleased with my proposal, as it would save the labour and expense of many thousands of oxen in the country; a matter of importance, since these animals are scarcely of any other use than working; for, though they are in pretty good condition, they are seldom killed for food, the Turks eating mutton, and the Arabs buffalo's flesh, when they can afford it. The Bashaw was just returned from Arabia, where he had conquered some of the Wahaby tribes, and delivered the holy cities of Mecca and Medina from the Infidels. He himself conducted the war till lately, when his son Ibrahim Bashaw conquered some of the great chiefs, who were taken prisoners, and sent to Constantinople, where they were executed. Notwithstanding this, I am of opinion, that Mecca will be to the Turks, what Jerusalem is to the Christians; for, unless a strong army be kept there, the croisades of Mahomet Ali will have no better effect, than that of our Godfrey of Bouillon.

During the time that I was engaged in preparing my hydraulic machine, one morning I went on the road towards Cairo, and, to my surprise, found a perfect silence, instead of the continual confusion of noise and bustle of every description. The boatmen were getting their boats ready, as if to set off immediately. No camels appeared to carry water to Cairo; no ass-drivers were seen; no shops open; and no person in the streets. I could not conceive what was the reason of this singularity, nor could I inquire of any one, as no person was in the way; but, being Friday, I concluded it might be some particular holiday with the Mahommedans. I went on, and still I met no one. The distance from Boolak to Cairo is about a mile, through an open country; and midway is a bridge, near which I found a group of soldiers. I continued my walk without noticing them; one of them, however, levelled a gun at me, and all the rest laughed at the idea of frightening a Frank.

I passed on till I entered Cairo. When I reached the Franks' quarter, both gates were shut; but through the small door I observd a Frank, engaged like myself in the act of peeping, and who proved to be Mr. Bocty, the Swedish consul-general, who was surprised to see me. I could not imagine what all this meant. At first I concluded, that a violent plague had broken out, and that every one kept his house: but the Mahommedans do not seclude themselves on such occasions; so I was at a great loss what inference to draw. Mr. Bocty anxiously inquired of me how I happened to be there, whence I came, and what I had seen on the road; and he was not a little surprised, when I told him, that I came from Boolak, and did not see any thing particular on the way. I had not been at the door long, before we heard a great noise in some of the streets, and a volley of musketry discharged. I was then hurried into the Franks' quarter, and the gates were closely shut. I was soon informed, that a revolution had broken out among the soldiers against the Bashaw, and that some of the troops were in pursuit of him to the citadel, whither he had retired for safety. Strange as it may appear, it proved, that by our not communicating with any body in Boolak, we knew nothing of what passed in the morning at Cairo; and it so happened, that at the very place where the revolution had begun, which was the seraglio, in the Esbakie, no one was visible when I passed; for after the Bashaw had retired into the citadel, all the soldiers ran after him; and as to the rest of the people, no one came out of their houses. All the Franks in their quarter were alarmed, and prepared for defence in case the gates should be attacked. I went to the house of Mr. Baghos, as I had business with him, and he was not a little surprised to see me, knowing where I lived.

I was much concerned for Mrs. Belzoni, whom I had left at home with only James and an Arab; and though Mr. Baghos endeavoured to persuade me to stop with them all night, I insisted on returning almost immediately. I went off unperceived by any one in the house; but at the gates of the quarter I found great difficulty in having the door opened; and no sooner was I out, than it was instantly closed after me. I took the same road that I came, and had not gone far, when I met a body of armed soldiers running towards the centre of the town. Advancing further I heard several muskets discharged in a street near, and many others at some distance; indeed there was a continual firing kept up. On my approaching the Esbakie, I saw several soldiers running towards the seraglio, and others hastening towards me. When they came up, one seized my bridle, while another took me by the collar, and the rest were busied in rifling my pockets. I had but a few dollars in my possession; and my pocket-book contained only letters and passports, of which I know not how they have disposed: but what principally drew their attention was a white topaz brooch, which I had in the frill of my shirt, and which they took for a brilliant. I kept in good humour with them; and when I perceived their attention to the topaz, I began to move in order to depart. I do not know whether I had reason to fear they would call after me, suspecting that I marked them so as to recognize them again: but I proceeded, and nothing further happened to me on the road.

For several days we kept ourselves close in the house, as we were advised by a friendly Turk, our neighbour, not to be seen. During this time, the soldiers plundered the shops in Cairo, and the Bashaw sent the Syrian horse against them, now known under the appellation of Tartoor. These were the only troops faithful to him; but being mounted, they could not follow the Albanians, who were posted in ploughed fields between Cairo and Boolak. One day the cavalry advanced, and the Albanians retired towards Boolak. Our house was so situated, that from the upper part of it we could see the firing of the troops on one side, and on the other the confusion of the people, who had taken to the boats, which were soon crowded with them, and in the hurry many of the boats went adrift. It was expected, that the troops would plunder the place, if they entered it: in such case, I depended on the appearance and ruined state of our habitation, which, I had reason to think, would rather deter the soldiers from entering it, lest it should fall on their heads, than invite them to plunder. Besides, we had no treasure with us, unless they had taken our kitchen furniture of earthen pots, &c. There was a universal cry among the people, and the troops advanced to the very entrance of the town; but, fortunately, they were prevented from coming in by the cavalry, who, by making a circuit, had taken post on the road. The confusion continued in this manner for several days: at last, after having plundered and ravaged Cairo at their pleasure, the troops retired to their camps, and in a few days more matters were arranged again. I have reason to think, that the Bashaw knew who the chief instigators of this insurrection were, for we found that several persons shortly after died of sudden deaths; and, indeed, many of the Chiefs and Beys disappeared. The discontented troops were all sent to encampments in various stations at a distance from Cairo, and part towards Mecca; but the European exercise, which was said to have been the cause of the revolt of the troops, was wholly abandoned, and consigned to oblivion. Turks are averse to control of any sort, and particularly to what is not the result of Mahommedan customs. I was never more amused, than when I saw our military evolutions attempted by men, whose large trowsers are peculiarly unsuited to our light motions.

When all was quiet again, I recommenced my hydraulic preparations. The place, where I was to erect my machine, was in Soubra, at the garden of the Bashaw, on the Nile, three miles from Cairo. We went to reside there, in a small house within the walls of the governor's palace, which was closed at night by large gates, something like the Occales in Alexandria. I had many provoking difficulties to encounter, before I became acquainted with the people of the place, as they supposed, that the introduction of such machines into the country would throw many of them out of work; consequently I was not welcome among them; and the very persons who were to furnish me with what was necessary in wood, iron, carpentry, &c. would be the first to suffer by it, if the machine succeeded. It may, therefore, easily be imagined that I had to contend with many obstacles, besides the prejudice against all strangers, or innovations in the customs of the natives. As a proof of this may be cited the hydraulic machine already in Soubra, sent as a present from England to the Bashaw of Egypt, which is said to have cost ten thousand pounds. It was neatly put up, though the engineer, who was in charge of it, met with many difficulties before he effected it. At last it was set to work; but as it was imagined, that an English machine would inundate the whole country in an hour, the quantity of water raised was not adequate to their expectation, and it has been left useless ever since. For my own part, I have no doubt, that the machine might have been made to draw up more water, if the person who constructed it could have seen the place and situation in which it was to act. The failure in this instance had given me an early surmise of what might be my own fate; and I was not mistaken.

During my stay at Soubra I became aquainted with many Turks, and in particular with the governor of the palace, as we had our house within his walls. The garden of the Bashaw was under his care, and a guard was kept at the gates. The seraglio is so situated, that the front looks over the hill: at the back of it is the garden, which is under the care of Greeks, who in a few years have brought it to great perfection. There are beautiful alcoves, made in form of cupolas, entirely covered with plants; and the water machines, which are constantly at work, keep up a perpetual verdure. There is a fountain in the European style, and a great quantity of fruit, particularly grapes and peaches, but they never grow to any size like ours, for many get rotten and fall before they are ripe; in consequence, the Turks eat them green.

The Bashaw is in continual motion, being sometimes at his citadel, and sometimes at his seraglio in the Esbakie; but Soubra is his principal residence. His chief amusement is in the evening a little before sunset, when he quits his seraglio, and seats himself on the bank of the Nile, to fire at an earthen pot, with his guards. If any of them hit it, he makes him a present, occasionally of forty or fifty *rubies*. He is himself an excellent marksman; for I saw him fire at and hit a pot only fifteen inches high, set on the ground on the opposite side of the Nile, though the river at Soubra is considerably wider than the Thames at Westminster Bridge. As soon as it is dark, he retires into the garden, and reposes either in an alcove, or by the margin of a fountain, on an

European chair, with all his attendants round him. Here his numerous buffoons keep him in continual high spirits and good humour. By moonlight the scene was beautiful. I was admitted into the garden whenever I wished, by which means I had an opportunity of observing the domestic life of a man, who from nothing rose to be viceroy of Egypt, and conqueror of the most powerful tribes of Arabia.

From the number of lights I frequently saw through the windows of the seraglio, I supposed the ladies were at such times amusing themselves in some way or other. Dancing women are often brought to divert them, and sometimes the famous Catalani of Egypt was introduced. One of the buffoons of the Bashaw took it into his head one day, for a frolic, to shave his beard; which is no trifle among the Turks; for some of them, I really believe, would sooner have their head cut off than their beard: he borrowed some Franks' clothes of the Bashaw's apothecary, who was from Europe, and, after dressing himself in our costume, presented himself to the Bashaw as a European, who could not speak a single word either of Turkish or Arabic, which is often the case. Being in the dark, the Bashaw took him for what he represented himself to be, and sent immediately for the interpreter, who put some questions to him in Italian, which he did not answer: he was then questioned in French, but no reply; and next in the German and Spanish languages, and still he was silent: at last, when he saw that they were all deceived, the Bashaw not excepted, he burst out in plain Turkish, the only language he was acquainted with, and his well known voice told them who he was; for such was the change of his person, particularly by the cutting off his beard, that otherwise they could scarcely have recognised him. The Bashaw was delighted with the fellow; and, to keep up the frolic, gave him an order on the treasury for an enormous sum of money, and sent him to the Kaciabay, to present himself as a Frank, to receive it. The Kaciabay started at the immensity of the sum, as it was nearly all that the treasury could furnish: but upon questioning this new European, it was soon perceived who he was. In this attire he went home to his women, who actually thrust him out of the door; and such was the disgrace of cutting off his beard, that even his fellow buffoons would not eat with him till it was grown again.

The Bashaw seems to be well aware of the benefits that may be derived from his encouraging the arts of Europe in his country, and had already reaped some of the fruits of it. The fabrication of gunpowder, the refining of sugar, the making of fine indigo, and the silk manufacture, are introduced, much to his advantage: he is constantly inquiring after something new, and is delighted with any thing strange to his imagination. Having heard of electricity, he sent to England for two electric machines, one with a plate, the other with a cylinder. The former was broken by the way; the latter was dismounted. The physician of the Bashaw, an Arminian, did not know, though it was so easy a matter, how to set it up. Happening to be at the garden one evening, when they were attempting it, and could not succeed, I was requested to put the several pieces together; and, having done so, I made one of the soldiers mount on the insulating stool, charged the machine, and gave the Turk a good shock; who, expecting no such thing, uttered a loud cry, and jumped off, as much terrified as if he had seen the devil. The Bashaw laughed at the man's jumping off, supposing his fright to be a trick, and not the effect of the machine; and when told, that it was actually occasioned by the machine, he affirmed positively that it could not be, for the soldier was at such a distance, that it was impossible the small chain he held in his hand could have such power. I then desired the interpreter to inform his Highness, that if he would mount the stool himself, he would be convinced of the fact. He hesitated for a while whether to believe me or not; however he mounted the stool. I charged well, put the chain into his hand, and gave him a pretty smart shock. He jumped off, like the soldier, on feeling the effect of the electricity; but immediately threw himself on the sofa in a fit of laughter, not being able to conceive how the machine could have such power on the human body.

The governor of Soubra, Zulfur Carcaja, was a Mamelouk of about sixty-five years of age, and an instance of the promotion of one of that body of men, who for so many centuries ruled Egypt. His political conduct towards the Bashaw procured him the place of governor of a village, which contained the residence of the Bashaw himself, and a vast tract of land, the cultivation of which was entirely under his direction. He was a learned man among the Turks, and had a considerable portion of knowledge in agriculture, which I suppose to be the cause of his continuing to enjoy the Bashaw's favour. He had travelled a great deal in the Ottoman dominions, and had acquired much information; which is uncommon for a Turk: but the prejudices of his nation, and the superstitions of his religion, notwithstanding all this, did not quit him an instant. At night I used to go to his divan, or *conversazione*, to chat, drink coffee, and smoke a pipe. We agreed in many points; but on that of the hydraulic machine I could make no impression upon him, as it was against his interest to be convinced. He was one day taken very ill; and as there was no physician nearer than Cairo, he sent to know whether we could not do something for him. As it was only a violent cold, Mrs. Belzoni sent him a negus, which he liked so well, that he continued the medicine for several days.

Some time after this, Mrs. Belzoni had a pain in her side. One evening, I went to his divan; and as he always inquired after the health of his physician, I informed him of the circumstance: upon which he assured me, that it was nothing but what he would find a remedy for immediately; and he rose and went into an inner room, from which with all imaginable pomp and devotion he brought out a book. The Sheik of the mosque was present; and, after turning over and over again the leaves of this book, they concluded on what was to be done. Three pieces of paper were cut in a triangular form, the size of a playing card, and the Sheik wrote on them several words in Arabic. Of these pieces of paper, he told me, that Mrs. Belzoni must fasten one to her forehead by a string, and one to each ear. He then fetched a piece of the skin of a lamb, that had been sacrificed during the feast of Bairam. The Sheik wrote on this also, and it was to be applied to the part affected. I thanked him very much for his kindness, and brought away the amulets, which we keep to this day, as a memorial of the Turkish method of curing pains. It happened, that Mrs. Belzoni was somewhat better a day or two after, and the old Turk exulted in having repaid the obligation he had incurred, when cured by her of his cold.

The Arabs of Soubra exhibit as much festivity, when a marriage of consequence takes place, as those of any of the villages in Egypt. Fortunately, one happened while we were there; and as the window of our house overlooked the very spot where the festival was to be celebrated, we had an opportunity of seeing the whole ceremony. Early in the morning of the grand holiday, a high pole was planted in the centre of the place, with a banner belonging to the village. A large assembly of people gathered under it, and preparations were made for an illumination with glass lamps, &c. The Arabs from other villages came to the feast in procession, beating their tambourines, and waving their flags. At some distance from the pole they halted, and did not advance till a deputation was sent to invite them to the feast. The elders of the village seated themselves around and under the pole, and the strangers at a little distance. One of those standing near the pole, who had an uncommonly good pipe, began to sing; while the rest divided themselves into two parties, forming two circles, one within the other, round the pole and facing each other. By each man putting his arms over his neighbours' shoulders, each circle formed a continuous chain. The outer circle stood still, while the people of the inner circle kept dancing and bowing in an orderly manner to those in the outer. Thus they continued three hours, and those who were not in the circles made separate rings by themselves. Some of the Hadgees, who were desirous of exhibiting their powers in ceremonial devotion, went on positively for two hours, and some minutes, bending their bodies nearly to the ground, and raising them up again with such quickness, that it would be impossible for any one, who was not accustomed to it, to undergo such exertion a quarter of an hour. All the women were at a distance by themselves, and among them was the bride. When the dancing and singing ended, they all sat down in large circles; and a great quantity of boiled rice was brought to them in large wooden bowls, beside a number of dishes of melokie and bamies*, and three or four large sheep roasted, which were immediately torn to pieces and devoured. For the drinking department they had a number of boys, who were fully employed in fetching water in large bardacks from the Nile; but some of the party I knew had a sly corner, to which to retire for a drop of horaky; for it is in this private way they drink it. At night, the pole and all the place around it was illuminated. The people seated themselves in an orderly manner, in the form of an amphitheatre, the women forming a part of the circle, separate from the men. A band of tambourines and pipes was continually playing; and the entertainment began with dancing, by two well-known and distinguished performers.

* Plants eaten in common by the Arabs as greens.

This particular mode of dancing, I believe, has never been described, and all who see it properly must be excused from giving a faithful picture of it. When the dancing was at an end, a sort of play was performed, the intent of which was to exhibit life and manners, as we do in our theatres. The subject represented an Hadgee, who wants to go to Mecca, and applies to a camel-driver, to procure a camel for him. The driver imposes on him, by not letting him see the seller of the camel, and putting a higher price on it than is really asked, giving so much less to the seller than he received from the purchaser. A camel is produced at last, made up by two men covered with a cloth, as if ready to depart for Mecca. The Hadgee mounts on the camel, but finds it so bad, that he refuses to take it, and demands his money back again. A scuffle takes place, when, by chance, the seller of the camel appears, and finds that the camel in question is not that which he sold to the driver for the Hadgee. Thus it turns out, that the driver was not satisfied with imposing both on the buyer and seller in the price, but had also kept the good camel for himself, and produced a bad one to the Hadgee. In consequence he receives a good drubbing, and runs off.—Simple as this story appears, yet it was so interesting to the audience, that it seemed as if nothing could please them better, as it taught them to be on their guard against dealers in camels, &c.—This was the play; and the afterpiece represented a European traveller, who served as a sort of clown. He is in the dress of a Frank; and, on his travels, comes to the house of an Arab, who, though poor, wishes to have the appearance of being rich. Accordingly he gives orders to his wife, to kill a sheep immediately. She pretends to obey; but returns in a few minutes, saying, that the flock has strayed away, and it would be the loss of too much time to fetch one. The host then orders four fowls to be killed; but these cannot be caught. A third time, he sends his wife for pigeons; but the pigeons are all out of their holes; and at last the traveller is treated only with sour milk and dhourra bread*, the only provision in the house. This finishes the play.

During my stay in Soubra, a circumstance took place, which I shall remember as long as I live, and which showed me plainly the country I was in, and the people I had to deal with. Some particular business calling me to Cairo, I was on my ass in one of the narrow streets, where I met a loaded camel. The space that remained between the camel and the wall was so little, that I could scarcely pass; and at that moment I was met by a Binbashi, a subaltern officer, at the head of his men. For the instant I was the only obstacle that prevented his proceeding on the road; and I could neither retreat nor turn round, to give him room to pass. Seeing it was a Frank who stopped his way, he gave me a violent blow on my stomach. Not being accustomed to put up with such salutations, I returned the compliment with my whip across his naked shoulders. Instantly he took his pistol out of his belt; I jumped off my ass; he retired about two yards, pulled the trigger, fired at my head, singed the hair near my right ear, and killed one of his own soldiers, who, by this time, had come behind me. Finding that he had missed his aim, he took out a second pistol; but his own soldiers assailed and disarmed him.

A great noise arose in the street, and, as it happened to be close to the seraglio in the Esbakie, some of the guards ran up; but on seeing what the matter was, they interfered and stopped the Binbasi. I thought my company was not wanted, so I mounted my charger, and rode off. I went to Mr. Baghos, and told him what had happened. We repaired immediately to the citadel, saw the Bashaw, and related the circumstance to him. He was much con-

---

* Dhurra is the common grain of Egypt.

cerned, and wished to know where the soldier was, but observed, that it was too late that evening to have him taken up. However, he was apprehended the next day, and I never heard or knew any thing more about him. Such a lesson on the subject was not lost upon me; and I took good care, in future, not to give the least opportunity of the kind to men of that description, who can murder an European with as much indifference as they would kill an insect.

Some little time after this, another circumstance took place, which I cannot omit relating. A charming young lady, about sixteen years of age, daughter of the Chevalier Bocty, now consul-general of Sweden, went out of her house, in company with her mother, sister, and some other ladies, to go to a bath. They formed a cavalcade on asses, as is the custom of the country; and had not proceeded far from their door, when they met a soldier, a monster I should say, who took a pistol from his belt, and, with the greatest coolness, fired and killed the young lady. She was one of the most amiable creatures, both in her manners and person, that ever lived; and was most deservedly lamented by every one who knew her. This is quite enough, surely, to invite young European ladies to that country! I must say, to the honour of Mahomed Ali, that the monster was taken and executed: but what satisfaction could this be to her afflicted parents?

About this time Mr. Bankes arrived in this country, and proceeded almost immediately to Mount Sinai, and thence to Upper Egypt; but returned in three months, and went to Syria. Mr. Burckhardt had for a long time premeditated the removal of the colossal head, or rather bust, known by the name of Young Memnon, to England, and had often endeavoured to persuade the Bashaw to send it as a present to the Prince Regent; but as it must have appeared to a Turk too trifling an article to send to so great a personage, no steps were taken for this purpose. Mr.

Burckhardt then proposed it to Mr. Bankes; but the reason why this gentleman did not take it away I am not acquainted with.

By this time the water machine was finished; and we waited the arrival of the Bashaw from Alexandria, to give his opinion on the advantages which might be derived from introducing it into the country. It was constructed on the principle of a crane with a walking wheel, in which a single ox, by its own weight alone, could effect as much as four oxen employed in the machines of the country. I accomplished this undertaking, notwithstanding the various species of intrigue and difficulty which were incessantly thrown in my way. The Bashaw arrived at Cairo, but did not come to Soubra till some time after.

At this period Mr. Salt, the consul-general from England, arrived in that capital, having business to transact in Cairo. I had frequent interviews with Mr. Burckhardt; and, knowing the wish he had for the removal of the colossal bust of Memnon, I repeatedly told him that I would undertake its conveyance from Thebes to Alexandria, so that it might be sent to England. On the arrival of Mr. Salt, Mr. Burckhardt proposed it to him; and shortly after having myself occasion to see that gentleman, I repeated to him, before Mr. Burckhardt, that I should be happy to undertake the removal of the bust, without the smallest view of interest, as it was to go to the British Museum. The consul seemed inclined to comply, but was indecisive for some time, saying he would think about it. A few days after this, he avoided all communication, keeping himself in strict seclusion, as the plague had begun to show itself in the streets of Cairo.

The Bashaw was now come to Soubra, accompanied with several connoisseurs in hydraulics. The machine was set to work; and, although constructed with bad wood and bad iron, and erected by Arabian carpenters and bricklayers, it was a question whether it did not draw six or seven times as much water as the common machines.

The Bashaw, after long consideration, gave his decision; and declared, that it drew up only four times as much. It is to be observed, that the water produced by this machine was measured by comparison with the water procured by six of their own; and that, at the time of measuring, the Arabs urged their animals at such a rate, that they could not have continued their exertion above an hour; and for the moment they produced nearly double the quantity of water, that was usually obtained. Notwithstanding all this, the calculation of the Bashaw was to my satisfaction, as it decided on the accomplishment of my undertaking. Still Mahommed Ali perceived plainly the prejudice among the Arabs, and some of the Turks, who were concerned in the cultivation of the land; for instead of four hundred people, and four hundred oxen, they would have only to command one hundred of each, which would make a considerable difference in their profits: but, as it happened, an accident occurred, that put an end to all their fears.

The Bashaw took it into his head to have the oxen taken out of the wheel, in order to see, by way of frolic, what effect the machine would have by putting fifteen men into it. James, the Irish lad in my service, entered along with them; but no sooner had the wheel turned once round, than they all jumped out, leaving the lad alone in it. The wheel, of course, overbalanced by the weight of the water, turned back with such velocity, that the catch was unable to stop it. The lad was thrown out, and in the fall broke one of his thighs. I contrived to stop the wheel before it did farther injury, which might have been fatal to him. The Turks have a belief, that, when such accidents happen in the commencement of any new invention, it is a bad omen. In consequence of this, exclusive of the prejudice against the machine itself, the Bashaw had been persuaded to abandon the affair. It had been stated to him, also, that it cost as much as four of the usual machines in making, while nothing was said of the advantages as to the oxen, that would be saved in the working of it. The business ended in this manner; and all that was due to me from the Bashaw was consigned to oblivion, as well as the stipulation I had made with him.

It was with considerable pain to my feelings, that I reflected on the idea of leaving a country, which has ever been one of the principal points of research among the learned. The fame of its antiquity excited in me the desire of investigation; but, under the circumstances I have mentioned, my purse would not afford the expenses of a journey to any great distance; and having Mrs. Belzoni with me, it required some deliberation, before I could decide, whether I should proceed to the north or to the south. I had been to visit the consul-general, but nothing more was said respecting the colossal head; so that the project of removing it seemed to have been forgotten. After having taken all matters into consideration, and made a proper calculation of the expenses, I found, that in an economical way I could make a voyage as far as Assouan and back again.

From the circumstances that follow, the reader will be able to form a proper idea of the motives by which I was induced to undertake the removal of the Memnion bust, which is now lodged in the British Museum; and for what purpose I made the researches, and accumulated the various remains of antiquity, which will find a place in this volume. There will be no occasion for me to enter into such particulars as would call for the evidence of others to the facts, as I am well assured, that a simple statement of the case will make the reader perfectly acquainted with it.

It has been erroneously stated, that I was regularly employed by Mr. Salt, the consul-general of his Britannic majesty in Egypt, for the purpose of bringing the colossal bust from Thebes to Alexandria. I positively deny that I was ever engaged by him in any shape whatever, either by words or writing; as I have proofs of the case being on the contrary. When I ascended the Nile, the first and second time, I had no other idea in my mind, but that I was making researches for antiquities, which were to be placed in the British Museum; and it is naturally to be supposed that I would not have made these excursions, had I been previously aware, that all I found was for the benefit of a gentleman, whom I never had the pleasure to see before in my life. But what has displeased me above all is, that while occupied in my researches, an advantage has been taken, and a notion promulgated, the very reverse of the real matter of fact; and I am sorry I cannot be silent on the subject, feeling it an indispensable duty to myself, as well as the public, to bring the truth to light. I am happy, however, to state, that I succeeded in putting all the articles of my discovery on their way to the British Museum, though not in the same manner in which I thought they were to be entered in that place at first, as was the case with the young Memnon head.

The indecision, whether I should go up or down the Nile, came at last to a point. I know not what to call it, whether curiosity, or that enthusiasm for antiquities, which I can trace from my younger days while in Rome, that spurred me on to decide to ascend the Nile.

Agreeably to the resolution I had taken, I hired a boat at a very cheap rate, with four sailors, a boy, and the Reis, or captain. I made provision for the voyage, and every thing was ready for our departure. Any one may ascend the Nile without being interrupted; but it is better to obtain a firman from the Bashaw, in case of the want of protection from any of his Beys, Cacheffs, or Caimacans, in Upper Egypt; and Mahomet Ali was always ready to give a firman to any one who asked for it. I communicated my intended departure to Mr. Burckhardt, who, on hearing that nothing more was said about taking away the colossal head, seemed to be quite disappointed. Being a native of that part of Italy which had lately come under the Austrian dominions, I might have applied to the Austrian consul, to obtain a firman from the Bashaw: but as I enjoyed the British protection, I applied to the British consul. Going to his house for the purpose, I found Mr. Burckhardt there: it seems he had persuaded the consul to avail himself of the opportunity of my ascending the Nile, by offering to pay half the expense. Accordingly, when I informed the consul of my intended journey, and that I came to request he would do me the favour to obtain a firman for me from the Bashaw, he expressed his joy by exclaiming, " This is a godsend indeed !" and I was then informed, that they had made up their minds to have the colossus conveyed down the Nile, and to offer it as a present to the British Museum, if I would kindly undertake the removal of it. I replied that my capacity was little, but that I would use all my efforts to succeed in the enterprise; adding that I should be happy at all times to increase the British Museum with the product of my exertions. To which the British consul answered, " And I shall be glad to do every thing in my power to promote your wishes." This was all that passed on either side.

As I was unacquainted with the upper country, I received instructions concerning the manner in which I was to proceed, to obtain information, and to provide myself with implements for the purpose in view. The instructions were as follow:

" Boolak, June 28, 1816.

" Mr. Belzoni is requested to prepare the necessary implements, at Boolak, for the purpose of raising the head of the statue of the younger Memnon, and carrying it down the Nile. He will proceed as speedily as circumstances will allow to Siout, there to deliver his letters, prepared for that effect, to Ibrahim Bashaw, or whoever may be left in the charge of the government; and he will, at that place, consult with Doctor Scotto on the subject of his further proceedings. He will take care to engage a *proper boat* for bringing down the head, and will request Mr. Scotto to provide him with a soldier to go up with him, for the purpose of engaging the Fellahs to work whenever he may require their assistance, as otherwise they are not likely to attend to Mr. Belzoni's orders; and he should on no account leave Siout without an interpreter.

"Having obtained the necessary permission to hire workmen, &c., Mr. Belzoni will proceed direct to Thebes. He will find the head referred to on the western side of the river, opposite to Carnak, in the vicinity of a village called Gornou, lying on the southern side of a ruined temple, called by the natives Kossar el Dekaki. To the head is still attached a portion of the shoulders, so that altogether it is of large dimensions, and will be recognized,— 1st, by the circumstance of its lying on its back with the face uppermost—2dly, by the face being quite perfect, and very beautiful —3dly, by its having, on one of its shoulders, a hole bored artificially, supposed to have been made by the French for separating the fragment of the body—and 4thly, from its being a mixed blackish and reddish granite, and covered with hieroglyphics on its shoulders. It must not be mistaken for another, lying in that neighbourhood, which is *much mutilated*.

"Mr. Belzoni will spare no expense or trouble in getting it as speedily conveyed to the banks of the river as possible; and he will, if it be necessary, let it wait there till the river shall have attained sufficient height, before he attempts to get it into the boat. But, at the same time, he is requested not to attempt removing it, on any account, if he should judge there would be any serious risk of either injuring the head, of burying the face in the sand, or of losing it in the Nile.

"If, on arriving at the ground, too, he should perceive that his means are inadequate, or that the difficulties of the undertaking, from the nature of the ground, or other causes, are likely to prove insurmountable, he will, at once, relinquish the enterprise, and not enter into farther expense on that account.

"Mr. Belzoni will have the goodness to keep a separate account of the expenses incurred in this undertaking, which, as well as his other expenses, will gladly be reimbursed; as, from the knowledge of Mr. Belzoni's character, it is confidently believed they will be as reasonable as circumstances will allow.

"The boat meant to carry the head should be hired for a sufficient time to allow of its being carried *directly* down to Alexandria; but, on the way, Mr. Belzoni will not fail to stop at Boolak for further instructions.

"If Mr. Belzoni should ascertain the certainty of his being able to accomplish his purpose, he is requested immediately to despatch an express with the gratifying intelligence to Cairo.

"HENRY SALT."

I beg leave to observe, that in the whole of these instructions, though written in an assuming style, not a word is said about any payment to myself, which would certainly have been the case, had I been employed in the way that has been represented.

Every thing was ready in the boat for our departure from Boolak. The whole of the implements for the operation consisted of a few poles and ropes of palm leaves, no other implements being to be procured in the place at that time. Seeing I undertook the enterprise cheerfully, the consul did me the honour to request something more, which was, to purchase whatever antiquities I could on the road. I assented to his wishes; and for this purpose he supplied me with money, as well as for the removal of the colossal head. On the 30th of June we left Boolak; and as Mrs. Belzoni determined to accompany me, we took with us the Irish lad, and a Copt interpreter, who had been in the French army.

The first ruins we arrived at were those of Shak Abade, or the ancient Antinoe; for I omit the pyramids for the present. Not to depreciate the works of Adrian, these ruins did not surprise me at all. There are few columns standing; many are fallen; and what are of granite were evidently taken from more ancient edifices. I made a drawing of one of the standing columns, merely to give an idea of the order, &c. (see Plate 32); and we crossed the same day over to Ashmounain. Here is the first Egyptian architecture that travellers meet with on the Nile above the pyramids; and I must say, that it has made a great impression on my mind, though it is only a portico of two rows of columns. The solitary place on which it stands, in the midst of the ruins of Hermopolis, and the majestic appearance of the columns, of a form so uncommon to a European, cannot fail to inspire veneration for the people that erected such edifices. It appears to me, that these ruins are of remoter date than those of Thebes; which does not agree with the opinion, that the temples in the Lower Thebais were of later date than those of Upper Egypt. From what I have seen of the tombs in these mountains, I am of opinion, that Hermopolis was inhabited by some great people, as nothing can give juster ideas of the condition of the Egyptians than the quality of the tombs in which they were buried.

On the 5th, in the evening, we arrived at Manfalût, where we met Ibrahim, Bashaw of Upper Egypt, son of Mahomet Ali, on his way to Cairo. Having presented my letters, he politely requested, that I would deliver them to the Defterdar, who was left in command in Siout. Along with him was Mr. Drouetti, the ex-consulgeneral of the late government of France. He was on his return from Thebes, and had been in the habit of making a collection of antiquities during the many years he resided in Egypt. He was already informed, that I had undertaken to remove the colossal bust, and he told me the Arabs would not work at Thebes, as he had occasion to try them. He then made me a present of a granite cover of a sarcophagus, which the Arabs had discovered in one of the tombs. He said that he had employed several of them for many days to take it out for himself, but they could not succeed; so that, if I could take it out, I was welcome to it. I thanked him for his present, and proceeded on my voyage.

On the 6th, in the afternoon, we arrived in Siout. The Defterdar Bey was not there, but was expected in two or three days. I waited upon the physician of Ibrahim Bashaw, Mr. Scotto, to whom I was referred for information respecting boats, carpenters, &c. This person had never seen Mr. Salt, by whom I was recommended to him. He behaved, however, very well to Mr. Bankes, as I have reason to believe, when he passed that way, and he did also to me; but as to taking away the colossal bust, after gradually introducing the matter, he made many difficulties: first, about obtaining permission to have the necessary workmen; then there were no boats to be had; and next, the bust was a mass of stone not worth the carriage: at last, he plainly recommended to me not to meddle in this business, for I should meet with many disagreeable things, and have many obstacles to encounter. I saw that I could obtain but little help from this quarter; so I procured all that I wanted by means of my interpreter, and a few words of my own. I provided myself with a Greek carpenter, who agreed to follow us to Thebes; and on the sixth day the Bey arrived. He received me very politely. I presented the letter to him which Mr. Salt had obtained from Mahomet Ali himself, and he furnished me with orders to the Casheff of the province of Erments, to whom the Fellahs of Thebes are subject.

While waiting for the Bey I visited the tombs of Issus. There are only two that are worth notice, and these are so decayed inside, that there is scarcely any remains of figures or painting; all the rest are small holes for the lower class of people. Siout is the capital of Sais, or Upper Egypt. There is a constant commerce kept up by the caravans from Darfoor. Negroes, feathers, elephants' teeth, and gum, are the principle articles brought to market. The viceroy of Upper Egypt is always the first to select what he pleases from the caravan; for which he fixes his own price, and pays what he likes. The rest is for the merchants, who dare not buy any thing till the viceroy has made his choice.

This place is celebrated for the making of eunuchs. As soon as the operation is performed the boys are buried in the ground, all but the head and shoulders; and many, who are not of strong constitutions, die with the excruciating pain. It is calculated, that the operation, during its performance or afterwards, proves fatal to two out of three.

Besides the usual produce of the country, wheat, beans, flax, and seeds, a great number of wax-candles are made; and it is from hence Cairo is supplied with this article. Ibrahim Bashaw has latterly been the terror of the people. When an unfortunate culprit was brought before him, after some few questions, he sent him to the Cady* to be judged. This was the signal for taking him to a particular cannon, to the mouth of which he was tied; and it was then fired off, loaded with a ball, so that the body was scattered about in pieces at a considerable distance. In the case of two Arabs, who had killed a soldier, not without provocation, this Bashaw had them fastened to a pole, like two rabbits on a spit, and roasted alive at a slow fire: yet this man is now heir to the government of Egypt on the death of Mahomet Ali.

* An Arab Sheik, who often decides trifling cases.

On our proceeding up towards Acmin, we saw the columns at Gow; which have since all fallen into the river, one excepted. I observed there the largest monolite I have seen any where. It was near twelve feet high, but of very rough workmanship. The temple had been very extensive, but the work not of the best sort.

Next day, the 15th, we went to Acmin, to visit the fathers of that convent. There is nothing interesting in the place, except some stairs, the only remains of the ancient temple. One of the fathers told me, that at some distance in the mountain there is a small lake, which he had visited himself, entirely surrounded by cassia trees. Among the rubbish in the town are found a few trifling antiquities, but nothing of any consequence. The fathers took me to see the Casheff, or governor of the place; who, hearing that I was in search of antiquities, said that he well knew there were many in the town, for the Fellahs had often told him so. I inquired of him where they were? "Oh! but you cannot have them," he replied: "they are all enchanted by the devil; and no one can take them from where they are!" I told him, if he would but tell me where they were, I would arrange the business in the other quarter. "That is very well," said he; "but no one here dares to tell you, for fear the devil should do him a mischief." He then informed me, that in the mountains, about six miles distant, there was a large gold ring stuck into the rock, which no one could take out: that some of his soldiers went with a cannon, and, after firing several balls at it, were returning without success, when by chance a man who was eating a cucumber threw a part of it at the ring, which immediately fell to the ground; so that it must have been fixed by enchantment there, and nothing but the rind of a cucumber could make it fall. This I received from the governor of a province! What sort of a country must that be, which allows itself to be ruled by a man of so elevated a mind!

On the 16th we passed before Manshia, and arrived at Georgia.

There we procured some provision, and continued our voyage. It was from this place I visited Arabat, the ancient Abydos, two years after, as I shall take a proper opportunity of relating.

Near Cossar el Sajats there is a narrow passage of the Nile, particularly at low water. The wind here was so strong, that we made considerable way against the current, even without sails; or, in nautical language, "scudding under bare poles."

On the 18th, at night, we arrived at Dendera, where we saw a phenomenon that I never before heard of. A meteor appeared over our heads, and took its course towards the south; but so slowly, that, from the time of its setting off to that of its dispersion, to the best of my reckoning, it was visible for about twenty seconds. It first appeared of a blueish colour, then became white, and lastly red; leaving, apparently, many sparks on the way it had passed.

On the 19th, early in the morning, my curiosity was at a high pitch, the noted temple of Tentyra being the only thought I had in my head. Accordingly, we set off on asses, as usual, and proceeded to the ruins. Little could be seen of the temple, till we came near to it, as it is surrounded by high mounds of rubbish of the old Tentyra. On our arriving before it, I was for some time at a loss to know where I should begin my examination. The numerous objects before me, all equally attractive, left me for a while in a state of suspense and astonishment. The enormous masses of stone employed in the edifice are so well disposed, that the eye discovers the most just proportion every where. The majestic appearance of its construction, the variety of its ornaments, and, above all, the singularity of its preservation, had such an effect on me, that I seated myself on the ground, and for a considerable time was lost in admiration. It is the first Egyptian temple the traveller sees on ascending the Nile, and it is certainly the most magnificent. It has an advantage over most others, from the good state of preservation it is in; and I should have no scruple in saying, that it is of a much later date than any other. The superiority of the workmanship gives us sufficient reason to suppose it to be of the time of the first Ptolemy; and it is not improbable, that he, who laid the foundation of the Alexandrian library, instituted the philosophical society of the Museum, and studied to render himself beloved by his people, might erect such an edifice, to convince the Egyptians of his superiority of mind over the ancient kings of Egypt, even in religious devotion.

This is the cabinet of the Egyptian arts, the product of study for many centuries, and it was here that Denon thought himself in the sanctuary of the arts and sciences. The front is adorned with a beautiful cornice, and a frieze covered with figures and hieroglyphics, over the centre of which the winged globe is predominant, and the two sides are embellished with compartments of sacrifices and offerings. The columns that form the portico are twenty-four in number, divided into four rows, including those in the front. On entering the gate the scene changes, and requires more minute observation. The quadrangular form of the capitals first strikes the eye. At each side of the square there is a colossal head of the goddess Isis with cows' ears. There is not one of these heads but is much mutilated, particularly those on the columns in the front of the temple facing the outside: but notwithstanding this disadvantage, and the flatness of their form, there is a simplicity in their countenance that approaches to a smile. The shafts of the columns are covered with hieroglyphics and figures, which are in basso relievo, as are all the figures in the front and lateral walls. The front of the door-way, which is in a straight line with the entrance and the sanctuary, is richly adorned with figures of smaller size than the rest of the portico. The ceiling contains the zodiac, inclosed by two long female figures, which extend from one side to the other of it. The walls are divided into several square compartments, each containing figures representing deities, and priests in the act of offering or immolating victims. On all the walls, columns, ceiling, or architraves, there is nowhere a space of two feet, that is not covered with some figures of human beings, animals, plants, emblems of agriculture, or of religious ceremony. Wherever the eyes turn, wherever the attention is fixed, every thing inspires respect and veneration, heightened by the solitary situation of this temple, which adds to the attraction of these splendid recesses. The inner apartments are much the same as the portico, all covered with figures in basso relievo, to which the light enters through small holes in the walls: the sanctuary itself is quite dark. In the corner of it I found the door, which leads to the roof by a staircase, the walls of which are also covered with figures in basso relievo. On the top of the temple the Arabs had built a village, I suppose to be the more elevated, and exposed to the air; but it is all in ruins, as no one now lives there. From the top I descended into some apartments on the east side of the temple. There I saw the famous zodiac on the ceiling. The circular form of this zodiac led me to suppose, in some measure, that this temple was built at a later period than the rest, as nothing like it is seen any where else. In the front of the edifice there is a propylæon, not inferior to the works in the temple; and, though partly fallen, it still shows its ancient grandeur. On the left, going from the portico, there is a small temple surrounded by columns. In the inside is a figure of Isis sitting with Orus in her lap, and other female figures, each with a child in her arms, are observable. The capitals of the columns are adorned with the figure of Typhon. The gallery or portico, that surrounds the temple, is filled up with rubbish to a great height, and walls of unburnt bricks have been raised from one column to another. Farther on, in a right line with the propylæon, are the remains of an hypæthral temple, which form a square of twelve columns, connected with each other by a wall, except at the door-way, which fronts the propylæon. The eastern wall of the great temple is richly adorned with figures in intaglio relevato: they are perfectly finished: the female figures are about four feet high, disposed in different compartments. Behind the temple is a small Egyptian building, quite detached from the large edifice; and from its construction I would venture to say, that it was the habitation of the priests. At some distance from the great temple are the foundations of another, not so large as the first. The propylæon is still standing in good preservation. My principal object did not permit me to stay here any longer; but I do not know that I ever quitted a place with so much regret and wish to remain.

When we again reached the Nile, the people of Dendera were assembled in great numbers, waiting our return from the ruins. On approaching them they surrounded my interpreter, and caught hold of him, some by the arms, others by the garments, and insisted that he should remain there, as he belonged to that village. The fact was, at the time the French were there, a boy from that place went along with them; and, as our interpreter told them that he had been in the French army, they concluded he must be the same person; nor could we persuade them to the contrary. I was not willing to part with him, as I was but little acquainted with the Arabic language; but no reasoning with them would avail, and they were too numerous for him to escape from them. At last, I told them to call for the mother of the boy in question. To this they answered, that she lived at six miles distance, and they would not take the trouble to go and fetch her. Presently, however, they consented; but they would not release their supposed old friend from their hands, telling him he had been long enough among christian dogs. Some brought him milk and bread, others dates, others sugar-canes, &c. At length the desired old woman arrived, accompanied with another son; and, on her coming up to my interpreter, he addressed her in such a manner, that she soon acknowledged he did not belong to her.

We set off the same morning, and arrived in an hour at Kenneh. This place is well known for its trade with India through Cosseir, and as it is a halting-place for the Hadgees, is always well supplied with provisions. The Aga has under his command five hundred soldiers, to escort the caravan through the desert to Cosseir. The Bashaw sends supplies of wheat to his troops in Arabia, beside the usual trade in sugar and silk; and they bring coffee from Mocha, with cottons and Cashmire shawls of India manufacture. The Hadgees here take a stock of provision sufficient to last them as far as Mecca, and in the proper season the town is crowded with them from all parts. The camels for the caravans are furnished by the Ababdy, who make it a profitable business with the Hadgees. The best vessels for cooling water are met with in this town. The slaves that come from the upper country pay a duty of four dollars for a boy, two for a woman, and one for a man.

We continued our voyage, and arrived at Gamola on the 21st at night. On the 22d, we saw for the first time the ruins of great Thebes, and landed at Luxor. Here I beg the reader to observe, that but very imperfect ideas can be formed of the extensive ruins of Thebes, even from the accounts of the most skilful and accurate travellers. It is absolutely impossible to imagine the scene displayed, without seeing it. The most sublime ideas, that can be formed from the most magnificent specimens of our present architecture, would give a very incorrect picture of these ruins; for such is the difference, not only in magnitude, but in form, proportion, and construction, that even the pencil can convey but a faint idea of the whole. It appeared to me like entering a city of giants, who, after a long conflict, were all destroyed, leaving the ruins of their various temples as the only proofs of their former existence. The temple of Luxor presents to the traveller at once one of the most splendid groups of Egyptian grandeur. The extensive propylæon, with the two obelisks, and colossal statues in the front; the thick groups of enormous columns; the variety of apartments and the sanctuary it contains; the beautiful ornaments which adorn every part of the walls and columns, described by Mr. Hamilton; cause in the astonished traveller an oblivion of all that he has seen before. If his attention be attracted to the north side of Thebes by the towering remains, that project a great height above the wood of palm trees, he will gradually enter that forest-like assemblage of ruins of temples, columns, obelisks, colossi, sphynxes, portals, and an endless number of other astonishing objects, that will convince him at once of the impossibility of a description. On the west side of the Nile, still the traveller finds himself among wonders. The temples of Gournou, Memnonium, and Medinet Aboo, attest the extent of the great city on this side. The unrivalled colossal figures in the plains of Thebes, the number of tombs excavated in the rocks, those in the great valley of the kings, with their paintings, sculptures, mummies, sarcophagi, figures, &c. are all objects worthy of the admiration of the traveller; who will not fail to wonder how a nation, which was once so great as to erect these stupendous edifices, could so far fall into oblivion, that even their language and writing are totally unknown to us.

After having taken a cursory view of Luxor and Carnak, to which my curiosity led me on my landing, I crossed the Nile to the west, and proceeding straight to the Memnonium, I had to pass before the two colossal figures in the plain. I need not say, that I was struck with wonder. They are mutilated indeed, but their enormous size strikes the mind with admiration. The next object that met my view was the Memnonium. It stands elevated above the plain, which is annually inundated by the Nile. The water reaches quite to the propylæon; and, though this is considerably lower than the temple, I beg leave to observe, that it may be considered as one of the proofs, that the bed of the Nile has risen considerably higher since the Memnonium was erected; for it is not to be supposed that the Egyptians built the propylæon, which is the entrance to the temple, so low as not to be able to enter it when the water was at its height. There are other proofs of this opinion, which I shall have an opportunity of introducing in this volume. The groups of columns of that temple, and the views of the numerous tombs excavated in the high rock behind it, present a strange appearance to the eye. On my approaching these ruins, I was surprised at the sight of the great colossus of Memnon, or Sesostris, or Osymandias, or Phameroph, or perhaps some other king of Egypt; for such are the various opinions of its origin, and so many names have been given to it, that at last it has no name at all. I can but say, that it must have been one of the most venerated statues of the Egyptians; for it would have required more labour to convey such a mass of granite from Assouan to Thebes, than to transport the obelisk, commonly known under the appellation of Pompey's Pillar, to Alexandria.

As I entered these ruins, my first thought was to examine the colossal bust I had to take away. I found it near the remains of its body and chair, with its face upwards, and apparently smiling on me, at the thought of being taken to England. I must say, that my expectations were exceeded by its beauty, but not by its size. I observed, that it must have been absolutely the same statue as is mentioned by Norden, lying in his time with its face downwards, which must have been the cause of its preservation. I will not venture to assert who separated the bust from the rest of the body by an explosion, or by whom the bust has been turned face upwards. The place where it lay was nearly in a line with the side of the main gateway into the temple; and, as there is another colossal head near it, there may have been one on each side of the doorway, as they are to be seen at Luxor and Carnak.

All the implements brought from Cairo to the Memnonium consisted of fourteen poles, eight of which were employed in making a sort of car to lay the bust on, four ropes of palm leaves, and four rollers, without tackle of any sort. I selected a place in the porticoes; and, as our boat was too far off to go to sleep in it every night, I had all our things brought on shore, and made a dwelling house of the Memnonium. A small hut was formed of stones, and we were handsomely lodged. Mrs. Belzoni had by this time accustomed herself to travel, and was equally indifferent with myself about accommodations. I examined the road by which I was to take the bust to the Nile. As it appeared, that the season of the inundation was advancing very fast, all the lands which extend from the Memnonium to the water side would have been covered in one month's time; and the way at the foot of the mountain was very uneven, and in some parts ran over ground to which the water reached, so that, unless the bust was drawn over those places before the inundation commenced, it would become impossible to effect it after, till the next summer; a delay which might have occasioned even still more difficulties than I had to encounter at that time; for I have reason to assert, that an intrigue was going on to prevent the removal of the head.

On the 24th of July, I went to the Cacheff of Erments to obtain an order to the Caimakan of Gournou and Agalta, to procure for me eighty Arabs, to assist in the removal of the young Memnon. He received me with that invariable politeness which is peculiar to the Turks, even when they do not mean in the slightest degree to comply with your wishes, and which often deceives a traveller, who only *en passant* takes coffee, smokes his pipe, and goes away. It is not so these people can be known. This requires an opportunity of dealing with them, and in matters in which their interest is concerned. There are exceptions among them, as there are among the Christians of Europe; and I often found myself deceived where I least expected it. The smooth-faced protestations of friendship and partiality for a person, whom they never saw before, is so common among them, that at last it becomes a matter of course; and no reliance is placed on it, except by those who are unacquainted with the customs of the country.

I presented the firman from the Defterdar at Siout. He received it reverently, and promised to do every thing in his power to get the Arabs to work; but observed that, at the present season, they were all occupied, and it would be better to wait till after the inundation of the Nile. I remarked, that I had seen a great many Arabs about the villages, who appeared perfectly idle, and who would be glad to gain something by being employed. "You are mistaken," he replied, "for they would sooner starve than undertake a task so arduous as yours; since, to remove that stone, they must be helped by Mahomet, or they will never stir it the thickness of a thumb. Now, at the rise of the Nile, the Arabs of these banks are quite unoccupied, and that is the very time for our purpose." The next objection was the Ramadan, which was just beginning; and the third, that he could not spare any Arabs, as they must work in the fields for the Bashaw, whose work could not be interrupted. I saw plainly, that I should have to encounter many difficulties, but I was determined to persist; and I told him, I should collect men myself, accompanied by my Janizary; and that all the Arabs I might find idle and willing to come, I should engage, according to the firman I had received. "To-morrow," he then replied, "I will send my brother to see if any men can be got." I told him I relied on his word, and gave him to understand, that, if he behaved in a manner conformably to the orders of the Bashaw, he would receive a present accordingly; and, leaving my Janizary there, to conduct the men who might be procured for me to the Memnonium the next morning, I withdrew.

The morning arrived, but no men appeared. I waited patiently till nine o'clock, and then mounted a camel, and went again to Erments. I gave my interpreter some powder, and about two pounds of raw coffee, to be produced when I should ask for them. I found the Cacheff occupied in giving directions to build a tomb for a Mahometan saint; but it was of no use to complain. I told him, therefore, that I came to drink coffee with him, and smoke a pipe. He was pleased, and we sat together on the divan. I pretended to be quite unconcerned about the removal of the colossus; and at a proper time I presented the powder and the coffee to him, with which he was much gratified. I then repeated to him, that, if he would obtain men for me, it would be much to his advantage; and if not, he would lose the chance of reward, and I should act accordingly. He promised again that, on the next morning, I should have the assistance I wanted, and gave me an order for the purpose. I returned to Gournou on the same evening, and sent the tiscarry, or order, to the Caimakan of the place, whose business it was to attend to it. This man was an old acquaintance of a certain collector of antiquities in Alexandria; and, as he had immediate command over the Fellahs, gave me much trouble. He had collected antiquities for this person for many years at Gournou, was married and settled there, so that I was by no means welcome to him. Agreeably to the order, he also promised, like his master, to furnish me with men; but again, on the 26th, not one appeared.

I then sent for him, and, with an air of indifference, he told me, that men could not be procured that day, but he would do what he could on the morrow or next day: at the same time the Fellahs, who were idle, would have been glad to be employed, as they came by twenty at a time to see if permission were granted for them to work. The Cacheff, too, instead of sending the assistance he had promised from his part of the country, sent only a soldier, to inquire whether I still wanted it; and I replied, that, if he did not supply me with some men the next morning, I should write to Cairo. I knew, that writing to Cairo would have been to no purpose, for it would take a month before I could receive an answer, and then it would be too late, in consequence of the rising of the Nile. I tried in vain to persuade those Arabs whom I saw unemployed to work; but, though they were desirous of earning money, they dared not do so, without permission either from the Cacheff or the Caimakan.

To the Cacheff I now applied again, and at last, on the 27th, he sent me a few men, but by no means sufficient for my purpose; yet, when others saw them at work, by permission, they were easily persuaded to join the party. I arranged my men in a row, and agreed to give them thirty paras a day, which is equal to fourpence halfpenny English money, with which they were much pleased, as it was more by one half than they were accustomed to receive for their daily labour in the fields. The carpenter had made the car, and the first operation was to endeavour to place the bust on it. The Fellahs of Gournou, who were familiar with Caphany, as they named the colossus, were persuaded, that it could never be moved from the spot where it lay; and when they saw it moved, they all set up a shout. Though it was the effect of their own efforts, it was the devil, they said, that did it; and, as they saw me taking notes, they concluded that it was done by means of a charm. The mode I adopted to place it on the car was very simple, for work of no other description could be executed by these people, as their utmost sagacity reaches only to pulling a rope, or sitting on the extremity of a lever as a counterpoise. By means of four levers I raised the bust, so as to leave a vacancy under it, to introduce the car; and, after it was slowly lodged on this, I had the car raised in the front, with the bust on it, so as to get one of the rollers underneath. I then had the same operation performed at the back, and the colossus was ready to be pulled up. I caused it to be well secured on the car, and the ropes so placed that the power might be divided. I stationed men with levers at each side of the car, to assist occasionally, if the colossus should be inclined to turn to either side. In this manner I kept it safe from falling. Lastly, I placed men in the front, distributing them equally at the four ropes, while others were ready to change the rollers alternately. Thus I succeeded in getting it removed the distance of several yards from its original place.

According to my instructions, I sent an Arab to Cairo with the intelligence, that the bust had begun its journey towards England. From the great heat of the day I was unwell at night, having never felt the sun so powerful before in my life. Being in the hottest season, the air was inflamed; and even at night the wind itself was extremely hot. The place I had chosen in the Memnonium was worse than any, as the whole mass of stones was so heated, that the hands could not be kept on it. In the course of time these places became familiar to me, as well as the climate; for I observed, three years after, that I was often on the same spot, and at the same season, without feeling the least inconvenience, or being sensible of the intense heat I had felt on my first arrival. When the Arabs found that they received money for the removal of a stone, they entertained the opinion, that it was filled with gold in the inside, and that a thing of such value should not be permitted to be taken away.

On the 28th we recommenced the work. The Arabs came pretty early, as they preferred to work in the morning, and rest in the middle of the day from twelve to two. This day we removed the bust out of the ruins of the Memnonium. To make room for it to pass, we had to break the bases of two columns. It was advanced about fifty yards out of the temple. In the evening I was very poorly: I went to rest, but my stomach refused any aliment. I began to be persuaded, that there is a great difference between travelling in a boat, with all that is wanted in it, and at leisure, and the undertaking of an operation, which required great exertions in directing a body of men, who in point of skill are no better than beasts, and to be exposed to the burning sun of that country from morning till night.

On the next day, the 29th, I found it impossible to stand on my legs, and postponed the work to the day following. I had all our household-furniture, beds, kitchen-pottery, and provisions, put on a camel, and returned to the boat, in hopes that the air might be cool at night; but I remained very ill the whole day, my stomach refusing to take almost any thing.

On the 30th we continued the work, and the colossus advanced a hundred and fifty yards towards the Nile. I was a little better in the morning, but worse again in the evening.

On the 31st I was again a little better, but could not proceed, as the road became so sandy, that the colossus sunk into the ground. I was therefore under the necessity of taking a long turn of above three hundred yards, to a new road. In the evening of this day I was much better.

On the 1st of August we still improved in our success, as we this day proceeded above three hundred yards. I was obliged to keep several men employed in making the road before us, as we went on with the head. The Irish lad that was with me I sent to

Cairo, as he could not resist the climate; but what is singular, Mrs. Belzoni enjoyed tolerable health all the time. She was constantly among the women in the tombs; for all the Fellahs of Gournou make dwelling-houses where the Egyptians had burial-places, as I shall have occasion to mention hereafter.

On the 2d the head advanced farther; and I was in great hopes of passing a part of the land, to which the inundation would extend, previous to the water reaching that spot.

On the 3d we went on extremely well, and advanced nearly four hundred yards. We had a bad road on the 4th, but still we proceeded a good way. On the 5th we entered the land I was so anxious to pass over, for fear the water should reach it and arrest our course; and I was happy to think, that the next day would bring us out of danger. Accordingly, I went to the place early in the morning, and, to my great surprise, found no one there except the guards and the carpenter, who informed me, that the Caimakan had given orders to the Fellahs not to work for the Christian dogs any longer. I sent for him, to know the reason of this new proceeding; but he was gone to Luxor. It is to be observed, that the spot where the head lay at this time was expected to be under water in a few days; and that by delay the risk would be incurred of having it sunk in the earth, so that it could not have been taken out till the following year, and then not without a great deal of additional trouble, exclusive of the tricks that might be played in the interval. Under these circumstances, it may be imagined I was uneasy upon the subject, and anxious for despatch. I afterwards learned, that the rogue of a Caimakan had suggested to the Cacheff to take advantage of the situation, when the head was to pass that spot, to put an end to our proceeding. I took the Janizary with me, and crossed the water to Luxor. I there found the Caimakan, who could give me no reason for his proceeding but saucy answers; and the more I attempted to bring him into good humour by smooth words and promises, the more insolent he became. My patience was great, and I was determined that day to carry it to its utmost length: but there is a certain point, which, if exceeded, these people do not understand; and, in a country where respect is paid only to the strongest, advantage will always be taken of the weak: consequently, if a man carry his policy beyond that point, they mistake him for a coward; he is despised, and will have the more difficulties to encounter.

This was the case on the present occasion: my patience was mistaken; and this man, after having said all that he could against my nation, and those who protected me, was so much encouraged by my forbearance, that he attempted to put his hands on me, which I resisted. He then became more violent, and drew his sword, though he had a brace of pistols in his belt. There was no time to be lost; and as I had received a good lesson at Cairo from another Albanian like himself, I gave him no leisure to execute his purpose. I instantly seized and disarmed him, placed my hands on his stomach, and made him sensible of my superiority, at least in point of strength, by keeping him firm in a corner of the room. The pistols and sword, which I had thrown on the ground, were taken up by my Janizary; and after giving the fellow a good shaking, I took possession of them, and told him, that I should send them to Cairo, to show the Bashaw in what manner his orders were respected. He followed me towards the boat, and was no sooner out of the crowd that had assembled, than he began to be quite humble, and talk of matters as if nothing had happened. He then told me, that the order he had given to the Fellahs not to work he had received from the Cacheff himself, and it could not be expected, that, being only a Caimakan, he could disobey his superior. I did not stop one instant, but ordered the boat to take me to Ermentes immediately.

The reader, perhaps, may think my narrative too minute; but I beg to observe, that it is in this way only the true character of these people can be known. I remarked, that in almost every thing he said to me nothing escaped him against my religion, which is generally the first thing with a Mahometan; but I found afterwards, that the friend in Lower Egypt, with whom he had trafficked in antiques, from whom he received money and presents, and who influenced him on this occasion, was a Christian; and if he could have found the means to interrupt my proceedings respecting the bust, he would greatly have obliged this friend.

I hastened to Erments, and arrived there before sunset. As it was the time of Ramadan, the Cacheff had many of his principal officers, and several Hadgees and Santons at dinner with him; it being the custom of these Turkish travellers, particularly at this season, to live at great men's tables. There were about thirty in all in the place. The dinner was prepared in a field before the house, as no room within it would contain so many persons. An old carpet, about twenty feet long and three wide, was spread on the ground; and where we should put plates, cakes were placed of fine white bread, made expressly for the occasion. On my arrival they were just going to begin, the hour of dining being always a little after sunset during the festival of Ramadan, as they are then not allowed to eat till the sun has wholly disappeared; so that I could introduce no business at that time. There is certainly something in the ceremonial manners of the Turks, that is often peculiarly provoking. At the very moment that they order your throat to be cut, they will not fail to salute you, apparently, with the utmost cordiality. The Cacheff received me very politely, and invited me to dine with him. I dared not refuse, as it would have been the greatest affront I could have offered him. Accordingly, we sat all round the carpet, on the ground. The Turkish cookery does not always suit a European palate; but there are a few dishes, that are equally agreeable with our own; particularly mutton roasted on a wooden pole, at a wood fire. They have a particular way of cooking it, putting it on the fire immediately after it is killed, and before it has lost its natural warmth; and in this way it has a particular flavour, quite agreeable to the taste. The soldiers and Hadgees tucked up their large sleeves, and with naked arms dipped the fingers of their right hands into the various dishes. They never employ the left hand in eating, nor do they eat much out of one dish, but taste of all that are within their reach. They always finish their dinner with pilau, and seldom drink while eating. They wash immediately after, and pipes and coffee being served all round, they begin to converse on their usual topics, horses, arms, saddles, or dress.

At a proper time I expressed to the Cacheff the necessity of my having an order for the Fellahs, to proceed with my operations the next morning. He answered with indifference, that they must work in the fields for the Bashaw, and that he could not spare one; but that, if I would wait till the next season, I might have as many as I liked. I replied to this, that as I could obtain no men from him, I would bring over some from Luxor, and he would thus lose the merit of what he had done; and as I had to return to Luxor that night, I must take my leave. He observed, I had no reason to be afraid, as I was armed with such a pair of fine English pistols. I answered, they were very necessary in that country, but they were at his service notwithstanding, if he would be pleased to accept of them; though I had written to Cairo for a better pair for him, which would soon arrive. At these words, he put his hands on my knees, and said, "We shall be friends." He ordered the firman to be written out immediately, and set his seal to it. I left him, returned to the boat, and arrived at Gournou before daylight. On passing before Luxor, we were in danger of being drowned. The pier, that protects these ruins from the force of the current, on the swelling of the Nile is always under water; and our boatman, not being acquainted with its situation, ran the boat against it. The current was very strong; no power could resist it; and the boat heeled so much, that the water kept running over the gunwale. As the rapidity in this spot is so great, that the most expert swimmer, being once in the stream, has no chance of reaching the shore, we appeared to have inevitable death before us, but Providence ordered it otherwise. At that moment a fresh breeze arose, the advantage of which was seized by the pilot, who hoisted the sail, got the boat under proper management, crossed the current, and escaped the danger.

Early on the morning of the 7th, I sent for the Sheik of the Fellahs, and gave him the Cacheff's order. The men were ready in an hour after, and we continued the operation. The bust advanced this day considerably more than usual, owing to the men having rested on the preceding day: and on the 8th I had the pleasure of seeing it out of danger of being overtaken by the water.

On the 9th, I was seized with such a giddiness in my head, that I could not stand. The blood ran so copiously from my nose and mouth, that I was unable to continue the operation: I therefore postponed it to the next day.

On the 10th and 11th, we approached towards the river; and on the 12th, thank God, the young Memnon arrived on the bank of the Nile. Besides their promised payment, I gave the Arabs a bakshis, or present, of one piastre each, equal to sixpence English, with which they were exceedingly pleased; and they well deserved their reward, after an exertion, to which no labour can be compared. The hard task they had, to track such a weight, the heavy poles they were obliged to carry to use as levers, and the continual replacing the rollers, with the extreme heat and dust, were more than any European could have withstood: but what is still more remarkable, during all the days of this exertion, it being Ramadan, they never ate or drank till after sunset. I am at a loss to conceive, how they existed in the middle of the day, at a work to which they were totally unaccustomed.

Next day, in the morning, according to my wish, some Arabs came to conduct me to the cave, where the sarcophagus was which Mr. Drouetti had attempted to take out, and had given to me as a present, if I could get it. I was conducted into one of those holes, that are scattered about the mountains of Gournou, so celebrated for the quantities of mummies they contain. The Janizary remained without, and I entered, with two Arabs and the interpreter.

Previous to our entering the cave, we took off the greater part of our clothes, and, each having a candle, advanced through a cavity in the rock, which extended a considerable length in the mountain, sometimes pretty high, sometimes very narrow, and without any regularity. In some passages we were obliged to creep on the ground, like crocodiles. I perceived, that we were at a great distance from the entrance, and the way was so intricate, that I depended entirely on the two Arabs, to conduct us out again. At length we arrived at a large space, into which many other holes or cavities opened; and after some consideration and examination by the two Arabs, we entered one of these, which was very narrow, and continued downward for a long way, through a craggy passage, till we came where two other apertures led to the interior in a horizontal direction. One of the Arabs then said "This is the place." I could not conceive how so large a sarcophagus, as it had been described to me, could have been taken through the aperture, which the Arab now pointed out. I had no doubt, but these recesses were burial-places, as we continually walked over skulls and other bones; but the sarcophagus could never have entered this recess; for it was so narrow, that on my attempt to penetrate it, I could not pass. One of the Arabs, however, succeeded, as did my interpreter; and it was agreed, that I and the other Arab should wait till they returned. They proceeded evidently to a great distance, for the light disappeared, and only a murmuring sound from their voices could be distinguished as they went on. After a few moments, I heard a loud noise, and the interpreter distinctly crying, "*O mon Dieu! mon Dieu! je suis perdu!*" After which, a profound silence ensued. I asked my Arab, whether he had ever been in that place? He replied, "Never." I could not conceive what could have happened, and thought the best plan was to return, to procure help from the other Arabs. Accordingly, I told my man to show me the way out again; but, staring at me like an ideot, he said he did not know the road. I called repeatedly to the interpreter, but received no answer; I watched a long time, but no one returned; and my situation was no very pleasant one. I naturally returned through the passages, by which we had come; and, after some time, I succeeded in reaching the place, where, as I mentioned, were many other cavities. It was a complete labyrinth, as all these places bore a great resemblance to the one which we first entered. At last seeing one, which appeared to be, the right, we proceeded through it a long way; but by this time our candles had diminished considerably; and I feared, that, if we did not get out soon, we should have to remain in the dark: meantime it would have been dangerous to put one out, to save the other, lest that which was left should, by some accident, be extinguished. At this time we were considerably advanced towards the outside, as we thought; but to our sorrow we found the end of that cavity, without any outlet. Convinced that we were mistaken in our conjecture, we quickly returned towards the place of the various entries, which we strove to regain. But we were then as perplexed as ever, and were both exhausted from the ascents and descents, which we had been obliged to go over. The Arab seated himself, but every moment of delay was dangerous. The only expedient was, to put a mark at the place out of which we had just come, and then examine the cavities in succession, by putting also a mark at their entrance, so as to know where we had been. Unfortunately, our candles would not last through the whole: however, we began our operations.

On the second attempt, when passing before a small aperture, I thought I heard the sound of something like the roaring of the sea at a distance. In consequence I entered this cavity; and as we advanced the noise increased, till I could distinctly hear a number of voices all at one time. At last, thank God, we walked out; and, to my no small surprise, the first person I saw was my interpreter. How he came to be there I could not conjecture. He told me, that, in proceeding with the Arab along the passage below, they came to a pit, which they did not see; that the Arab fell into it, and in falling put out both candles. It was then that he cried out, " Mon Dieu! je suis perdu!" as he thought he also should have fallen into the pit; but, on raising his head, he saw at a great distance a glimpse of daylight, towards which he advanced, and thus arrived at a small aperture. He then scraped away some loose sand and stones, to widen the place where he came out, and went to give the alarm to the Arabs, who were at the other entrance. Being all concerned for the man who fell to the bottom of the pit, it was their noise that I heard in the cave. The place by which my interpreter got out was instantly widened; and in the confusion the Arabs did not regard letting me see that they were acquainted with that entrance, and that it had lately been shut up. I was not long in detecting their scheme. The Arabs had intended to show me the sarcophagus, without letting me see the way by which it might be taken out, and then to stipulate a price for the secret. It was with this view they took me such a way round about.

I found that the sarcophagus was not in reality a hundred yards from the large entrance. The man was soon taken out of the well, but so much hurt in one of his hips, that he went lame ever after. Finding that the cover of the sarcophagus could be taken out, I set several men at work to clear the passage; but on the third day, on my return from the king's tombs, I found that the Cacheff had recommenced his old tricks. He came to Gournou from Erments; and, seeing the Arabs at work, he took them all to the latter place, bound like thieves, and put them into prison. I could not imagine the reason of all this, after the promises I had made him, and the protestations on his part which he had made to me; but, on inquiry, I found that some agents of Mr. D—— had just arrived from Alexandria and brought him presents. I do not know what passed between them; I only state the case as it appeared. On my applying to him again, he said that the sarcophagus was sold to the French consul, and no one else should have it. I feigned to be quite unconcerned about the matter, as well as about the Arabs he had put into prison; for, if I had appeared anxious, he would have kept them longer, as his motives were all mercenary. I told him I should write to Cairo about the sarcophagus. In fact, I had to write to Mr. Salt, to have a boat sent to convey the colossus down the Nile, as none could be had at that season in Upper Egypt; for they were all engaged, and mostly for the Bashaw.

After having sent a courier to the consul about the boat, I thought I could not employ my time better than in going up the Nile, as no extra expense would be incurred. The boat which I had engaged might go where I pleased; and, by the time the answer from Cairo arrived, I should be back again. I always had two guards kept at the colossal bust day and night; but when I found that I could not get a boat to embark it without writing to Cairo, I formed an inclosure of earth all round it; and on the 18th we set off for Esne. Our number was diminished in this voyage, as I had sent the Irish lad to Cairo, and discharged the carpenter; so that we remained only with the Janizary and the interpreter. The next day we reached Esne, and I landed just in time to see Khalil Bey on the same evening, whom I knew some time before in Soubra. He was appointed to the government of the upper provinces, from Esne to Assouan; and having married one of the Bashaw's sisters, he was quite independent of the orders of the Deftardar Bey at Siout. It was nearly night when I went to him. He was just returned from an excursion into the country. I found him seated on a sofa made of earth, covered with a fine carpet and satin cushions, surrounded by a great number of his chiefs, Cacheffs, and Santons. They had just finished their dinner; and I could not have arrived at a better time for conversation. He was much pleased to see me, and offered to give me letters to all the people under his command. Understanding that I might perhaps proceed as far as Ibrim, he caused a letter to be written to Osseyn Cacheff, who was one of the three princes residing in Nubia: and as Khalil Bey received a yearly contribution from the Nubians, he had sent his soldiers thither; so they were now on friendly terms. The moment the troops of Egypt enter Nubia to receive the tribute, the princes march higher up the Nile, and are never to be seen.

The usual conversation on horses, &c. was laid aside; and, as I was going to Nubia, the topics were the various personages I should meet with in that country, and the risk I ran of being robbed by them, &c. After smoking a few pipes, and drinking as many cups of coffee, I left the Bey, and returned to the boat.

The next day I made a cursory inspection of the temple in that town. It is much encumbered with rubbish, and only the portico of it is now to be seen; but the beautiful variety and fine shaped capitals of the columns, as well as the zodiacal figures on the ceiling, announce that it was one of the principal temples of Egypt. The figures and hieroglyphics are somewhat larger than those of Tentyra; and it is a great pity that such beautiful edifices should be inhabited by dirty Arabs and their cattle.

On the 20th we passed Elethias with a strong wind, and therefore did not stop till we arrived at Edfu. This temple may be compared with that of Tentyra in point of preservation, and is superior in magnitude. The propylæon is the largest and most perfect of any in Egypt: it is covered on all sides with colossal figures of intaglio relevato, and contains several apartments in the interior, which receive light by square apertures in the side. We have here one of those curious subjects of inquiry, which, in my opinion, have never yet been explained. These square holes, or windows, viewed from the inside of the chambers, appear to have been made for the purpose of giving light to these apartments, or to hold some particular ornaments or emblems, placed in them occasionally on festival days; consequently, it might be concluded that they were made at the same time with the building. Yet, on the outside, these very windows come in contact with the colossal figures which are sculptured on the walls; and part of these appear as if cut off where the windows have been made: so that, from the appearance on the outside, it is to be inferred, that these apertures were formed after the building was finished. For my own part, I think they were cut long after that period, and made to give light to the apartments, which were inhabited by people of a different religion from those who built the temple. The pronaos is very wide, and is the only one to be seen in Egypt in such perfection, though completely encumbered with Arab huts. The portico is also magnificent; but, unfortunately, above three-fourths of it covered with rubbish. Through some holes in the upper part of the sekos I entered the inner apartments; but they were so obstructed, that I could not proceed far. The Fellahs have built part of their village on the top of it, as well as stables for cattle, &c. The temple is surrounded by a high thick wall, which extends from each side of the propylæon, so as to inclose the whole building. Not only the temple, but every part of the wall, is covered with hieroglyphics and figures. On the side wall of the pronaos I observed the figure of Harpocrates which is described by Mr. Hamilton, seated on a full-blown lotus, with his finger on his lips, as in the minor temple at Tentyra; and on the west side of the wall is the figure of an unicorn. This is one of the few figures of beasts I observed in Egypt. The elephant is to be seen only in the entrance to the temple of Isis, in the island of Philoe: the horse, as a hieroglyphic, is on the northern exterior wall at Medinet Aboo; and the camelopard is on the wall of the sekos of the Memnonium, and on the back of the temple at Erments. On looking at an edifice of such magnitude, workmanship, and antiquity, inhabited by a half savage people, whose huts are stuck against it, not unlike wasps' nests, and to contrast their filthy clothes with these sacred images, that once were so highly venerated, makes one strongly feel the difference between the ancient and modern state of Egypt. The minor temple is but of small dimensions. It had a portico in the front; nothing of which is to be seen but fragments of columns buried in the rubbish. Some say this temple was dedicated to Apollo: but I do not know why there is not as much reason to suppose that it was dedicated to Typhon, as that the temple at Tentyra was dedicated to Isis. The square capitals on the columns at Tentyra are adorned with heads of Isis; and this is one of the principal circumstances, that indicate the deity to whom the temple was dedicated. In the temple at Edfu the figure of Typhon is placed on the capitals in a similar manner; and though there are representations of the beneficent deeds of nature on the walls, these may have been placed there by way of contrast, to elucidate the destroying power of the cruel god. Farther on to the south is part of a building, which no doubt was a second propylæon, as it faces the one now standing. Farther still is a small temple, almost unnoticed by travellers, which has an avenue of sphinxes leading in a right line towards the great temple. The sphinxes, several of which I cleared from the surrounding sand, have a lion's body and female head as large as life. There are vast heaps of ruins all round these temples, and many relics of antiquity may be buried there.

On our passing by Djebel Cilcilly we did not stop, as we had a fair wind; and I deferred visiting that place till our return. On the 22d we arrived at Ombos. The ruins that are now left give a clear idea of what it has been. The columns of the portico form one of the richest groups of architecture I have seen: the hieroglyphics are well executed, and some still retain their colours. On the water-side are the remains of a smaller temple, part of which is fallen into the Nile. The stones of this little temple are not so large as most of the rest; which proves, that the Egyptians paid great attention to the proportion of masses, as one of the principal points in the effect they were intended for. The aspect of this little temple is somewhat graceful; and some of the figures retain part of their colours, though exposed to the open air. In this temple the same state of decay was apparent as in various others. The altar is fallen down, and may be seen when the water is low. It is a piece of gray marble, without hieroglyphics. Close to the water-side are some landing-places, with covered staircases, leading up to the temple; but these are quite filled up with sand. We have reason to suppose this little temple to have been dedicated to Isis, as there are the heads of that goddess on the capitals of the two pillars, like those on the columns at Tentyra.

Before our arrival at Assouan, we landed on the western bank of the Nile. Here the country has a more pleasing aspect than any we had passed since the Chained Mountains. There are palm-trees in great abundance, on each side of the river, and some cultivated spots of ground, which extend from the Nile to the mountains. The distant view of Assouan presents a very gratifying aspect, perhaps increased by the barrenness of the preceding lands. The old town of Assouan stands on a hill, which overhangs the Nile. On its left is a forest of palm-trees, which hides the modern town; and on its right a distant view of the granite mountain that forms the cataract. The island of Elephantine seems to interfere with the barrenness of the western bank, and fills the ground with picturesque groups of various trees; and the high rock on the left, with the remains of a Coptic convent nearly on the summit of it, forms a view, to which travellers in Egypt are not accustomed; and this may be the cause of their describing it with so much partiality. We landed at the foot of the hill on the left of the Nile, and went to see the ruins of the convent, where I observed many grottoes, which had served as chapels for the Christian worship. The convent is formed of several small arched cells, separate from each other; and commands a very pleasing view of the cataract, Assouan, and the lower part of the Nile. One of the Arabian traditions relating to this place, I think worth notice.

There is in this spot, say the Arabs, great treasure, left by an ancient king of the country, previous to his departure for the upper part of the Nile, on a war against the Ethiopians. He was so avaricious, that he did not leave his family any thing to live on; and he was in close friendship with a magician, whom he appointed to guard his treasure till his return. But no sooner was he gone, than his relations attempted to take possession of the treasure: the magician resisted, was killed in the defence of his charge, and changed to an enormous serpent, which devoured all his assailants. The king is not yet returned, but the serpent still keeps watch over the treasure; and once every night, at a particular position of the stars, he comes out of the caves, with a powerful light on his head, which blinds all that attempt to look at it. He is of an enormous size; descends to the Nile, where he drinks; and then returns to his cave, to watch the treasure till the king returns.

The 24th, on our arrival at Assouan, I made application to the Aga for a boat to proceed to Nubia; but, it being the last two days of Ramadan, none could be had, for every body was feasting. I went the same evening to the outer town of Assouan, and found it more extensive than it appeared from an external view. It stands on a granite rock, and its situation is extremely pleasant. The higher part commands a view over the cataract, the Elephantine, and the New Town. The granite quarries of the ancient Egyptians are to be seen every where. From this spot we have a full view of the cataract, which, when the water is high, scarcely deserves the name; for it consists merely of several rapids, where the river is divided in its course by various granite islands scattered about, and ascending gradually to the island of Philoe, distant from Assouan about three hours' journey by water, but two only by land. When the Nile is low, the cataract has a different appearance, as I shall have to describe in my subsequent excursions. Above the New Town are the remains of a small Egyptian temple, so buried in the rubbish and stones, that it has escaped the notice of many travellers.

On my return to the boat, I found the Aga and all his retinue seated on a mat under a cluster of palm-trees close to the water. The sun was then setting, and the shades of the western mountains had reached across the Nile, and covered the town. It is at this time the people recreate themselves in various scattered groups, drinking coffee, smoking their pipes, and talking of camels, horses, asses, dhourra, caravans, or boats. The Aga came on board, with as many of his followers as the boat could hold. We treated them indiscriminately with coffee, and a small portion of tobacco each. As a present to the Aga, I sent to his house about a pound of tobacco, some soap and raw coffee, which he gladly accepted. His manners were pretty free; and, from motives of self-interest, he proposed to furnish us with a boat of his own. This I preferred, because I supposed we should be the more respected by the people of Nubia, whither we were going. He promised, that I should see the Reis of the Nubian boat the same evening, but he did not appear. Showy as the appearance of the Aga was, the inside of his house was not in conformity with his dress, which by no means corresponded with that of many persons in Cairo employed by the Turkish government; who dare not make the least show of riches, lest they should incur the suspicion of having defrauded their master. This proves, that the fear of the Turks has in a great measure lost its influence here. While remaining with our boat, Mrs. Belzoni took an opportunity to visit his harem, or seraglio, which consisted of two houses; for the old Aga had separated the old wives from the young, though he still visited them.

Next morning early I went to see the island of Elephantine,

named by the Arabs El-Shal. As I could get no boat from the shore where we were, we went to the old town, and crossed in the ferry-boat, which is made of branches of palm-trees, fastened together with small cords, and covered on the outside with a mat pitched all over. There were nine of us in this boat. Its length was ten feet, its breadth five, and it might weigh about fifty pounds. It cost, when new, twelve piastres, or six shillings.

On my arrival at the island, I went to see the temple, supposed to be dedicated to the serpent Knuphis; and, I may truly say, the only antiquity in it worthy of mention. It consisted of one chamber, with two doors facing each other, and a gallery of square pillars all round. The walls are adorned with hieroglyphics, and it has a staircase in the front. I could not see the pedestal with Greek inscriptions, mentioned by Mr. Norden. There was a subterraneous staircase leading from the temple to the river; and, a little above it, two lateral parts of a gateway, made of square blocks of granite, sculptured with hieroglyphics. Several large pieces of granite are lying about, apparently as if there had been a building of some magnitude. Towards the centre of the island is a kind of gallery, built of several square pillars of sandstone, full of hieroglyphics. The rocks of blue granite, that project out of the earth, serve as foundations. Not far from this temple, I saw a statue of granite, I believe of Osiris, about double the size of life. It is sitting on a chair, with some hieroglyphics on it, and its arms crossing the breast: but it was so mutilated, that it did not appear worth taking away.

I crossed the island, and on the west bank found it to contain many trees of cassia and sycamore. The ground is well cultivated, and altogether it is pleasant enough; but it has not those beauties, which have been ascribed to it by some travellers. In crossing the river, I saw the rocks of granite, with the hieroglyphics and the

Nilometer cut on them. I returned to our bark, and prepared for our departure.

August 25, in the morning, I waited to see the Reis, whom the Aga had promised to send to me the night before; but no one came. In the afternoon I went to the Aga, who repeated, that I should see the Reis in a few minutes. I waited patiently some time; at length the Aga himself came on board. After the usual ceremonies and protestations, he gave me to understand, that we must make an arrangement about the money to be paid for the boat. I told him, that I should be very glad to see the Reis himself on the business. He answered, that if I agreed with him, it was the same thing. He added, that the bark was ready: but he demanded so exorbitant a sum, that I told him I never would pay it, and that I would contrive to provide myself with a Reis, who knew the cataract, and would draw up our own bark. He seemed very much dissatisfied with my answer, and said, that the Reis of the Shellal could agree with no sailors but their own.

I went with my Janizary and the interpreter to the upper part of the cataract at Morada, which is two hours distant. Two soldiers of the Aga offered to accompany us, but I told them we were not afraid, as we were well armed. They almost insisted on going, but I would not permit them; for I was aware, that they wanted only to see what we were doing, and to interrupt my plans if possible. When we arrived, we found the boat not ready, without a mast, and the Reis not there. On inquiry we met with a man, who undertook to pilot our bark up the first cataract, and as far as the second, and back again, for twenty pataks, which are equal to forty-five piastres, or four dollars and a half. As we were returning, the Reis of the first boat came, and protested, that his boat would be ready early next morning. I asked him about the price, but he said, that this was left entirely to the Aga. I was now certain of the Aga's tricks, and felt pleased, that I had a Reis to pilot our own bark; but I found myself much mistaken. While I was absent on this expedition, the Aga had threatened our Arab Reis, if he proceeded any farther with his bark; and he was glad to obey, for he thought I should leave him and his bark to wait at Assouan till my return, and pay him his monthly money during the whole time. I had scarcely arrived on board, when the Aga came with great speed, attended by his whole train of courtiers, in their rags and finery. They were all clad in their gala attire, as this was their grand feast of the Ramadan.

I cannot describe the motley confused manner, in which this great divan was decorated: one had a new tunic of their brown cloth, and a ragged turban: another had a fine turban, and a ragged tunic: a third, without turban or tunic, had a fine red woollen shawl round his body; the Aga himself was uncommonly dirty and showy, being dressed in green and red, and without a shirt on his back. He came on board with all his suite. I observed the Reis, whom I had brought from Morada, advance to kiss the hand of the Aga; but he refused with an angry look, saying to him, "Do you dare to hinder me from letting a boat."—I then told the Aga that, if my taking a boat from any one but himself would cause a disturbance, I would rather return back, as I was not anxious to see a country, where there was nothing to interest me, and which would occasion me such enormous expense. At this he became all at once very mild; and still more so when I told him, that I was determined to return, and not go any farther, as my patience was worn out with the number of obstacles thrown in my way. The result was, that he offered me his boat at the price a Nubian would have paid; and with the positive condition, that it should be entirely at my disposal, to stop where I pleased, go where I pleased, and take us to the second cataract and back again; that it mattered not how long I should stay in a place, even a fortnight if I liked it; that the Reis should be obliged to bring on board four other sailors besides himself, supply them with provision, and give us all the assistance and information in his power; and for all this accommodation I was to pay the sum of two hundred piastres, or twenty dollars, which was less than I should have had to pay, if I had kept the former boat from Cairo, as I incurred no extra expenses. The first demand of the Aga was fifty thousand paras, equal to about a hundred and twenty dollars. Our luggage was to be sent on board the next morning on camels, and we ourselves set off in the evening.

Early in the morning the Aga came again to our boat, begging for a bottle of vinegar, which I gave him, accompanied with a trifling sum of money for his trouble, to induce him to take care of the baggage we left behind till our return. He was well satisfied, and promised to do all in his power to expedite our departure. The boat I had from Cairo was to go back; and I embraced the opportunity to write to the consul, informing him of my scheme of ascending the Nile to the second cataract, during the interval required for the arrival of the boat from Thebes, which was to convey the colossal bust.

We arrived at Morada in the evening, and accommodated ourselves in the boat as well as we could for the night.

In the morning of the 27th, long before the rising of the sun, I stood at the stern, waiting the light to unveil that goodly sight, the beautiful island of Philœ. My anxiety to see the ruins was as great as my expectations; but, when I beheld them, they surpassed every thing that imagination could anticipate. We crossed the water, and three hours elapsed, which appeared to us as so many minutes; but, as I intended to inspect these ruins minutely on our return, I only took a hasty view of the island. I observed several blocks of stones, with hieroglyphics on them in great perfection, that might be taken away, and an obelisk of granite about twenty-two feet in length, and two in breadth. I think this also might easily be removed, as it lies in a good situation, and not far from the water-side. On our return to the boat we set sail, and in about three hours arrived at Debod: but I would not go to see the temple there, as the wind was so favourable I did not like to lose the advantage of it. This, therefore, I also deferred to my coming back. We stopped near the shore above Sardeeb el farras.

28th.—We passed several ruins this day on the western bank of the Nile, which I shall mention hereafter, and about noon we stopped at a village on the eastern bank, I believe to take in provision for the crew. The Reis, the Janizary, and the sailors went on shore; Mrs. Belzoni, the interpreter, and myself, remained on board. Some time after, a few natives came to our boat, and seemed anxious to see what we had in it; but as it was covered with mats, they could not look into it so well as they wished. After one of them had approached, and examined every thing with attention, they all retired; but a few minutes had scarcely elapsed, when we saw several of them returning armed with spears and shields of crocodile skins. As they came straight towards us, and were joined by some others, their appearance was rather alarming, and I thought it was time to be on our guard. Though we were well armed, we were only three in the boat: accordingly I took a pistol in each hand; Mrs. Belzoni also seized one, and the interpreter another. They approached us in their boats, as if with intention to come on board. We asked them what they wanted; but, as they had no knowledge of the Arabic language, they did not understand us. I made signs to them to keep off; but they appeared indifferent to all we said or did. I then stepped forward, and with my right hand prevented the first of them from entering the boat, while I held the pistols in my left. He began to be rather rough in his manner, but kept his eyes on the pistols, while the others behind were urging him on. At last I pointed a pistol at him, making signs, that, if he did not retire, I would shoot at him. On this he drew back, and remained with the rest for some time, apparently in consultation. The Reis, the crew, and the Janizary, now came on board. I told the Reis what had happened to us, and he talked to the men in their own language; but, at the same time, untied the boat, and we went from the shore into the middle of the Nile. On my expostulating with him upon the impropriety of leaving the boat without any one who could speak the language of the country, he said, that these people had a dispute with their neighbours, which was the reason of their being armed; and that they only wanted our boat to go to another island, to fight with the inhabitants, their adversaries. Whatever might have been their intention, whether to attack us, or to fight others, neither would have been a pleasant adventure to us.

Proceeding on our voyage, we passed Taffa, and entered the rocks of granite above that place. Here the Nile seems as if a passage had been cut for it through a chain of high mountains, which rise nearly perpendicular on each side of the river, and open gradually to the south, into another country. As we advanced forward, the view extended more and more. On the right of the Nile were several groups of palm-trees; on the left, the distant ruins of Kalabshe; and in the centre, the island of the same name, which has a formidable appearance at a distance, owing to the ruins of some Saracenic houses, which give it the resemblance of a castle. We arrived at this island the same evening.

29th. This day we arrived at a village named El Kalabshe. At the foot of a rock, and facing the river, stand the ruins of a temple, which certainly must have been of later date than any other in Nubia; for it appeared to me to have been thrown down by violence, as I did not see that decay in its materials, which I have observed in other edifices; and what remained standing clearly proved, that time had had nothing to do with the destruction of it. On the water-side, before the temple, is a landing-place, which leads straight to the propylæon, as the gate of this does to the portico. The propylæon is in good preservation, but the portico is quite destroyed. There are two columns, and one pedestal, on each side of the door into the pronaos. They are joined by a wall raised to nearly half their height, which proves the late period when this temple was erected, as such a wall is clearly seen in all other temples of later date; and I would not hesitate to say, that Tentyra, Philœ, Edfou, and this temple, were erected by the Ptolemies: for though there is great similitude in all the Egyptian edifices, yet there is a certain elegance in the forms of the more recent, that distinguishes them from the older massy and enormous works; whence they appear to me to have been executed by Egyptians under the direction of Greeks. The pronaos and the cella are detached from the main wall all round; the intermediate space forms a gallery, so as to leave them isolated from the rest of the wall. The roof has fallen down, except a small portion on the chamber behind the adytum, in the wall of which there are several cells, merely large enough to contain a single person in each. They must have been either prisons for men, or places for the sacred animals. There are groups of figures on the walls of the cella, which retain their colours remarkably well; better indeed than in any other temple in Egypt; which I think is another proof of its being of later date than many others. As we entered this temple immediately on our landing, there were none of the people at its door: but when we were coming out, we found a great number of natives assembled at the entrance of the propylæon; and as we attempted to pass through it, they closed it entirely, and demanded money. They were all armed with spears, shields, halberts, &c. I told them that I would not be forced to part with money thus; but if they would let us pass, I would do what I thought proper. I did not allow them time to reflect, but immediately walked forward, staring them in the face, and no one touched us. When on the outside, I gave them a bakshis, and told them, I was ready to give them a farther present, if they would bring me some antiquities. This they did, and I bought several tombstones with Greek inscriptions.

They took us to see a smaller temple, a quarter of a mile distant; and we passed a great deal of rubbish and stones, which indicate the ruins of an ancient town, extending about a mile. Mr. Burckhardt says, this seems to have been the town of Talmis. The quantity of pottery in the ruins is all of Greek manufacture; scarcely any thing Egyptian is found among them: but if this be not sufficient evidence that the town was built by the Greeks, I can produce an incontrovertible proof that the temple was a place of their worship. It was only a few months previous to our arrival there, that one of the natives, raising a stone among the ruins of the temple, saw a piece of metal. He did not know what it was; but as whatever is found in the ruins the natives always suspect to be gold, he took this to be so. Not being certain of it, however, he communicated his discovery to others, who immediately claimed a share of it, and of course a scuffle ensued. Some time after, the circumstance came to the ears of Ibrahim Bashaw, or his soldiers at Assouan, who did not fail to take possession of it, on their first tour to collect the Miri in that country. The piece turned out to be a golden lamp of Grecian form, with part of a chain attached to it. It was sent to Cairo, and I believe money was made of it. This will prove two points; one, that the temple was used by the Greeks; and the other, that it was destroyed by violence; for if the temple had fallen gradually by decay, the lamp would not have been left there, to be buried under the ruins. The small temple we saw cut out of the rock, I think, is considerably older than this, and of a construction more conformable with the others of that country.

On the south of the large temple stands the village, which consists of a few huts built of earth and of stones from the ruins. Near the temple I observed an ancient wall, parallel with the front of it, and having several divisions, apparently the habitations of the priests. The country round has a pleasing aspect, owing to the groups of palm-trees, and their contrast with the barren rocks every where else; but the cultivated grounds are very scanty. Behind the mountain are valleys with some acacia trees, of which the natives make charcoal: when the Nile is at its height, they make rafts of the same wood; and the charcoal, put into sacks fabricated of palm leaves, or of a kind of rush, is conveyed on them to Cairo for sale; dhourra, salt, and tobacco, being brought back in return.

We arrived on the same day at Garba Dandour, where are the ruins of a small temple, consisting only of a pronaos and two chambers in the front. There is a small portal, and a species of platform, which extends from the propylæon to the river, one hundred feet long and fifty wide. This could not have been built as a landing-place, as there are no marks of stairs any where. The inner apartments have a few hieroglyphics, and two columns. The rocks here are pretty close to the water, and for some miles without a spot of cultivated land.

We proceeded on to Garba Merieh, and early the next morning landed at Gyrshe. This temple is partly hewn out of a rock, which rises perpendicularly, facing the east, a quarter of a mile from the river. In our way to it we crossed the ruins of a small ancient town. I observed the fragments of four lions, probably sphinxes, which stood before the temple; and a mutilated statue, apparently of a woman. The portico consists of five pilasters on each side of the door, cut out of the rock, each of which has a striking figure before it, I believe representing Hermes. In the front of the portico are four columns, formed of several blocks of stone: the pronaos is hewn out of the rock, and has three square pillars on each side, in a line from the door to the entrance into the cella. In front of each of these pillars stands a colossal figure, about eighteen feet high, elevated four feet above the ground. We may here see how the sculpture of primitive ages differs from that of the more modern school. The figure of these colossi indicates that the artist meant to represent men; but this is all: their legs are mere shapeless columns, and their bodies out of all proportion: their faces are as bad as the artist could make them from the model of an Ethiopian: they have the usual mitres on their heads; and are adorned on the lower part of their bodies with curious appendages, not unlike the tobacco pouches used among the Highlanders; though I hope no one will suppose, that I mean to suggest a comparison between the two nations. The place is blackened with smoke, I presume from the fires made by the natives. Behind the pillars are several niches cut in the rock, but all mutilated. In the cella are two small chambers, one on each side, cut also in the rock; and at the end two lateral doors leading into smaller apartments, independent of the adytum. In the wall at the end of this are four figures seated, as large as life, and an altar before them, as I have seen in other places, without hieroglyphics or any inscription. The floor is in many places dug up, I suppose by the Barabra or other nations, in search of treasure. The natives of this place are rather rough in their manners, but were easily satisfied with a piece of soap, a pipe of tobacco, and a few paras. Here we bought some gryadan, a grain of the size of a small shot, which the Nubians use as coffee. It is a good substitute where no coffee is to be had, and is much cheaper. A little above this place is a dangerous passage of the Nile, a chain of rocks running across the river, and making it very alarming, when the waters are low; but as they were now high, we passed without danger. The country here still continues quite barren.

In the afternoon of the next day we arrived at Dakke, (see plate 21). The mountains at this place stretch far from the Nile, and leave a spacious plain, which no doubt has been formerly cultivated, but is now covered with sand. A stratum of vegetable mould is visible, three feet under the sand on the banks of the Nile. The temple stands about a hundred yards from the river, and has a very elegant appearance. There are no hieroglyphics on the outside wall, but the interior is adorned with beautiful figures in basso relievo: it has a pronaos, an adytum, and a cella. On the west side of the adytum is a small staircase which leads to the top of the temple; and on the east a small chamber, with figures uncommonly well executed: the walls of the cella are well covered with religious processions. In the lower part I observed several figures, not unlike hermaphrodites. From the cella a door in a line with the first entrance leads into an area, formed by a wall which surrounds the edifice, except in front. On the east side of the exterior wall is a door, which leads to a passage across the temple, that separates the pronaos from the adytum. The temple faces the north, and at the distance of forty-eight feet is a propylæon, with the gateway facing the entrance to the pronaos. The isolated situation of this edifice renders it still more graceful to the eyes of the traveller, as it is entirely free from any other building near it. On the propylæon are several Egyptian, Coptic, and Greek inscriptions, one of which is as follows:

ΔΟΜΙΣΙΟCΑΡΡΙΑΝΟC
CΤΡΑΤΙCΠ;ΙΡΗ;ΙΤΟΥΡΑΝ,
ΦΗΛΙΚΟΚΑΙΔΟΜΙΤΙ
ΟΥΙΟCΜΟΥCΥΝΤωΠΑΝΓΑ
ΟΙΚωΠΡΟC;ΚΥΝΗΟΛ
Φ;ΟΝΜ;ΓΙCΤΟΝ;ΡΜΗ
ΚΑΔΡΙΑΝΟΥΚΑΙCΑΡΟC
ΤΟΥΚΥΡΙΟΥΤΥΒΙΙΗ

We continued our voyage, and arrived in the afternoon at Meharraka, or Offelina, where stand the ruins of a small Egyptian temple, but evidently built by the Greeks. It consists of only a single portico, forty-two feet long and twenty-five wide, with a row of columns round the two sides and the back. On the right is a winding staircase, the only one I recollect having seen in any temple in Egypt or Nubia. The columns are fourteen in all. It has served as a christian chapel, as is shown by many figures of the apostles which remain perfect on the walls; but on close examination I observed clearly the Egyptian figures under the saints. The main entrance is closed by an altar, no doubt built by the Copts or Greeks after the christian epoch. The wall facing the south is fallen down, but the stones still adhere to each other. On one of them I saw the following inscription.

NH ᴸᴸ
VICIHROΥNᴸ cTTc
TIωTOΥKAITωNE*t*·CEBEC
TATωNFONEωNKAIF·AIOΥ
Υ WIKΓOΥAAEAΦCΥKN
AOITFωNAAEAΦII

A few paces to the east stands part of another temple, on which is the figure of Isis, dressed in the Greek costume, sitting under a tree. Before her stands the figure of Orus, in the act of offering to his mother. In a niche further to the east is the figure of the Egyptian Isis; and in another small niche above are a Greek priest and priestess, and the Egyptian Priapus. A greater proof than this I never saw of the religion of the Egyptian and Greek nations united (see Plate 29). On the south of this temple is a large pedestal of granite, formed by three steps, which appears to have been erected for the purpose of supporting some large statue or obelisk.

We proceeded with a fair wind to Wowobat; and the next day, the 31st of August, brought us to Seboua. On our landing, the first thing that attracted my notice was a propylæon, at a small distance from the Nile; in the middle of which interval are two standing figures eleven feet high. These form the entrance to an avenue of sphinxes with lions' bodies and men's heads, that leads to the propylæon, which is much decayed. There is the usual entrance or gateway into the pronaos, at each side of which are five columns, with figures in the front of each, not unlike those in the pronaos at Medinet Aaboo. The wind has accumulated a great quantity of sand, which has not only covered the court, but closed the entrance to the adytum and the cella. From what I could discover, after a close examination from the top part of this temple, it deserved to be opened; but as my principal views were bent on other objects, which I thought of greater importance, we continued our voyage towards Deir. The country here is very barren, and few habitations are to be seen any where.

Next day we arrived at Korosko. A few miles above this place the Nile turns towards the north-west, and as the wind blew mostly from that quarter, we had it right against us, besides a very strong current, for the Nile was nearly at its height. Though the day was very hot, the night was exceedingly cold, considering the climate we were in. At this place we found it very difficult to advance, for the wind still continued strong ahead, and the sailors could not track the boat by ropes on the shore, as the bank was covered with thorns and acacia-trees, so that it took us two days to reach the territory of Deir, where the river resumes its course again to the south. From the trees I have mentioned we gathered a little gum-arabic; and the Reis of the boat caught some cameleons, which we intended to keep alive. They feed on flies and boiled rice, and drink water; but they do not agree together in confinement, for they bit off the tails and legs of each other. If put into the water, they swell like bladders, and swim faster than they can crawl. They generally live on palm-trees, and descend in the evening to drink. We caught about thirty, but they all gradually died. I saw a female full of eggs, of the size of large peas, eighteen in number, all attached to the matrix.

The 5th of September brought us to Deir, the great capital of Lower Nubia. The town consists of several groups of houses, built of earth intermixed with stones. They are in general not higher than eight or ten feet, a few excepted, which are the habitations of the Cacheffs of the country. The town is close to the water-side. At the foot of the sloping and rocky hill is a small temple; but I could not venture to go to see it, as I observed we were closely watched. I went immediately to Hassan Cacheff, who received me with an air of suspicion, and wanted to know our business. I told him, that we ascended the Nile merely to seek for antiquities, and that we wished to proceed as far as the Shellal, or second cataract. This he said was impossible, for the people in the upper country were at war with each other. He then ordered his mat to be brought to him, seated himself close before the door of his house, and invited me to sit also. The first question he put to me was, if I had any coffee. I replied we had a little on board for our own use, but that he was welcome to half of it. He next asked for soap, and I made the same reply. Then he inquired if we had any tobacco. I told him we had but a few pipes, and we would smoke it together; with which he was exceedingly pleased. The next question was, if I had any powder. To which I answered, that I had very little, and could not spare any. At this he laughed, and put his hand on my shoulder, saying, "You are English, and can make powder wherever you go." I was glad that he thought so, and deemed it prudent to leave him with this impression; but I told him I did not come there either to make powder or to waste any. By this time my Janizary had brought me some tobacco from on board; so we began to smoke; and coffee of gryadan was served; but, notwithstanding this, he said my sailors would not advance any farther, for they were afraid to go into the upper country. I told him, that if he gave me a letter to his brother Osseyn, we should be out of any danger. I then showed him the letter of Callil Bey at Esne to his brother: on which he observed, that this letter did not mention where I was going. Perceiving that the affair was likely to proceed very dilatorily, I frankly told him, if he meant to let me pursue my journey, I would make him a very handsome present of a fine looking-glass, some soap, and some coffee; on the contrary, if I were to return, he would lose all, and incur the displeasure of the Bey of Esne besides. His reply was, " We will talk of this tomorrow." So I returned to our boat without any positive answer.

Early in the morning I went to him again. When he asked me for the looking-glass, I replied, that it was ready, if he gave me the letter to his brother at Farras, which at last he did. Previous to our departure from Cairo, I took occasion to obtain all the information possible concerning the country of Nubia, from the natives who came to that city with dates and charcoal; and from them I learned, that a looking-glass and a few Venetian beads would be equal there to silver plate and pearls. Accordingly we took a good stock with us, though I was not certain of entering Nubia. The looking-glass I gave the Cacheff was twelve inches long and ten broad, and was the largest the people there had ever seen. It made a great impression on them. Many, who never came down as far as Assouan, had not seen a looking-glass before, and it astonished them greatly. The Cacheff was never tired of admiring his bear-like face; and all his attendants behind him strove to get a peep at their own chocolate beauty, laughing, and much pleased with it. The Cacheff gave it, not without fear, to one of them, with a strict charge to be careful not to break it.—On my way to our boat I met a very old man, who knew Baram Cacheff, the tyrant of Deir in the time of Norden. He said, that Baram died in his bed, but all his descendants were slain by the Mamelukes; and that he was a boy when Baram died.

We left Deir about noon; and a few hours brought us to Hafee, where the river flows from the south-west. The country all the way from Deir to this place is tolerably productive of dhourra and dates, and furnishes also a great deal of cotton, which is gathered, and sent to Cairo. The sugar-cane is not cultivated here, which I know not whether to attribute to the laziness of the natives, or to the country being too hot for that plant; but I am inclined to think the former is the real cause.

Proceeding onward, we came to Ibrim. This place stands on a high rock, nearly perpendicular, and forming the bank of the Nile. The town is surrounded by a wall of sun-baked bricks. The houses are all in a ruined state, having been uninhabited ever since the Mamelukes made it their abode on their retreat to Dangola. Close to the water-side are several chambers, not unlike sepulchres, hewn out of the rock; some of which have been painted, apparently by the Greeks, and retain their colour remarkably well. The cultivated land on the south side of the river in some parts extends not more than two hundred yards in width; but it is thickly set with palm-trees, producing dates, which are esteemed the best in Egypt, and in which the Nubians carry on a considerable trade. The northern bank is quite barren, except a few date and acacia trees.

In my voyage from Ibrim to the second cataract I must entreat the reader's indulgence. I noted down the names of all the villages we passed, as they were given to me; and thus I lay them before the public, as I am not aware, that they have been yet described by any traveller. Messrs. Legh and Smelt, who were the first to penetrate to any extent up this country by water, did not proceed beyond Ibrim; and Norden has given a correct account of all the villages and districts he passed only as far as Deir. About a league above Ibrim we came to the village of Vady Shubak on the east, and Mosmos on the west. The country on the east continued to be covered with dates as far as Bostan, but on the west it is quite a desert. From Toske we saw several rocks in the plain toward the east, which resembled so many pyramids of various sizes; and I should not wonder if these suggested to the Egyptians the first idea of this form. Some of them appear to be about two hundred feet high.

We went on shore at Ermyne, on the west of the river. The banks here are covered with the thorny acacia, tamarisks, and palm-trees, and some cultivated ground. Next day we saw the island of Hogos. On this island are the ruins of an ancient tower, which must have commanded the whole Nile, as the river is not very narrow here, and the island is exactly in the centre of it. The blocks of stone are not so large as those in the temples in Egypt, but they are well connected together. After this we reached Formundy, a district extending on both sides of the Nile as far as Saregg. At Formundy the river turns to the north-east, for two leagues only; but we had as much trouble to pass this place as we had at Korosko, the current and wind being both against us.

I cannot omit mentioning the hard labour the barbarian boatmen had on this occasion. They were continually in the water; and, though good swimmers, they had great trouble in wading against the current to pull the rope from under the trees, which cover the banks of the Nile in such a manner, that it is impossible to track it along on the shore. They are a people living very hardly, and eat any thing in the world. They chew the rock salt, or natron, mixed with tobacco, putting the mixture between the front teeth and the lower lip. The natron is found in several parts of Egypt, and is one of their articles of trade. The Laplanders are said to be very filthy in their food, and I am sure these people are not unlike them in that respect. When we killed a sheep, I had sometimes the pleasure of seeing the entrails opened, pieces of which, dipped once into the water, were eaten by them raw. The head and feet, with the skin, wool, hoofs, and all, were put into a pot, which is never washed, to be half-boiled, when they drank the broth, and devoured the rest.

We fastened our bark to the shore in the district of Formundy, and I mounted a high rock, to have a view of the country round. I found, on the west of the Nile, an extensive plain, with low, isolated hills, in the form of sugar-loaves, covered with black, smooth stones, something approaching to basalt. Some of the stones are above five feet in length. The country is every where barren; there are only a few date-trees near the water.

Next morning we reached Faras, which we left on the east, and went to see the temples of Ybsambul on the west. As we crossed the Nile exactly opposite these temples, we had an opportunity of examining and having full views of them at a distance (see Plate 42). In the front of the minor temple are six colossal figures, which make a better appearance at a distance than when near them. They are thirty feet high, and are hewn out of the rock; as is also the large temple, which has one figure of an enormous size, with the head and shoulders only projecting out of the sand; and notwithstanding the great distance, I could perceive, that it was beautifully executed. On the upper part or frieze of the temple was a line of hieroglyphics, which covered the whole front; and above this, a range of figures in a sitting posture, as large again as life. The sand from the north side, accumulated by the wind on the rock above the temple, and which had gradually descended towards its front, choked the entrance, and buried two-thirds of it. On my approaching this temple, the hope I had formed of opening its entrance vanished at once; for the amazing accumulation of sand was such, that it appeared an impossibility ever to reach the door. We ascended a hill of sand at the upper part of the temple, and there found the head of a hawk projecting out of the sand only to its neck. From the situation of this figure, I concluded it to be over the door. From the size of the head, the figure must have been more than twenty feet high; below the figure there is generally a vacant space; so that, with the cornice over the door and the frieze, I calculated, that the doorway could not be less than thirty-five feet below the surface of the sand; and this distance would have accorded in proportion with the front of the temple, which is one hundred and seventeen feet wide. The sand ran down in a slope from one side to the other, and to attempt to make an aperture straight through it to the door would have been like making a hole in the water. It was necessary, therefore, to remove the sand in such a direction, that it might fall off from the front of the door: but in doing this the sand from above would continue to fall on the place whence that below was removed, and render it an endless task. Besides, the natives were wild people, totally unaccustomed to such labour, and knew nothing of working for money; indeed they were ignorant of money altogether. All these difficulties seemed such insurmountable obstacles, that they almost deterred me from the thought of proceeding: yet perseverance, stimulated by hope, suggested to me such means, that at last, after much exertion and two voyages thither, I had the satisfaction of entering the great Temple of Ybsambul.

Having taken a proper measurement of the front of the temple, and made a calculation, I found, that, if I could persuade the people to work with persevering steadiness, I might succeed in the undertaking. I did not examine the small temple that night, as I wished early to reach the village of Ybsambul, and to see Osseyn Cacheff. The rocks out of which the temple is hewn continue for about two hundred yards southward, and then open into a flat country, where are some good spots of cultivated land on the banks of the Nile, abounding with palm-trees. We embarked, and soon landed at the village. I perceived a group of people assembled under a grove of trees, who, when I came near them, seemed to be somewhat surprised at the sudden arrival of a stranger. Having desired to see Osseyn Cacheff, for some time I received no answer; but at last was told, that he who sat there was Daoud Cacheff, his son. I saw a man about fifty years of age, clad in a light blue gown, with a white rag on his head as a turban, seated on a ragged mat, on the ground, a long sword and a gun by his side, with about twenty men surrounding him, who were well armed with swords, spears, and shields. A younger brother, of much inferior rank and dignity, was among them, who behaved very roughly towards me. Some had garments, others had none, and they all together formed a ragged assembly, by no means of most encouraging aspect. These people have no other employment, than to gather the imposts of their master from the poorer sort of natives. The Cacheff himself has nothing to do but to go from one place to another to receive his revenue; and in every place to which he goes he has a house and a wife. He is absolute master to do what he pleases: there is no law to restrain him; and the life of a man here is not considered of so much worth as that of a cat among us. If he have not what he wants, he takes it wherever he can find it: if refused, he uses force; if resisted, the opponent is murdered: and thus the Cacheff lives.

They are not easily led by promises, for there is so little faith among them, that what is not obtained is considered as imaginary. It was with such a race of people I had to deal; and from whom I had to obtain permission to penetrate into a place, and to carry on operations, the thought of which appeared to them like that of a madman. To persuade them to undertake work for money was still worse, as their only mode of buying and selling is by bartering dhourra for dates, or dates for salt. It will be recollected that Messrs. Legh and Smelt did not think proper to go any higher than Ibrim, as it was useless to penetrate into a country, where money was of little or no use, which in fact was the case at that time at Deir, and much more so above that place. Daoud Cacheff demanded of me what business brought me there. I told him I had a letter from the Cacheff, his uncle, directed to Osseyn Cacheff, his father; and that I came into the country in search of ancient stones. He laughed, and said that a few months before he had seen another man, who came from Cairo in search of treasure, and took away a great deal of gold in his boat; and that I came for the same purpose, not to take stones: what had I to do with stones, if it were not that I was able to procure gold from them? I answered, the stones I wished to take away were broken pieces belonging to the old Pharaoh people; and that by these pieces we were in hopes of learning, whether our ancestors came from that country; which was the reason of my coming in search of ancient stones. I thought this might serve as a good explanation of the motives by which I was induced to open the temple. He then asked where I meant to go in search of these stones. I told him the place in the rock had a door, and by removing the sand we could enter, and perhaps should find many stones there. Accordingly I proposed to have the place opened; and on a promise, that, if I succeeded, he should receive a bakshis, he consented on his own part; but still his father remained to be persuaded, and then people to be procured, who would work at such a place without fearing harm from the devil. I told him, that those who worked would gain money. "What money do you mean?" said he, "money from Mahomet

Ali, Bashaw of Cairo? what can we do with it? we cannot buy any thing here, or at Dongola." I said, the money may be sent to Assouan, and there dhourra could be purchased with it. "But," replied Daoud, "if we do so, they keep the money, and send us no dhourra." I could scarcely believe, that they had so little faith, or notion of commerce: but the fact is, that what produce they carry to Cairo, Siout, or Esne, they exchange for other articles, which they send to the southern country of Nubia, and never receive any money for it.

I produced a piastre, and showed it to some of the people, who by this time had increased in number all round, seated themselves in form of a crescent before us, and were staring me in the face, observing all my motions. I went on endeavouring to persuade them of the advantages they would derive from such money, if they introduced it into their country. The Cacheff, however, seemed convinced, that it would do no good; for then, he observed, the people who were not contented to stay in Nubia could sell their cows and goats, and go and live in Egypt. I believe he was right in this point; but it was certainly impolitic in him to make such a remark before his subjects. One of them took the piastre from my hands, and, after looking at it for some time, asked me who would give any thing for that small piece of metal. "Any one," I answered, "will give you a measure of dhourra for it, quite enough for a man to eat in three days." "That may be so in your country," replied he; "but here I am sure no one will give six grains of dhourra for so small a bit of iron." I told him, if he went on board our boat, and presented it to any one there, he would get for it dhourra enough to suffice him for the time I had mentioned. Off he ran like a deer, and in a few minutes returned with the dhourra folded in a rag fastened to his waist.

I had previously instructed the Reis of our boat what he had to do, if any of the natives should come with money to fetch dhourra; and accordingly he gave him the measure so ordered for a piastre. This experiment had a good effect, not only on the minds of the people, but also on that of the Cacheff; though, barbarian-like, he was not yet thoroughly satisfied. He observed, that a man who laboured a whole day ought to have four times that measure for his share; therefore, if I would give them four piastres a day each, he would persuade the people to work. At length, with much ado, I made a bargain for two piastres a man. Daoud told me, that a man who came there a few months before had left in his hands three hundred piastres, to open that place for him; but the people would not undertake the business, as no one cared for such small pieces of metal. On the traveller's return from Wady Halfa, he expected to have found the place open; but Daoud gave him his pieces of metal back again, as he did not know what to do with them. I found afterwards, that the person who had been there was Mr. D., the ex-consul of France in Egypt; and that in fact he received his money back, as the people would not work for it.

The next and greatest difficulty was to persuade Osseyn Cacheff to let us proceed; for without his consent nothing could be done. He lived at Eshke, a day and half up the Nile. That night we slept at Ybsambul, as I wished to strengthen the disposition of the Cacheff in my favour. Accordingly I sent him a measure of rice, about four pounds weight, three ounces of coffee, half a pound of sugar, and a few leaves of a particular sort of tobacco, called Tunny Djebel, from Syria, which the Barabra chew, and consider it a great luxury.

In the evening we received on board some sour milk, and warm thin cake of dhourra bread. This is baked on a flat stone, eighteen inches square, raised from the ground by a small stone at each corner, so as to admit a fire under it; and when it is at a certain degree of heat, the paste is laid on it, which being quite soft, or nearly liquid, spreads in a sheet all over the stone, and in one minute is firm enough to be turned, which is done with great dexterity without breaking it. As soon as one is baked, another is placed on the stone; and they are pretty good if eaten while hot, but when cold they are quite sour and disagreeable. They are generally eaten with sour milk; but if allowed to get cold they are broken to pieces, put into a bowl, and boiled lentils poured on them. This forms the general food of the country.

In the morning of the 11th, we passed near the ruined town of Adda, in a pleasant situation, commanding a view of the Nile, and a considerable part of the country. It contains a great number of houses, built like those at Ibrim; but the land on the east side is covered with sand. The western bank of the Nile is fertile, abounding with trees of various sorts, acacias, tamarisks, and many thorny groups. Farther on we came to the district of Kosko, on both sides of the Nile; then to Enhana, or Oddenham, Garba, Zarras, and, a little farther, to the island of the same name; beyond which was Antero on the south, and above it on the same side Diberet, and the island so called. In almost all these parts we observed the left side of the Nile quite barren, except at Zarras. On the right it is pretty full of palm-trees, and some dhourra is seen. The soil of the islands, however, seems to be the most fertile.

We next reached Eshke, the residence of the Cacheff, and certainly the best spot of land above Ibrim and Assouan. The trees are very thick here, and a large tract of land is cultivated along the Nile, producing a great deal of dhourra and cotton, which, being cleaned and sent to Cairo, are exchanged for ready made lines, salt, and tobacco. On our arrival we were told, that Osseyn Cacheff was not now at Eshke, but would return in a few days, as he was only at a small distance. As I did not like to go back to Ybsambul till I had an interview with him, we advanced to the second cataract, situated a little higher up. The Nile here turns to the south-west, the lands as we advanced still continued to be well cultivated, and the few huts, which were visible among the trees, were stronger and better built than those of the Arabs of Egypt. We fastened our boat to the shore, in the same district.

We set off early next morning, and with a good north wind soon saw Aloanortis on the right, and above it on the left Debrous. A little farther on was an island of the same name; and higher up on our left the district of Angosh or Sukoy. I had expected, judging from the rocky nature of the country about the first cataract, to have seen the mountain of the second at a great distance; but to my surprise we arrived at the very last district, without perceiving any thing but a flat country before us. The territory of Wady Halfa is the last on the Nile, on this side of the cataract. In the middle of the river is an island called Givarty, after this another called Mainarty, and beyond these two others, named Genesap and Ennerty. These four are cultivated; but there are others innumerable, which form the shellal or cataract, that are all barren. Some present nothing to the eye but bare stones and sand; others a few sycamore trees and sunt; but there are no palm-trees, except in the four islands first mentioned.

About nine in the morning we made to the shore, as near as possible to the last cultivated land on the left, which is Wady Halfa. A few of the natives came to see us, whom I requested to bring some asses, that we might ride to the cataract, a request they complied with without any difficulty. Mrs. Belzoni and myself (the Janizary and interpreter advancing before us) proceeded as far as the day would permit us, so as to return in proper time to the bark at night. We had many views of the cataract, and in different directions. I mounted one of the rocks, to have a distant view of the deserts;

and as far as I could see it is a flat country, except a few rocks that project here and there, particularly at the river's side, but they are of small dimensions. Towards the desert we saw several wild antelopes, which kept at a great distance from us. As the Nile was high, the current had not so great a fall, as when it is low; but I believe the cataract is not navigable at any time of the year. The rock forming this cataract differs from that of the first, for here is no granite, but a kind of black marble quite as hard. Some say it is black granite, but I cannot consider it as such: the grain of it is too coarse, and not so compact as that of granite.

We returned to the bark after sunset, and immediately crossed to the island Mainarty, where we arrived at dusk. We saw fires and people at a distance; but when we arrived we could not find any one. Their huts were left with all they had, which consisted only of dry dates, and a kind of paste made of the same, which they kept in large vases of clay baked in the sun, and covered with baskets made of palm-leaves. A baking-stove and a mat to sleep on were the whole of their furniture. They had pots and leathern bags to bring water from the Nile for their lands. Their settlement consisted of four men and seven women, with two or three children. They have no communication with the main land, except when the water is low, for at any other time the current, being immediately under the cataract, is so rapid, as to render it impossible to ford it; and boats never go to these islands, seldom passing farther than Wady Halfa. They are poor but happy: knowing nothing of the inticing luxuries of the world, and resting content with what Providence supplies as the reward of their industry. There are a few sheep and goats, which furnish them with milk all the year round; and the few spots of land they have are well cultivated, producing a little dhourra, which forms their yearly stock of provision. The wool they spin into yarn; wind the threads round little stones, and thus suspend them to a long stick fixed in an horizontal position between two trees, to form a warp; and by passing another thread alternately between these fabricate a kind of coarse cloth, with which they cover the lower part of their bodies.

I visited along with the Reis the whole of the rock, which is about an eighth of a mile in length, and half as much in breadth. It was quite late when we found this poor but truly happy people. They had lighted a fire to make their bread, and it was this fire which directed us to that quarter. They were all hidden in a hole under some ruins of an old castle, which stands on the south side of the island; and when we approached them, the women set up a loud scream through fear. Our Reis, who was a native of the lower part of Nubia, could talk their language, and pacified them: yet, notwithstanding this, we could not entice more than one man out of the place. Their fear was owing to some depredations committed by the robbers of Wady Halfa a few years before, who, at low water, forded over to the island, and did all the injury that could be done to such people. We assured them, that we were not like the robbers of Wady Halfa, but came only to get some one to show us the way to the cataract. At this, they were more afraid than ever; and said, that it never appeared, that boats passed higher than Wady Halfa, which is at the beginning of the cataract; it being impossible to proceed farther, owing to the quantity of rocky islands. The Reis himself opposed my wish to ascend higher, fearing more for his boat than for our lives. At last it was concluded, that the Reis should leave his son on the island as a hostage for the two men, while they came on board, to show us the way up. They knew their way to these islands; for at low water they frequent them, to collect some of the earth, from which they extract a sort of saltpetre, which they use in their food. I had reasons for not remaining at night with the boat fastened to the main land, and consequently preferred staying at the island.

Early in the morning of the 14th, we took on board the two men of the island, to pilot us towards the cataract as far as the boat could go, and then to show us the way we should proceed. We went on with the same strong north wind; and as we had plenty of water, advanced with our bark till we found ourselves so tossed about by the different currents and eddies, as to prevent our farther progress; and at the same time were so situated, that we could not return back, for fear of being driven against some of the rocks, which abounded on each side. Thus we were confined to one spot for about an hour. Sometimes we had a rapid start for a hundred yards; then all at once were stopped, and turned round, in spite of all our efforts, and of the north wind, which blew very hard. At last we were caught on a sudden in one of the eddies of water, and driven against a rock concealed about two feet below the surface. The shock was terrible; and I must confess, having Mrs. Belzoni on board, I felt no small degree of alarm, as I thought the boat was split in two. For my own part, perhaps I might have swam on shore; but Mrs. Belzoni was no small charge to me on this occasion. However, as it pleased God, and to my astonishment, there was no harm done. We succeeded in getting to the other side of the river as quickly as possible, and when we arrived, forgot all the danger we had just passed. We landed, and took our route on foot; Mrs. Belzoni, myself, the interpreter, the Janizary, the two men from the island, and four boys belonging to the bark; carrying with us some provision and water. We proceeded, on the rocks, and over a plain of sand and stones, till we arrived at the rock called Apsir, which is the highest in the neighbourhood of the cataract, and commands a complete view of the falls. The prospect from this spot is magnificent. The several thousand islands you see, of various sizes and forms, with as many different falls of water, running rapidly onward, while counter-currents return with equal velocity, exhibit a diversified appearance, truly grand. The blackness of the stones, the green of the trees on the islands, intermixed with the white froth of the water, form a fine picture, which can scarcely be described or delineated.

Hence you see the four cultivated islands, which lie on the south, or the most remote part of the cataract. They are named as follows: Nuba, Gamnarty, Ducully, and Suckeyr: on the north side are two others, called Dorge and Tabai. These islands are inhabited by a race of people who may be looked on as living in the most primitive state; for no one ever goes to them, nor do they ever quit their island. They are very few in number—in some of the islands not more than five or six; and they live on the produce of the few spots of ground they find on them, which they continually irrigate with the common machine named hade, consisting only of a piece of sheepskin and two sticks, by which they draw up the water. They have also a few sheep; and fabricate a cloth from cotton produced in the islands, in the same manner as they make that of wool.

On the left of the cataract the soil differs from that on the right. It consists of soft whitish stones and sand. From this spot it may be seen, that the course of the river is for a considerable extent among the rocks; and the summits of two high mountains are to be seen at a great distance. This part is not frequented by travellers; for there is no mode of conveyance, and no inhabitants on that side of the cataract. Boats never venture thither: when the water is low, it is impossible; and, when high, it would require a very strong north wind, to stem the rapid current against you.

We returned slowly to the bark, and took our course towards

the island we had left in the morning; but unfortunately the wind, being very strong, drove us to the island of Gulgé. The Reis wished to pass the whole night there; but in the evening the wind shifting a little, we returned to the island we were at before. But again, notwithstanding the proof we had given of our harmless intentions, the natives were not to be seen; and even the two men who had been with us in the boat no sooner landed than they disappeared. The son of the Reis, however, was preparing some food; and we were glad to have escaped the danger of so many eddies and rocks.

I forgot to mention that on the island Gulgé I perceived the remains of an ancient wall, in the form of a church, and built of sun-baked bricks. It was in the centre of the island, and consisted of three divisions.—See Plate 32.

15th.—In the morning we would not leave the island without seeing the inhabitants. The men soon appeared for their bakshis; and at last came the women, to see Mrs. Belzoni, who made them presents of glass bead-necklaces, with which they were wonderfully pleased: though, as it is their custom to take all, and give nothing, they did not even return us thanks for what they received; but took their presents, laughed, and ran away immediately.

We now descended the river with a strong north wind against us; and though some authors assert, that the Nile has no waves, but runs quite smooth, I can assure the reader, that we were this day tossed about as if by a gale at sea. The wind blowing fresh against a strong current naturally caused this effect.

We arrived in the afternoon at the village of Iskus, and went to see Osseyn Cacheff, who was returned, and to whom we had a letter from his brother Mahomet at Deir. I had landed with my interpreter and the Janizary, and entered a kind of house made in the shape of an angle of a propylæon. These houses would not stand the weight of an upper apartment, if they were built perpendicularly; for the clay walls, of which they are made, would fall outward. The Cacheff's house was adorned with an old mat spread on the ground as usual, a water jar, and a chain with two hooks made in a particular manner. This was that same Osseyn, who was one of the two brothers that caused Mr. Burckhardt to return from Tinareh. He was about sixty-eight years of age, five feet eleven inches high, stout and robust, and able to support the charge he was born to hold. He was surrounded by thirty men, all armed, some with matchlock guns and long swords, and some with spears and shields intead of guns. He was clothed in a long tunic down to his feet, made of white woollen cloth, with a belt round his waist, to which his sword, flint, and steel were attached. Over his shoulder he had a long shawl, made of the same stuff as the tunic, thrown partly over his head, so as to cover it from the sun. He had also a red turban, and on his feet a pair of ragged shoes. Notwithstanding his dress, there was an air of superiority about him, which distinguished him at once above all the rest. It is worthy of observation, that even among barbarians great respect is paid to superiors; and those very men, who would murder a fellow-creature in a difference about a few pipes of tobacco, almost tremble at the frown of a single and sometimes harmless old man. His inquiries concerning my business were very minute; but I soon brought the affair of the temple forward, which did not a little surprise him. He said he knew the entrance into the place very well; that the round ball on the large head was the door of the great Dere, as he named it, and if removed I could immediately enter. This round ball was no other than the globe on the head of the hawk-headed Osiris, which stood over the door, as I mentioned before. At first he stated to me the great difficulty, if not impossibility of opening this place; and at last, when I had endeavoured to remove these obstacles, he made me promise, that, if I found the temple full of gold, I should give him half. To this I agreed, on condition that if I found only stones, they should be all my own property; and he immediately assented, for he said he wanted no stones. Upon this he gave me a letter to his son at Ybsambul, and when I left him, and went on board, I sent him some trifling presents, which he received with pleasure, and sent us a lamb.

When I came to the bark I found it crowded with women, who had learned from our crew, as we passed upwards, that there was a woman on board; and as soon as we arrived, on our return, they all ran to the shore. Mrs. Belzoni, not supposing they would come in such numbers, made a present of some glass beads to one of the wives of the Cacheff. This was enough: they increased in crowds, and we had to please them all.

Next morning we continued our voyage, and arrived very early at Ybsambul. I went to see a small temple on the south side, opposite the village; but it is of no consequence, only it may be remarked as the last on the Nile on this side of the cataract. It has served as a chapel to the Christian Greeks; and the figures of the Apostles remain nearly perfect painted on the wall and roof. We crossed the river, and I went immediately to Daoud Cacheff. Having presented the letter from his father, he sent for the men who were intended to work. I found these people complete savages, and entirely unacquainted with any kind of labour. They had changed their minds since I was there last; and, though I had the authority of the Cacheff, they would not work. My persuasion was of no avail; first, because they were not inclined to such labour; secondly, they did not know the value of money, &c. At last I pretended to give up my project, and go away. When the Cacheff saw that I meant to go, and that he should lose many a good present, he began to talk to them; and at last, with much difficulty, reduced the payment to one half of what they had demanded before. On my agreeing to this, they immediately insisted, that I should employ as many as they chose. It was in vain I told them, thirty were more than sufficient for my purpose; they would not hear of less than a hundred. With this it was impossible for me to comply; so I rose, and took leave of the Cacheff, ordering the Reis to go on board, and set off immediately. This, however, was not satisfactory to the parties; they had still more to say, and at last it was concluded, that I should take forty men, who were to be at the bark before the sun rose next morning, as it was nearly two miles from the village to the temple. I went on board heartily wishing I had done with these people.

17th.—Early in the morning when I expected to see these wild men, for such I must call them, I was greatly disappointed: the sun was very high, and no one appeared. I then returned to the Cacheff, to inquire whether the men meant to make a joke of the business, or to work. Not being accustomed to be disturbed so early, he rose very slowly, and sent a party of his soldiers to search for the men, some of whom at last made their appearance, while others pretended they could not come. Their excuse was, that they saw a Bedoween in the desert, and they were all on the watch. The day before they wanted to be employed to the number of a hundred, and to-day they were unwilling to be employed at all. At length some arrived by land, some by water, but very late, and we went at last to the temple. I took it patiently, and began the work in such a direction, that the sand should fall off from the centre of the front of the temple, where naturally the door must be. They had a long stick, with a cross piece of wood at the end, at each extremity of which was a rope. One man drew the long stick back, and another pulled it forward. This is the method they use in removing the earth in their cultivated ground, and I found it very useful in clearing away sand also. As it was the first day of our enterprise, they went on better than I expected; and all their thoughts and talk were on the quantity of gold, pearls, and jewels, we should find in the place. I did not discourage them in their supposition, as I considered it to be the best stimulus they could have to proceed. At noon I gave them some boiled lentils, and bread soup, with which they were pretty well pleased. The Cacheff, who attended to the work himself, partook of what I ate. At night I paid the men, and recommended them to be there again early in the morning. The Cacheff and part of his court came on board, and we returned to the village for the night.

18th.—In the morning we went to the temple, and the Fellahs came after us rather late, and we began the work again very slowly. I had to use a great deal of persuasion this day; for the savages were led to think, they had laboured too hard on the first day, so that they were obstinate, and I had much ado to prevail on them to continue. As they complained of being very much tired, I promised, that they should not work the next day, but be allowed to rest themselves. We ended this day's work before sunset, and returned to the village. Finding ourselves but ill supplied with provision in this place, I offered more than usual for a sheep, but to no purpose: I was obliged to eat rice and water, and very little of that, as we had not much on board. Our stock of butter was quite finished, and milk was very scarce.

19th.—In the morning I went to see the Cacheff, to speak about some palm wood. I found him quite changed in his behaviour, starting a thousand difficulties; in particular, that the Fellahs would not come to work any more, as it was useless for them to fatigue themselves for a little money; adding, that it was impossible to get any palm wood; though at the same time we were surrounded by it. I answered, that this was not our agreement; and, as I kept my word, and paid the Fellahs according to our first engagement, I expected them to perform their part of the bargain. After much debate, it was at last concluded, that I should see the Fellahs at night, and try myself what could be done, for he could not serve me. In short, I could make nothing of him; but his interpreter soon gave me to understand, that all this difficulty arose from my not having made him any considerable present; and the soldier who was with me from Siout told me, that I ought not to omit giving him a brace of pistols, or some other valuable thing. I saw through the plot immediately; and I also knew that these people never feel grateful for any thing after they receive it, but think only of contriving new tricks to extort more, if possible; so that it is just the same whether you give or not. However, I took a middle course, and told the interpreter, that I would provide a good bakshis both for his master and himself, if they would interest themselves in my favour. In the afternoon the savages were all assembled, and I was sent for. The brother of the Cacheff, whom I saw the first time we arrived at Ybsambul, was there: his behaviour however was altered, and much for the better; so that he, who at first was rough, became smooth, and the smooth became rough. I inquired about the wood, and was told, that I must go to a place two leagues off, where I should find some; but this was said only to start new difficulties, as I knew there was plenty in the village. With respect to the savages, I was informed, that they would not come to work so hard, unless I doubled the numbers. It was in vain for me to tell them, that a man does not work more when alone, than when accompanied by multitudes. They were obstinate, and I could do nothing with them; for had I consented to employ a hundred, I should soon have been called on to make it up two hundred. I promised to give bakshis to the brother of the Cacheff, who began to talk to them in their own language; and to my astonishment all at once they agreed to come to the number of forty only; on condition, however, that I should give them the sixth part of an ardep of corn to make bread with. The Cacheff seemed displeased with the influence of his brother, and rose and walked off. A barbarian from Deir, who was a stranger in the island, and had come thither to cultivate a piece of ground, had bought some wood to build a sakias, or water machine; but as he could not agree with the savages at Ybsambul, and was going away, he proposed to sell his wood to me; and I gladly availed myself of the opportunity, and thus got over this difficulty.

20th.—Next day in the morning the people came slowly to work, but upon the whole we went on very well, though I had much ado to make them proceed in the right way. The Cacheff, with his attendants, came to see how we were proceeding, and gave me to understand, that he intended dining with me. I told him I was very glad of his company, but had nothing except boiled rice, unless he would order his people to kill a sheep for us, which I would gladly pay for. They consulted about who could afford to part with a sheep, and receive piastres in payment, and at last the order was given to an old man, who had five, which was a greater number than any body else. When the sheep was brought to us, the difficulty was to fix the price of it. Being the first ever sold for money in that place, to put a high price on it would have increased the value of sheep in general, and consequently would have been against the interest of the Cacheff; for when he receives his revenue in these animals, he sets them at a very low price, that he may have the more given him. To estimate it at a low price would be worse, for it would be against them all in the exchange of sheep for dhourra with the other villages. Finding it a dangerous point to decide, it was at length resolved, that no price at all should be put upon the sheep, but that the man should make me a present of it, and I should give any thing I pleased in

o

return. To prevent any standard being established from what I gave the man, I paid him in soap, tobacco, and salt.

At dinner the sheep was brought in pieces in two wooden bowls and the Cacheff and his attendants seated themselves in a circle on the sand near the temple. The extremities of their filthy hands were soon washed in the liquor, and in a few seconds the whole was devoured. Not being accustomed to this unceremonious sort of feasting, I stood but a poor chance; but in subsequent occurrences of this kind I contrived to take my share without interfering with their scramble. Soon after dinner coffee was brought up from the boat, and I went on board to take my dinner with Mrs. Belzoni, who had boiled rice and water for her fare, in preference to the chieftain's mess of mutton. In a short time the Cacheff approached, and signified his wish to speak to me in secret. We retired, and his principal interpreters were called to us. The great secret was this: on the night before, as he stood on the bank close to our boat, he saw me drinking a coffee cup of red liquor that I poured out of a bottle; and having inquired what it was, was told it was *nebet* (wine). Now he had heard that the wine of the English was much better than what they made in their own country with dates; he wished, therefore, to have some to drink also, but in a secret way. Fortunately I had a few bottles left from our stock in Cairo, which we preserved for extraordinary occasions; and I sent my interpreter down to the boat to fetch one. When the wine was first poured out into a cup and presented to the Cacheff, he sternly looked at the interpreter, and told him to drink first. The interpreter, who was a Copt, and had been in the French army for several years, did not want much persuasion to make a libation to Bacchus; so with a smile he soon convinced the Cacheff of the purity of the contents of the bottle, and the Cacheff did not hesitate to drink the next cup.

At the first taste it did not appear to him so strong as he had supposed; but at last he found it so good, that in three days my scanty stock was nearly finished. I had much reason to repent having taken a Janizary with me, for instead of assisting me in my dealing with these people, he was the first to suggest to them what they never would have thought of. It is not to be supposed that a Mussulman will ever take the part of a Christian dog, against any of his own religion, unless he is responsible for the life of the stranger; and then he does it for his own sake, and not from any attachment to the European. The work went on very slowly this day; but altogether we had made a considerable advance in the sand, towards the centre of the front of the temple.

21st.—Next morning, the people took it into their heads to come in such numbers, that I could not employ them all, as the work was directed only to one point. There was warm debating on the subject; but, as I would not spend one farthing more than I had promised from the first, they agreed at last that the pay should be divided amongst them all; and thus, instead of forty men, I had eighty for the same price, which was less than sixpence a day. The anxiety to see the inside of the temple, and to plunder all that it might contain, brought the two brothers on board very early in the morning. They soon gave me to understand plainly, that all that was there was their own property; and that the treasure should be for themselves. Even the savages began to lay their account in the division of the spoil. I assured them that I expected to find nothing but stones, and wanted no treasure. They still persisted, that, if I took away the stones, the treasure was in them; and, if I could make a drawing, or likeness of them, I could extract the treasure from them also, without their perceiving it. Some proposed, that, if there were any figure discovered, it should be broken before I carried it away, to see the inside of it. Thus I plainly perceived, that, on entering the temple, I should not be at liberty either to take notes of what was in it, or to make any drawings, much less to take away any statue, or any thing else that might be found. We went on with our labour, however, and, as I made a palisade with the palm wood I had bought, I had no need of so many men, as they had only to clear the space between the palisade and the temple.

In the course of the morning, two of the men left the work, and went down the Nile to our boat. Finding Mrs. Belzoni on board, with only a little girl from the village, they were rather impertinent to her, and attempted to go on board in spite of all she could say to them, intending to rob the boat. At last she presented a pistol to them, on which they immediately retired, and ran up the hill. She followed, but they mixed with a number of their fellow savages, and it was impossible to find them out; for they were all like so many lumps of chocolate seated on the sand at work, and not to be distinguished the one from the other. At night, when I paid the men, the Cacheff's brother said, the money must be counted all in one heap, before it was divided among the people. My interpreter, who was also my treasurer, accordingly counted the money on a piece of a ragged shawl, which he had no sooner done, than the Cacheff's brother threw himself on it, and seized every piastre. The men looked at each other, but no one dared to say a word about it; and he took it all away with him. I observed to him, that his magic was much more sure in its operation than mine, for obtaining money. But I was pleased to find they had begun to know the worth of it so well.

I naturally expected, that no one would come to work the next morning; but in this I was mistaken. As much of the sand had been taken away, the first palisade was insufficient. I made another, therefore, directly before the place where I supposed the entrance of the temple to be, to prevent the sand from falling against it. I now began to perceive clearly, that this work would employ more time than I could spare in that country, and the period I had meant to dedicate to it was already elapsed; but this would not have deterred me from proceeding, and no doubt I should have accomplished my undertaking, had it not been for a material cause which compelled me to quit the work for a time. This was the want of that very article which, a few days before, was so despised and unknown; and now I absolutely could not proceed without it. It was money, which, even here, had shown its usual power among mankind, of exciting avarice, and of which those wild people soon became very fond. I had some water brought up from the Nile, and poured down close to the wall over the door. This stopped the sand from running, till I had a hole made so deep, that I could perceive it required a longer time than I could stay, and more money than I could then afford. I had by this time removed so much sand, as to uncover twenty feet in the front of the temple. The colossal statues above the door were completely exposed; and one of the great colossi sitting before the temple, on the north side, which was buried in the sand, appeared with his face and shoulders like his companion on the south. Having obtained a promise from the Cacheff, that he would not let any one touch the place till my return, which would be in a few months, I contented myself with putting a mark where the sand was before I commenced the operation; and after taking a drawing of the exterior of the temple, quitted it, with a firm resolution of returning to accomplish its opening. We brought our boat to the village, and, after making some trifling presents to the Cacheff, set off the same evening.

We descended the Nile rapidly, as the current was very strong, which was a fortunate circumstance for us, for we were almost without provisions on board. Two hours after we left Ybsambul, a Turkish soldier on a dromedary hailed us from the right bank of the

Nile; but, without attending to him, we continued our voyage. He turned back, and followed us a considerable way; and when he came to a place, where the current brought us near the shore, he fired a pistol, as a signal to stop. We were greatly at a loss to conjecture who he could be, as it was not to be supposed, that a Turkish soldier would venture alone into this country. At length, as we drew near the bank, he said he had letters for me from the Bey of Esne. This was not true. He produced two letters in Arabic, signed by two different persons not in existence, which ordered me, in an insolent tone of command, to desist from any work I might have begun in Nubia, and return to Cairo. The reason why these letters were sent to me, by whom, and for what purpose, is one of those mysteries which, for the present, must remain unknown.

The soldier came on board, and sent the dromedary back by his servant; for in that country every soldier has a servant, to take care of his camel, horse, or asses, if he have any. Thus, when a body of five thousand men marches against an enemy, there are always at least six thousand people more to encumber it, and eat up the provision: for not only every common soldier has a man, but every officer has two or three; and those of the higher rank, as Beys, Cacheffs, &c. have ten or more.

As the current was so rapid, the next day, in the evening, we arrived at Ibrim, and early on the day after at Deir. I went to see the temple, but in a cursory way, reserving my observations to my next visit. We took in some provision, set off immediately, arrived in the evening at Nobat, and the next night stopped at El Kalabshe. Here we visited the temple a second time, but rather too late for much inspection. Mrs. Belzoni went to see the women of this place; of whom an account, given by her, will be found in the Appendix.

Next day we visited the two temples at Todfa, my humble observations on which I shall give in my next voyage in Nubia. Here a barbarian, armed with a spear and shield, called to me to stop, which I did, as he said he had something to communicate. He demanded my money in a resolute manner, and with a savage look; but when I made the interpreter inquire of him if he demanded the money per force, or as a voluntary bakshis, he laughed and ran off.

Continuing our voyage, at Cardassy I saw the remains of some very extensive buildings, and of some quarries, where a small chapel is cut in the rock, containing many Greek inscriptions, which I regretted I had not time to copy. We next came to Gamby, where, on the east, is a small temple, but almost even with the ground, and a few figures and hieroglyphics on the stones. This temple, that of Deir, and the one opposite Ybsambul are all I have seen on the eastern side of the Nile above the first cataract. We came down to Deboude in the afternoon, and went to see the ruins of that place.

Next day brought us to the Shellal, or first cataract. The soldier of Derow, who brought the letters, set off immediately, and I never saw him afterwards. I took particular notice of a large obelisk which was lying before the propylæon, and which, if brought to England, might serve as a monument in some particular place, or as an embellishment to the metropolis. I sent for the Aga of Assouan, and a Reis who knew the channels in the Shellal, and in the meantime took a general view of these superb ruins. I observed in the southern part of the island the remains of a small temple, quite in ruins, with blocks of stone scattered here and there, and remarked, that a part of the remaining wall contained the legs of several figures in basso relievo finely finished. I examined the blocks that had been thrown down from the wall, and found they contained the remaining parts of the figures, which had formed a group of seven in all. When the Aga and the Reis came, I made an agreement with them to have the obelisk taken down the cataract; but, for want of a boat, it could not be effected that season. The obelisk is twenty-two feet long, by two wide at the base; so that it required a pretty large boat to convey it. It was agreed, and perfectly understood, that I took possession of this obelisk in the name of his Britannic Majesty's consul-general in Cairo; and I gave four dollars to the Aga, to pay a guard for it till my return.

I entreat the reader here to pause, and to recollect what caution I took in securing this piece of antiquity; as he will find, in the course of this volume, that the obelisk in question has caused me more trouble and persecution than any thing else I succeeded in removing from Egypt. Indeed, it nearly cost me my life; and for such disinterested exertions I received, in return, the meanest insults. Unfortunately such was my situation in Egypt, that some of the very people I had to deal with, though I was acting for the credit both of their country and of themselves, could not restrain the impulse of jealousy, which they nourished in their breasts, and which always operated to my disadvantage. In a future work, that I intend to lay before the public, I shall unfold these matters; so that any one who has common feeling will wonder how I could persist so long in my researches under such circumstances.

The blocks of stone, which formed the compartment of fourteen feet long and twelve wide, were twelve in number. When they were put together on the ground, they were a beautiful group, consisting of the great god Osiris seated on his chair, with an altar before him, receiving offerings from priests and female figures; the whole surrounded by flowers and hieroglyphics. The blocks were three feet six inches long, and three feet wide: but as they were two feet three inches thick, they were too bulky to be embarked whole. As they could be easily cut, being a calcareous gritstone, I made an agreement for one hundred piastres, to have them cut to six inches. I left the money in the hands of the Aga; and it was understood, that these stones were to be embarked by the first opportunity of a boat, and sent down to Luxor. The Aga hinted, that he should be happy to know what I meant to give him for permission to take away the obelisk; for though I was authorised by the firman of the Bashaw to take what stones or statues I pleased, yet these fellows think they have a right to demand something; and if they cannot openly refuse, still they have it in their power to throw such obstacles in the way, as to entirely defeat your undertaking. It was agreed, that he should give orders to the Sheik of the island, to guard the stones and the obelisk, so that no one should injure them; for which guard, as before stated, he received four dollars; and that on the removal of the obelisk he should receive three hundred piastres, equal to thirty dollars.

Next day, the 27th of September, we came to Assouan by land; just one month from the day on which we first entered that place. On our arrival, we were informed, that there were no boats to take us to Esne; and, in spite of all our haste, we were obliged to wait till some came from the North. We therefore took another tour in the island of Elephantine, and on the next morning I set off for the granite mountain, about two hours and a half south-east of Assouan. I took an Arab of Assouan with me as a guide, and walked about the greater part of the day. I saw a great many granite quarries, which plainly showed, that the ancients took the granite intended for the temples, statues, and ornaments, from these places; and in one of these excavations I saw two large basins in the rough cut out of the rock, one of which was ready to be taken away, as it was nearly finished. It appeared to me, by what I could observe, that the pieces of granite were procured by cutting a line with a chisel, about two inches deep, round the stone intended to be removed,

P

and then by giving a great blow with some machine, which separated the part like glass when cut with a diamond. In this basin were pieces, which plainly showed the fact of this operation. On my return towards the west, I was fortunate enough to find a column lying on the ground, with a Latin inscription, as in the annexed plate. It proves, that the Romans used to take granite from these quarries, and, no doubt, chiefly for religious purposes, like the Egyptians.

On my return to Assouan, no boat had arrived, and I became impatient, for I wished to reach Thebes. We were seated under a grove of palm-trees, eating our soup of rice and meat with the Aga, when an Arab came to him, and whispered in his ear, as if he had something of great importance to communicate. The Aga rose, though his dinner was not finished, and went away with the air of a man of great business. Half an hour after he returned, accompanied by two other persons of distinction, and the old man who came before. They all seated themselves round me, and after introducing the affair with a degree of caution, I was asked, whether I wished to purchase a large piece of diamond. I considered, that I was no diamond merchant; but in a case like this, I would have contrived to become a jeweller, and have procured the money from Esne, if it had been to my advantage; for, in the times in which we live, jewels are no despicable articles, if they can be obtained at a cheap rate. I told the Aga, that if the article were good, I would purchase it, if we could agree; but it was necessary that I should see it. He said, the piece had been found by one of the natives of that place; and, as he was not in want of money, it had been preserved in the family for many years. This original proprietor being now dead, his successors wished to dispose of it. I requested to see it; so we retired some

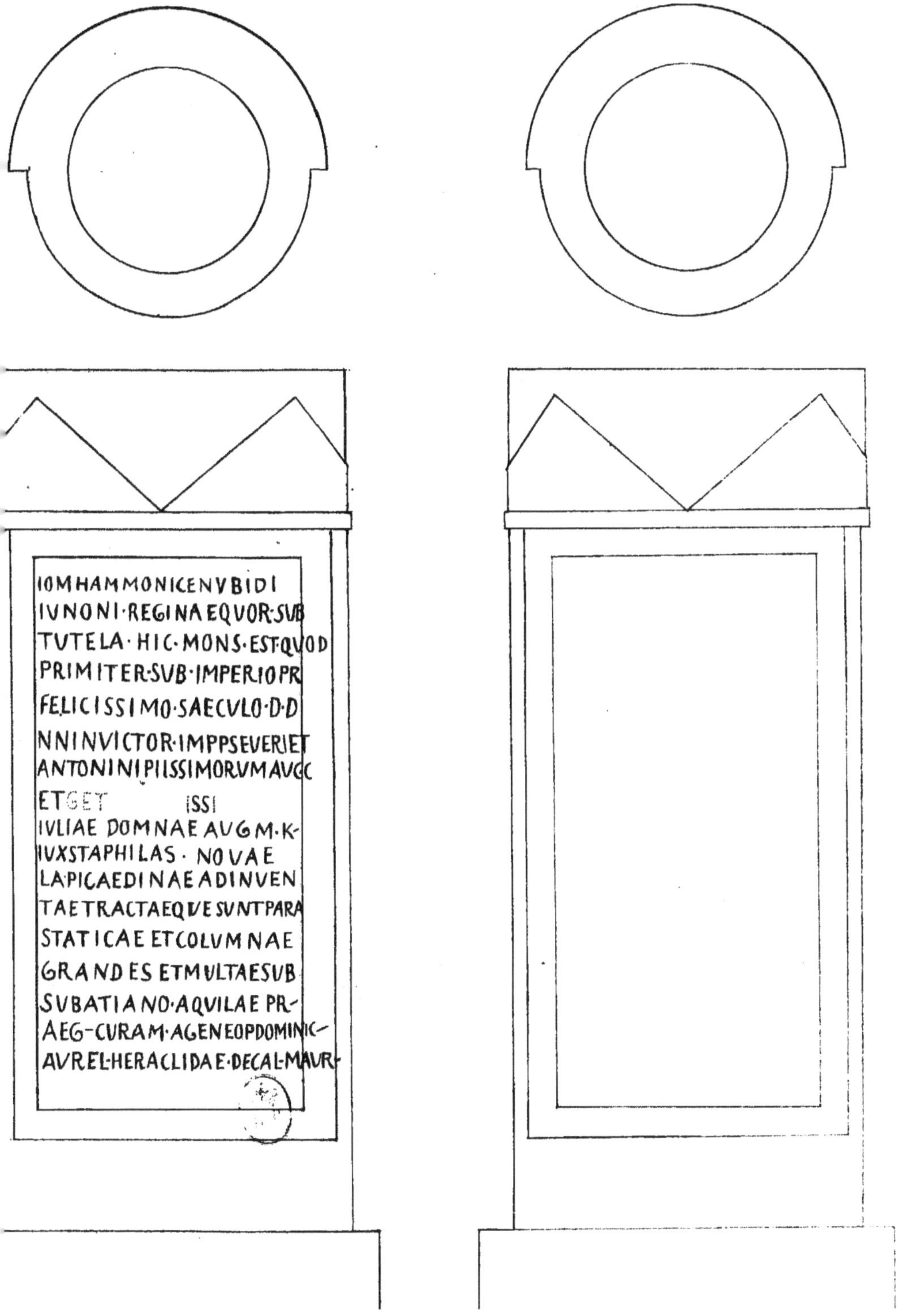

IOM HAMMONI CENUBIDI
IUNONI·REGINAE QUOR·SUB
TUTELA·HIC·MONS·EST QUOD
PRIMITER·SUB·IMPERIO PR
FELICISSIMO·SAECULO·D·D
NN INVICTOR·IMPP SEVERI ET
ANTONINI PIISSIMORUM AUGG
ET GET   ISSI
IULIAE DOMNAE AUG M·K·
IUXSTA PHILAS · NOVAE
LAPICAEDINAE ADINVEN
TAE TRACTAEQUE SUNT PARA
STATICAE ET COLUMNAE
GRANDES ET MULTAE SUB
SUBATIANO·AQUILAE PR
AEG·CURAM·AGENE OP DOMINIC
AUREL·HERACLIDAE·DECAL·MAUR

distance out of the way of the people. The old man then with great solemnity took a small wooden box from a pocket in his leathern belt. In this was a paper, which he unfolded; after that, two or three others, till at last he opened the sanctum sanctorum. I took its contents in my hands with no small degree of expectation: but, alas! how did I look, when I saw it was only part of the stopple of a common glass cruet, of the size of a hazel-nut, with two or three little gilt flowers on it! All my hopes vanished; and as the others were anxiously observing my motions, they could not fail to see disappointment so strongly marked in my countenance, as decided their fate, and destroyed their great expectations of wealth from this invaluable jewel. When I told them, that it was only a piece of glass, the words affected their minds like the unhappy tidings of some great misfortune: they walked off in solemn silence, not without giving me an inquiring look, to learn whether I were really in earnest. But I also shared their disappointment, and no smile on my face could give them any hopes.

Another day passed, but no boat appeared. At last I thought of bespeaking two camels, and proceeding to Esne by land, with Mrs. Belzoni and the interpreter, and letting the Janizary remain there, to follow by the first boat, and bring the implements we should leave behind. But when the Aga saw, that I had taken this resolution, he sent for a boat, which was hidden about a league distant, and there were two or three more concealed in other places. I found, that all this was done to keep us a few days in that place for the benefit of the town, strangers being of course obliged to spend money while they are there. After the boat was hired, at a great price, I found it belonged to the Aga himself; and the Captain or Reis told us, afterwards, that he ordered him to hide it, to compel me to give what he liked for the hire of it.

Some travellers give us the notions they have formed of the

Arabs and Berberys; but it is to be observed, that there is a very great difference in the manner in which different persons travel; and the methods pursued in going through a country may afford one more opportunities of seeing and judging than another.

A traveller who has all the accommodation possible, and nothing to do with these people but in passing, can never judge of their ideas, their system of conduct, and their rapacious manners; for in the little interval, and the limited business he has to transact with them, they do not appear to be the people they really are. Some travellers even receive civilities, with which they are mightily pleased; without having time to discover, that the very persons, whom they suppose to be naturally civil, are so only to serve their own interested views. They pass on, and in their journal of remarks just say, that they were received civilly at such and such a place. But let a traveller deal with them in any transaction, where their interest is concerned, and where their execution of any undertaking is required, he will soon find, that in every point they are the most cheating people on earth. Their deception is extreme. A traveller passing by a village stops his bark for an hour or two: what good people he finds! Some bring him a small basket of dates, others a few eggs, another some bread and milk; with which he is so pleased, that he immediately gives them five or perhaps ten times more than the worth of what he receives, without being aware, that it is through such an expectation they bring him these things; but exclaims, that in Europe they do not treat a stranger so civilly. But let him take the smallest of these presents without giving any thing in return, or even no more than it is worth, they will not fail to murmur at him. If he give only double the price, they have the art of returning the money with scorn and contempt, in order to shame him to give more:—and if he take the money returned, or give them nothing from the beginning, he must not expect, that they will let him go away without paying them for what they brought him. All this is unknown to a traveller merely passing by; for there is no one in this character, who would be so mean as to accept any thing, without returning double or treble its value. From these trifles it may be presumed what they are in all their dealings: to night one word for such a thing, to morrow another: their intrigues are beyond description: they have the art of making one thing appear like another so well, that it is very difficult to avoid falling into their trap.

There are two extremes in travellers. One who is just arrived, has never before been in the country, and of course has no knowledge of customs and things, cannot see one-fourth of what he should see: the other is so thoroughly initiated into their customs and manners, that those which shock at first sight, lose their effect on him; he almost forgets his own ways, and does not reckon any thing he beholds extraordinary or worth attention, though perhaps even of the greatest consequence.

At last, after settling all my affairs with the Aga, and satisfying his demands of oil, vinegar, and some empty bottles, we left Assouan in the morning of the 29th, and two days brought us to Esne, the current being very strong. Khalil Bey was not there, and his Hasnadar or treasurer did not know any thing about the orders, which were sent to me in Nubia: but on seeing the Bey sometime after, he said he never sent me any such. On the morning of the fourth day we arrived at Luxor. I set off next morning in the same boat to Gheneh, arrived there the next day, and went to see Mr. Sokiner, a person whom I knew, and who served me much in this business. We went to the Cacheff, who could not give me a boat, in consequence of a fresh order from Cairo to press all boats that passed; and I was therefore obliged to despatch a courier to Cairo, for an order from the Consul to obtain one.

On the 7th, in the morning, we were preparing for our return to Gournou, when the courier came, and said he had been bitten by a dog, and could not proceed on the journey. I was not pleased at this circumstance, as it tended to retard the embarkation of the bust, and sent immediately to seek for another courier, but could not find one. We lost the whole day in this manner, and I was nearly despairing of success; but, repairing the next morning to the Cacheff, I begged him to give me an order to press a courier, and he complied immediately, for he was of a very different cast from the Cacheff of Erments. The courier received his despatch about noon, and was to go and return from Cairo in sixteen days. All was ready for his departure, and he was on the point of setting off, when a large boat appeared, which brought Messrs. Jacque and Caliad, two agents of the French consul, who were going to Assouan. On inquiry I found that the boat was at liberty to be engaged after it arrived at Assouan. Accordingly I bespoke it of the Reis, before the Aga, who made him promise not to retract his agreement. Fortunately, the courier had not yet set off, and there was now no necessity of sending to Cairo, as I was assured of having this boat.

On our arrival at Thebes, the boat happened to be fastened to the bank, where the colossal head was. I will not waste my time in describing the remarks made by the two French agents of Mr. D., on seeing the head: suffice it to say, they positively declared, in spite of the evident mark it bore on its breast, that the French army did not take it away, because they thought it not worth the taking! On hearing of my fortunate success in collecting several valuable pieces of antiquity, their Dragoman, a renegado Frenchman, observed to me, that, if I persevered in my researches, I should have my throat cut, by order of two personages; one was the Cacheff of Erments, the other I shall not mention at present. I told him I was greatly obliged to him for his information, but did not believe any one would make such an attempt. They went to visit the soldiers, who lived in the tombs among the people at Gournou, and assembled several Arabs of that place before the two agents, who told them plainly in my presence, that, if they sold any article of antiquity to the English party, they would have them well beaten by the Cacheff of Erments, who commanded over them. From this moment I perceived, that I should have much opposition and many difficulties to encounter; but as my stay there was to be short, I did not regard them, and continued my business. Mrs. Belzoni was lodged in the house of an Arab at Luxor.

The same day I went to Carnak, and set twenty men at work on a spot of ground, that I chose according to a simple calculation I made, of which I shall have to speak hereafter. I re-embarked for Esne again, as I had to conclude the contract with the Reis of the boat, and to pay a part of the money as earnest. The two Frenchmen were on board also. We proceeded during the whole night, being favoured with a good strong wind, and arrived at Esne the next day at noon.

I hope the reader will not think that I employ my pen in useless accounts, or to make a display of the difficulties I encountered in my operations, merely to enhance any merit on my part: on the contrary, I can assure him, that I study by all means possible to be brief, and not to insert the least thing but what is necessary to be known. I went to the house where all the owners of the boats were assembled, who at first were of one accord, that it was impossible to put the head on board the boat, alleging that it would break it to pieces, if such a mass of stone were placed in it. They then strove to persuade me to leave the stone, as they were disposed to believe that there was no gold in it; and, if I took it, and found none after I had spent so much, I should lose all. Notwithstanding their simplicity, when I persuaded them that no accident would happen, and that I took all risks upon myself, they did not fail to ask me an enormous sum for the hire of the boat. I was in a dilemma, fearing, that, if I missed this boat, I might lose the high water, which would have obliged me to wait till next year; and in a country like this, changing from one day to another its government and way of thinking, I did not know what might happen. I therefore thought it best to secure myself from any future extortion, and give an enormous hire for the boat. This was three thousand piastres, equal to seventy-five pounds sterling, from that place to Cairo.

After all this was settled, and half the money paid down, the boat was to ascend the Nile as far as Assouan, to unload at that place, and to return immediately. I sent my Janizary with some presents to the Aga, and some trifles for Osseyn Cacheff, to be forwarded to him at Ybsambul, by the first opportunity from Assouan to that place; thinking by this trifle he would be convinced, that I intended to return to that country to finish the operation, and be induced to keep his promise, not to let any one undertake the accomplishment of what I had begun. The Janizary was likewise to take on board the twelve stones which I left there to be cut, &c. When all this was arranged, I set off for Thebes at night, and arrived there the next morning. On my arrival, I went immediately to Carnak, to see what had been done the day before by the twenty men.

Here, reader, was the beginning of those discoveries, which have caused me so much trouble, not from the exertion and arduous labour required in these researches, but in the atrocious persecution they have drawn on me, from malice, jealousy, and envy, to such a degree, that to this day, the very goddess Fortune, who has been apparently so propitious to me, I had reason to call barbarous and unkind. Notwithstanding which, I did not relinquish my undertaking, till I reached the accomplishment of my wishes. Let me add, I have further enterprises in view, which, I hope, will convince my adversaries, that their persecution has had no other effect on me, than that of strengthening me to perseverance in my undertakings. Had I not determined to stand, like a pyramid defying the wind, against all their numerous attacks, which poured on me like a torrent, I should not have been able to proceed, even from the commencement. On the other hand, I must acknowledge, that at the moment when I was persecuted on one side, I received marks of kindness and good wishes on the other; and fortunately, thank God, the well-disposed far outnumbered the others, though few like to enter into, or interfere with matters which do not concern themselves. Many travellers of various nations, at the time of my researches, witnessed, that the greatest difficulties I had to encounter were not in the discovery of antiquities, which I consider the smallest part of my task, but in controlling the complicated intrigues of my enemies and false friends. I am more inclined to excuse Count Forbin, as the erroneous and false accounts he gives are so confused and contradictory to the facts, that he openly exposes himself to ridicule and contempt, than to pardon some others, who should have been above such paltry proceedings.

The works in Carnak were begun when I returned from Esne, but nothing was found, and there was no likelihood of finding any thing. The place whence the French had taken their lion-headed statues, at the time of the invasion, is where a temple stood, surrounded on three sides by a lake. It faces the avenue of the great sphinx to the north, and not a single wall or column remains standing. On the exterior side of the wall are several fragments of the above statues, which were there before the French army invaded Egypt, but they made some excavations on the east side of the temple, and made discoveries, the fruits of which are now to be seen in the British Museum, they having been captured at sea. The Count de Forbin asserts, that after all these sphynxes had been discovered they were covered up again by some French gentlemen who superintended the work. But the Count did not mention the names of those persons, for he knew very well that no such thing ever took place. The account he published of the statues, which he acknowledges to have been found twenty feet below the surface, and backed by a strong ancient wall, was taken from my own letters, which I gave him myself in Cairo, of which I shall have to speak hereafter, and which he promised to give to the world as they were. Instead of this, the only use he made of them was to throw all the facts into confusion, and prevent the real truth from coming before the public.

Now to more obvious facts. According to a calculation I had made, I dug on the west side of the temple, where no one had ever made any excavation before, nor did any traveller previous to me take any thing thence but what was in sight. The earth, bricks, and stones, were so strongly cemented together by time, particularly on the surface, that it clearly proved the ground never to have been touched from the earliest ages. In the course of a few days I discovered about eighteen statues, six of which were perfect, and among them a white statue as large as life, supposed to be of Jupiter Ammon, which is now also in the British Museum.

I here beg leave to make an observation which I hope will convince the world of the false statement of Count de Forbin. The French Consul, Monsieur Drouetti, who had been making researches for fifteen years in that country, and who was naturally attached to the interest of France, had been to Thebes twice previous to my arrival in Egypt. How was it, that, in the course of so long a period, he never came to know from the natives, that such statues had been found there by the French, and covered up again? and how happened it, that the person who covered them up never mentioned it to him, or to any one else, even after a general peace took place? We should suppose, that as soon as the seas were cleared of the English cruizers, whose watchful eyes did not let even a water-rat pass into France, there was no fear that these statues should have been taken, and thus a second loss incurred: but independent of all this, there was nothing to prevent Mr. Drouetti from bringing them safe to Alexandria, as he did other antiquities, which were the sole object of his ascending the Nile. I should not enter on this subject, had it not been for the petty means which have been employed to depreciate every thing I have done, and which are a compound of erroneous assertions, that I believe originated in the volcanic brains of Count de Forbin himself.

The place where I found these statues must have been the interior of the pronaos; but there were many others in various places, and it is difficult to determine their original stations. In another temple in Gournou, which is yet unknown, and of which I shall speak in this volume, I found several statues of the same sort, and by the pedestals it appears they were within the place surrounded by the columns. The same may have been the case in this temple. The situation in which I found them was by no means their original place, and it was clearly to be seen by their irregular positions, that they had been brought thither in great hurry and confusion. Some brick walls had been built, as if to hide them from the destructive hands of an invader, and the white statue lay among the rest in an irregular manner.

During the time of this excavation I scrutinized the ruins of Carnak, and perceived a great number of spots that deserve digging. I saw the famous altar, with the six deities mentioned in the great French work, and the colossal arm, both of which I formed the project of removing even at that period. Fortunately on this side of the water the difficulty of obtaining people to work was less than I had found it on the other. The Cacheff was ready to do all he could for me, and every thing went on very smoothly. The only impediment here was that the Fellahs of Carnak would insist upon coming to work in greater numbers than those of Luxor; for they said the others had no right to come to labour on these grounds, and sometimes this dispute ended in blows. These people were quite the reverse of those in Gournou, who, having become opulent by the trade in antiquities, and tricking travellers, were not so anxious to gain thirty paras a day. During the same excavation I turned up a fine standing colossus without a head, part of which projects above the ground, and which had not been seen by any body. For my part I think it one of the most finished pieces of Egyptian sculpture I ever saw.

It would be too tedious to the reader, to mention all the particulars that occurred during my researches. Unfortunately I was without money to proceed, and had to go to Esne, to borrow some from a Greek I happened to know in that place, who would supply me with any sum; but as I expected a remittance from the Consul, I only took what was necessary to transport the lion-headed statues from Carnak to Luxor, ready for embarkation. On my return to Carnak, I found, that an order had come from the Cacheff of Gous to the Caimakan of Luxor, not to let me take any thing away: this being contrary to the order I had from Mahomet Ali Bashaw, I set off for Gous immediately; and finding, on my arrival, that the

Cacheff was gone to Gheneh, I directed my course to that place. As the current was very strong, we went on pretty fast. About midnight we saw two cangias coming up. I inquired what party it was, and was told it was Calil Bey, my good friend, on his return from Cairo. I was pleased at this circumstance, as I meant to complain against the conduct of the Cacheff; but, on approaching the cangias, I found that the Cacheff was there also. Calil Bey was well pleased to see me returned from Nubia, and was anxious to inquire how they received me in that country. I told him, that they obeyed his firman, and that I had done all I wished to do in respect to the temple at Ybsanibul; but not being able to finish my undertaking that year, I should return the next. He desired to know, whether the two brothers, Mahomet and Osseyn Cacheff, were friends again; a question to which I was unable to reply; but I told him the country was perfectly quiet at that time.

I returned to Gous with him, and the next morning took an opportunity to inquire of the Cacheff the reason of his sending the order to the Sheik not to let the English take away any thing that was found. He said, he knew nothing about it; although I had seen the order myself. However, he was ready to give me any order I pleased. No doubt this was in consequence of the Bey being there, otherwise I should not have found him so easy to deal with.

Calil Bey was an Albanian, who had married the sister of Mahomet Ali, Bashaw of Egypt, and held the command of the provinces in Upper Egypt from Esne to Assouan; and for a Turk was much attached to European travellers. He was continually inquiring concerning things he did not know, and had a degree of sound judgment; a quality very scarce among Turks: but for all this he was a complete slave to superstition, and to the belief of magical powers. On our arrival at Gous, he took his seat in the garden of the Cacheff, under an arbour of grape-vines, shaded all round by plantain trees, which formed a very pleasing and cool recess. A large mat was spread on the ground, and on this a fine carpet, and cushions, as usual. The Cacheff was seated at his right, and a Turkish Sheik on his left. Two Hadgees sat by the Cacheff, and I was requested to take my seat near the Holy-man. Next to me was a Turkish merchant, and after him a fool or Santon quite naked. All the rest of the followers, soldiers, and attendants, stood in a crescent before us. Pipes were brought in for the Bey, the Cacheff, the Holy-man, and myself. Coffee was served all round to the persons who were seated, and the conversation turned on the harvest, that was to be the next season, according to the inundation of that year. It was then the beginning of November. They were wondering at the great quantity of corn the Bashaw was sending continually to be embarked at Alexandria, particularly at this season. Some supposed, that the Europeans were about to make war against the Porte, and that, previous to the declaration, they made provision of corn, as without a supply from Egypt they would be unable to feed their troops. Others observed, if this were the case, Mahomet Ali would not send them corn, till he knew for what purpose it was wanted. One said, he thought the corn was sent into Russia, as he heard that the French had set all that country on fire; and he then inquired of me, whether it were not so. I told him, that I did not know what the French did in that country; but I knew that the corn was sent into Europe, in consequence of a scarcity in the harvest that year, through the whole of that quarter of the globe. The Bey agreed it must be so, and asked whether it would be the same the next season. I told him I hoped not, for, in general, after a scarcity came a plenty. Yes, says the Bey, but the Bashaw will sell the corn at a high price for three or four years to come, till your granaries are filled again. "But pray," added he, smiling, "have you a scarcity of stones also in Europe, that you come here to fetch them away?" I answered, that we had plenty of stones, but we thought those of Egypt were of a better sort. "O ho!" replied he, "it is because you find some gold in them perhaps, thank God!" This is the first instance of my hearing the word "perhaps" employed; for they are so positive on this point, that they never make any doubt of it.

The dinner was brought in a large tray. It consisted, as usual, of very poor rice soup, which, after eating three spoonsful, was taken away, and a dish of roast mutton brought forward. No sooner had we begun to eat of that, than a man came in with his hand full of large green peppercorns, and let them fall on the tray, which, being of metal, sounded like a drum-head. After him came another, with half-a-dozen onions peeled, which he let fall in like manner, and they rolled about the tray like billiard balls; and a third followed with peeled garlic, &c. After eating the mutton, a dish of very small fried fish was served up. They were about half-a-dozen, and we were eight of us, so that we could not eat too much of this. It was soon removed, and a kind of tart was produced; but neither the Bey, the Cacheff, the Sheik, nor myself, could eat a single bit of it. The fruit consisted of a water melon, which having demolished, they finished their repast by washing their beards. It was rather too mean to set before the Bey, as I have seen the Cacheff take a better for himself at other times; but it is a general system among these people, both Turks and Arabs, always to make themselves appear poor in the presence of their superiors. As the Cacheff had furnished me with an order for the Caimakan of Luxor to let me carry away what stones I pleased, I took my leave of the Bey and set off.

On my arrival at Carnak, the work to be done consisted only in transporting the six sphinxes and the white statue to Luxor for embarkation, a distance of nearly a mile, without a road. In many parts the water had left a soft ground where the statues had to pass; and, as there was no mechanical power to assist, the Arabs had enough to do to carry them to the place of destination. With this all my labour at Carnak ended; and while thus waiting for the boat from Assouan, and the cash from Cairo, I paid a daily visit to the tombs in Gournou. These sepulchres are excavated in all directions in the rocks, but generally with the entrance facing the east, as the chain of these mountains runs from north to south. They are intermixed of all sizes; and some of them have porticoes hewn out of the rocks before the entrance; but, generally, they are within the outer door, which is mostly adorned with well-finished figures and hieroglyphics, and generally the watchful fox is represented at each side of the inner door leading to the grotto. Some of them are very extensive, and run down in various directions, something like winding stairs, having on each side, at regular distances of a few paces, small chambers to deposit the mummies. Some have deep shafts, or wells, with excavations on each side of the shaft to receive the mummies; and at the bottom of the wells are passages leading to smaller apartments, with endless winding recesses. It was here that I had first leisure to examine and find the means of ascertaining where the entrances were to many of the tombs, which had been hidden for centuries from the eye of mankind.

The extensive ruins of Medinet Aboo are, in my humble

opinion, best worthy the attentive scrutiny of a traveller of any on the west of Thebes. The descriptions given by Messrs. Hamilton and Denon are sufficient to convey a correct idea of these edifices, which contain propylæa, temples, and dwelling-places. It seems that here was the residence of some of the sovereigns of Egypt; for in no other edifices of ancient Egypt have I seen the remains of habitations as they are in this place. There are two separate temples, of which the first that meets the view going from the Memnonium is of a less ancient date than the other. On the west side of the portal are stones with hieroglyphics upside-down, evidently belonging to a former temple. The pronaos is surrounded by a portico of pilasters, at each side of which are two chambers: one on the right of the entrance has been used as a Christian chapel. The cella contains various apartments, quite dark; in one of which, on the right side, is a monolite temple of red granite, without hieroglyphics. It is wider than the door, and must have been placed there before the cella was erected. The hieroglyphics and figures of this edifice differ from those of the other temple in proportion as the two temples differ from each other. On the north side of this little temple was a small lake, or rather a tank for water, which is now filled up with earth and rubbish; and there must have been statues all round it, as I found part of one and fragments of others in an excavation I made in that place. Perhaps it might have been used for the same purposes as the small lakes near the temple of Carnak, which may be supposed to have been the public baths destined for the religious visitors to the temple. On the south of these ruins is a building something like a square tower, with a large gateway, which I opened and went through. It is nearly in a line with the gates leading into the great temple. Above the gateway is a chamber with two square windows, looking over it at each side. There are also two doors opposite each other on the

R

sides. Above this chamber was another, with two windows like those below; but the fore part of the upper chamber is fallen in. There are recesses at the sides of the windows, no doubt to place the shutters. No hieroglyphics are to be seen within this building, though on the outside it is every where covered with them. The two lateral walls in front of this place form an avenue to the gateway.

Further on, about two hundred yards to the west, stands the great temple. There is a large propylæon, with the entrance into the inner yard. The walls are covered with hieroglyphics, deeply cut. The gateway, which is also adorned in like manner, leads into a large yard, with a wall opposite to the propylæon, and a gateway into another yard. At each side of this yard is a portico. On the right are seven pilasters, with colossal figures before them; and on the left eight columns, with capitals in the form of the lotus. Both of these porticoes are also adorned with hieroglyphics, deeply cut. The next yard has a gallery, or area, all round it, of pilasters and columns. The walls are beautifully embellished with battles, men on chariots, captives, and slaves; together with which are distinctly visible procession offerings, initiations, and sacrifices, so well described by Mr. Denon. The excavation of these works shows, that they are of a very ancient period. The hieroglyphics are uncommonly deep, more so than any I have seen in other buildings in Egypt. In some parts the figures retain their colours pretty well, particularly in the ceiling on the capitals of the columns. This edifice has been used as a Christian church; and the rude columns, employed in a more modern building within this yard, show the wonderful difference between the arts of the two ages. Further on, through the last gate, was the entrance to the pronaos and cella: but now these are buried under the earth, and several Saracenic buildings have been raised on it. The exterior wall of these ruins is filled with historical subjects, such as land and sea fights, lion hunting, processions of captives, and various national emblems. Further to the south of the town is a small temple, which now serves for the shepherds to keep their cattle in at night. The whole town, in my opinion, appears to have been rebuilt twice or three times successively on the ruins of the former.

It was at this period, that I began to make some researches in the valley adjacent to that of Beban el Malook. I had seen all the tombs of the kings: as I did not go there, however, with any intention of making researches, my curiosity must have been greater than that of many who had been there before, as I went into every little recess of these valleys. It was in the western valley that one of the French savans discovered a large tomb, which he found open, but was quite unknown before his time. I went to visit this tomb, and found it very extensive, and in pretty good preservation. My curiosity did not end here. I went farther on in the valley; and in one of the most remote spots saw a heap of stones, which appeared to me detached from the mass. The vacancies between these stones were filled up with sand and rubbish. I happened to have a stick with me, and on thrusting it into the holes among the stones, I found it penetrate very deep. I returned immediately to Gournou, and procured a few men, to open these places. Unfortunately, both Mrs. Belzoni and myself had been much afflicted for some time with the ophthalmia, which was so severe on me at this time, that I could scarcely see any thing before me.

I took the men into the same valley the next morning; but in consequence of my eyes being so bad, it was some time before I could find the spot again. On removing a few stones, we perceived, that the sand ran inwards; and, in fact, we were so near the entrance, that in less than two hours all the stones were taken away. I had caused some candles to be brought, and I went in, followed by the Arabs. I cannot boast of having made a great discovery in this tomb, though it contains several curious and singular painted figures on the walls; and from its extent, and part of a sarcophagus remaining in the centre of a large chamber, have reason to suppose, that it was the burial-place of some person of distinction. The tomb consists of three chambers, two corridors, and a staircase; but the remote situation in which it was found renders it remarkable: and I declare, that I owe this discovery merely to fortune, not to any premeditated research, as I went into these mountains only to examine the various places, where the water descends from the desert into the valleys after rain. It is singular to observe, that though rain falls very seldom, perhaps not more than once or twice a year, yet such is the effect of the climate and the sun on the spots where the water passes, that they are as strongly marked, as if it were continually running over them, and much harder than the rest of the masses.

The higher part of the mountain on the west of Thebes extends in wide plains, which rise gradually towards the west; and when rain falls upon them, the water takes its course towards the Nile, descending into the valleys of Egypt. There are very few places in these mountains where water gathers in such quantities, as in the valley of Beban el Malook, and its adjoining branch on the west side. For some time the water forms a small torrent, that carries every thing before it. Mr. Salt superintended the making of a road from the tombs of the kings to the Nile, for the purpose of transporting a large sarcophagus, and one of these falls of water from the desert destroyed the whole road. For the present, however, I shall leave this valley, as I shall have to speak of it in another part of this volume, on my second journey to Thebes and Nubia.

The time having elapsed, in which I expected to receive letters from Cairo, I was rather uneasy, and resolved to return to Kenneh. On my arrival at this place, I found the courier had just entered it. He brought me letters from Mr. Salt, with an order for money on the Seraf, or banker, of Kenneh. I quickly finished my business there, and speeded to Luxor, where I was pleased to find the boat returned from Assouan, to take the colossal bust on board: but I was soon informed by the proprietor, that it was loaded with dates, and that he was come himself from Esne, to return the money I had paid as earnest; for they could not think of taking that large stone into the boat, as it would crush it to pieces. All my persuasions were useless; and though I had a written agreement in my hands, they signified to me, that it was of no use, they never would take the stone on board. I had much to say to them, as may be imagined in such a case; for I was so circumstanced, that if the present opportunity of transporting the bust were lost, the water in the Nile would have become much too low, and the conveyance could not have been effected till the next season. At the same time I was informed by my Janizary, whom I sent to Assouan in the same boat with the two agents of Mr. D., that it was owing to them the owner would not take the stone on board: for they told him he would lose his boat, and never receive any recompense for it; and that the agreement I made with them was good for nothing when in Cairo. In fact, these gentlemen had so much the minds of the crew, that they were resolved not to perform their contract.

The twelve stones I had left in the island of Philœ, and which were to have been conveyed in the same boat, in like manner could not be embarked, as the Reis said there were no small boats to take them down the cataract: and I afterwards learned, that this also was owing to the same influence. The unfortunate history of these stones will not be read without exciting sentiments of detestation towards the parties concerned: they had been mutilated, and rendered useless, how, and by whom, I shall mention hereafter. My situation with regard to the boat was far from pleasant, and I had no resource, but to take the owner to Esne and lay the case before Khalil Bey, who by this time must have arrived at that place: but even then I did not know how far he would interfere in compelling these people to keep to their agreement, as he had himself observed, that he thought the stone would break the boat. This, however, was the only step I could take.

Fortune sometimes brings troubles on mankind merely that they may taste the fickleness of her nature and uncertainty of the favours she condescends to bestow on them. My vexation was great, thinking all my efforts and exertion in bringing the bust to the Nile were to no purpose, and that very probably it would never reach England, as the underhand machinations against it were so powerful. At that moment, however, a soldier arrived from Erments, acquainting me that the Cacheff was returned from Cairo; and he gave me at the same time a letter from him, with a present which he had sent of two small bottles of anchovies and two of olives. Strange as it may appear, it will be seen that the effects of a few salted little fish contributed the greatest share towards the removal of the colossus, which I had so much at heart, and which, in all probability, but for them, would not have been in the British Museum to this day. The letter contained a very gratifying invitation to a feast to be given by the Cacheff, and the present was in token of a friendly disposition towards me. I was not a little surprised at this change, but I soon discovered the reason. The soldier acquainted me, that the Cacheff was in a terrible rage with a certain correspondent and friend of his, a Frank, who for some time had raised his expectation of having some valuable presents sent him; but, instead of this, he received at last only a few bottles of insignificant fish, which may be had in plenty from the Nile, and a few olives, not worth a pipe of tobacco. I took care, that this should not be told to the owner of the boats; and, as it was arranged that we should go to Esne for the decision of the affair, I took them on board the little boat which I had hired, and we set off for that place, leaving the large one at Luxor. Knowing in what humour the Cacheff must be in from his disappointment, I thought to strike while his mind was hot.

On our arrival before Erments I begged the two owners of the boat to wait a little, as I had business with the Cacheff of the village. It was already an hour after sunset, and the village is about a mile from the Nile. I took my interpreter and Janizary with me, and set off alertly to my anchovy and olive man. I found him seated on a mat in the middle of a field, a stick fastened in the ground with a lantern attached to it, and all his attendants standing before him. On seeing me, he made a great parade of compliments; I suppose because he thought, that, as he was disappointed of presents from one quarter, he would make the best market he could by trying the other. Pipes and coffee were brought as usual; and an offer was made me, to send as many men as I liked to have to work, that I might take away the great head early the next morning, and the cover of the sarcophagus, or any thing else I pleased. Had I requested him to let me take the two large colossi of Thebes, Tommy and Dummy, as the Arabs call them, he would have had no objection to my putting them on board my little boat that night. I then introduced the affair of the boat, produced the written agreement I had drawn up at Esne with the two owners, and mentioned the money I had paid, which amounted to half the sum of what they were eventually to receive. He immediately said, I need not go to Esne for the decision, the affair belonging to himself, as the boat was to be loaded on a bank in his province. The two gentlemen from Esne were sent for, and when they heard, that the cause was to be tried at Erments, they were thunderstruck. They considered the boat lost to them, though I repeatedly told them, that I would be answerable for any damage that might be incurred in the embarkation or landing; but it was all to no purpose. The Cacheff, however, insisted that they should keep their agreement with me; and still more to accommodate matters, as they were at a loss what to do with the dates, offered them his canja, which would contain as much as was necessary to be taken out of the boat, as I did not wish to unload it entirely. Meanwhile, as he did not like to appear too openly decided in my favour, he proposed that in the morning the owners should be summoned, and the case brought to a fair hearing. They then retired to pass the night on board. In continuing his civilities and protestations of friendship, the Cacheff came to an explanation of his former conduct, and, in particular, of the letter he sent to his brother respecting the sarcophagus. It was written, he said, before he saw Mr. D.; but now that he found how things were, I might have the sarcophagus, or any thing else; that he would guard it for me as long as I desired; that no one else should have it; and added a thousand other obliging things.

So extraordinary a change led me to suppose, that Mr. Salt had made him some handsome present when in Cairo; but I was mistaken, for, a little after, asking him what he thought of the consul, to my surprise he told me, that he did not see him. The consul invited him, he said, to his house, and prepared a dinner for him; but that, on the day he was to go, news arrived of the death of Tusoon Bashaw, the eldest son of Mahomet Ali; and he was ordered to come away immediately, which put an end to the pleasure of seeing the consul, for he loved him like his right eye. The story was equally well invented, and well told; and I saw plainly he was so ashamed of his late conduct towards me, that he could not face the consul. He caused dinner to be brought, and carried his civilities to such a height, that I began to be alarmed, suspecting him of some diabolical trick. On my thanking him for the bottles of anchovies and olives, he said, they were the whole of the French consul's present to him while he was in Cairo. I took the opportunity of observing, that it would have been well for him, if, while he was there, he had called on the English consul. To which he replied, that he had been told the consul had a fine brace of pistols for him; but that unfortunately it was out of his power to go to see him. I answered, I had no doubt he would make him some present when the stone should reach Cairo; on which he immediately rejoined, that there was nothing he would not do either for him or for me; but I must not think that what he did was with any view of interest. I said, I was quite persuaded of the contrary; and should trouble him for an order to be given to the people at Gournou to come to work. He protested he would comply with all I wished; but added, with a smile, " What will you do, if the trial should go against you?" I told him I should proceed to Esne, where the agreement was made in the presence of the Sharif, and show that I was in the right. He laughed, put his hand on my shoulder, and said, " You may sleep in peace, for to-morrow I will myself see the boat unloaded of every date that is in it, and you may re-load it at your pleasure." I answered, that I had no doubt he would do what was just, and, taking leave, I returned on board the little boat for the night.

13th.—In the morning I found him in his chamber of audience, surrounded by several Arabs, Sheiks of the village. He made me sit down on his right hand, and coffee and pipes were brought; for no judgment could be pronounced without these luxuries. He had explained the cause to the gentlemen of the jury, who said, without hearing the other side, that what he intended to do was perfectly equitable, and they would have said the same whether I had been right or wrong; for these juries are not so deficient in politeness as to contradict the judge. The other parties came, and he received them politely, but with a frown on his brow, from which I have no doubt they sufficiently augured their fate. However, not to keep them in suspense, they were soon plainly told, that the bark, except only eighty ardeps, an indulgence to which I had agreed, must be unloaded; and he saw no other way of settling the business. He then referred to the gentlemen of the jury, to know whether they had any thing to say. To my astonishment they answered, that, as the other parties made no defence, they of course acknowledged themselves wrong; and, having nothing more to do, they all instantly rose and walked off. The defendants then partook of what was before them; but I believe never made a worse breakfast in their lives. They began to talk about where to find a boat, though they were obliged of necessity to hire one of the Cacheff, being fully aware of his design, which was to get the best part of the money for himself. The contract was soon made, and they paid him two-thirds of what they were to receive from me, which, indeed, they were glad to do, lest he should scrutinise the business, and, finding the freight to be double what was mentioned in the bill of lading, they should thus lose still more. I then took leave of the Cacheff, that I might hasten to Gournou, to settle what business was to be done there. He had given me a tiscary for the soldier to furnish me with what I wanted, gave orders to the Fellahs to do all I desired, and take out the sarcophagus; and on going on board, I found that he had sent me two sheep, a jar of cheese, and some bread. We set off immediately. One of the sheep died in the evening, the other next day, and the cheese was full of vermin. We arrived at Luxor in the afternoon, and a few hours after went to Gournou, and saw the Sheik el bellad of that place. I sent my Janizary to the soldier, and it was concerted, that the Fellahs I wanted should be ready for me in the morning.

Early on the 14th, I went again to Gournou to begin the work, and was not a little surprised when I saw no Fellahs assembled. By one whom I met, I was told, that they were afraid, being ordered not to work for the English. I applied as before to the soldier, who sent a man to collect the Fellahs; but it was too late: they were all dispersed. Accordingly, I contented myself this day with only having the apparatus, necessary to embark the head, conveyed over from Luxor. The Cacheff's boat from Erments arrived, and that at Luxor came also to Gournou to unload.

15th.—The next day we collected, though not without trouble, a hundred and thirty men; and I begun to make a causeway, by which to convey the head down to the river side; for the bank was more than fifteen feet above the level of the water, which had retired at least a hundred feet from it.

Next morning a soldier came from the Cacheff, to say that I was not to pay the Fellahs any thing, as they were ordered to work for me for nothing as long as I required, and that he made me a present of their labour. I thanked him, but desired the soldier to tell him, at the same time, that it was not my custom to have the labour of men for nothing, nor would the consul of England accept of such a present. I this day finished the causeway down the bank, and had the head brought to the edge of the slope, ready to be embarked.

On the 17th of November, I succeeded in my attempt, and the head of the younger Memnon was actually embarked. I cannot help observing, that it was no easy undertaking to put a piece of granite, of such bulk and weight, on board a boat, that, if it received the weight on one side, would immediately upset; and, what is more, this was to be done without the smallest help of any mechanical contrivance, even a single tackle, and only with four poles and ropes, as the water was about eighteen feet below the bank where the head was to descend. The causeway I had made gradually sloped to the edge of the water close to the boat, and with the four poles I formed a bridge from the bank into the centre of the boat, so that when the weight bore on the bridge, it pressed only on the centre of the boat. The bridge rested partly on the causeway, partly on the side of the boat, and partly on the centre of it. On the opposite side of the boat I put some mats well filled with straw. I necessarily stationed a few Arabs in the boat, and some at each side, with a lever of palm-wood, as I had nothing else. At the middle of the bridge I put a sack filled with sand, that, if the colossus should run too fast into the boat, it might be stopped. In the ground behind the colossus I had a piece of a palm-tree firmly planted, round which a rope was twisted, and then fastened to its car, to let it descend gradually. I set a lever at work on each side, and at the same time that the men in the boat were pulling, others were slackening the ropes, and others shifting the rollers as the colossus advanced.

Thus it descended gradually from the main-land to the causeway, when it sunk a good deal, as the causeway was made of fresh earth. This, however, I did not regret, as it was better it should be so, than that it should run too fast towards the water; for I had to consider, that, if this piece of antiquity should fall into the Nile, my return to Europe would not be very welcome, particularly to the antiquaries; though I have reason to believe, that some among the great body of its scientific men would rather have seen it sunk in the Nile, than where it is now deposited. However, it went smoothly on board. The Arabs, who were unanimously of opinion that it would go to the bottom of the river, or crush the boat, were all attention, as if anxious to know the result, as well as to learn how the operation was to be performed; and when the owner of the boat, who considered it as consigned to perdition, witnessed my success, and saw the huge piece of stone, as he called it, safely on board, he came and squeezed me heartily by the hand. "Thank heaven!" I exclaimed, and I had reason to be thankful; for I will leave it to the judgment of any engineer, whether it would not be easier to embark a mass ten times larger on board a competent vessel, where all sorts of mechanical powers can be procured, instead of being destitute, as I was, of every thing necessary.

The boat then crossed the water to Luxor, for what was to be taken in there, which was done in three days, and on the 21st we left Thebes on our return to Cairo.

I had just finished my business, when I was again so affected with ophthalmia, that for twelve days I kept myself shut up in the cabin of the boat, so that I can give no account of this voyage, till we reached Siout. I could then just peep at the light; but it gave me great pain whenever I attempted to open my eyes. At Siout I went to see the Deftardar Bey, to return him thanks for the firman he had given me when I ascended the Nile. I found him in his tent in the middle of a field of high clover, which had nearly reached its growth, and his horses were all out at grass. He was pleased to hear that I had succeeded in my undertaking, and requested to be remembered to the English Consul, to whom he sent a letter by me.

Next morning we set off for Cairo, and reached it on the 15th of December, having been twenty-four days from Thebes. Thus I had been five months and a half in continual activity and exertion; but I must not let pass the unjust observation made by the ever veracious Count de Forbin, who asserted, that I employed six months solely in taking the colossal bust on board the boat. It is true, I was absent five months and a half from Cairo, and six months had elapsed before I reached Alexandria; but this time was not all devoted to the removal of the bust, as I employed only eighteen days in that operation, and but a single day in embarking it: the greater part of the time was spent in more arduous researches; and the various pieces of antiquity which I brought down the Nile will bear infallible testimony to my labour.

At Cairo I found that the consul was gone to Alexandria, but had left with Mr. Beechey, his secretary, instructions and letters for me. He requested, that every thing might be landed and lodged in the consulate except the bust. I could not conceive the reason of this distinction, as I thought that all the articles I collected were to go to the British Museum. However, I made no inquiry into the business, and every thing was deposited as desired. The first hour of my arrival I had the pleasure of seeing my good and much lamented friend, Burckhardt, whose death has been a great loss to me. He was the most candid, disinterested, and sincere being I have ever met with; totally free from that invidious and selfish disposition, which is so often to be found in travellers, who wish to be alone in one quarter of the world, to relate their story agreeably to the suggestions of their own imagination to the people of another. But Burckhardt had none of that littleness of mind: he was a true explorer, and a hardy one, without pride, or the ambition to be thought more than he was. He made no parade of his knowledge, as his works plainly evince.

Having prepared for my departure for Alexandria, we left Boolak on the 3d of January, 1817, and arrived in Raschid, or Rosetta, on the 10th. There I had to land the colossus, and embark it again on board a djerm; but as I had now some tackle, of which I was destitute before, and proper people to work, I found it quite an easy operation. Besides, I took care to land it in a situation, that was advantageous for embarking it again. Having finished, I set off on board the same djerm, with the bust, and was fortunate enough to reach Alexandria two hours after sunset of the same day, which was the fourth after our arrival in Rosetta. That very day, above two hundred djerms came out of the Nile, some of which had been waiting for an opportunity of passing the bar above eighty days. Mrs. Belzoni went by land, accompanied by the Irish lad, and arrived the next day. I will not mention the kind reception of the consul-general, and the under-consul, Mr. Lee; I was fortunate enough to become acquainted with a gentleman, Mr. Briggs, who received me into his house in the most hospitable manner, and was as much concerned for the success of my affairs as it was possible to be; for he felt the pleasure of a true Englishman, in seeing one of the most finished monuments of Egyptian art ready to be embarked for his native country.

The next and final operation with respect to the bust, on my part, was to land it, and have it conveyed in safety to the Bashaw's magazine, there to await its embarkation for England. I had some difficulty in landing it, as the pier was much higher than the djerm, and the motion of the sea did not permit me to erect any bridge. I was so fortunate as to procure the crew of a British transport, which was there at the time; and with their help, with proper tackle, and a hundred men besides, it was landed safely.

Having finished my operations, and whatever was necessary respecting the head, I proposed to the consul, to make another trip into Upper Egypt and Nubia, to open the temple at Ybsambul. Nothing could be more pleasing to me, than to find, that my proposal was accepted; as I thought I might have an opportunity of accomplishing the wishes I had formed, which, to a certain extent, were with particular views; though, as the consul has proved, no interested motives governed my mind. The only stipulation I made was, that, if I were successful, he should give me an official letter of introduction to the Society of Antiquaries, when

I should return to England; with which he promised to comply. Thinking, however, I might be indulging hopes that would not be realised, he cautioned me against any expectations from that quarter. I told him, I was not rich; but as I had no other view, than to serve the nation at large, I intended to make certain proposals to the members of that honourable society. On this he again promised me the letter requested, and in a few days we all set off for Cairo. There the worthy Burckhardt would insist, that I should receive a present, half of which he obtained from the consul, as an acknowledgment for my success with regard to the colossus; of the general expenses attending which he paid a moiety.

It was at this period that Captain Cabillia had ventured into the well of the first pyramid of Gaza. His enterprise was hazardous and bold, and nothing but an enthusiasm for discovery could induce a man to take such a step. The consul, with Mr. Briggs, Mr. Beechey, and myself, went to see the operations that were going on. Captain Cabillia's circumstances were much better than mine; but he had no superfluous wealth at command, to continue what he had begun, which required a supply beyond his means. Mr. Briggs was the first who generously offered to furnish money for this purpose; and, after a consultation with Mr. Salt, they agreed to support the work to any extent that might be required. This gentleman not only encouraged the undertaking at the pyramid, but has exerted his influence with Mahomed Ali for the general advantage of the commerce of Europe, as I shall have occasion to mention hereafter. The enterprise of Captain Cabillia is worthy the attention of every one interested in antiquities, as he has solved a question, by which the learned world has been puzzled for many centuries. The famous well, which has given rise to so much conjecture, turns out to be a communication with a lower passage leading into an inferior chamber, discovered and opened by himself. He first descended the well to the depth of thirty-eight feet, where his progress was stopped by four large stones. Three of these being removed, there was space enough for a man to pass through; but the fourth he could not stir, though he had the help of Mr. Kabitsch, a young man in the employment of Mr. Baghos, who bore a share of the expense with the captain. Twenty-one feet below this place they found a grotto, seventeen feet long and four high; and seven feet below this, a platform, from which the well descended two hundred feet lower. The captain went down, and at the bottom found earth and sand: but from the hollow sound under his feet, he judged, that the passage must communicate with some other apartment below. He then set some Arabs at work, to remove the sand; but the heat was so great, and the candles so incapable of burning, for want of oxygen, that they were compelled to desist. The captain then turned his researches to another quarter, and began to enlarge the entrance into the first passage of the pyramid. For this operation he was well rewarded; for by it he found, that the passage continued downward; and having employed several men, and taken out a great deal of earth and rubbish, at last, after a long and arduous toil, he came in contact with the bottom of the well, where he found the baskets and rope which had been left there. The same day that this occurred, was that on which we had agreed to visit the pyramids, and I had the pleasure to be an eye-witness of the arduous task of Captain Cabillia. Proceeding in his laborious researches, he found, that the passage led into a chamber cut out of the rock, under the centre of the pyramid.

Captain C. made several researches round the pyramids also, but none exceeded his toil in uncovering the front of the great sphinx. He found a small temple between the two paws, and a large tablet of granite on its breast. The tablet is adorned with several figures and hieroglyphics, and two representations of sphinxes are sculptured on it. Before the entrance into the small temple was a lion, placed as if to guard the approach. Farther on from this front of the sphinx is a staircase of thirty-two steps, at the bottom of which is an altar, with a Greek inscription, of the time of the Ptolemies. At each side of the altar was a sphinx of calcareous stone, much mutilated. From the base of the temple to the summit of the head is sixty-five feet: the legs of the sphinx are fifty-seven feet long from the breast to the extremity of the paws, which are eight feet high. Forty-five feet from the first altar, he found another, with an inscription, alluding to the emperor Septimus Severus; and near to the first step was a stone, with another Greek inscription, alluding to Antoninus. Notwithstanding his own occupation about the sphinx, Captain Cabillia employed other people to carry on other researches. He opened some of the mausoleums which were choked up with sand, and found several small chambers, with hieroglyphics and figures, some of them pretty well executed, and in good preservation. In one of the pits he found some mummies, in their linen envelopes, and various fragments of Egyptian antiquity. He also opened some of the smaller pyramids, and from the suggestion of Mr. Briggs to follow a certain direction, he succeeded in finding the entrance into one of them: but it appears, that it was so decayed in the interior, he could advance only a few feet in it. No doubt this led into some chamber, or apartment, containing, perhaps, a sarcophagus, &c.

I was then merely a spectator of the works of Captain Cabillia. The consul, Mr. Salt, proposed to me, to enter into the researches in concert with the Captain; but as I thought it would not be right to attempt to share the credit of one, who had already exerted himself to the utmost of his power, I declined. Besides, it would have been a poor victory on my part to enter into the field after the battle had been fought, and conquest gained by another. I contented myself, therefore, with hoping for a better opportunity to try my skill, independent of any one. Having got all things ready for my departure, the consul proposed that I should take Mr. Beechey with me up the Nile. Nothing could suit me better than to have a companion in a young gentleman, with the prospect of whose society, from what I had seen of him, I had much reason to be pleased. I was fully satisfied that, after having weaned himself from those indulgences to which he was accustomed, he would make a good traveller; though it is not easy, to one who is not accustomed to an arduous life, to pass on a sudden from the accommodation of a comfortable house to that of a rough uneasy boat, and much less to a life that is so irregular. However, Mr. Beechey soon accustomed himself to the change, and in a few months became quite indifferent to the many inconveniences he had to undergo. As to Mrs. Belzoni, I left her at Cairo, in the family of Mr. Cochini, the British chancellor; and when all was ready, we took leave of the consul and Mr. Burckhardt. Alas! I little thought it was the last time I should see my friend; but so it was ordained.

END OF THE FIRST JOURNEY.

RESEARCHES AND OPERATIONS

IN

EGYPT, NUBIA, &c.

SECOND JOURNEY.

Having thus finished the account of my first journey up the Nile, I shall proceed to the narrative of my second. We set off from Boolak on the 20th of February, 1817. Mr. Beechey had the stern of the boat well covered with mats, and close lined all round, with a curtain to the door from which we had light, which was occasionally shut up, to prevent the dust or wind from penetrating from any quarter; beside, another cover over all, rendering it entirely secure, not only from the wind and dust, but also from the rain, if any should happen to fall. We had on board a Greek servant, a Janizary from the Bashaw, and a cook; all persons who never saw any necessity for economy in the article of provision, and who would make as much waste at Deir in Nubia as they would in Cairo. The result was, our provision, which was to last six months, began to fail at the end of one; consequently, with all the caution we took, we were obliged to live on what the country afforded. Indeed, while we were at Thebes we had no reason to complain; for there is a good supply to be had of meat, fowls, and pigeons; and, after the inundation, some greens, such as bamies, malokies, beans, &c.

Our Reis and crew were Barabras, engaged to go and stop where we pleased. They were hired by the month, and had to find themselves in provisions. As to the Janizary from the Bashaw, we found him of so little use (as he did scarcely any thing except treat the Christian dogs with insolence), that we sent him back after a few days trial.

Our departure from Boolak was attended with a contrary wind, which very seldom happens in going up the Nile, as the north winds prevail there at least nine months in the year. We passed the island of Roda, old Cairo, and all the pyramids; but such was the slowness of our progress, that in four days we only reached Tabeen, a village on the eastern bank, opposite Dajior. We stopped at this place pretty early, as the wind would not permit us to proceed; and it happened to be a situation so elevated, that it commanded a distant view of Cairo, the pyramids of Ghizeh, Saccara, and Dajior. I took this opportunity to make a sketch, which I humbly present to the reader (See Plate 22). One day more brought us near Lafachie, where we went to see a Bedoween camp. Hearing we were only travellers in search of antiquities, the Bedoweens were quite civil to us, as far as these people can be. Our business was immediately known to them from our servants and the crew; for no secrecy can be kept in that country, owing to these persons. The Bedoweens told us, that at Boorumbol, the next village, there was a statue half buried in the sand, which they had seen themselves. Next day we came to this village; and as we could not proceed, owing to a calm, we landed, and went in quest of the said statue. On our arrival we were shown a piece of rock, which had not the form of any thing. The Fellahs told us it was once a camel; that God turned it into a stone; and that the smaller ones which lay round it were water-melons, with which it was loaded, and which were metamorphosed into stones also. Perfectly satisfied with the story, we returned to our bark.

In the evening we arrived at Meimond; and, hearing the tambourine, went to see an Arabic feast in the village (See Plate 30.) We were introduced in front of the spectators. The performers consisted of about thirty men, all in a row, clapping their hands in concert, so as to form a kind of accompaniment to their song, which consisted of three or four words; and with one foot before the other keeping a sort of perpetual motion, but without changing their positions. Before the men were two women with daggers in their hands, also in continual action, running toward the men and then returning from them with an extraordinary motion, brandishing their daggers, and waving their garments. In this they persevered for such a length of time, that I wondered how they could support the exertion. This is a sort of Bedoween dance, and is the most decent of all that I ever saw in Egypt;—but no sooner was it ended, than, in order I suppose to please us, they immediately began another, in the fashion of the country, which fully compensated for the extraordinary modesty of the first: but we returned to our boat more disgusted than pleased with it.

For three days we had a strong southerly wind, so that we advanced but a few miles, and did not arrive at Minieh till the 5th of March. It was necessary for us to land there, to see Hamet Bey, who has the command over all the boats on the river. He styles himself admiral of the Nile, and thinks himself as great as any British admiral on the sea. One day at a christian party in Cairo, the discourse happened to fall upon Sir Sydney Smith; "Ah!" said Hamet Bey, "Sir Sydney is a very clever man, and holds the same rank as myself." From this great commander we had to obtain a protection for our Reis, to secure him from having his boat pressed while we employed it. We found him sitting on a wooden bench, attended by two or three of his sailors. He complied with our request, and gave a hint for a bottle of rum. We sent him two, and he made a feast in high glee with them. We went to the house of Doctor Valsomaky, who distils aqua vita, and sells medicines wholesale and retail. He also collects antiquities from the Fellahs round the country, and disposes of them to any one, who chooses to buy them; and it was in hope of purchasing something of this sort, that we visited him. There we saw two Copts dressed like Franks, as they had been in France with the army. They were employed by Mr. Drouetti, the ex-French consul in Alexandria, who sent them up the Nile in search of antiquities.

As we did not wish to interfere with these men, we set off from Minieh immediately, and on the evening of the next day arrived at Eraramoun near Eshmounein, the ancient Hermopolis, where we went to see Mr. Brine, an Englishman, who had introduced sugar-baking into the country. After encountering many obstacles, he had succeeded in purifying and refining the sugar to great perfection. His chief difficulties were to surmount the tricks played off against him by the Arab sugar dealers in that country, and to free the sugar from a particular smell occasioned by the soil, which, though not disagreeable, might retard its introduction into Europe. At his house we learned, that the two agents of Mr. Drouetti were making a forced march to Thebes, of their motives for which I was aware. They wished to arrive there before us, and purchase all that had been accumulated by the Arabs in the preceding season; so that we should have had no chance of buying any thing on our arrival. It was not on this account however I was uneasy, but because the spot, where I had been digging and found the sphinxes and statues, was so evidently pregnant with objects worthy the risk of excavation, that I had no doubt, if they reached Thebes before us, they would take possession of that ground, and we should have no longer a right to explore it.

The mode of travelling on asses or horses is much more speedy than the progress of our boat could be, so that we should certainly have no chance of regaining my old spot of ground where I found the statues. I was not long therefore in considering the matter, and resolved to set off immediately, and by travelling day and night was in hopes to reach the place before them. Accordingly a horse and an ass were got ready, and taking with me the Greek servant, I left Mr. Beechey to come up in the boat at his leisure. By this time it was midnight, yet we set off immediately, and forced marches brought us on the next evening to Manfalout. From this place we hastened without delay, and arrived at Siout before daylight. At sunrise we mounted again, and arrived at dark at Tahta. Here we rested in the convent for four hours, started afresh by the light of the moon, and arrived at Girgeh in the night. We resumed our journey at one o'clock in the morning, reached Farshiout at noon, and after a delay of four hours, in consequence of not finding beasts immediately, arrived at night at a village three leagues above Badjoura. Here we rested two hours, set off by moonlight, and arrived at Gheneh at three. Having dined, we proceeded onward, rested a couple of hours at Benut at night, and arrived at Luxor the following noon.

The whole of our journey occupied five days and half, during which I slept eleven hours, and all the rest of the time we were hastening on with asses, horses, or camels, as we could procure them on the road. The principal places we passed in this journey were Manfalout, Siout, Aboutij, Tahta, Menshieh, Girgeh, Farshiout, Badjoura, Gheneh, Copt, and Ghous. Any one who has been in the country may form some idea of the hardships a person must undergo, travelling through a tract entirely destitute of the necessaries of life. The fathers of the convents of Propaganda at Tahta, Girgeh, and Farshiout, afforded great accommodation to me on this forced march. They provided me with beasts and provisions for the road immediately on my arrival, for which I felt myself deeply indebted to them. The Arabs make every stranger welcome when they are at their meals; and I generally took advantage of the custom, whenever opportunity served; but on this occasion it would have caused the loss of that time I was so eager to gain. In places where there was no convent I went to the house of the Sheik el balet, where travellers of all sorts assemble at night. I was so fatigued and stiff, that any place of rest was acceptable to me. The bare earth generally afforded me a bed, and when I could procure a mat it was a luxury. I was refreshed one night with a few pieces of sugar-cane, which, after passing the torch where the juice has been extracted, becomes pretty soft, and affords a tolerable bed. I was also regaled with sugar-canes as a dessert after a repast of bread and onions. The sugar-cane is pleasant at the first taste, but on pressing it to extract the juice, it gives an acid that is not agreeable, and the flavour is rather insipid. The people of the country eat of it continually, and are very fond of it. It is sold in the markets as fruit when in season.

On the road between Sious and Tahta I met a body of Bedoween horsemen. I never had an opportunity of viewing these people to more advantage than at this time; and I must observe, that I never saw a finer set of men in my life. The horses were very strong, though not in full flesh. The riders were clothed only with a kind of mantle, made of white woollen, of their own manufacturing, which covered the head, and part of the body. They had very small saddles, contrary to the custom of this country; were armed with guns, pistols, and swords; and were going to

Cairo to enter into the service of the Bashaw, who could find no other expedient for suppressing this body of freebooters, than offering to give them good pay, horses, and arms, and to send them to Mecca. This proposal has had its due effect; for all the young men have embraced it, and left the old men and women in the deserts. In this manner the Bashaw entertains hopes of getting rid of the greater part, if not all, of these people, who are detested in the country, and, in case of any insurrection, always avail themselves of it to plunder. I passed through their camp, at the time of their convention with the Bashaw, so that I escaped unmolested, and perhaps unnoticed, as I was covered with a large burnoose of their own fashion, and my beard was pretty long. Their tents consist of four sticks set in the ground, about a yard in height, to which is fastened one of their shawls as a cover, with another behind, so as to form a kind of shelter from the sun, wind, or dew. They generally pitch their camps near a fertile spot, but always at the foot of the desert, so that in case of surprise they are soon in their native country: like the crocodile, which enjoys the land, but when disturbed, or at the approach of any person, immediately plunges into the river, as a place of safety. The women were all uncovered, and the children entirely naked. They are very frugal in their diet, and never drink any strong liquor. They are Arabs, but no more like the Arabs of Egypt, than a freeman is like a slave. The Egyptian Arabs are accustomed to obey, but will not do any thing unless compelled by force. They are humbled, because they are continually under the rod; and indolent, because they have no interest in any thing. But the wild Arabs, on the contrary, are constantly in motion, and labour to procure provision for their beasts and themselves; and being in perpetual war with each other, their thoughts are incessantly employed in improving their arts of defence, or in obtaining plunder.

I must here mention a circumstance, which occasioned me so many unpleasant events, and so much loss of time, and unnecessary labour, that I would not undertake to go through the business again for the discovery of another tomb of Apis. This was merely in consequence of an interpreter's not choosing to take the trouble of writing a few lines. It will be recollected, that, on my return from Thebes to Cairo, I stopped at Siout; and that the Defterdar Bey sent a letter on board our boat for the consul. Previous to my return into Upper Egypt, I urged to the consul the necessity of sending some presents to the Bey, and in particular an answer to his letter from Siout. The consul, naturally thinking that his interpreter, who had been many years settled in the country, should know the customs of it better than myself, consulted him; and this man, merely to save writing, told the consul there was no occasion for it. Relying on him, my remonstrances were of no avail. The Bey, whose pride was touched to the quick at not seeing any present, or receiving any letter, was exasperated at every thing belonging to our party. I do not mean to impute any neglect to the consul for not sending a present to the Bey, as I know he intended to make him one; but the avaricious mind of the Defterdar did not place any reliance on the future, particularly when he found no reply to his letter, which he certainly had a right to expect. On the other hand, our opponents took every advantage, and neglected no means of attracting the good will of the Bey, sending him continually something or other, so that he openly promoted their interest in every respect. Such, with what follows, is the real state of the case; and let the Count de Forbin invent some other story to disguise the truth, if he can. On my arrival at Luxor, I found the Defterdar Bey had just passed, and, after having inquired which was the ground where I discovered the sphinxes, ordered it to be excavated, and returned to Siout, leaving his physician, Doctor

Moroki, a Piedmontese, and countryman of Mr. Drouetti, to superintend the work. I was not a little surprised, to see the advantage which had been taken of us by this intrigue; and the Doctor, who was in the plot, ashamed, I suppose, of his own mean conduct, told me, that what he found was for the Bey, who had taken it into his head to be an antiquary. Several Sphinxes had been uncovered, and more were to be found, while I was obliged to be a mere spectator of the operation, made on the very ground I first opened. Yet the Count de Forbin had impudence enough to assert, that they were discovered by a gentleman, and covered up again, with other idle stories from his own school. Many sphinxes had been found in the Doctor's excavation, but only four were worth taking out. Having finished his operation, he left a guard to the statues, and returned to Siout, as he was ordered by his master; but previous to his departure he went to the west side of Thebes, and forbade the Fellars with threats to sell any thing to the English. On finding that I had already purchased some articles, which I did immediately on my arrival, he took such a spite against me, as he has not forgotten to this day. The conclusion of all this parade about the Bey, the Doctor, the statues, and the excavation, was, that though the statues were for the Bey, yet on the arrival of the agents of Mr. Drouetti (as will be seen hereafter), they took possession of them. Some time after the Doctor wrote me a letter, to inquire whether it were really true, that the agents of Mr. Drouetti had taken away the statues he had found in Carnak, and pretending to be quite shocked at their proceeding. I plainly saw that the Doctor did not wish to open my eyes, but, on the contrary, sent me the letter to blind me entirely, and make me believe, that he had no hand in the plot. But what could he say, when he as well as we saw Mr. Drouetti himself come to Luxor, and with great coolness take away these very statues or sphinxes, pretended to have been found for the Defterdar? I leave the farce to be explained by the veracious Count de Forbin, who may invent some other puff to cover a trick so openly executed.

During this time I was not idle. I set a few men to work on both sides of Thebes, and went to Erments to present to the Cacheff the letter I had from Cairo. On my arrival he received me with much politeness; and after the usual ceremonious protestation of friendship, I took the first opportunity of presenting to him the letter of the Bashaw. He was a little alarmed at first, and very anxious to know the contents; but was relieved when he heard, that I had made no complaint against him, as his good behaviour just before my departure retrieved in part the faults he had committed before. I then reminded him of the behaviour of the Caimakan of Gournou. He swore that he would punish him, and, if I pleased, would turn him out of his place. I said I did not desire him to do either on my account, but for the future wished to proceed in my business undisturbed, and we concluded, that the next morning he should come to Gournou, and settle the affair in a proper manner.

He afterwards introduced to me one of those wonderful saints, who work miracles by dozens, catching scorpions, serpents, &c. This fellow brought a serpent with no teeth, and the Cacheff was much alarmed when he put it into his lap. I took it, and opened its mouth without uttering a word; but the wonder-worker understood me very well. We then went into a dark room to see a miracle. He began with a long prayer, and after a few minutes stretched out his hand in a corner of the room, and to the great astonishment of the beholders produced a scorpion. I observed closely this wonder-working saint, and saw clearly what was passing. The scorpion was kept in the enormous large sleeve of his garment, and being produced in an instant, it appeared as if it came out of the wall. We were now taken to see the apartments all through the house, and he practised the same deception over again. In a particular lower room the son of this Santon pretended to find a small serpent, but not being so adroit as his father, he contented himself with protesting that it had no teeth, which made me ask where serpents could be found in this country without teeth. The Cacheff, I perceived, was a man who would swallow the grossest impositions. He told me many stories truly ridiculous; among the rest, he said that his caste were subjects to a king in the mountains of Cassara, and had such power, that if caught in a storm at sea, a calm was restored in a minute; and if a cannon ball made a hole in the ship, a Santon could stop it; that the Venetian zechins are made by the magic of these Santons; and that one of them being with the Sultan at Constantinople, where the Persian Ambassador had been to announce war against the Porte, he said, that they would conquer the Persians, and that on his thrusting out his finger, the sovereign of Persia should become blind.

I left Erments and went to Luxor; and the next morning I met the Cacheff at Gournou, according to his promise. He gave orders to the Caimakan on every necessary subject; not to threaten the Fellahs, if they sold me any papyri, &c. and to furnish me with men to excavate in whatever place I pleased. The works in Carnak were going on, and I had begun to uncover one of the sitting colossi before the second propylæon, beyond the large avenue of sphinxes leading into the great temple. I had it cleared all round, and found it to be twenty-nine feet high from the bottom of the chair; it is of a white calcareous stone, and very hard. At the foot of the chair I found a sitting statue seven feet high. It represented a female figure, perhaps of Isis. Its head-dress, of enormous size, differed from that of the generality of the Egyptian statues, and from its style appeared to be of a very remote age. The bust was divided at the waist from the rest of the body and chair. I took out the bust, and intended to take out the chair, as soon as the boat arrived with the implements. Having then set the people to work in another direction, where also I had hopes, I took the opportunity to examine at leisure the superb ruins of this edifice. In a distant view of them nothing can be seen but the towering propylæa, high portals, and obelisks, which project above the various groups of lofty palm-trees, and even at a distance announce magnificence. On approaching the avenue of sphinxes, which leads to the great temple, the visiter is inspired with devotion and piety: their enormous size strikes him with wonder and respect to the Gods, to whom they were dedicated. They represent lions with heads of rams, the symbols of strength and innocence, the power and purity of the Gods. Advancing farther in the avenue, there stand before it towering propylæa, which lead to inner courts, where immense colossi are seated at each side of the gate, as if guarding the entrance to the holy ground. Still farther on was the magnificent temple dedicated to the great God of the creation. It was the first time that I entered it alone, without being interrupted by the noise of the Arabs, who never leave the traveller an instant. The sun was rising, and the long shades from the various groups of columns extended over these ruins, intermixed with the rays of light striking on these masses in various directions, formed such delightful views all round as baffle description. Plate 24 will give a general idea of these extensive ruins; and the small sketch, Plate 31, exhibits a small part of the interior of the great temple. I was lost in contemplation of so many objects; and being alone in such a place, my mind was impressed with ideas of such solemnity, that for some time I was unconscious whether I were on terrestrial ground, or in some other planet.

I had seen the temple of Tentyra, and I still acknowledge, that nothing can exceed that edifice in point of preservation, and in the beauty of its workmanship and sculpture; but here I was lost in a mass of colossal objects, every one of which was more than sufficient of itself alone to attract my whole attention. How can I describe my sensations at that moment! I seemed alone in the midst of all that is most sacred in the world; a forest of enormous columns, adorned all round with beautiful figures, and various ornaments, from the top to the bottom; the graceful shape of the lotus, which forms their capitals, and is so well proportioned to the columns, that it gives to the view the most pleasing effect; the gates, the walls, the pedestals, and the architraves, also adorned in every part with symbolical figures in basso relievo and intaglio, representing battles, processions, triumphs, feasts, offerings, and sacrifices, all relating no doubt to the ancient history of the country; the sanctuary, wholly formed of fine red granite, with the various obelisks standing before it, proclaiming to the distant passenger, "Here is the seat of holiness;" the high portals, seen at a distance from the openings to this vast labyrinth of edifices; the various groups of ruins of the other temples within sight; these altogether had such an effect upon my soul, as to separate me in imagination from the rest of mortals, exalt me on high over all, and cause me to forget entirely the trifles and follies of life. I was happy for a whole day, which escaped like a flash of lightning; but the obscurity of the night caused me to stumble over one large block of stone, and to break my nose against another, which, dissolving the enchantment, brought me to my senses again. It was quite late when I returned to Luxor, to the hut of an Arab, who ceded to me part of his chamber, and a mat, which afforded me an excellent bed.

The change from those ruins to the Arab's hut was not less than that from the elevated ideas the sight of them inspired, to the thought of procuring my supper, if I could.

By this time the two agents of Mr. Drouetti had arrived. They immediately set to work to take out the lower Sphinxes, which the Doctor had discovered, and commenced their labours on a very extensive scale. The Bey had left his orders with the Caimakan and the Sheiks, and now scarcely a Fellah could be gotten for us. Mr. D.'s agents had employed them all, and my remonstrances were to little purpose. From the moment these personages came to Thebes, I had a continual series of disagreeable circumstances to encounter, which I could not describe, were I to attempt it. Suffice it to say, that the Bey, who had the command of the whole country, made it a particular point, I have no doubt, to thwart our views; and consequently took care to express his wishes, as to each party, to the Cacheffs and Caimakans, who could not avoid obeying their superior. The petty advantage taken on this occasion soon showed me the characters of the persons I had to deal with. I do not mean the first two agents alone, who had arrived in Thebes, but those who had given them instructions, and others who were sent after them, consisting of European renegadoes, desperadoes, exiles, &c. People of this sort, under no restraint in any thing they do, were sent to obstruct my proceedings; and met with every encouragement from the Bey, and of course from his subalterns.

The first two agents, as I have said, begun their researches extensively; and, as I could get but a few men to employ on the east side of the Nile, I determined to try what could be done on the west, as I had the good-will of the Cacheffs there; but unfortunately the boat with Mr. Beechey had not arrived, and I could not proceed for want of money, having, from prudence, as I came by land, taken but little with me. Accordingly, I left my interpreter, with instructions how to act with the few men I had engaged, and set off in a small boat to meet him. In twenty-four hours I arrived at Gheneh, as the wind happened to be in my favour, and had the good fortune to find him at that place.

It took us three days to reach Thebes, when we moored our bark at Luxor, and I recommenced my operations with what Fellahs I could obtain. The work at Gournou was continued also; and I must confess occupied a greater share of my attention than that at Carnak. Could it but be accurately known, with what a wretched set of people in these tribes travellers have to deal, their mean and rapacious dispositions, and the various occurrences that render the collection of antiquities difficult, whatever came from thence would be the more prized, from the consideration of these circumstances.

The people of Gournou are superior to any other Arabs in cunning and deceit, and the most independent of any in Egypt. They boast of being the last that the French had been able to subdue, and when subdued, they compelled them to pay the men whatever was asked for their labour; a fact which is corroborated by Baron Denon himself. They never would submit to any one, either the Mamelukes or the Bashaw. They have undergone the most severe punishments, and been hunted like wild beasts, by every successive government of Egypt. Their situations and hiding-places were almost impregnable. Gournou is a tract of rocks, about two miles in length, at the foot of the Libyan mountains, on the west of Thebes, and was the burial-place of the great city of a hundred gates. Every part of these rocks is cut out by art, in the form of large and small chambers, each of which has its separate entrance; and, though they are very close to each other, it is seldom that there is any interior communication from one to another. I can truly say, it is impossible to give any description sufficient to convey the smallest idea of those subterranean abodes, and their inhabitants. There are no sepulchres in any part of the world like them; there are no excavations, or mines, that can be compared to these truly astonishing places; and no exact description can be given of their interior, owing to the difficulty of visiting these recesses. The inconveniency of entering into them is such, that it is not every one who can support the exertion.

A traveller is generally satisfied when he has seen the large hall, the gallery, the staircase, and as far as he can conveniently go: besides, he is taken up with the strange works he observes cut in various places, and painted on each side of the walls; so that when he comes to a narrow and difficult passage, or to have to descend to the bottom of a well or cavity, he declines taking such trouble, naturally supposing that he cannot see in these abysses any thing so magnificent as what he sees above, and consequently deeming it useless to proceed any farther. Of some of these tombs many persons could not withstand the suffocating air, which often causes fainting. A vast quantity of dust rises, so fine that it enters into the throat and nostrils, and chokes the nose and mouth to such a degree, that it requires great power of lungs to resist it and the strong effluvia of the mummies. This is not all; the entry or passage where the bodies are is roughly cut in the rocks, and the falling of the sand from the upper part or ceiling of the passage causes it to be nearly filled up. In some places there is not more than a vacancy of a foot left, which you must contrive to pass through in a creeping posture like a snail, on pointed and keen stones, that cut like glass. After getting through these passages, some of them two or three hundred yards long, you generally find a more commodious place, perhaps high enough to sit. But what a place of rest! surrounded by bodies, by heaps of mummies in all directions; which, previous to my being accustomed to the sight, impressed me with horror. The blackness of the wall, the faint light given by the candles or torches for want of air, the different objects that surrounded me, seeming to converse with each other, and the

Arabs with the candles or torches in their hands, naked and covered with dust, themselves resembling living mummies, absolutely formed a scene that cannot be described. In such a situation I found myself several times, and often returned exhausted and fainting, till at last I became inured to it, and indifferent to what I suffered, except from the dust, which never failed to choke my throat and nose; and though, fortunately, I am destitute of the sense of smelling, I could taste that the mummies were rather unpleasant to swallow. After the exertion of entering into such a place, through a passage of fifty, a hundred, three hundred, or perhaps six hundred yards, nearly overcome, I sought a resting-place, found one, and contrived to sit; but when my weight bore on the body of an Egyptian, it crushed it like a band-box. I naturally had recourse to my hands to sustain my weight, but they found no better support; so that I sunk altogether among the broken mummies, with a crash of bones, rags, and wooden cases, which raised such a dust as kept me motionless for a quarter of an hour, waiting till it subsided again. I could not remove from the place, however, without increasing it, and every step I took I crushed a mummy in some part or other. Once I was conducted from such a place to another resembling it, through a passage of about twenty feet in length, and no wider than that a body could be forced through. It was choked with mummies, and I could not pass without putting my face in contact with that of some decayed Egyptian; but as the passage inclined downwards, my own weight helped me on: however, I could not avoid being covered with bones, legs, arms, and heads rolling from above. Thus I proceeded from one cave to another, all full of mummies piled up in various ways, some standing, some lying, and some on their heads. The purpose of my researches was to rob the Egyptians of their papyri; of which I found a few hidden in their breasts, under their arms, in the space above the knees, or on the legs, and covered by the numerous folds of cloth, that envelop the mummy. The people of Gournou, who make a trade of antiquities of this sort, are very jealous of strangers, and keep them as secret as possible, deceiving travellers by pretending, that they have arrived at the end of the pits, when they are scarcely at the entrance. I could never prevail on them to conduct me into these places till this my second voyage, when I succeeded in obtaining admission into any cave where mummies were to be seen.

My permanent residence in Thebes was the cause of my success. The Arabs saw that I paid particular attention to the situation of the entrance into the tombs, and that they could not avoid being seen by me when they were at work digging in search of a new tomb, though they are very cautious when any stranger is in Gournou not to let it be known where they go to open the earth; and as travellers generally remain in that place a few days only, they used to leave off digging during that time. If any traveller be curious enough to ask to examine the interior of a tomb, they are ready to show him one immediately, and conduct him to some of the old tombs, where he sees nothing but the grottoes in which mummies formerly had been deposited, or where there are but few, and these already plundered; so that he can form but a poor idea of the real tombs, where the remains were originally placed.

The people of Gournou live in the entrance of such caves as have already been opened, and, by making partitions with earthen walls, they form habitations for themselves, as well as for their cows, camels, buffaloes, sheep, goats, dogs, &c. I do not know whether it is because they are so few in number, that the government takes so little notice of what they do; but it is certain, that they are the most unruly people in Egypt. At various times many of them have been destroyed, so that they are reduced from three thousand, the number they formerly reckoned, to three hundred, which form the population of the present day. They have no mosque, nor do they care for one; for though they have at their disposal a great quantity of all sorts of bricks, which abound in every part of Gournou, from the surrounding tombs, they have never built a single house. They are forced to cultivate a small tract of land, extending from the rocks to the Nile, about a mile in breadth, and two and a half in length; and even this is in part neglected; for if left to their own will, they would never take a spade in their hands, except when they go to dig for mummies; which they find to be a more profitable employment than agriculture. This is the fault of travellers, who are so pleased the moment they are presented with any piece of antiquity, that, without thinking of the injury resulting from the example to their successors, they give a great deal more than the people really expect. Hence it has arisen, that they now set such an enormous price on antiquities, and in particular on papyri. Some of them have accumulated a considerable sum of money, and are become so indifferent, that they remain idle, unless whatever price they demand be given them; and it is to be observed, that it is a fixed point in their minds, that the Franks would not be so liberal, unless the articles were worth ten times as much as they pay for them.

The Fellahs of Gournou who dig for antiquities are sometimes divided into parties, and have their chiefs over each; so that what is found by any of the party is sold, and the money divided among them all. They are apparently very true to each other, and particularly in cheating strangers; but when they can find a good opportunity, they do not scruple to cheat each other also. One day when I had to purchase some antiquities according to appointment, and was going to the tomb of one of these companies, my guide told me by the way, that he had some papyri to sell, which he had himself found, previous to his entering into partnership with his associates; and it was agreed, that I was to repair to his house alone to see them. However, I took Mr. Beechey with me, and we had great difficulty to prevent those by whom we were observed from following us; as it is the common custom among these people to enter each other's houses as they please, and see and hear all that passes. In spite of all his caution, they suspected that the old man had a considerable hoard of papyri, and were persuaded that he wished them not to know the large sum he was to receive for them. Accordingly they did not fail to watch our coming out, so that they might see what we purchased; and when they saw we had nothing they were all surprised and disappointed. One of the chiefs, who was a favourite with the English, approached the interpreter, to know what had passed; and when he heard that nothing had passed but words, he said, the old man dared not sell any papyri without the consent of the company, and that all they had to sell, and all he had, must be brought to us conjointly. They had no idea how this veteran had deceived them; for other articles of consequence are so very seldom found, that they did not suspect his having any thing but papyri to dispose of. Age and experience, however, had naturally rendered him a greater adept in the art of deceit. When Mr. Beechey, myself, and the interpreter, entered his cave, his wife walked out to watch if any one approached. The donkey-men, who brought us, were at some distance from the cave, and not a single being was near us. His dwelling was a grotto cut in the rock like the rest, and black as any chimney. He made us sit down on a straw mat, which is a luxurious thing in Gournou, and after a little ceremony, put into my hands a brazen vessel, one of the finest and most perfect pieces of Egyptian antiquity I have ever seen of the kind. It was covered with hieroglyphic engravings, very finely executed. It was about eighteen inches high and ten in diameter.

The composition is extremely fine, and it sounds not unlike the Corinthian brass. I was most agreeably surprised, and could scarcely believe that I had such a treasure in my hands. I conceive it to be a sacred vessel used by the Egyptians. It has a handle something like our common baskets. We were examining it with astonishment, when the old man took it from our hands, and presented us with another exactly similar to it. The sight of a pair of antiques like these, their admirable preservation, and the opportunity we had of purchasing them, delighted us so much, that the bargain with the old man was made in a few words. The great difficulty was to take them to our boat, which the old man promised to do in the night, after all were asleep. We returned to Luxor in high glee, from the expectation of having in our possession two of the finest articles of metallic composition, that ever were to be found in Egypt. At night the old man did not come, which made me uneasy; but he came in the morning, and said, that he could not bring the vases with him, as his companions were watching, but that he would not fail to bring them at night, meanwhile he should be glad, he added, to receive the money and the present we had promised; and we paid him without hesitation, that he might not retract his bargain. At night, however, no old man; nor the next day did he make his appearance. I thought it necessary therefore to go to his habitation. I found him at home, and he said, as before, he would not fail to come to us at night. Night, however, again arrived without him; but early the next morning he brought the vessels to our boat. Some time after, one of his companions inquired of me what the old man had received for his antiques. We wondered how he came to know any thing of the matter; when he informed us, the vessels belonged to the company, and the pretence of secrecy was a scheme of the old man to extract from us the present of a turbouse*, in which he had succeeded.

* A red cap, or bonnet.

After having described the tombs, the mummies, the rocks, and the rogues of Gournou, it is time to cross the Nile, and return to Carnak. Here we continued the work, as I mentioned before. Our opponents had taken away the four sphinxes, which the doctor had dug up, in the name of the Defterdar-bey, from the ground I had opened the year before, but had found nothing more, which is somewhat singular, considering the number of men they had employed in their excavation. I now opened another piece of ground, in a line parallel with the point of the temple, and I was fortunate enough to find another line of sphinxes. From the fragments there were probably twenty, but five only were in good preservation. Among them was a sitting figure of a young man nearly of the size of life, of gray granite; but though the face, hands, and arms, were in good condition, the chest and lower parts were quite decayed, and the bust detached from the rest of the body. In the same place I found two small sitting figures of red granite, nearly two feet high, and a stone irregularly shaped, but flat and smooth on the surfaces. It is divided by lines into many little squares of half an inch, in each of which is a hieroglyphic, but all different from each other. This piece in my opinion might be of much service to Dr. Young in his undertaking of the discovery of the alphabet of the Egyptians, particularly in the advanced state at which he has at present arrived. Two other articles were found in this excavation, of which one is a tombstone, and the other an iron sickle, that I think worthy the attention of the antiquary. It is certain, that the burial-places of the Egyptians were on the west side of the Nile, for not a single place is to be found on the eastern side to indicate there having ever been a burial-ground there: yet among these sphinxes was a tombstone similar to those which are found in the tombs on the other side of the Nile, and probably, therefore, made to be taken to the tomb of some family on the west. But the iron sickle to which I would call the attention, was found under the feet of one of the sphinxes on its removal. I was present; one of the men took it up and gave it me. It was broken into three pieces, and so decayed, that the rust had eaten even to the centre. It was rather thicker than the sickles of the present time, but exactly of the common shape and size of ours. It is now in the possession of Mr. Salt. The question is, at what time were these statues placed there? They could not have been deposited subsequently to the age of the Ptolemies; for it appears, that since the time of Cambyses, who destroyed the Gods of Egypt, the country has never been invaded, so as to compel the people to conceal their idols; and it is evident, that these statues had been hidden in a hurry, from the irregular and confused manner in which they lie. Now, as the sickle was found under the statue above mentioned, I think it a sufficient proof, that there was iron in the country long before the invasion of the Persians, since the Egyptians had enough to make instruments of agriculture with it. Sickles of the same form are to be seen in many agricultural representations in the tombs; but it does not follow, that they were taken from sickles of iron, like the one in question. I do not mean to decide this point by my own suppositions: I lay the fact before the reader, that he may form his own opinion upon it; yet there are circumstances that would destroy the conjecture, that might be drawn from this discovery. It is very singular, if the Egyptians had iron in such abundance, as to make sickles, that they did not make instruments of war, and other articles for their common use, of the same metal; and if they had done so, it is strange, that none are to be found among the various specimens of their manufacture.

I continued the work as fast as I could with the few men I had, as I foresaw, that when the Defterdar came to the knowledge of my success he would put a stop to our proceedings by some intrigue or other. My daily employment kept me in continual motion. In the morning I used to give my directions for the works at Carnak. The Arabs generally come to work at the rising of the sun, and leave off from noon till two or three o'clock. When I had many employed, I divided them into parties, and set an overseer over each, to see that they worked at the proper hours, and on the allotted spots of ground, which I had previously marked out; but generally some of our people were obliged to be there, for no trust is to be reposed in the Arabs, if they should find any small pieces of antiquity. Before noon I used to cross the river and inspect the works at Gournou. Having been there the year before, and had dealings with these people, I was at home in every part of Thebes, knew every Arab there, and they knew me as well. Mr. Beechey had taken possession of the temple at Luxor, without requesting permission from the Gods, and we made a dwelling-place of one of the chambers: I believe it must have been the sekos. By the help of some mats we procured a very tolerable accommodation, but could not prevent the dust from coming on our beds, and clothes, to which for my part I had long before become indifferent. We could not sleep any longer in the boat; for in consequence of the provision we had on board, such quantities of large rats accompanied us all the way to Luxor, that we had no peace day or night, and at last they succeeded in fairly dislodging us. We thought to have been a match for them, however, for we caused all the provision to be taken out, and the boat to be sunk at Luxor, but as they were good swimmers, they saved their lives, and hid themselves in the holes of the pier; and when the provision had been put on board again, they all returned cheerfully, a few excepted, and were no doubt grateful to us for having given them a fresh appetite and a good bathing.

In Gournou, our researches continued among the mummies. The

Arabs had become quite unconcerned about the secret of the tombs; for they saw it was their interest to search, as they were rewarded for what they found, and those who were duly paid were indifferent whether we or their brethren found a tomb. The men were divided into two classes. The most knowing were making researches on their own account, employing eight or ten to assist them. They indicated the ground where they hoped to find a tomb, and sometimes were fortunate enough to hit on the entrance of a mummy pit in the first attempt. At other times, after spending two or three days, they often found only a pit filled with mummies of the inferior class, which had nothing among them worthy of notice: so that, even to the most skilful explorer, it was a mere chance what he should find. On the other hand, in some of the tombs of the better class they found very good specimens of antiquity, of all sorts. I met with some difficulty at first in persuading these people to work in search of tombs, and receive a regular daily payment; for they conceived it to be against their interest, supposing I might obtain the antiquities at too cheap a rate: but when they saw, that sometimes they received their pay regularly, and I had nothing for it, they found it was rather in their favour, to secure twenty paras (three pence) a day, than run the risk of having nothing for their labour, which often happened to those who worked at adventure.

It was from these works that I became better acquainted with the manner in which the Egyptians regulated their burial-places; and I plainly saw the various degrees and customs of the divers classes, from the peasant to the king. The Egyptians had three different methods of embalming their dead bodies, which, Herodotus informs us, were according to the expense the persons who presented the dead bodies to the mummy-makers chose to incur. This father of history thus expresses himself on the subject: " Certain persons were appointed by the laws to the exercise of this profession. When a dead body was brought to them, they exhibited to the friends of the deceased different models, highly finished in wood. The most perfect of these, they said, resembles one, whom I do not think it religious to name on such an occasion; the second was of less price, and inferior in point of execution; the other was still more mean. They then inquired after which model the deceased should be represented. When the price was determined, the relations retired, and the embalmers proceeded in their work. In the most perfect specimens of their art, they extracted the brain through the nostrils, partly with a piece of crooked iron, and partly by the infusion of drugs. They then, with an Ethiopian stone, made an incision in the side, through which they drew out the intestines. These they cleansed thoroughly, washing them with palm-wine, and afterward covering them with pounded aromatics. They then filled the body with powder of pure myrrh, cassia, and other spices, without frankincense. Having sown up the body, it was covered with nitre for the space of seventy days; which time they were not allowed to exceed. At the end of this period, being first washed, it was closely wrapped in bandages of cotton, dipped in a gum, which the Egyptians used as a glue. It was then returned to the relations, who enclosed the body in a case of wood, made to resemble a human figure, and placed it against the wall in the repository of their dead. This was the most costly mode of embalming.

"For those who wished to be at less expense, the following method was adopted. They neither drew out the intestines, nor made any incision in the dead body, but injected a liniment made from the cedar. After taking proper means to secure the injected oil within the body, it was covered with nitre for the time above specified. On the last day they withdrew the liquid before introduced, which brought with it all the intestines. The nitre dried up and hardened the flesh, so that the corpse appeared little but skin and bone. In this state the body was returned, and no further care taken concerning it.

"There was a third mode of embalming, appropriated to the poor. A particular kind of lotion was made to pass through the body, which was afterward merely left in nitre for the above space of seventy days, and then returned." Such is the account given us by Herodotus.

Nothing can more plainly distinguish the various classes of people, than the manner of their preservation: but there are many other remarks, that may be made to the same effect. I shall describe how I have found the mummies of the principal class untouched, and hence we may judge how they were prepared and deposited in their respective places. I am sorry that I am obliged to contradict my old guide Herodotus; for in this point, and many others, he was not well informed by the Egyptians. In the first place, speaking of the mummies in their cases, he mentions them as erect: but it is somewhat singular, that in so many pits as I have opened, I never saw a single mummy standing. On the contrary, I found them lying regularly, in horizontal rows, and some were sunk into a cement, which must have been nearly fluid when the cases were placed on it. The lower classes were not buried in cases: they were dried up, as it appears, after the regular preparation of the seventy days. Mummies of this sort were in the proportion of about ten to one of the better class, as near as I could calculate by the quantity I have seen of both; and it appeared to me, that, after the operation of the nitre, adopted by the mummy-makers, these bodies may have been dried in the sun. Indeed, for my own part, I am persuaded it was so; as there is not the smallest quantity of gum or any thing else to be found on them. The linen in which they are folded is of a coarser sort, and less in quantity; they have no ornaments about them of any consequence, and they are piled up in layers, so as to crowd several caves excavated for the purpose in a rude manner. In general, these tombs are to be found in the lower grounds, at the foot of the mountains of Gournou; and some extend as far as the border to which the inundation reaches. They are to be entered by a small aperture, arched over, or by a shaft four or five feet square, at the bottom of which are entrances into various chambers, all choked up with mummies: and though there is scarcely any thing to be found on them, many of these tombs have been rummaged, and left in the most confused state.

I must not omit, that among these tombs we saw some which contained the mummies of animals intermixed with human bodies. There were bulls, cows, sheep, monkeys, foxes, bats, crocodiles, fishes, and birds, in them: idols often occur; and one tomb was filled with nothing but cats, carefully folded in red and white linen, the head covered by a mask representing the cat, and made of the same linen. I have opened all these sorts of animals. Of the bull, the calf, and the sheep, there is no part but the head which is covered with linen, and the horns projecting out of the cloth; the rest of the body being represented by two pieces of wood, eighteen inches wide and three feet long, in an horizontal direction, at the end of which was another, placed perpendicularly, two feet high, to form the breast of the animal. The calves and sheep are of the same structure, and large in proportion to the bulls. The monkey is in its full form, in a sitting posture. The fox is squeezed up by the bandages, but in some measure the shape of the head is kept perfect. The crocodile is left in its own shape, and after being well bound round with linen, the eyes and mouth are painted on this covering. The birds are squeezed together, and lose their shape except the ibis, which is found like a fowl ready to be cooked, and bound round with linen, like all the rest.

It is somewhat singular that such animals are not to be met with in the tombs of the higher sort of people; while few or no papyri are to be found among the lower order, and if any occur they are only small pieces stuck upon the breast with a little gum or asphaltum, being probably all that the poor individual could afford to himself. In those of the better classes other objects are found. I think they ought to be divided into several classes, as I cannot confine myself to three. I do not mean to impute error to Herodotus when he speaks of the three modes of embalming; but I will venture to assert, that the high, middling, and poorer classes, all admit of farther distinction. In the same pit where I found mummies in cases, I found others without; and in these, papyri are most likely to be met with. I remarked, that the mummies in the cases have no papyri; at least, I never observed any: on the contrary, in those without cases they are often obtained. It appears to me, that such people as could afford it would have a case to be buried in, on which the history of their lives was painted: and those who could not afford a case, were contented to have their lives written on papyri, rolled up, and placed above their knees. Even in the appearance of the cases there is a great difference: some are exceedingly plain, others more ornamented, and some very richly adorned with figures, well painted. The cases are generally made of Egyptian sycamore: apparently, this was the most plentiful wood in the country, as it is usually employed for the different utensils. All the cases have a human face, male or female. Some of the large cases contain others within them, either of wood or of plaster, painted. The inner cases are sometimes fitted to the body of the mummy: others are only covers to the body, in form of a man or woman, easily

z

distinguishable by the beard and the breast, like that on the outside. Some of the mummies have garlands of flowers, and leaves of the acacia, or sunt tree, over their heads and breasts. This tree is often seen on the banks of the Nile, above Thebes, and particularly in Nubia. The flower, when fresh, is yellow, and of a very hard substance, appearing as if artificial. The leaves, also, are very strong, and though dried and turned brown, they still retain their firmness. In the inside of these mummies are found lumps of asphaltum, sometimes so large as to weigh two pounds. The entrails of these mummies are often found bound up in linen and asphaltum. What does not incorporate with the fleshy part, remains of the natural colour of the pitch; but that which does incorporate becomes brown, and evidently mixed with the grease of the body, forming a mass, which on pressure crumbles into dust. The wooden case is first covered with a layer or two of cement, not unlike plaster of Paris; and on this are sometimes cast figures in basso relievo, for which they make niches cut in stone. The whole case is painted; the ground generally yellow, the figures and hieroglyphics blue, green, red, and black. The last is very seldom used. The whole of the painting is covered with a varnish, which preserves it very effectually. Some of the colours, in my humble opinion, were vegetable, for they are evidently transparent; besides, I conceive it was easier for the Egyptians to produce vegetable colours than mineral, from the great difficulty of grinding the latter to such perfection.

The next sort of mummy that drew my attention, I believe I may with reason conclude to have been appropriated to the priests. They are folded in a manner totally different from the others, and so carefully executed, as to show the great respect paid to those personages. The bandages are stripes of red and white linen intermixed, covering the whole body, and forming a curious effect from the two colours. The arms and legs are not enclosed in the same envelope with the body, as in the common mode, but are bandaged separately, even the fingers and toes being preserved distinct. They have sandals of painted leather on their feet, and bracelets on their arms and wrists. They are always found with the arms across the breast, but not pressing it; and though the body is bound with such a quantity of linen, the shape of the person is carefully preserved in every limb. The cases in which mummies of this sort are found are somewhat better executed, and I have seen one, that had the eyes and eyebrows of enamel, beautifully executed in imitation of nature. Among the various tombs, I discovered one of this description in the valley adjacent to Beban el Malook on the west of it, of which I shall have to speak hereafter.

I found eight mummies, all untouched since they had been deposited in their resting-place. The cases lay flat on the ground, facing the east, in two equal rows, imbedded four inches deep in mortar, which must have been soft when they were put into it; for when I had them removed the impression of them remained perfect. The opening of them I shall describe, with that of the tomb.

The tombs containing the better classes of people are of course superior to the others. There are some more extensive than the rest, having various apartments, adorned with figures representing different actions of life. Funeral processions are generally predominant. Agricultural processes, religious ceremonies, and more ordinary occurrences, such as feasting, &c. are to be seen every where. I shall not enter into a minute account of these paintings, as they have been so often described, particularly by Mr. Hamilton, whose perspicuous observations upon them give the best idea of their various representation. It would be impossible to describe the numerous little articles found in them, which are well adapted to show the domestic habits of the ancient Egyptians. It is here the smaller idols are occasionally found, either lying on the ground, or on the cases of the mummies. Vases are sometimes found containing the embalmed entrails of the mummies. These are generally made of baked clay, and painted over: their sizes differ from eight inches to eighteen: their covers represent the head of some divinity, bearing either the human form, or that of a monkey, fox, cat, or some other animal. I met with a few of these vases of alabaster in the tombs of the kings, but unfortunately they were broken. A great quantity of pottery is found, and also wooden vessels in some of the tombs, as if the deceased had resolved to have all he possessed deposited along with him. The most singular among these things are the ornaments, in particular the small works in clay and other composition. I have been fortunate enough to find many specimens of their manufactures, among which is leaf gold, beaten nearly as thin as ours. The gold appears to me extremely pure, and of a finer colour than is generally seen in our own. It is somewhat singular that no instruments of war are found in these places, when we consider what a warlike nation the Egyptians were. What has become of their weapons I cannot conjecture; for in all my researches I found only one arrow, two feet long. At one extremity it had a copper point well fixed in it, and at the other a notch as usual to receive the string of the bow: it had been evidently split by the string, and glued together again.

Among other articles too numerous to be mentioned, the beetle, or scarabæus, to all appearance a highly sacred animal, is found in the tombs. There are various sorts; some of basalt, verde antico, or other stones, and some of baked clay. They are scarce, particularly those with hieroglyphics on them, which no doubt contain some particular prayers, or the commemoration of striking events in the life of the deceased. It is supposed, that the Egyptians hung the scarabæus to their necks when they went to war; but of this we have no clear proofs. I must mention a circumstance on this subject, which perhaps will solve the doubt. The scarabæi are of such a peculiar form, that, if they were among the ornaments of the warriors, they would be easily distinguished. One solitary instance of this kind I have observed. There is a sitting figure in the tomb of Samethis, which I discovered in the valley below Beban el Malook, that, by its splendid dress and ornaments, may be intended to represent a king. It has a square plate of basalt hung to its neck, with an obelisk in the centre, and a figure on each side of it. I was extremely fortunate in meeting with one of these plates, I believe the only one that ever was found of the kind. It has the form of an Egyptian temple, and in the centre is an elevated scarabæus on a boat, guarded by two figures, one at each side; and on the reverse of the scarabæus is an inscription over a boat, on which are two other figures, exactly like the former. The plate has the holes by which it was hung to a chain or string. I found also other scarabæi, with human heads, which I never saw before.

The Egyptians were certainly well acquainted with linen manufactures to a perfection equal to our own; for, in many of their figures, we observe their garments quite transparent; and among the folding of the mummies, I observed some cloth quite as fine as our common muslin, very strong, and of an even texture. They had the art of tanning leather, with which they made shoes as well as we do, some of which I found of various shapes. They had also the art of staining the leather with various colours, as we do Morocco, and actually knew the mode of embossing on it, for I found leather with figures impressed on it, quite elevated. I think it must have been done with a hot iron while the leather was damp. They also fabricated a sort of coarse glass, with which they made beads and other ornaments.

Beside enamelling, the art of gilding was in great perfection among them, as I found several ornaments of the kind. They knew how to cast copper as well as to form it into sheets, and had a metallic composition not unlike our lead, rather softer, but of greater tenacity. It is much like the lead which we see on paper in the tea-chests from China, but much thicker. I found some pieces of it covered on both sides with a thin coat of another metal, which might be taken for silver, but I cannot believe it to be so. It certainly is a proof of the scarcity of this metal in Egypt, where, in my opinion, it was less common than gold; for it is seldom found, whereas the latter is quite common on the ornaments.

Carved works were very common, and in great perfection, particularly in the proportion of the figures; and it is to be observed, that though the Egyptians were unacquainted with anatomy, yet in these, as well as in their statues of marble, they preserved that sweet simplicity peculiar to themselves, which is always pleasing to the beholder.

In one of the tombs of the kings I found two wooden figures, nearly seven feet high, of very fine workmanship. They are in a standing posture, with one arm extended, as if holding a torch. They had many other carved works, hieroglyphics, ornaments, &c.

The art of varnishing, and baking the varnish on clay, was in such perfection among them, that I doubt whether it could be imitated at present. Articles of the best sort of this manufacture, however, were rather scarce, as there are but few to be found; while, on the contrary, there are great quantities of the inferior sorts. Indeed, the few good ones I met with were all in the great tomb of Samethis, and these are of the most beautiful colour.

The art of painting was but simple among the Egyptians, as they had no knowledge of shadowing to elevate their figures; but great credit is due to them for their taste in disposing their colours. There is great harmony even in the red and green, which do not always agree with us, and which they knew how to mingle so well, that it produced a very splendid effect, particularly by candle-light. As I observed before, I am of opinion, that these colours were from the vegetable kingdom, and think I can produce a pretty strong proof of the fact. The present natives of Egypt, who manufacture indigo, make it up in cakes of the size of a sea biscuit, in a very rough manner. Not knowing how to extract the colour from the plant without mixing it with sand, the cake glitters all over, the light being reflected from every particle. Of this imperfection the ancient Egyptians could not get the better; for whenever there is blue in any of their paintings, which is evidently indigo, the same sparkling sand is to be seen, as in the modern cakes. Their drawings and sculpture are but simple, and systematically done; notwithstanding which, they knew how to impart a certain vivacity to their posture, which animates their figures. They knew little or nothing of perspective, and all that was done was in profile. The wall or whatever other place was to be ornamented was previously prepared, by grinding it very smooth. The first lines were done in red by a scholar, or one not so expert as the master, who examined the outlines, and corrected them in black. Specimens of this are to be seen in the tomb of Samethis, as I shall have to mention hereafter.

When the outlines were completed, the sculptor began his work. He raised the figure by cutting away the stone all round it. The angles are smoothly turned, and the ornaments on the figure or garments are traced with a chisel, which leaves a slight impression, and adorns the wholefigure. The last was the painter, who finished the piece. They could not find any other colours than red, blue, yellow, green, and black. The blue is divided into two sorts, the dark and the light. With these colours they adorned their temples, tombs, or whatever they wished to have painted. As there is no colour among these that could imitate the living human flesh, they adopted the red for this purpose. The ornaments were decorated with the other colours; and, though so few, I am sure they are not all used in the same piece.

As to their architecture, I can only say it is in conformity with their ideas. It is to be recollected, that they had a notion of returning to life again, body and soul, after a period of three thousand years: whence we may presume, that they intended to make their edifices last so long, that they might see them again in good preservation. As to arches, can we not prove, from the circumstance of their having made them in a different form from ours, that they could also have made them of a larger size, than we see to this very day in Thebes? Yes, I say, in Thebes there are Egyptian arches. If any reader will observe Plate 44, he will see an Egyptian arch which exists at Gournou, under the rocks that separate this place from the valley Beban el Malook. The arch is made in a manner entirely different from our own; but if the Egyptians were inclined to have arches, they might soon have constructed them in this manner, and of considerable sizes, equal in proportion to the enormous blocks which we see in their edifices. No, they did not want arches—they preferred having their temples crowded with columns, which formed the finest embellishments of their edifices; and I assert, that the number of these columns is no detriment to the beauty or magnificence of these sacred places. On the contrary, without these columns, their architecture would not have appeared to the Egyptians so substantially firm, which was their principal object. This, in my opinion, was their reason for not erecting arches. But I shall endeavour farther to prove, that they knew how to make an arch with the key-stone as well as we do. A traveller may wander among the ruins of Thebes, and his attention be so much taken by the magnificence of the great edifices, as to overlook what is inferior, especially what is constructed of simple bricks, baked in the sun. Besides, he has a preconceived notion, that the Egyptians were ignorant of the art of turning an arch; so that, if he should see one, or even pass under an archway, he would take it for granted, that it was the work of a later people. I shall now describe the situation of several arches, which are to be seen in Thebes; point out the purpose for which they were evidently erected; and leave the reader to conjecture whether they were made by the Egyptians, or by any other people.

The mode of building enormously strong walls with unburnt bricks is peculiar to the Egyptians. Of this I trust there can be no doubt, from the many instances clearly before our eyes; but if it be questioned, I would inquire of any traveller, who has seen Thebes, whether he thinks that the wall, which surrounded the avenue of sphinxes, or lion-headed statues, which I discovered at Carnak, could have been made by any other people. There are even some of these walls that enclose their sacred places: and if it be objected, that some subsequent nation, who adored the same gods, may have erected these walls to preserve the holy edifices, I can boldly say: No, this was not the fact; for the walls are so connected with the Egyptian works, that it is plain they were constructed at the same time with them. But what is still more to the point, at Gournou there are various and extensive tombs, excavated not in the rocks themselves, but in the plains at their foot, twelve or fourteen feet below the surface, and extending a considerable length under ground. The way to these tombs is generally by a staircase, which led into a large square hall, cut in the rock, in some instances ninety or a hundred feet long; and opposite the stairs is generally the entrance into the tomb. It is to be observed, that these halls entered into the original plan of the structure: there was nothing to protect or to enclose them on any side but a wall, by which they were completely covered. Without this, they would have been exposed to all the rubbish of

A A

other tombs, which might have fallen in. The necessity of building these walls is evident; and I have no doubt many travellers will plainly see, that no other succeeding nation would have built these enormous walls to preserve the tombs of the Egyptians. Now over the stairs, which lead into the hall, there are some very high and majestic arches, not only made of the same bricks, but connected with the walls themselves; consequently, made by the Egyptians, and constructed with the same key-stones as our own in the present day. There is also at Gournou a great number of other buildings of sun-burnt bricks, of a later date, which I hope will not be confounded with the others. Some of these are built with a smaller sort of bricks; others with bricks taken from the Egyptian walls; but their construction plainly shows the difference of the people who erected them.

If we extend our observations on the Egyptian architecture, it will appear, that the Egyptians undoubtedly have the merit of invention, which I consider as the source of improvement, &c. The Greeks may claim their having brought the art to great perfection; but it is well known, that they took their principal hints from the Egyptians.

The Egyptians were a primitive nation. They had to form every thing without any model before them to imitate. Yet so fertile was their inventive faculty, that to this day new orders of architecture might be extracted from their ruins. If we observe the Egyptian capitals, do we not see a complication of orders in one mass, which, if divided, would produce numerous hints for new ideas? If the lover of truth will but inspect the various representations of the lotus on the capitals, he will plainly see, that not only the Doric and the Corinthian orders have been extracted from them, but that more might still be formed. There is reason also to believe, that the Ionic order originated in Egypt. The capitals of the columns of Tentyra, those in the small temple of Edfu, and, lastly, the others in the small temple of Isis, in the island of Philœ, sufficiently indicate this. The name of the deity, to which the first and third of these temples are dedicated, seems to strengthen this supposition. We well know, that Isis is the Io of the Greeks, from whom the name of Ionic was no doubt derived; and it is very probable, that he who introduced the order gave it that name, as having been taken from the temple of the goddess.

The wonderful sculptures of the Egyptians are to be admired for the boldness of their execution. Their enormous sizes rendered it difficult for the artists to maintain their due proportions, which were according to the height of the figure. For instance, if a statue were erected of the size of life, the head was of the natural size; if the statue were thirty feet high, the head was larger in proportion to the body; and if fifty feet high, the magnitude of the head was farther increased. Had it been otherwise in statues of so great height, the distance from the eyes of the spectator would have so much diminished the size, that the head would have appeared too small in proportion to the legs. The tedious work of the endless hieroglyphics which are to be seen in every part of every edifice, the numberless figures on the temples, tombs, obelisks, and walls, must have required wonderful labour. They had only four sorts of stones in general use for sculpture, the sandy, the calcareous, breccia, and granite. All except the first are very hard, and what is most singular is, we do not know with what tools they were cut out. We have ocular demonstration, that the tools of the present day will not cut granite without great difficulty, and I doubt whether we could give it that smoothness of surface we see in Egypt. But I would observe it is not unreasonable to suppose, that the granite and other stones were less hard at the time of the Egyptians, than they are at present. On the calcareous stone the figures have angles so sharp, that the best tempered chisel of our time could not produce the like; it is so hard that it breaks more like glass than stone; and the granite is almost impenetrable.

At the end of the above mentioned plain in Gournou, at the foot of the rocks which divide that valley from Beban-el-Malook, the excavation was going on at the end of an avenue where sphinxes must have been. Here was found a causeway gradually rising to some ruins, which being uncovered, proved to be a temple, with columns doubly octangular, the only one of such form I saw in Egypt. The temple is evidently ancient, but I dare not affirm it to be Egyptian, though it has hieroglyphics, &c. on the walls; for the proportions of the plan, as far as I could see, and the order of the columns, being totally different from any others of the Egyptians, lead me to suppose this temple to be of a later date. Farther on, just under the rocks, we discovered a granite door nine feet high by five wide, and one and a half thick. It is covered with hieroglyphics and figures neatly cut, and on the top it has the winged globe and a cornice. It had been painted, and was buried entirely under ground.

While my men were at work, I was in the habit of searching among these tombs, and entered all the places and holes I could possibly squeeze myself into. In the large tombs I caused the side wall or rock to be struck with the large sledge hammer, to discover by the sound if any cavity were near. One day the hammer not only gave a hollow sound, but made an aperture a foot and half wide into another tomb. Having enlarged the hole sufficiently to pass, we entered, and found several mummies, and a great quantity of broken cases. The stones which had fallen from the roof were as sharp as a razor, and as my shoes were not very strong, my feet were cut in several places. These stones detach themselves from the roof in flakes, which proves them to be much harder than when first cut. In an inner apartment of this tomb is a square opening, into which we descended, and at the bottom found a small chamber at each side of the shaft. In one was a granite sarcophagus with its cover quite perfect, but so situated, that it would be an arduous undertaking to draw it out. Among the mummies I found some small papyri, and one extraordinarily large.

When I did not choose to pass the river in the night to our habitation at the temple of Luxor, I took up my lodging in the entrance of some of the tombs along with those troglodytes. Nothing could be more amusing to me. Their dwelling is generally in the passages between the first and second entrance into a tomb. The walls and the roof are as black as any chimney. The inner door is closed up with mud, except a small aperture sufficient for a man to crawl through. Within this place the sheep are kept at night, and occasionally accompany their masters in their vocal concert. Over the doorway there are always some half-broken Egyptian figures, and the two foxes, the usual guardians of burial-places. A small lamp, kept alive by fat from the sheep, or rancid oil, is placed in a niche in the wall, and a mat is spread on the ground; and this formed the grand divan, wherever I was. There the people assembled round me, their conversation turning wholly on antiquities. Such a one had found such a thing, and another had discovered a tomb. Various articles were brought to sell to me, and sometimes I had reason to rejoice at having stayed there. I was sure of a supper of milk and bread served in a wooden bowl; but whenever they supposed I should stay all night, they always killed a couple of fowls for me, which were baked in a small oven heated with pieces of mummy cases, and sometimes with the bones and rags of the mummies themselves. It is no uncommon thing to sit down near fragments of bones; hands, feet, or sculls are often in the way; for these people are so accustomed to be among the mummies, that they think no more of sitting on them, than on the skins of their dead calves. I also became indifferent about them at last, and would have slept in a mummy pit as readily as out of it.

Every human being can be happy if he likes, for happiness certainly depends on ourselves. If a man be satisfied with what he has, he is happy; but much more so when he thinks, that there is nothing more to be got. It is somewhat singular to talk of happiness among people who live in caves like brutes, or rather who live in sepulchres among the corpses and rags of an ancient nation, of which they know nothing. But this is trifling compared with their slave-like state, subject to the caprice of a tyrannical power, who leaves them no chance of receiving any remuneration for their labour, and no prospect of any change except for the worse. But custom reconciles all this. The labourer comes home in the evening, seats himself near his cave, smokes his pipe with his companions, and talks of the last inundation of the Nile, its products, and what the ensuing season is likely to be. His old wife brings him the usual bowl of lentils and bread moistened with water and salt, and when she can add a little butter it is a feast. Knowing nothing beyond this, he is happy. The young man's business is to accumulate the amazing sum of a hundred piasters (two pounds and ten shillings) to buy himself a wife, and to make a feast on the wedding day. If he have any children, they want no clothing: he leaves them to themselves till mother nature pleases to teach them to work, to gain money enough to buy a shirt or some other rag to cover themselves; for while they are children, they are generally naked or covered with rags. The parents are roguishly cunning, and the children are schooled by their example, so that it becomes a matter of course to cheat strangers. Would any one believe, that in such a state of life luxury and ambition exist? If any woman be destitute of jewels, she is poor, and looks with envy on one more fortunate than herself, who perhaps has the worth of half-a-crown round her neck; and she who has a few glass beads, or some sort of coarse coral, a couple of silver brooches, or rings at her arms and legs, is considered as truly rich and great. Some of them are as complete coquettes, in their way, as any to be seen in the capitals of Europe. I often noticed, that modesty was most apparent among the ugliest. These do not care to let a stranger see their faces; as they have nothing to gain by it, they deem it better to keep it covered: on the contrary, one who hopes to excite admiration in the stranger, takes care that some accident or other shall cause the veil, or cloth, or rag, covering her face, to fall or turn aside. The artifice having succeeded, she pretends to be quite anxious to cover herself again; but she is satisfied the stranger has had his peep, and she passes on, proud that he knows her to be pretty.

When a young man wants to marry, he goes to the father of the intended bride, and agrees with him what he is to pay for her. This being settled, so much money is to be spent on the wedding-day feast. To set up house-keeping nothing is requisite but two or three earthen pots, a stone to grind meal, and a mat, which is the bed. The spouse has a gown and jewels of her own; and, if the bridegroom present her with a pair of bracelets of silver, ivory, or glass, she is happy and fortunate indeed. The house is ready, without rent or taxes. No rain can pass through the roof; and there is no door, for there is no want of one, as there is nothing to lose. They make a kind of box of clay and straw, which, after two or three days' exposure to the sun, becomes quite hard. It is fixed on a stand, an aperture is left to put all their precious things into it, and a piece of a mummy case forms the door. If the house do not please them, they walk out and enter another, as there are several hundreds at their command; I might say several thousands, but they are not all fit to receive inhabitants.

While I was thus occupied in my researches at Thebes, we received news that the Defterdar was to come up the Nile again. By this time I had arranged my operations, and they were going on very well. At Carnak, one morning previous to my crossing the Nile to Gournou, I set several men to work on a spot of ground at the foot of a heap of earth, where part of a large colossus projected out. Mr. Beechey, who sometimes visited the ruins, did me the favour to superintend the work on that day; and, on my return from Gournou, I had the pleasure to find the discovery had been made of a colossal head, larger than that I had sent to England. It was of red granite, of beautiful workmanship, and uncommonly well preserved, except one ear, and part of the chin, which had been knocked off along with the beard. It is detached from the shoulder at the lower part of the neck, and has the usual corn measure, or mitre, on its head. Though of larger proportion than the young Memnon, it is not so bulky or heavy, as it has no part of the shoulder attached to it. I had it removed to Luxor, which employed eight days, though the distance is little more than a mile.

I had by this time accumulated at Luxor articles enough to fill another boat, as large as that of the preceding year. Besides this head, which is ten feet from the neck to the top of the mitre, I procured an arm belonging to the same colossus, which measures also ten feet, and with the head, will give a just idea of the size of the statue.

I brought also the famous altar, with the six divinities, in alto relievo, which are the most finished works of any I have seen in Egypt. It was thrown from its pedestal in a small temple in the north-east angle of the wall inclosing the great temple of Carnak. The pedestal is still there, and is of a kind of whitish marble. I had also four large statues with the lion-heads; and the cover of the sarcophagus, of which so much was said on my first visit. It cost much trouble, as may be supposed, to remove a heavy piece of granite from those abysses, through a place scarcely high enough to allow a man to sit on the ground, up an uneven and craggy ascent, by the assistance of people, strangers to every sort of order, and who had to contend with the dust that rose under the feet, and the excessive heat from the number of labourers. I had it conveyed over the water to Luxor, ready to embark, and it was well that I did so.

Fortune seemed to favour me so far this time; for, no sooner had I finished the operation, and made the above collection, than an order came from the Defterdar Bey, who had arrived at Gamola, three miles north of Thebes, to all the Cacheffs and Caimakans, who commanded on both sides of Thebes, not to permit the English party to accumulate any more antiquities, nor to allow the Arabs to work or sell any thing more to them on any account.

I must inform my reader, that the two agents for the opposite party had gone to Gamola on the arrival of the Bey, and requested him to send this order, under the pretext, that they could not find or buy a single article in consequence of the English, who laid their hands on every thing. He did not want much persuasion to this; and immediately sent for the chiefs of Gournou, Luxor, and Carnak, to whom he gave strict orders as above.

The Sheik of Gournou came to tell us of the order the Bey had issued. The poor fellow, who was rather attached to us, was sorry for his part, but said he must obey. It was too late to set off that evening to see the Bey, so I waited till early the next morning. On my arrival, I found the mighty potentate seated on his divan, surrounded by his Cacheffs, and a number of other attendants. He received me more coolly than on my former visit. He inquired whether I had not yet made up my collection. I answered, that, as long as I had his permission, I would still endeavour to find something more.

I presented the letter from the Bashaw; but, if I had brought him a present, it would have had a better effect. As he saw the address previous to taking the letter into his hands, he dexterously turned the discourse on other business; and half an hour passed before I could bring the subject on again, which he still contrived to divert. I was at a loss what to think of his behaviour, and began to inquire, if there were any reasons why our works were stopped at Carnak, and orders given at Gournou, that the English should not purchase any thing, and on what account they were to be distinguished from the opposite party. He looked at the letter a second time; and, with a smile, told the Cacheffs what the Bashaw had written, but the letter was expressed in a manner as if the old Bashaw were in his dotage and quite childish; so that the Bey might do as he pleased in the affair. He then put the letter aside, and began to talk of other matters. I saw that he wanted an excuse for his conduct towards us; for he said he had been informed that the Fellahs had complained of being so exceedingly ill-treated by us, that we drew our swords every moment to cut off their heads, and that we beat them continually. At this I rose from my seat, and said I was surprised that a man of his good understanding could believe such reports, and condemn us without proof; that, if he would inquire into the matter, he would find it to be all false; and that it was his duty to do me justice. He answered, that we had bought nearly every article of antiquity that could be obtained in Gournou, while the other party could purchase nothing, and therefore it was time to stop our proceedings. I replied, what we had bought had been voluntarily sold us by the Arabs, and begged him not to believe what he heard from our opponents, who played such tricks, that we could not be aware of them. He continued to talk of other things, till at last I asked him what he intended to do with respect to the order for Carnak: to which he made no reply, but inquired whether Gournou were far off. On being shown the place out of the window, six miles distant, he ordered horses, and in a few minutes we set off for that place. We arrived in two hours, and he went straight on to Memnonium; where he inquired about these great " mosquees," as he named them, and put several questions concerning the buildings and the colossi that are there. He then proceeded to the two colossi, and from them to Medinet, whither I followed him, as I was determined to have the order he gave to the Sheiks recalled. I sought an opportunity to speak to him tête-à-tête, and indeed I had many, but all to no purpose; for the moment I began to mention the business he put some other question, so that my words were of no effect. Still I was determined not to lose my patience, as I saw this was what he wanted, and resolved not to leave him a moment; for it is the character of the Turks, that they must be importuned into compliance with whatever is against their inclination. After a general survey of the ruins, he seated himself before the famous battle painted on the wall, and gave his opinion respecting it; observing, it was impossible that the colouring could have been done at the time the figures were made, as it was so fresh, and the stones were so much broken. I told him, it was owing to the climate of the country that these things were preserved; but he persisted in his opinion, that it was impossible it could be so. Then, quitting his station, he seated himself under the archway of the first entrance, and called the Sheik of Gournou, whom he knew to be our friend, and who had received the order the night before. The poor Sheik, trembling all over at this call, was asked how many men there were in Gournou who dug the ground in search of mummies. The Sheik answered six or seven. I saw the Bey did not know what to do to gratify his spleen; and, as he could not avoid retracting the order, the poor Sheik was to suffer, and our party to be mortified. A diabolical thought came into his head; and he asked the Sheik if he could find in Gournou a mummy that had not been opened. The Sheik answered, that one might be found, if he gave him time to search; but the people who find them always open them instantly. On this the Bey flew into a great rage, and insisted that one should be found immediately; and, if he did not find it, he would give him the bastinado. The poor Sheik was ordered to dig directly under his feet, and take out a mummy; but he answered, that the mummies were in Gournou, and none were ever found in the place where he stood: and it was well for him that one of the attendants and a Cacheff confirmed what he said. The Bey then sent him to Gournou, and told him to see that he found a mummy, in its case and unopened; and he allowed him an hour for doing it. The poor Sheik attempted to speak, but was turned out by three or four soldiers. A little after, the Bey began to ask some other questions respecting the temple, particularly if we had taken any drawings; adding, that he could draw himself, if he had paper and pencils. I told him I had no doubt he might make some good sketches from what was before him; on which he asked me for a pencil and some paper, which I gave him from my pocket-book, and he made a sketch of the capital of one of the columns that are before the gate. When finished, it was shown to all around with great parade. He praised it himself highly, and every one agreed, that it was very fine indeed. He then gave it me, with an air of self-conceit, saying, " There, see what I can do!" I took it, put it into my pocket, and have preserved it, as it may give an idea of the person by whom it was executed. We left Medinet Abou and came to Gournou, and under a doum-tree saw the Sheik and some of the Janizaries, with the mummy ready for his highness. Before he drew near to ascertain, the Bey began to cry out that he was sure it had been opened by one of the fellows who search for mummies; and it was in vain he was told otherwise, and that he had himself found it. I did not imagine things would be carried to such an extreme. That the case had been opened no one could suspect; but the Bey wanted a pretence to beat the poor Sheik for being our friend. Accordingly, he ordered him to be immediately stretched on the ground; and such a scene ensued, that I heard from the Turks themselves expressions both of displeasure and disgust. I perceived that all this was owing to the intrigues of our opponents, who had told the Bey, that the Sheik was our friend; and as they brought him some trifling presents to back their assertion, of course he listened to what they said. I did not fail to intercede for the poor unfortunate wretch, who all this time was under the stick, but it was useless; and I was persuaded, the more I entreated, the more beating he would receive. The interpreter, not reflecting on what he did, ventured to intercede in the name of Mr. Salt, the British consul; at which the Bey laughed. He then begged in the name of his father-in-law, the Bashaw; and the Bey made answer, that he was the sole commander in all business there; adding, to the man who was punishing the Sheik, " Go on, go on, and hard."

By this time the poor fellow was like the mummy that lay by his side, deprived of sense and feeling; and with a little more beating I have no doubt would have remained there for ever, and been buried where he lay. I leave to the imagination of any friend of humanity to what a height my blood rose, and what my feelings must have been at that moment. I can assure the reader I did not think I could have stood so long without openly declaring them; but I reflected, that my losing my patience would answer no good purpose, and only expose me to insults from the Bey, for all he wanted was an opportunity to justify him in acting as he liked towards us. Reason, however, subdued not my rage, but it restrained the mere action of my body, and I stood for a long time motionless. The Bey was smiling, and I was afraid might discover the state of my feelings, which would have increased his pleasure. At last he told the man to stop, and the miserable Sheik was carried to his cave as into his tomb; and was, indeed, more fit for the tomb than for a house. The Bey then caused the mummy to be opened, and finding nothing, he exclaimed, if they did not bring him one that was entire, he would throw the Sheik into the river. Observing that I avoided speaking to him, for I was too much disgusted even to continue near such a being, he called another Sheik, and ordered, that henceforth whatever antiquities were found in Gournou should be sold to our opponents. On my representing to him, that I now felt myself under the necessity of writing to Cairo that very night, he mounted his horse, called my interpreter, and bade him despatch a man to Gamola, and he would send an order by him, to have the men at work the next day. I told him, that I should send to Cairo notwithstanding this apparent change in his sentiments; as it was incumbent on me to let the Bashaw know how his commands were obeyed. I then went to see the Sheik, whom I found unable to speak; I did all I could for him; but there was such fear amongst the Arabs, that they dreaded having any thing to do with us.

In the morning I was about to send the interpreter to Gamola, when we saw the cangiar of the Bey passing before Luxor, and the Cacheff of Gheneh just landing the man from Gamola, who brought an order, that we might have twenty men to work for eight days.

When I perceived that the Bey did not stop, I spoke to the Cacheff, to use his influence, that the order might be enforced; but he seemed desirous of evading it, as he was aware it was merely a pretext on the part of the Bey. He told us plainly, that our opponents had calumniated us to the Bey; and protested, that if it had been in his power, he would have befriended us. Accordingly I gave him to understand, that it would be to his advantage to be friendly to our party, as well as to the other, and that the Bey's enmity would not last much longer, as it was simply owing to some business which had prevented the Consul from coming, who intended to bring with him presents both to the Bey and to himself, when all would be set to rights again. At length my persuasions prevailed; he ordered the men to work; and in a few days I collected all the pieces of antiquity together on the quay of Luxor; and caused a mud wall to be made round them.

At this time the Fellahs of Gournou were all in great consternation, in consequence of another order they had received from the Bey, not to sell any thing either to us, or to the French; and to get three unopened mummies ready for him on his return, which would be in a few days. This was a pretext they had no doubt for a general bastinadoing, as it was expressly said, that the mummies were to be procured by the men who worked for the English. The poor Sheik, who still could scarcely move, began to fear that he should receive another beating; and we had just finished some works at Carnak and Luxor, when, on the 3d of May, in the morning, our gentleman made his appearance at Luxor on his return from Derou. On landing, he came to see our collection of antiques, which certainly formed no inconsiderable group. He made a remark or two, that the head was a very fine piece, &c. and then, like a being bewildered, ran here and there among the ruins, to seek for antiquities, without knowing where he went. As he appeared to be a little more disposed to hearken to what we had to say to him, we complained of our situation; stating to him, that in consequence of what he had done to the Sheik on the other side of the water, the Fellahs would not work, and that, although we had brought strong letters of recommendation from the Bashaw himself, we were without protection, exposed to the insolence of our opponents, and every one else, who thought they might act as they pleased towards us with impunity. He inquired if any one had done us any injury; and we informed him, that our interpreter had been beaten by the Fellahs of Carnak, and that the Caimakan, after it had been proved, said he could do nothing to the assailants, as he was afraid of incurring the displeasure of the Bey. He next asked, if I were displeased because he had beaten the Sheik of Gournou. I said, it was not pleasant to see any one beaten without cause, for the Sheik had had no dealings with us, had not sold us a single article of antiquity; but he might treat his own people as he liked, for we had no business to interfere either with his orders, or with them, so long as they were not injurious to us. He then wished to know what we wanted. We said, that we wanted to be respected, and to be allowed to proceed in our researches. We did not wish to be treated with more favour than our opponents; but we were desirous of an order to the people of Gournou, that we might purchase antiquities as well as others; and a farther order for the Cacheffs of Assouan and Ibrim, as we intended to ascend the Nile; with which he complied, and set off.

On our return to Luxor I found two of the fathers of the Propaganda whom I had met with on my first journey from Redamont to Luxor, and who were come to see the antiquities. As they had treated me with civility on my journey, I felt it my duty to return the obligation. Accordingly I went with them to all the places I knew, and in particular to the tombs of the kings, the Memnonium, Medinet Abou, Carnak, Luxor, &c. To me it was in general a source of pleasure to show these things to strangers, to hear their remarks, and to observe their astonishment and satisfaction, after coming so far to view what cannot be seen any where else; at the same time no vexation can be greater to a lover of antiqutiy, when, which is often the case, he witnesses indifference even to what is most striking. These two holy fathers had been in the country for about ten years, and their place of residence was only at the distance of three days' journey from Thebes; yet they had never thought of taking the trouble of such a journey during all that time, and probably never would have done it, had it not been for my persuasion when I first saw them. Such neglect of antiquities would be not a little provoking to the travellers who come from London, Paris, Vienna, and Petersburgh, to see these magnificent ruins. On arriving at the first tombs through the entrance, which is truly magnificent, the holy fathers, who had as much taste for antiquity as the animals that brought them, complained of being very much fatigued, though they had been carried by two very good asses. My attention was on the alert for the first bursts of their astonishment; but how I was disappointed! They dismounted without taking any more notice of these magnificent places, than of a common building, or of the cloister of a convent. They sent immediately for the boy who had the bottle of aquavitæ, and drank a glass each. I thought they meant to take it easily, and to examine every thing minutely, but I was soon undeceived, for the only observation they made was on the name of a friend they happened to know, which was scrawled on one of these sacred walls in charcoal. They expressed their wonder how he had come thither, when he had been there, and so on; and although they were surrounded by Egyptian antiquities, hieroglyphics, figures, fine paintings, &c. all their occupation was to inspect the numerous other scrawls on the stones, to see whether any more of their friends had been there. On our arrival at the great hall, they could not help observing the immense sarcophagus that lies there, and immediately inquired whether the body were still in it. On advancing a little farther, and perceiving it had been emptied, they concluded there was nothing worth seeing, as there were none of the kings' bodies to be found. At my request they cast their eyes on the painting, otherwise they would have walked out without knowing whether it were a tomb or a cellar: in the mean time a friend of theirs, who not being quite so anxious as the fathers to see these antiquities, had seated himself near the entrance, as he cared not about coming any farther, was calling to the holy friars to make haste, and wondered why they would waste so much time in examining such things. It may easily be imagined, that I was not only disappointed in the taste of my companions, but also provoked at their indifference; and as I saw there was no remedy, I hurried them out of the tomb as fast as I could, to show them another more magnificent, in hopes to have better success. Accordingly I took them to see the most remarkable of the tombs, and that which is reckoned the best. This tomb is truly grand; it is distinguished from the others not only by its excellent state of preservation, but because it contains eight small cells cut in the rock, in the first passage on each side of it, in which are painted a multitude of articles used by the ancient Egyptians, such as implements of war, domestic and ceremonial dresses, decorations, musical instruments, and in short all that was conducive to utility, ornament, or convenience, in their time, so as to give perfect ideas of their mode of living, &c. The ground is white, and the colours are so lively and striking, that we cannot fail to wonder at them. Farther on you pass through a long gallery, painted with the most beautiful hieroglyphics, in as good perfection as the former; and in the great hall lies an enormous sarcophagus, of one single piece of granite, measuring ten feet long, five wide, six high, and six inches thick, covered with hieroglyphics inside and out. This is one of the largest sarcophagi remaining in perfection at this day. There are other apartments communicating with the great hall, all of which deserve the attention of the traveller, for in them he sees various groups of figures and hieroglyphics indicating the manner of living, agriculture, &c. of the ancient inhabitants of the country.

On our entering I informed the fathers that this was the finest tomb, and that it contained paintings of the implements and other things of the ancients, which are very interesting. They passed the first corridor with the same apathy as the first tomb, holding a candle into each of the cells as they passed, and peeping in with their heads, but without entering. The only thing that struck their attention were the hasps on a little box, somewhat like those which contain large flasks for liquors. On coming out I took the road over the mountain, which is a little troublesome, but in a few minutes it brings you to the summit, and then descends to Medinet Abou. Having no better success here, I returned with them to Luxor.

A strong wind that arose this day leads me to mention some particulars of the phenomena that often happen in Egypt. The first I shall notice is the *whirlwinds*, which occur all the year round, but especially at the time of the camseen wind, which begins in April, and lasts fifty days. Hence the name of camseen, which in Arabic signifies fifty. It generally blows from the south-west, and lasts four, five, or six days without varying, so very strong, that it raises the sands to a great height, forming a general cloud, so thick that it is impossible to keep the eyes open, if not under cover. It is troublesome even to the Arabs; it forces the sand into the houses through every cranny, and fills every thing with it. The caravans cannot proceed in the deserts; the boats cannot continue their voyages; and travellers are obliged to eat sand in spite of their teeth. The whole is like a chaos. Often a quantity of sand

and small stones gradually ascends to a great height and forms a column sixty or seventy feet in diameter, and so thick, that were it steady on one spot, it would appear a solid mass. This not only revolves within its own circumference, but runs in a circular direction over a great space of ground, sometimes maintaining itself in motion for half an hour, and where it falls it accumulates a small hill of sand. God help the poor traveller who is caught under it!

The next phenomenon is the *mirage*, often described by travellers, who assert having been deceived by it, as at a distance it appears to them like water. This is certainly the fact, and I must confess, that I have been deceived myself, even after I was aware of it. The perfect resemblance to water, and the strong desire for this element, made me conclude, in spite of all my caution not to be deceived, that it was really water I saw. It generally appears like a still lake, so unmoved by the wind, that every thing above is to be seen most distinctly reflected by it, which is the principal cause of the deception. If the wind agitate any of the plants that rise above the horizon of the mirage, the motion is seen perfectly, at a great distance. If the traveller stand elevated much above the mirage, the apparent water seems less united and less deep, for, as the eyes look down upon it, there is not thickness enough in the vapour on the surface of the ground to conceal the earth from the sight. But, if the traveller be on a level with the horizon of the mirage, he cannot see through it, so that it appears to him clear water. By putting my head first to the ground, and then mounting a camel, the height of which from the ground might have been about ten feet at the most, I found a great difference in the appearance of the mirage. On approaching it, it becomes thinner, and appears as if agitated by the wind, like a field of ripe corn. It gradually vanishes as the traveller approaches, and at last entirely disappears when he is on the spot.

The third phenomenon is the *locusts*. These animals I have seen in such clouds, that twice the number in the same space would form an opaque mass, which would wholly intercept the rays of the sun, and cause complete darkness. They alight on fields of corn, or other vegetables, and in a few minutes devour their whole produce. The natives make a great noise to frighten them away, but in vain; and, by way of retaliation, they catch and eat them when fried, considering them a dainty repast. They are something like the grasshopper in form, about two inches in length. They are generally of a yellow or gold colour, but there are some red and some green.

To return to our proceedings at Luxor. By this time our opponents were preparing to depart for Cairo, at which we rejoiced, as we thought we should remain quite alone. We had written to Cairo, informing Mr. Salt, the consul, of all that passed with the Bey; but indeed, unless a person is present at such occurrences, he can feel no interest in them, nor understand the disgust they excite. I had written also to Mr. Burckhardt on the subject, and from his answer I perceived, that the Bey's conduct excited in him no surprise.

When at last we thought we should remain alone, and pursue our researches in peace, I made preparations for recommencing our work at Gournou. After having in some measure persuaded the Sheiks and the people of the place, that they would not incur the displeasure of the Bey, as I had an order from himself, which permitted them to work for us, and sell us antiques, it was agreed, that all the Sheiks should meet in the morning, and hear the order read. Accordingly, we assembled in the grotto, that usually serves as a public place for strangers, and a sort of exchange for buying and selling antiques. A great number of the Fellahs also came to hear the firman, which the great man had written with his own hand; and in consequence of the example that had recently been made of their Sheik, they were very attentive. The firman had been kept by our interpreter well secured in his pocket, as the most mighty order that had ever been given; and he often boasted of having it in his possession. At last it was produced, and put into the hands of the only person among the Sheiks who could read it. He first perused it to himself, that he might read it fluently to the assembly; but had not gone far, when he turned towards me a look of astonishment: however, he proceeded to the end, and then asked me whether he should read it aloud to the assembly; and upon my answering in the affirmative, read nearly as follows:

" It is the will and pleasure of Hamed, the Defterdar Bey and present ruler of Upper Egypt, that no Sheiks, Fellahs, or other persons, shall from this moment sell any article of antiquity to the English party, or work for them; on the contrary, it is hereby ordered, that every thing that may be found shall be sold to the party of Mr. Drouetti; and whoever disobeys this order will incur the displeasure of the Bey."

I need not inform the reader how I felt on hearing this mandate, the very reverse of what the Bey had given me reason to expect. Were I sure of not returning to Egypt again, I would explain farther how this happened, and what means had been employed to influence the Bey: but as I do not know what fate may attend my future proceedings, I shall say nothing on the subject till the proper season, when this and many other things, of which the world has not the smallest idea, shall be explained, and the various intrigues be exposed to light, that were darkly carried on against me by more than one description of persons.

Under the circumstances I have stated, we deemed it of no use to attempt a renewal of our labours, and contented ourselves with writing to Cairo, and entering on our intended journey to the island of Philœ. I had suggested to Mr. Salt, that, if he could send us a supply of money, we would proceed to open the temple of Ybsambul; a project that was deemed nearly imaginary, a castle in the air, as no one supposed any temple really existed there. After having secured all our collection in one spot, and built a mud wall round it, and covered it with earth, we left an Arabian Sheik to guard it, and, on the 23d of May, set off for Assouan.

As we intended to examine every thing on our return, we went straight on, seeing scarcely any thing except Edfu and Ombos. At Assouan, we took a general view of Elephantine, and the other islands, and proceeded to Philœ, as our station to await the answer to the letters we had sent from Luxor to Mr. Salt. On our way, we took a good view of the cataract. One of the principal falls at this season is about thirty feet in length, forming an angle of fifteen degrees. Small boats and cangiars can be drawn up or down at all times of the year.

The prospect of the island of Philœ and its ruins is truly magnificent, particularly at some distance, though it is extremely barren. It is surrounded by rocks of granite in all directions, forming part of the main land, and part of other islands. The style of the hieroglyphics proves, that the edifice on it is of the last era of the Egyptian nation: in my opinion, of the time of the Ptolemies. There are reasons enough to remove all doubts of this, if any were entertained: in particular, the peripteral temple, supposed to have been at the landing-place at the east of the island, is evidently of the last school, and not half finished. The work of the columns is in a much lighter style than the old Egyptian, evincing, if that nation had continued its existence, it would have improved gradually; and in due course of time, by amalgamating the Grecian elegance with the vast and lofty magnificence of its own works of art, would have formed an architecture of which we have no idea, but, no doubt, most sublime. There are other proofs that this temple is a more modern structure, formed of the materials of an older edifice. In one of the columns, opposite the gate in the portico which leads to the sanctuary, there is in the centre a stone, sculptured with hieroglyphics inverted; and another stone of this kind is to be seen in the same column on the west side, near the ground. The whole ruins consist of two temples, nearly united together. The small temple, dedicated to Isis, is within the peristyle of the larger, which was dedicated, I believe, to the same goddess, to Serapis, and to the rest of the gods. The building faces the south, with a large portal or propylæon, flanked by two porticoes or colonnades, the capitals of the pillars of which are different from each other. At the entrance of the first portal lies the obelisk of granite, thrown down, as mentioned before, its pedestal having a Greek inscription on it, which is a complaint of the priests, addressed to Ptolemy and Cleopatra, against the soldiers and the government of the place, and proves that the Egyptian priests had no influence in the government at that period. The inscription was discovered by an English traveller, Mr. Banks, who, not having time to dig it out, left it, and Mr. Beechey took a copy of it. Part of another obelisk and pedestal are to be seen in the mud wall opposite. There are also two lions, of granite, which were at the sides of the stairs formed by four steps, that must have been in this situation, as I observed, that the bases of the colonnades are lower than the bases of the propylæa.

After passing the first portal is the entrance to the pronaos; on the west of which is the small temple of Isis, surrounded by square pillars, with the head of the goddess as the capital. The inner part consists of three apartments: the portico, the cella, and the adytum. The hieroglyphics on it are nearly perfect, but almost covered with mud, as it has served as a Greek chapel. On the east of the pronaos is a gallery with several cells, no doubt for the use of the priests; and the north is the second portal, covered with colossal figures like the first. On passing this we come to the portico, which is reckoned the most perfect and beautiful part of this building. The hieroglyphics are entire and highly painted, as are the capitals of the columns, which are ten in number. The figures on the wall of this portico are all divided into several groups, forming compartments of five feet high; those on the columns forming the ornaments of this hall are highly beautiful. There are other ruins on the west of the island, which formed the entrance into the temple by the water-side; and on the north-east are the remains of three arches made by the Romans. Here must have been the landing-place to the island. The middle arch has fallen down. On the key-stones the words " sanctum, sanctum, sanctum," are cut; affording clear evidence, that this island served as a holy seat not only to the Egyptians and Greeks, but also to the Romans. There are palpable marks of the whole temple having been fitted up for Christian worship. The walls are covered with mud, to hide the hieroglyphics on them; and some figures peculiar to the Christian religion were painted on this; but time uncovered the hieroglyphics again, as the mud lost its hold in several places. At the back of the temple, or on the north side of it, are the foundations of a building that served for a Greek church, and was formed of the stones from the ruins of the other buildings, as is obvious from the hieroglyphics on them. I cannot avoid observing, that this island is the most superb group of ruins I ever beheld together in so small a space of ground. The whole island, which is not more than a thousand feet in length, and less than five hundred in breadth, is richly covered with ruins; and being detached from the other barren islands which surround it at some distance, has a very superb appearance. On the island to the west of Philœ are the remains of a small temple, which has also served for Christian purposes. There are but few hieroglyphics to be seen, and the remains of two sitting figures in granite much mutilated. On the south of this temple is a burying-ground, so much like that of Gournou, that I was led to suppose it may have been the burying-place of the inhabitants of Philœ, though there are other tombs in the mountains on the east of the island.

During our stay in Philœ I made a model in wax of the portico of the great temple. The beautiful capitals and other ornaments of the columns induced me to do this. It was the month of May, and the heat was so great, that wax incorporated with resin could scarcely be kept in a mass of sufficient solidity to be reduced into form. The thermometer stood as high as 124° of Fahrenheit; but the mercury had risen to the top of the glass, so that we could not judge what degree it would have reached had the tube been longer.

An Arab now arrived from Cairo with a letter from Mr. Salt. He had performed his journey in eighteen days, all by land. The letter brought us a supply of money; and, to my great satisfaction, Mr. Salt complied with my wishes of opening the temple of Ybsambul, which I had so often suggested to him; and I must give him much credit for risking the expense of such an undertaking, the uncertainty of which would have deterred most people from doing it, particularly as he himself entertained strong doubts of the existence of a temple there; for he said, in the same letter, that he thought we should find no entrance, but that it would turn out to be like some of the mausoleums round the pyramids.

A few days previous to this the two captains, Irby and Mangles, had arrived in the island. They were going up the Nile, as far as the second cataract, and as there was some difficulty in obtaining two boats, we made a joint party, and contented ourselves with one only. We had to send our interpreter to Esne for provision, nothing being to be had at Assouan. The fourth of June arrived, and our jolly companions, Captains Irby and Mangles, proposed to commemorate the birth-day of his Majesty George III. Accordingly we took an old flag we had in the boat, and planted it on the highest propylæon in the island. At noon we brought out all our fire-arms, and went through the regular salute of twenty-one guns. Having only five, we had to load them again immediately after being fired; and from the heat of the fire and that of the sun, the barrels soon became so hot, that we could not touch them with our hands. At night we repeated our rejoicings, and frightened all the natives round, who could not imagine why we wasted so much powder without killing somebody. However, it convinced them, I believe, that we were well prepared in case it should be requisite to make our defence. The next day Mrs. Belzoni arrived from Cairo, a voyage which she performed accompanied only by the Irish lad, James. I could not contrive to take her higher up the Nile with us, as we had only one boat; and therefore left her in the island till our return. The account of her stay there will be given by herself.

On the 16th of June we left the island of Philœ. Our company consisted of Captains Irby and Mangles, Mr. Beechey, and myself; two servants, and Mahomed, a soldier sent to us by Mr. Salt. On our voyage up we had much trouble with our crew, who were five men and three boys, all of one family.

On our arrival at Ybsambul, opposite Deir, we found that the Cacheffs were not there, but at Tomas. We sent an express to inform them, that we were to open the temple, and meanwhile we proceeded to the second cataract. Previous to our arrival at Wady Halfa we followed the west side of the Nile, as far as we could go with the boat, and then landed, and walked three or four miles to the Rock Upsir; for as I had seen such beautiful views there on my first voyage, when the water was high, I wished to see how they appeared at this season and to show them to my companions. I found them not so interesting as the first time; the islands did not appear so numerous; nor did the water form those foaming eddies, which so finely interspersed the views with white and green. Notwithstanding this, the whole was very grand, and I was gratified in seeing it again.

Having returned to our boat, we passed the night on the same side of the river. The next morning we crossed the water, and entered into an inlet of the Nile, where we moored our boat near the village of Wady Halfa. The crew took it into their heads to extort money from us by force, for which purpose they landed, and said we might return by ourselves if we liked. They knew we could not effect this without some difficulty, as the boat was surrounded by sand banks. We had intended to proceed by land to see the cataract on the east side, as I had done the year before, but under the present circumstances we deemed it imprudent to leave the boat, lest all we had in it should be plundered; for the crew had collected several of the natives, who were apparently disposed to aid them in their undertakings. We would not give up to them, and they protested that they would not come on board, unless we first gave them some money. We then took the resolution to try what we could do ourselves, but it was more in appearance than reality, for we never could have got the boat out of that place. However, the appearance of our attempt to strike the sail, which must be done to fall down the river with the current, had the intended effect; for these fellows immediately sent one of the crew to a parley. We told him, if they took the boat out into the middle of the river, we would give them a bakshis, but not till then. This was agreed on, and at last, after losing the whole day in this business, we returned toward Ybsambul. During this day the natives came to examine every thing we had on board; but they perceived that we were too well armed for them, and quite ready for defence in case of necessity.

On our reaching Ybsambul we found that no answer had been sent from Mosmos. We waited three days, and on the fourth a messenger arrived on a camel. He said he came to see whether I were the same person, from the English consul, who was there the preceding year and wished to open the temple. On recognizing me, he returned immediately.

Three days after the two Cacheffs appeared, and took up their abode in small huts made of rushes, on a sandy bank of the river. We waited on their highnesses, and were well received, as we were much respected for what we might bring with us. We presented Daoud Cacheff with a fine gun, powder and ball, a shawl, some soap, and some tobacco. This distinction unfortunately caused a jealousy between the two brothers. Khalil considered himself his brother's equal since the absence of his father. I was not aware of this, as the first year he was merely an attendant on his brother Daoud. He was in a terrible rage, and informed us, that he was as great a man as his brother. We told him, that we would give him one of our guns; but our endeavours to appease him were all to no purpose. We passed the whole day without knowing our fate. Daoud kindly insisted that we should stop and dine with him; but I declined it on account of his brother's not being there, who had retired to his hut. He went over to bring him to dinner, but in vain. I then went myself to speak to him, and after much ado, I succeeded in making peace with this great potentate. He took one of our guns, and some powder and ball; and it was concluded, that we should begin to work in the morning with thirty men.

In the morning the men appeared rather late, but we recommenced the work at the temple with much enthusiasm and good hopes. I perceived the necessity of drawing the sand from the sides of the door, so that it might run off from the centre; toward which, on the contrary, if the sand were taken from the centre, that from the sides would continually run. The enterprising Count de Forbin, who never was within five hundred miles at least of the place, judged that the sand might have been easily thrown into the river. I wish he had been there once in his life, and then he might have seen, whether it were such a trifle as he represents it. It was a mass of sand accumulated by the winds for many centuries, and to have had it removed, and thrown into the river, would have been an undertaking, that all the people the adjacent country afforded could not have effected in twelve months. I was contented to make it my principal object to reach the door, as the most speedy means of entering the temple.

This day I divided the men into two parties, and stationed one on each side of the colossal figure that stood over the entrance. They worked pretty well, but were so few that the little sand they removed could scarcely be perceived. Seeing that it would be a very tedious business that way, in the evening I made a proposal to the Cacheff to pay three hundred piastres for opening the temple, which was agreed to by the Cacheff and the working men. They continued their labour for three days with much ardour, for they supposed they could finish it in that time, as their number was increased to eighty by order of the Cacheff; but on the evening of the third day there was as little prospect of seeing the door as on the first. They got tired at last, and under the pretext that the Ramadan was to commence on the next day, they left us with our temple, the sand, and the treasure, and contented themselves with keeping the three hundred piastres, which were partly paid to them previously to their beginning, and partly on the third day. During this time the Cacheffs dined with us. Our mess was in company with them and all their followers. Our banquet consisted of a small piece of mutton, the water in which it was stewed, some bread, and a little butter or fat. No sooner was the dinner set on the ground, than a scramble took place. Every one crowded round the earthen bowl: the Cacheff was the first to dip in his hand, and immediately the rest followed his example. We four, the two Captains Irby and Mangles, Mr. Beechy, and myself, contrived to keep as close together as possible, that we might all eat out of the same side of the dish, and by this means have some chance of a cleaner meal. The Cacheff seeing that we stood no chance against his people, who at last plunged their hands into the dish from all quarters, politely picked out the most fleshy parts from the bowl, which he distinguished from the bones by a squeeze with his hand, placed them on the sleeve of his gown, and then continued to eat till the bowl was nearly emptied. When all had done eating, he presented each of us with a piece of the fleshy parts he had reserved as a compliment, which we gladly devoured, as there was no other chance of our having a morsel to eat till the next morning.

This day being the first of Ramadan, the Fellahs could not work, but they could feast according to their holy law; for, though they know very little of religion, they keep their own festivals as correctly and as regularly as an European. The next day again nobody came near us, and the two Cacheffs Daoud and Khalil went away.

From that time we took the resolution to work at the sand ourselves. We were only six, but the crew offered their services, and thus our party amounted to fourteen in all. Finding that one of us did as much work as in the proportion of one to five of the

Barabra, we were well satisfied, and resolved to continue. We rose every morning at the dawn of day, and left off two hours and half after sunrise. Our perseverance and independence drew some of the peasants, to offer their services, which we accepted; but as many of them were from the opposite side of the Nile, they could not agree with those of Ybsambul, and there was a perpetual warfare between them; besides, from jealousy, they increased to such a number, that we could not employ them all, which gave rise to fresh disputes, so that we resolved to dismiss them all, and continue the work by ourselves. They still persisted in offering their services to what number we pleased; but we saw it would not prevent their having quarrels and fighting every day, and we therefore refused their offer.

One day we observed a boat on the opposite side of the Nile steering toward us, and as it approached we perceived, that it was filled with well armed men. After the Cacheffs of Ybsambul left us, there was a man of that village, who, in spite of their orders, still remained with us, and occasionally helped us in the work. His name was Musmar, which in English signifies nail. Mr. Nail was a great man; told us wonderful stories of his astonishing courage; gave us to understand, that, when the Bedoweens from the Desert attacked the village of Ybsambul he was the first to resist them; and vaunted, that he was not afraid of any man in the world. We were of course charmed at having such a gallant knight with us. On the approach of the boat he seemed agitated, and was very anxious to know who the people were. While they were at a distance, he said no one dared come where he was. When they were nearer, and he might see distinctly who they were, he could not conceive what they wanted on this side of the water. As soon as they had nearly reached the shore, still pretending he was unable to guess who they could be, he would ascend the mountain to observe them better. With this he took to his heels, and ran off as fast as he could scamper. The men landed, and ascended the hill of sand where we were. We seized our arms, for this is the only way to be respected by these gentry. They approached.—The first was an elderly man, who had strong traits of resolution in his countenance. He held out his hand, which I immediately shook according to the custom of the country. They were the Cacheffs of Ibrim, father and son. They seated themselves on the sand, and the others stood.

They appeared in greater style than our sovereigns of Ybsambul, and had more swords and fire-arms. We were pleased to find them friends, particularly as we knew they were at war with Hassan Cacheff and his sons Daoud and Khalil. I perceived their disappointment, for our attire did not bespeak riches. Besides, seeing us at work like labourers, they concluded we were but poor people. They told us they were afraid of Mahomed Ali, Bashaw of Egypt, and presented us with two small and meager sheep. I was not pleased at this, for I knew how the politeness of such gifts always ends: we returned this civility by paying the servant who brought the sheep twice as much as they were worth, and told the Cacheffs, that we were sorry we had nothing to give them, as we had exhausted every thing, but that we should recollect them on our return to the country. They said, they did not come thither to have any thing from us, and hoped on our return to Cairo we would speak to the Bashaw in their favour. We answered, we could not say any thing against them, as they never did us any harm, or ever saw us before. Soon after they rose, and we gave them the usual salute, but they said they were going to see the small temple below. Our interpreter followed them, as the boat was near that place; and when they reached the temple they took him aside, and told him, that they were the masters of the country; if the other Cacheffs killed one man, they killed two; they could stop, or let us proceed on our works, as well as the other Cacheffs, for they were more powerful; adding, they knew we gave guns, powder, shot, soap, and tobacco to the others—therefore they expected we should do more for them, as they were superior, and we might expect the consequences of refusing to comply with their demands. At such proceedings I thought we were in as bad a situation as ever respecting our works at the temple, for we had nothing left to give these people. Accordingly we sent them an answer, that we had nothing for them at present, but that they might depend on our words, that we would bring them something on our future visit to Nubia. They replied, we had no business to come into the country without written orders directed to them, as they were the true masters of it. We informed them we had a firman from the Bashaw, and sent our interpreter with it to show it them. They opened it, and looking at it said they could not understand one word in it; besides it was not for them, and therefore was good for nothing, and even if we had one, it would be to no purpose, unless it was accompanied with presents of more value than we had given to the other Cacheffs. While all this was passing, the great potentates and their honourable followers walked towards their boat, and hinted, that we must think on the business while they were going to the village of Ybsambul.

We left off work at our usual time, and resumed our labour in the afternoon, expecting that we should have some interruption in our proceedings; but on the next day to our astonishment we heard, that the great men were off at night. We continued our operations regularly, and in the course of a few days more we perceived a rough projection from the wall, which indicated apparently that the work was unfinished, and no door to be found there. At this the hopes of some of our party began to fail; nevertheless we persevered in our exertions, and three days after we discovered a broken cornice, the next day the torus, and of course the frize under, which made us almost sure of finding the door the next day; accordingly I erected a palisade, to keep the sand up, and to my utmost satisfaction saw the upper part of the door as the evening approached. We dug away enough sand to be able to enter that night, but supposing there might be some foul air in the cavity, we deferred this till the next morning.

Early in the morning of the 1st of August we went to the temple in high spirits, at the idea of entering a newly discovered place. We endeavoured as much as we could to enlarge the entrance; but our crew did not accompany us as usual. On the contrary, it appeared that they intended to hinder us as much as lay in their power; for when they saw, that we really had found the door, they wished to deter us from availing ourselves of it: the attempt however failed. They then pretended, that they could not stop any longer with the boat in that place, and if we did not go on board immediately, they would set off with her and leave us. On our refusal they knelt on the ground, and threw sand over their faces, saying, that they would not stop an instant. The fact was, they had promised to the Cacheffs to play some trick to interrupt our proceedings, in case we should come to the door. But even all this would not do. We soon made the passage wider, and entered the finest and most extensive excavation in Nubia, one that can stand a competition with any in Egypt, except the tomb newly discovered in Beban el Malook.

From what we could perceive at the first view, it was evidently a very large place; but our astonishment increased, when we found it to be one of the most magnificent of temples, enriched with beautiful intaglios, painting, colossal figures, &c. We entered at first into a large pronaos, fifty-seven feet long and fifty-two wide, supported by two rows of square pillars, in a line from the front door to the door of the sekos (See Plate 43). Each pillar has a figure, not unlike those at Medinet Aboo, finely executed, and very little injured by time. The tops of their turbans reach the ceiling, which is about thirty feet high: the pillars are five feet and a half square. Both these and the walls are covered with beautiful hieroglyphics, the style of which is somewhat superior, or at least bolder, than that of any others in Egypt, not only in the workmanship, but also in the subjects. They exhibit battles, storming of castles, triumphs over the Ethiopians, sacrifices, &c. In some places is to be seen the same hero as at Medinet Aboo, but in a different posture. Some of the columns are much injured by the close and heated atmosphere, the temperature of which was so hot, that the thermometer must have risen to above a hundred and thirty degrees. The second hall is about twenty-two feet high, thirty-seven wide, and twenty-five and a half long. It contains four pillars about four feet square; and the walls of this also are covered with fine hieroglyphics in pretty good preservation. Beyond this is a shorter chamber, thirty-seven feet wide, in which is the entrance into the sanctuary. At each end of this chamber is a door, leading into smaller chambers in the same direction with the sanctuary, each eight feet by seven. The sanctuary is twenty-three feet and a half long, and twelve feet wide. It contains a pedestal in the centre, and at the end four colossal sitting figures, the heads of which are in good preservation, not having been injured by violence. On the right side of this great hall, entering into the temple, are two doors, at a short distance from each other, which lead into two long separate rooms, the first thirty-eight feet ten inches in length, and eleven feet five inches wide; the other forty-eight feet seven inches, by thirteen feet three. At the end of the first are several unfinished hieroglyphics, of which some, though merely sketched, give fine ideas of their manner of drawing. At the lateral corners of the entrance into the second chamber from the great hall is a door, each of which leads into a small chamber twenty-two feet six inches long, and ten feet wide. Each of these rooms has two doors leading into two other chambers, forty-three feet in length, and ten feet eleven inches wide. There are two benches in them, apparently to sit on. The most remarkable subjects in this temple are, 1st, a group of captive Ethiopians, in the western corner of the great hall: 2d, the hero killing a man with his spear, another lying slain under his feet, on the same western wall: 3d, the storming of a castle, in the western corner from the front door. The outside of this temple is magnificent. It is a hundred and seventeen feet wide, and eighty-six feet high; the height from the top of the cornice to the top of the door being sixty-six feet six inches, and the height of the door twenty feet. There are four enormous sitting colossi, the largest in Egypt or Nubia, except the great Sphinx at the pyramids, to which they approach in the proportion of near two-thirds. From the shoulder to the elbow they measure fifteen feet six inches; the ears three feet six inches; the face seven feet; the beard five feet six inches; across the shoulders twenty-five feet four inches; their height is about fifty-one feet, not including the caps, which are about fourteen feet. There are only two of these colossi in sight, one is still buried under the sand, and the other, which is near the door, is half fallen down, and buried also. On the top of the door is a colossal figure of Osiris twenty feet high, with two colossal hieroglyphic figures, one on each side, looking towards it. On the top of the temple is a cornice with hieroglyphics, a torus and frize under it. The cornice is six feet wide, the frize is four feet. Above the cornice is a row of sitting monkeys eight feet high, and six across the shoulders. They are twenty-one in number. This temple was nearly two-thirds buried under the sand, of which we removed thirty-one feet before we came to the upper part of the door. It must have had a very fine landing-place, which is now totally buried under the sand. It is the last and largest temple excavated in the solid rock in Nubia or Egypt, except the new tomb. It took twenty-two days to open it, beside six days last year. We sometimes had eighty men at work, and sometimes only our own personal exertions, the party consisting of Mr. Beechey, Captains Irby and Mangles, myself, two servants, and the crew, eleven in all, and three boys. It is situated under a rock about a hundred feet above the Nile, facing the south-east by east, and about one day and a half's journey from the second cataract in Nubia, or Wady Halfa.

The heat was so great in the interior of the temple, that it scarcely permitted us to take any drawings, as the perspiration from our hands soon rendered the paper quite wet. Accordingly, we left this operation to succeeding travellers, who may set about it with more convenience than we could, as the place will become cooler. Our stock of provision was so reduced, that the only food we had for the last six days was dhourra, boiled in water without salt, of which we had none left. The Cacheffs had given orders to the people not to sell us any kind of food whatever, hoping that we might be driven away by hunger. But there was an Abady, who lived in the village, and as he was of a different tribe, he was not so much afraid of disobeying the Cacheffs. He sometimes came at night, and brought us milk; but he was at last detected, and prevented from bringing any more.

Great credit is due to Mr. Beechey, and the two Captains, for their laborious exertions in assisting me in the above operation. I must not omit to mention, that, in the temple, we found two lions with hawks' heads, the body as large as life; a small sitting figure, and some copper work belonging to the doors.

We left Ybsambul on the 4th of August, and did not stop at

Ibrim, as we had seen it before. On passing Tomas, a village on the western banks of the Nile, we were told, that Daoud Cacheff was there. We found he was ready to receive us, and came himself on board, entreating us to go on shore, which we did, though not without hesitation, as he had not behaved well to us. He wished us to stop all night, and attempted to be very civil. We stated to him, that we had not been well treated by the people of Ybsambul; to which he replied, hastily, that he knew nothing of the matter. But how could he be ignorant of it, when one of his men, who came to see us at work, and inquired whether we atest one, was at that moment standing by his side, as well as others, whom we recognized to have been of the party, and who came there to raise a disturbance? Perceiving we knew what he had done to us, he attempted to make us amends, presenting us with a sheep and a basket of bread; and on quitting the place, I received a present from his wife for Mrs. Belzoni, of a milch goat, two small baskets, and a carpet made of palm leaves. I gave in return two pair of Turkish women's boots, and two small looking-glasses.

On our arrival at Deir, we met Khalil Cacheff, who crossed the Nile in a boat, and hailed us, saying he would return to us very soon. By this time it was quite dark, and we went to see the temple immediately with candles, as we hoped to set off early in the morning, and avoid meeting such a sincere friend. On our return, we attempted to procure some provision, but it was too late at night. About ten o'clock, Khalil returned, but we were asleep. Early in the morning we were told, that he had sent us some aqua vitæ and a lamb. We were sorry for this, as it retarded us. Some time after he came on board, accompanied by his party. We returned him thanks for what we had received, but told him, that we could not give him any thing in return, as we were destitute ourselves, and that at Ybsambul we had lived on boiled dhourra for several days, as the peasants had refused to sell us any thing to eat. We knew very well that all this was done by his order, but he pretended, like his brother, not to know any thing of it. We did not think proper to say much, as we wished to be gone, and leave these affectionate friends on peaceful terms. At last, after examining our boat, and the strange figure we had found in the temple, he with great sorrow quitted us, and we set off immediately. It is to be remarked, that all his civility was out of opposition to his brother Daoud, in hopes that we should bring him something on our coming up again; for it was plain to be seen, that it was all forced politeness.

The temple at Deir is in a very ruinous state. I saw but one or two figures entire: the fragments of the rest indicate, that it was dedicated to Osiris. There was a portico, with sixteen pillars, twelve of which are fallen down. It has a chamber, and a sanctuary, with two small chambers, one on each side.

In about two hours we arrived at Almeida, the ruins of a small temple on the north of the Nile. The river there takes its course from north-west to south-east. It is a small temple, and has served for a Greek chapel. The hieroglyphics are pretty well finished, but nearly covered with plaster by the Greeks. There are other apartments, of unburnt bricks, which served as a monastery to the works. Toward evening we arrived at Seboua. The ruins of the temple here I have described before.

Four days more brought us down to El Kalabshe. We landed, to visit the temple; but the Fellahs, seeing our boat at some distance, gathered together at the entrance to the temple, determined that we should not go in, unless we first paid them for leave. We were accordingly stopped, and money was demanded.

We refused to comply, but promised, that, if they would let us in, we would give them a bakshis afterward. As this did not satisfy them, and they behaved in a very insolent manner, we were returning to our boat, when our soldier said, that he would remember them. On this their daggers were instantly drawn, and his gun was seized. A scuffle took place, which gave us something to do to rescue the gun from the one who had taken it from the soldier, and was endeavouring to decamp with it. On our approaching the boat, some of them, perceiving our indifference whether we saw the temple or not, came to offer to let us enter, while others were of a different opinion; but, as we had seen the temple before, we did not think it worth our while to venture to force our way into it. While all this was going on at the temple, others attacked the boat; but, as our people were armed with pistols and guns, they retreated. One man entered the boat with a drawn sword, but was turned out.

Having left El Kalabshe, we passed by Taffa, but could not land there, as the narrow passage of the Nile did not permit us to approach the shore. There are two small temples at Taffa, which I had seen before. One consists of a single chamber, and two columns, one of which is not finished. The other has some few hieroglyphics in a good style: it serves as a stable for sheep and cows. We arrived the same evening at Hindau, where we saw an extensive wall, apparently made to enclose a vast building, or probably more than one. There are the remains of a portal on the north side, and a great quantity of ruins within. Coming down, we saw several quarries and ruins; in one of which is a door cut in the rock in the Egyptian style, and a number of Greek inscriptions, written, I suppose, by some Greek workmen, and which I think serve to prove that the Greeks procured stones from this place. We observed the remains of a temple, of which six columns are standing, beautifully adorned with the lotus and other emblematic devices of the Egyptians. Farther down there is another column standing alone.

In a few hours we arrived at Debod. This temple has a portico and a sekos, which leads into the cella, at each side of which is a small chamber. In the portico also are two chambers, and a staircase leading to the top. There are a few hieroglyphics; and in the sekos are two monolite temples of granite. In the porch of the building are three portals, one before another. The whole building is surrounded by a wall. On the water-side is a quay, with an entrance toward the temple.

We arrived on the same day at the island of Philœ: Mrs. Belzoni went to Assouan by land, and we resolved to pass the cataract in the boat in which we came. The barbarians made objections and took some advantage, but they will do any thing for money. Accordingly we set off from the island, and began to take our course gradually among the rapids and rocks of the Shellal. As we advanced, we expected every moment to arrive at the spot where the great fall is; but having passed over several rapids, one, in particular, a little stronger, but not more extraordinary than are seen in other rivers, we were agreeably surprised to find, that in less than an hour we were out of all danger. I have seen the great cataract on the west side when the water is low; and its fall was then, in length, about six hundred yards, forming an angle of thirty or thirty-five degrees, divided by the interspersed rocks into various branches. On our arrival at Assouan we prepared immediately for our departure; but meanwhile we visited the island of Elephantine once more, and in the evening went to see the column with the Latin inscription, which I discovered in the mountain of Assouan. We had some difficulty to find it again, as the guide conducted us by another road, different from that which I took the first time. Next day we left that place; and as the current of the Nile (it being now near its height) was very strong, we reached Thebes in three days.

On our passage we visited Edfu once more; and, farther down, we landed at Elethias, and took a cursory view of its ruins and grottoes. There is a high thick wall of unburnt bricks, which surrounds the whole town. It is a square enclosure of six hundred and seventy yards. We saw the ruins of three or four temples. One appears to have been very extensive; but only six columns of the portico remain (See Plate 41), and part of the sekos of another. This town was formerly much more extensive than it is at present, as appears by its ruins. I observed part of the walls of ancient buildings at some distance from the great wall which surrounds the town. Among the ruins of the largest temple I noticed part of a large sphinx of white marble, with the head of a woman and body of a lion. There were also fragments of several statues, and other ornaments of the temple, part of which are covered by its own ruins. On the east of this temple was a small lake, or rather tank, which perhaps was a public bath, as we may likewise presume of those near the temple in Carnak; but at present there is no water in it. On the west of the town is another building, of a later date, which extends from the great wall to the river. There are many ruins of houses with arches, but the walls are inferior in point of size. The remains of a pier or landing-place are visible when the water is low; and it appeared to me, that there had been a causeway from the stair at the water-side to the temple.

The country round the town is pretty flat, and extends above a mile from the Nile to the mountains. It must have been all cultivated and fertile, as the few spots that are now in cultivation are very productive. Some excellent grapes are produced in this place; and it is to be remarked, that, from the representations in the grottoes or sepulchres in the mountains, the dressing of vines appears to have formed one of the chief occupations of the people. The sepulchres in these rocks are numerous, and several are much on the same plan as those of Gournou. Some contain various agricultural representations; from which may be formed a more exact idea of their manner of living than I have seen any where else. The figures and colours are in pretty good preservation. I cannot say, however, that they can boast of any great perfection in their sculpture; and it is evident that the dead deposited in those places must have been husbandmen. I am of opinion that this town had a communication with the Red Sea; my reason for which I shall state hereafter.

One mile to the north of the town is a small peripteral temple, situated in the midst of an extensive plain, now covered with sand, but which evidently was once cultivated. The rock in which the tombs are cut forms a solitary hill, that commands the surrounding country. From its summit I could see an extensive plain of sand, extending north and south of the town nine or ten miles along the banks of the Nile, and a mile and a half in breadth from the river to the foot of the mountain. When the whole of this land was cultivated, it must have produced provisions sufficient for a town of considerable importance. Three miles to the north of Elethias the rocks reach close to the Nile. There is a village named El Khab, which includes the whole of the above-mentioned land, with the ruins of Elethias.

On our arrival at Luxor we took up our former abode in the sekos of the temple, and found ourselves at home again; for Thebes was now become quite familiar to me. We received letters from Mr. Salt, by which we learned that he was purposing to ascend the Nile.

The two Captains, Irby and Mangles, set off for Cairo, Mr. Beechey began to take drawings of the different places, and I recommenced my researches.

At Gournou I found two more agents of Mr. Drouetti busied in digging the ground in all directions, and who had been tolerably successful in their researches for mummies. These agents were of a different cast from the two Copts who had been there before. Both of them were Piedmontese. One a renegado who had deserted from the French army when in Egypt, and entered the service of the Bashaw; the other had left Piedmont after the fall of the late government. I did not like to begin my work in any place near these people, and therefore gave up the idea of prosecuting my researches in Gournou. It was fortunate for me I did so, and from that time I made the valley of Beban el Malook the scene of my researches, which is completely separated from Gournou by the chain of mountains, that divides Thebes from the valley. I went to this plain quite alone, and spent the whole day in making observations, the result of which confirmed me in the opinion, that there was a sufficient prospect to encourage me to commence my work.

It will be recollected, that, when we left Thebes for the island of Philœ, we could not obtain any labourers, in consequence of the orders of the Bey. Supposing the same would be the case at this time, I sought the Cacheff of Erments, to obtain an order to allow the men to work. I found that the old Cacheff had fallen into disgrace with the Defterdar Bey, and was displaced and gone; consequently I applied to the Cacheff of Ghous, who had become ruler over the great city of a hundred gates. He was well aware, that to allow us to engage men to work would not please the Defterdar Bey; but reflecting on the firman we had from the Bashaw himself, and the barefaced distinction made in favour of the opposite party, who had many men at work, he could not well refuse me a small number of

Arabs. I accordingly obtained from him a firman to the Sheiks of Gournou, to furnish me with twenty men, with whom I began my operations in the valley above mentioned. Here I entered upon an undertaking, that appeared rather presumptuous, when I recollected, that many travellers had been there, and many had inquired as to the possibility of discovering more tombs, than were already known, even from the time of Herodotus and Strabo. The former speaks of the tombs as being above forty in number. In the time of Strabo not half so many were known to exist. Having found by experience, that the reports of ancient authors are not always to be depended upon, particularly when they speak from hearsay, I put them out of the account, and proceeded entirely on my own judgment to search for the tombs of the monarchs of Thebes.

I began in the valley to the westward of Beban el Malook, near the same place where I discovered the tomb the year before. Here I must acquaint my reader, that the only guide I had in these discoveries was the knowledge I had acquired in the continued researches for tombs I made in Gournou. In these I found, that the Egyptians had a particular manner of forming the entrance into their tombs, which gave me many leading ideas to the discovery of them. Besides, the supposition that many of these tombs must have been buried under the stones and rubbish, which continually fall from the upper parts of the mountains, the great quantity of materials cut out of the tomb accumulated in considerable heaps in different parts of the valley, might give various suggestions of the spots where the entrance to the tombs was to be found, as is justly observed by Mr. Hamilton. But all these striking reasons it appears were insufficient to lead any traveller to persevere in the attempt, or to make the attempt at all; and indeed it would have been the same with me, had I not been acquainted with a more secure mode of proceeding.

After a long survey of the western valley, I could observe only one spot, that presented the appearance of a tomb. Accordingly, I set the men to work near a hundred yards from the tomb which I discovered the year before; and when they had got a little below the surface, they came to some large stones, which had evidently been put there by those who closed the tomb. Having removed these stones, I perceived the rock had been cut on both sides, and found a passage leading downwards. I could proceed no farther that day, as the men were much fatigued, and we had more than four miles to return to Thebes. The next day we resumed our labour, and in a few hours came to a well-built wall of stones of various sizes. The following day I caused a large pole to be brought, and by means of another small piece of palm-tree laid across the entrance, I made a machine not unlike a battering-ram. The walls resisted the blows of the Arabs for some time, as they were not Romans, nor had the pole the ram's head of bronze at its end; but they contrived to make a breach at last, and in the same way the opening was enlarged. We immediately entered, and found ourselves on a staircase, eight feet wide and ten feet high, at the bottom of which were four mummies, in their cases, lying flat on the ground, with their heads toward the outside. Farther on were four more, lying in the same direction. The cases were all painted, and one had a large covering thrown over it, exactly like the pall upon the coffins of the present day.

I went through the operation of examining all these mummies one by one. They were much alike in their foldings, except that which had the painted linen over it. Among the others I found one, that had new linen, apparently, put over the old rags; which proves, that the Egyptians took great care of their dead, even for many years after their decease. That which was distinguished from all the rest, I observed was dressed in finer linen, and more neatly wrapped up. It had garlands of flowers and leaves, and on the side over the heart I found a plate of the metal which I have already described, soft like lead, covered with another metal, not unlike silver leaf. It had the eyes of a cow, which so often represents Isis, engraved on it; and in the centre of the breast was another plate, with the winged globe. Both plates were nearly six inches long. On unfolding the linen, we still found it very fine, which was not the case with the other mummies; for, after three or four foldings, it was generally of a coarser kind. At last we came to the body, of which nothing was to be seen but the bones, which had assumed a yellow tint. The case was in part painted; but the linen cloth covering it fell to pieces as soon as it was touched, I believe owing to the paint that was on it, which consisted of various devices and flowers. The cases were sunk four inches into the cement I have already mentioned. Some of the painting on the inside of the cases appeared quite fresh, as if recently done; and there was generally a coat of varnish, whether laid on over the colours, or incorporated with them, I do not know. For what purpose this tomb might have been intended, I cannot pretend to say: perhaps it was originally designed for one of the royal blood. It appeared by the entrance to have been commenced on a scale similar to those of the kings; though it seems to have been finished for a more humble family.

The result of my researches gave me all the satisfaction I could desire, of finding mummies in cases, in their original position: but this was not the principal object I had in view; for, as I was near the place where the kings of Egypt were buried, I thought I might have a chance of discovering some of their relics.

The sacred valley, named Beban el Malook, begins at Gournou, runs toward the south-west, and gradually turns due south. It contains the celebrated tombs of the kings of Egypt, and divides itself into two principal branches, one of which runs two miles farther to the westward, making five miles from the Nile to the extremity. The other, which contains most of the tombs, is separated from Gournou only by a high chain of rocks, which can be crossed from Thebes in less than an hour. The same rocks surround the sacred ground, which can be visited only by a single natural entrance, that is formed like a gateway, or by the craggy paths across the mountains. The tombs are all cut out of the solid rock, which is of hard calcareous stone, as white as it is possible for a stone to be. The tombs in general consist of a long square passage, which leads to a staircase, sometimes with a gallery at each side of it, and other chambers. Advancing farther we come to wider apartments, and other passages and stairs, and at last into a large hall, where the great sarcophagus lay, containing the remains of the kings. Some of these tombs are quite open, and others incumbered with rubbish at the entrance. Nine or ten may be reckoned of a superior class, and five or six of a lower order. Strabo may have counted eighteen, as may be done to this day, including some of an inferior class, which cannot be esteemed as tombs of the kings of Egypt from any other circumstance, than that of having been placed in this valley. For my part, I could distinguish only ten or eleven that could be honoured with the name of the tombs of kings, nor do I suppose when Strabo was told by the Egyptian priests, that there were forty-seven tombs of the kings of Egypt, they meant to say, these tombs were all in the place, now named Beban el Malook. In confirmation of this I would observe, that similar tombs, and perhaps even more magnificent ones, are to be found out of this valley, which are open to this very day. I do not mean the tombs in the western valley, that forms the other branch of Beban el Malook; but those in Gournou, which the traveller seldom fails to see. There are various tombs at that place, which are worthy to be compared with those in Beban el Malook; and I will venture to say, that there is one in Gournou far superior to any in that valley, being more extensive, and, from the fragments that remain, apparently of greater magnificence. But the frequent exposure to all sorts of injury from the various visitors, owing to their being nearer to the Nile, has reduced the tombs at Gournou to a state of the greatest dilapidation. From the besmoked and defaced walls it is easy to see, that they have been frequently visited and perhaps inhabited by herds of Arabs at a time, who retired to these recesses to escape the violent hands of their pursuers. If we add the tombs in the valley above mentioned to those of the superior class at Gournou, I will allow, that the Egyptian priests were right in their reports; otherwise I must say, it is my firm opinion, that in the valley of Beban el Malook, there are no more than are now known, in consequence of my late discoveries; for, previously to my quitting that place, I exerted all my humble abilities in endeavouring to find another tomb, but could not succeed; and what is a still greater proof, independent of my own researches, after I quitted the place, Mr. Salt, the British consul, resided there four months, and laboured in like manner in vain to find another. I think therefore I may venture to assert, that the whole forty or forty-seven tombs of the kings of Egypt could not be in this valley, but some of them were in various other places.

One argument more I shall offer on this subject. If the tombs of Gournou above mentioned, which are superior to those in the valley of Beban el Malook in size, in variety of apartments, consequently in number, and I will add, from what now remains to be seen, in the excellence of the sculpture, were not for the kings of Egypt, what other person in that country could aspire to such high honours, and presume to have tombs superior to those of the kings? If I may be permitted to give my humble opinion on the subject, I should conclude, that the tombs in the valley of Beban el Malook were erected subsequently to those in Gournou; for I could scarcely find a spot in the latter place adapted to the excavation of one of the great tombs, and it may be supposed, that when all the best spots for large tombs in Gournou had been occupied, the Egyptians went over the rocks to seek another situation in which to deposit their kings. Certain it is, that the tombs in the valley of Beban el Malook are in far better condition than those in Gournou.

Under these circumstances, reflecting on the possibility of discovering some of the tombs of the kings, I set the few men I had to work.

On the 6th of October I began my excavation, and on the 9th discovered the first tomb: the apparent arrangement of the entrance indicated it to be a very large one; but it proved to be only the passage of one that was never finished. The Egyptians, however, would not lose their labour, for they used it as a tomb notwithstanding. Though it is not extensive, they plastered it very finely with white, and painted some very fine figures on it in the most finished style. This passage is ten feet five inches wide, and seventy-five feet from the entrance to the part where we come to evidently the unfinished work. From the appearance, as it stands, it is plain, that they intended to proceed, and that some particular event caused the work to be stopped. The painted figures on the wall are so perfect, that they are the best adapted of any I ever saw to give a correct and clear idea of the Egyptian taste. This tomb lies south-east from the centre of the valley, and quite at the foot of the large rocks, that overlook Gournou. As I had several parties of Fellahs at work in different directions, I hoped to make farther discoveries; and indeed this first success gave me much encouragement, as it assured me, that I was correct in my idea of discovering the tombs. On the same day we perceived some marks of another tomb in an excavation, that had been begun three days before, precisely in the same direction as the first tomb, and not a hundred yards from it. In fact, I had the pleasure to see this second tomb on the same day, the 9th. This is more extensive, but entirely new, and without a single painting in it: it had been searched by the ancients, as we perceived at the end of the first passage a brick wall, which stopped the entrance, and had been forced through. After passing this brick wall you descend a staircase, and proceed through another corridor, at the end of which is the entrance to a pretty large chamber, with a single pillar in the centre, and not plastered in any part. At one corner of this chamber we found two mummies on the ground quite naked, without cloth or case. They were females, and their hair pretty long, and well preserved, though it was easily separated from the head by pulling it a little. At one side of this room is a small door, leading into a small chamber, in which we found the fragments of several earthen vessels, and also pieces of vases of alabaster, but so decayed that we could not join one to another. On the top of the staircase we found an earthen jar quite perfect, with a few hieroglyphics on it, and large enough to contain two buckets of water. This tomb is a hundred feet from the entrance to the end of the chamber, twenty feet deep, and twenty-three wide. The smaller chamber is ten feet square: it faces the east by south, and runs straight towards west by north.

Several days before we received news, that there were some English people coming up from Cairo, and we were anxiously expecting them, as we knew by letter from that place, that they were three English gentlemen. Early on the morning of the 10th they reached Beban el Malook, accompanied by Mr. Beechey, who was at Luxor, where they arrived the evening before. They were the first to enter into the two discovered tombs, and observed, that the painted figure in the first was the best to be seen in Egypt, in point of preservation. We were just quitting the valley, to go over the mountain to Medinet Abou, when I was informed, that there was some other discovery in one of the excavations near the centre of the valley. Thither we went immediately, and I perceived that there was another tomb; but as it could not be opened that day, the travellers proposed to return the next morning. That night I went over to Luxor also, where we arrived very late in the evening.

Early on the next morning, the 11th, we began the tour of Thebes. We went to see the tombs in Gournou, and the little temple in the valley behind the Memnonium. About twelve o'clock word was brought me, that the tomb discovered the day before was opened, so that we might enter it. On this we took the road over the rocks immediately, and arrived in less than three quarters of an hour. I found the tomb just opened, and entered to see how far it was practicable to examine it. Having proceeded through a passage thirty-two feet long, and eight feet wide, I descended a staircase of twenty-eight feet, and reached a tolerably large and well-painted room. I then made a signal from below to the travellers, that they might descend, and they entered into the tomb, which is seventeen feet long, and twenty-one wide. The ceiling was in good preservation, but not in the best style. We found a sarcophagus of granite, with two mummies in it, and in a corner a statue standing erect, six feet six inches high, and beautifully cut out of sycamore-wood: it is nearly perfect except the nose. We found also a number of little images of wood, well carved, representing symbolical figures. Some had a lion's head, others a fox's, others a monkey's. One had a land-tortoise instead of a head. We found a calf with the head of a hippopotamus. At each side of this chamber is a smaller one, eight feet wide, and seven feet long; and at the end of it is another chamber, ten feet long by seven wide. In the chamber on our right hand we found another statue like the first, but not perfect. No doubt they had been placed one on each side of the sarcophagus, holding a lamp or some offering in their hands, one hand being stretched out in the proper posture for this, and the other hanging down. The sarcophagus was covered with hieroglyphics merely painted, or outlined: it faces south-east by east.

Next day, the 12th, the party could not proceed on their voyage, the wind being foul. On the 13th I caused some spots of ground to be dug at Gournou, and we succeeded in opening a mummy-pit on that day, so that the party had the satisfaction of seeing a pit just opened, and receiving clear ideas of the manner in which the mummies are found, though all tombs are not alike. This was a small one, and consisted of two rooms painted all over, but not in the best style. It appeared to me that the tomb belonged to some warrior, as there were a great number of men enrolling themselves for soldiers, and another writing their names in a book. There are also several other figures, &c. In the lower apartment we saw the mummies lying here and there one on another, without any regularity. To all appearance therefore this pit had been opened by the Greeks, or some other people to plunder it.

The same day we visited another mummy-pit, which I had opened six months before. The construction is somewhat similar to what I have just described, a portico and a subterraneous cavity where the mummies are. Here the paintings are beautiful, not only for their preservation, but for the novelty of their figures. There are two harps, one with nine strings, and the other with fourteen, and several other strange representations: in particular, six dancing girls, with fifes, tambourins, pipes of reeds, guitars, &c.

On the 16th I recommenced my excavations in the valley of Beban el Malook, and pointed out the fortunate spot, which has paid me for all the trouble I took in my researches. I may call this a fortunate day, one of the best perhaps of my life; I do not mean to say, that fortune has made me rich, for I do not consider all rich men fortunate; but she has given me that satisfaction, that extreme pleasure, which wealth cannot purchase; the pleasure of discovering what has been long sought in vain, and of presenting the world with a new and perfect monument of Egyptian antiquity, which can be recorded as superior to any other in point of grandeur, style, and preservation, appearing as if just finished on the day we entered it; and what I found in it will show its great superiority to all others. Not fifteen yards from the last tomb I described, I caused the earth to be opened at the foot of a steep hill, and under a torrent, which, when it rains, pours a great quantity of water over the very spot I have caused to be dug. No one could imagine, that the ancient Egyptians would make the entrance into such an immense and superb excavation just under a torrent of water; but I had strong reasons to suppose, that there was a tomb in that place, from indications I had observed in my pursuit. The Fellahs who were accustomed to dig were all of opinion, that there was nothing in that spot, as the situation of this tomb differed from that of any other. I continued the work however, and the next day, the 17th, in the evening, we perceived the part of the rock that was cut, and formed the entrance. On the 18th, early in the morning, the task was resumed, and about noon the workmen reached the entrance, which was eighteen feet below the surface of the ground. The appearance indicated, that the tomb was of the first rate: but still I did not expect to find such a one as it really proved to be. The Fellahs advanced till they saw that it was probably a large tomb, when they protested they could go no farther, the tomb was so much choked up with large stones, which they could not get out of the passage. I descended, examined the place, pointed out to them where they might dig, and in an hour there was room enough for me to enter through a passage that the earth had left under the ceiling of the first corridor, which is thirty-six feet two inches long, and eight feet eight inches wide, and, when cleared of the ruins, six feet nine inches high. I perceived immediately by the painting on the ceiling, and by the hieroglyphics in basso relievo, which were to be seen where the earth did not reach, that this was the entrance into a large and magnificent tomb. At the end of this corridor I came to a staircase twenty-three feet long, and of the same breadth as the corridor. The door at the bottom is twelve feet high. From the foot of the staircase I entered another corridor, thirty-seven feet three inches long, and of the same width and height as the other, each side sculptured with hieroglyphics in basso relievo, and painted. The ceiling also is finely painted, and in pretty good preservation (See Plate 2). The more I saw, the more I was eager to see, such being the nature of man: but I was checked in my anxiety at this time, for at the end of this passage I reached a large pit, which intercepted my progress. This pit is thirty feet deep, and fourteen feet by twelve feet three inches wide. The upper part of the pit is adorned with figures, from the wall of the passage up to the ceiling. The passages from the entrance all the way to this pit have an inclination downward of an angle of eighteen degrees. On the opposite side of the pit facing the entrance I perceived a small aperture two feet wide and two feet six inches high, and at the bottom of the wall a quantity of rubbish. A rope fastened to a piece of wood, that was laid across the passage against the projections which form a kind of door, appears to have been used by the ancients for descending into the pit; and from the small aperture on the opposite side hung another, which reached the bottom, no doubt for the purpose of ascending. We could clearly perceive, that the water which entered the passages from the torrents of rain ran into this pit, and the wood and rope fastened to it crumbled to dust on touching them. At the bottom of the pit were several pieces of wood, placed against the side of it, so as to assist the person who was to ascend by the rope into the aperture. I saw the impossibility of proceeding at the moment. Mr. Beechey, who that day came from Luxor, entered the tomb, but was also disappointed.

The next day, the 19th, by means of a long beam we succeeded in sending a man up into the aperture, and having contrived to make a bridge of two beams, we crossed the pit. The little aperture we found to be an opening forced through a wall, that had entirely closed the entrance, which was as large as the corridor. The Egyptians had closely shut it up, plastered the wall over, and painted it like the rest of the sides of the pit, so that but for the aperture, it would have been impossible to suppose, that there was any farther proceeding; and any one would conclude, that the tomb ended with the pit. The rope in the inside of the wall did not fall to dust, but remained pretty strong, the water not having reached it at all; and the wood to which it was attached was in good preservation. It was owing to this method of keeping the damp out of the inner parts of the tomb, that they are so well preserved. I observed some cavities at the bottom of the well, but found nothing in them, nor any communication from the bottom to any other place; therefore we could not doubt their being made to receive the waters from the rain, which happens occasionally in this mountain. The valley is so much raised by the rubbish, which the water carries down from the upper parts, that the entrance into these tombs is become much lower than the torrents; in consequence, the water finds its way into the tombs, some of which are entirely choked up with earth.

When we had passed through the little aperture, we found ourselves in a beautiful hall, twenty-seven feet six inches by twenty-five feet ten inches, in which were four pillars three feet square. I shall not give any description of the painting, till I have described the whole of the chambers. At the end of this room, which I call the entrance-hall, and opposite the aperture, is a large door, from which three steps lead down into a chamber with two pillars. This is twenty-eight feet two inches by twenty-five feet six inches. The pillars are three feet ten inches square. I gave it the name of the drawing-room; for it is covered with figures, which, though only outlined, are so fine and perfect, that you would think they had been drawn only the day before. Returning into the entrance-hall, we saw on the left of the aperture a large staircase, which descended into a corridor. It is thirteen feet four inches long, seven and a half wide, and has eighteen steps. At the bottom we entered a beautiful corridor, thirty-six feet six inches by six feet eleven inches. We perceived, that the paintings became more perfect as we advanced farther into the interior. They retained their gloss, or a kind of varnish over the colours, which had a beautiful effect. The figures are painted on a white ground. At the end of this corridor we descended ten steps, which I call the small stairs, into another, seventeen feet two inches by ten feet five inches. From this we entered a small chamber, twenty feet four inches by thirteen feet eight inches, to which I gave the name of the Room of Beauties; for it is adorned with the most beautiful figures in basso relievo, like all the rest, and painted. When standing in the centre of this chamber, the traveller is surrounded by an assembly of Egyptian gods and goddesses. Proceeding farther, we entered a large hall, twenty-seven feet nine inches by twenty-six feet ten inches. In this hall are two rows of square pillars, three on each side of the entrance, forming a line with the corridors. At each side of this hall is a small chamber: that on the right is ten feet five inches by eight feet eight inches; that on the left, ten feet five inches by eight feet nine inches and a half. This hall I termed the Hall of Pillars; the little room on the right, Isis' Room, as in it a large cow is painted, of which I shall give a description hereafter; that on the left, the Room of Mysteries, from the mysterious figures it exhibits. At the end of this hall we entered a large saloon, with an arched roof or ceiling, which is separated from the Hall of Pillars only by a step; so that the two may be reckoned one. The saloon is thirty-one feet ten inches by twenty-seven feet. On the right of the saloon is a small chamber without any thing in it, roughly cut, as if unfinished, and without painting: on the left we entered a chamber with two square pillars, twenty-five feet eight inches by twenty-two feet ten inches. This I called the Sideboard Room, as it has a projection of three feet in form of a sideboard all round, which was perhaps intended to contain the articles necessary for the funeral ceremony. The pillars are three feet four inches square, and the whole beautifully painted as the rest. At the same end of the room, and facing the Hall of Pillars, we entered by a large door into another chamber with four pillars, one of which is fallen down. This chamber is forty-three feet four inches by seventeen feet six inches; the pillars three feet seven inches square. It is covered with white plaster, where the rock did not cut smoothly, but there is no painting on it. I named it the Bull's, or Apis' Room, as we found the carcass of a bull in it, embalmed with asphaltum; and also, scattered in various places, an immense quantity of small wooden figures of mummies six or eight inches long, and covered with asphaltum to preserve them. There were some other figures of fine earth baked, coloured blue, and strongly varnished. On each side of the two little rooms were some wooden statues standing erect, four feet high, with a circular hollow inside, as if to contain a roll of papyrus, which I have no doubt they did. We found likewise fragments of other statues of wood and of composition.

But the description of what we found in the centre of the saloon, and which I have reserved till this place, merits the most particular attention, not having its equal in the world, and being such as we had no idea could exist. It is a sarcophagus of the finest oriental alabaster, nine feet five inches long, and three feet seven inches wide. Its thickness is only two inches; and it is transparent, when a light is placed in the inside of it. It is minutely sculptured within and without with several hundred figures, which do not exceed two inches in height, and represent, as I suppose, the whole of the funeral procession and ceremonies relating to the deceased, united with several emblems, &c. I cannot give an adequate idea of this beautiful and invaluable piece of antiquity, and can only say, that nothing has been brought into Europe from Egypt that can be compared with it. The cover was not there: it had been taken out, and broken into several pieces, which we found in digging before the first entrance. The sarcophagus was over a staircase in the centre of the saloon, which communicated with a subterraneous passage, leading downwards, three hundred feet in length. At the end of this passage we found a great quantity of bats' dung, which choked it up, so that we could go no farther without digging. It was nearly filled up too by the falling in of the upper part. One hundred feet from the entrance is a staircase in good preservation; but the rock below changes its substance, from a beautiful solid calcareous stone, becoming a kind of black rotten slate, which crumbles into dust only by touching. This subterraneous passage proceeds in a south-west direction through the mountain. I measured the distance from the entrance, and also the rocks above, and found, that the passage reaches nearly half way through the mountain to the upper part of the valley. I have reason to suppose, that this passage was used to come into the tomb by another entrance; but this could not be after the death of the person who was buried there, for at the bottom of the stairs just under the sarcophagus a wall was built, which entirely closed the communication between the tomb and the subterraneous passage. Some large blocks of stone were placed under the sarcophagus horizontally, level with the pavement of the saloon, that no one might perceive any stairs or subterranean passage was there. The door-way of the sideboard room had been walled up, and forced open, as we found the stones with which it was shut, and the mortar in the jambs. The staircase of the entrance-hall had been walled up also at the bottom, and the space filled with rubbish, and the floor covered with large blocks of stone, so as to deceive any one who should force the fallen wall near the pit, and make him suppose, that the tomb ended with the entrance-hall and the drawing-room. I am inclined to believe, that whoever forced all these passages must have had some spies with them, who were well acquainted with the tomb throughout. The tomb faces the north-east, and the direction of the whole runs straight south-west.

To give an accurate description of the various representations within this tomb, would be a work above my capacity. I shall therefore only endeavour to describe the most remarkable that are to be seen in the various parts of it. From these the reader may form some idea of this magnificent excavation.

The entrance into the tomb is at the foot of a high hill, with a pretty steep ascent. The first thing the traveller comes to is a staircase cut out of the rock, which descends to the tomb. The entrance is by a door of the same height as the first passage. I beg my kind reader to observe, that all the figures and hieroglyphics of every description are sculptured in basso relievo, and painted over, except in the outlined chamber, which was only prepared for the sculptor. This room gives the best ideas that have yet been discovered of the original process of Egyptian sculpture. The wall was previously made as smooth as possible, and where there were flaws in the rocks, the vacuum was filled up with cement, which, when hard, was cut along with the rest of the rock. Where a figure or any thing else was required to be formed, after the wall was prepared, the sculptor appears to have made his first sketches of what was intended to be cut out. When the sketches were finished in red lines by the first artist, another more skilful corrected the errors, if any, and his lines were made in black, to be distinguished from those which were imperfect. When the figures were thus prepared, the sculptor proceeded to cut out the stone all round the figure, which remained in basso relievo, some to the height of half an inch, and some much less, according to the size of the figure. For instance, if a figure were as large as life, its elevation was generally half an inch; if the figure were not more than six inches in length, its projection would not exceed the thickness of a dollar, or perhaps less. The angles of the figures were all smoothly rounded, which makes them appear less prominent than they really are. The parts of the stone that were to be taken off all round the figure did not extend much farther, as the wall is thickly covered with figures and hieroglyphics, and I believe there is not a space on those walls more than a foot square without some figure or hieroglyphic. The garments, and various parts of the limbs, were marked by a narrow line, not deeper than the thickness of a half-crown, but so exact, that it produced the intended effect.

When the figures were completed and made smooth by the sculptor, they received a coat of whitewash all over. This white is so beautiful and clear, that our best and whitest paper appeared yellowish when compared with it. The painter came next, and finished the figure. It would seem as if they were unacquainted with any colour to imitate the naked parts, since red is adopted as a standing colour for all that meant flesh. There are some exceptions indeed; for in certain instances, when they intended to represent a fair lady, by way of distinguishing her complexion from that of the men, they put on a yellow colour to represent her flesh; yet it cannot be supposed, that they did not know how to reduce their red paints to a flesh colour, for on some occasions, where the red flesh is supposed to be seen through a thin veil, the tints are nearly of the natural colour, if we suppose the Egyptians to have been of the same hue as their successors, the present Copts, some of whom are nearly as fair as the Europeans. Their garments were generally white, and their ornaments formed the most difficult part, when the artists had to employ red in the distribution of the four colours, in which they were very successful. When the figures were finished, they appear to have laid on a coat of varnish; though it may be questioned, whether the varnish were thus applied, or incorporated with the colour. The fact is, that nowhere else except in this tomb is the varnish to be observed, as no place in Egypt can boast of such preservation, nor can the true customs of the Egyptians be seen any where else with greater accuracy.

With the assistance of Mr. Ricci, I have made drawings of all the figures, hieroglyphics, emblems, ornaments, &c. that are to be seen in this tomb; and by great perseverance I have taken impressions of every thing in wax: to accomplish the work has been a laborious task, that occupied me more than twelve months.

The drawings show the respective places of the figures, so that if a building were erected exactly on the same plan, and of the same size, the figures might be placed in their situations precisely as in the original, and thus produce in Europe a tomb, in every point equal to that in Thebes, which I hope to execute if possible.

Immediately within the entrance into the first passage, on the left hand, are two figures as large as life, one of which appears to be the hero entering into the tomb. He is received by a deity with a hawk's head, on which are the globe and serpent. Both figures are surrounded by hieroglyphics; and farther on, near the ground, is a crocodile very neatly sculptured. The walls on both sides of this passage are covered with hieroglyphics, which are separated by lines from the top to the bottom, at the distance of five or six inches from one another. Within these lines the hieroglyphics form their sentences; and it is plainly to be seen, that the Egyptians read from the top to the bottom, and then recommenced at the top. The ceiling of this first passage is painted with the figure of the eagles, as in Plate 2. Beyond the first passage is a staircase with a niche on each side, adorned with curious figures with human bodies and the heads of various animals, &c. At each side of the door at the bottom of the stairs is a female figure kneeling, with her hands over a globe. Above each of these figures is the fox, which, according to the Egyptian custom, is always placed to watch the doors of sepulchres. On the front space over the door are the names of the hero and his son, or his father, at each side of which is a figure with its wings spread over the names to protect them, as is seen in Plate 3. The names are distinguished by being inclosed in two oval niches. In that of Nichao is a sitting figure, known to be a male by the beard. He has on his head the usual corn measure, and the two feathers; on his knees the sickle and the flail: over his head is a crescent with the horns upward: above which is what is presumed to be a faggot of various pieces of wood bound together, and by its side a group twisted in a serpentine form. Behind the figure are what are thought by some to be two knives, by others feathers; but as the feathers are of a different form, I for my part think they are sacrificing knives, which may have served as emblems of the priesthood, for we know, that the heroes or kings of Egypt were initiated into the sacred rites of the gods. Below the figure is a frame of two lines drawn parallel to each other, and connected by similar lines, beneath which is the emblem of moving water.

In the next oval on the right is a sitting female figure with a band round the head fastening a feather, and on her knees she holds the keys of the Nile. Above the head is the globe, and beneath the figure the form of a tower, as it is supposed to represent strength. The faces of both figures are painted blue, which is the colour of the face of the great God of the creation. On each of the oval frames there is the globe and feathers, and beneath it two hieroglyphics not unlike two overflowing basins, as they are under the two protecting figures at each side of the oval frame.

Next is the second passage, on the right hand side of which are some funeral processions, apparently in the action of taking the sarcophagus down into the tomb, the usual boat, which carries the male and female figures upon it, and in the centre the boat with the head of the ram drawn by a party of men.

The wall on the left is likewise covered with similar processions. Among them is the scarabæus, or beetle, elevated in the air, and supported by two hawks, which hold the cords drawn by various figures; and many other emblems and symbolical devices. The figures on the wall of the well are nearly as large as life. They appear to represent several deities; some receiving offerings from people of various classes.

Next is the first hall, which has four pillars in the centre, at each side of which are two figures, generally a male and a female deity. On the right hand side wall there are three tiers of figures one above the other, which is the general system almost all over the tomb. In the upper tier are a number of men pulling a chain attached to a standing mummy, which is apparently unmoved by their efforts. The two beneath consist of funeral processions, and a row of mummies lying on frames horizontally on the ground. On the left is a military and mysterious procession, consisting of a great number of figures all looking toward a man who is much superior to them in size, and faces them. At the end of this procession are three different sorts of people, from other nations, evidently Jews, Ethiopians, and Persians. Behind them are some Egyptians without their ornaments, as if they were captives rescued and returning to their country, followed by a hawk-headed figure, I suppose their protecting deity. For this procession see Plates 6, 7, and 8.

I have the satisfaction of announcing to the reader, that, according to Dr. Young's late discovery of a great number of hieroglyphics, he found the names of Nichao and Psammethis his son, inserted in the drawings I have taken of this tomb. It is the first time that hieroglyphics have been explained with such accuracy, which proves the doctor's system beyond doubt to be the right key for reading this unknown language; and it is to be hoped, that he will succeed in completing his arduous and difficult undertaking, as it would give to the world the history of one of the most primitive nations, of which we are now totally ignorant. Nichao conquered Jerusalem and Babylon, and his son Psammethis made war against the Ethiopians. What can be more clear than the above procession?

The people of the three nations are distinctly seen. The Persians, the Jews, and the Ethiopians, come in, followed by some captive Egyptians, as if returning into their country, guarded by a protecting deity. The reason why the Egyptians must be presumed to have been captives is, their being divested of all the ornaments, which served to decorate and distinguish them from one another. The Jews are clearly distinguished by their physiognomy and complexion, the Ethiopians by their colour and ornaments, and the Persians by their well-known dress, as they are so often seen in the battles with the Egyptians.

In the front of this hall, facing the entrance, is one of the finest compositions that ever was made by the Egyptians, for nothing like it can be seen in any part of Egypt. It consists of four figures as large as life. The god Osiris sitting on his throne, receiving the homages of a hero, who is introduced by a hawk-headed deity. Behind the throne is a female figure as if in attendance on the great god. The whole group is surrounded by hieroglyphics, and inclosed in a frame richly adorned with symbolical figures. The winged globe is above, with the wings spread over all, and a line of serpents crowns the whole. The figures and paintings are in such perfect preservation, that they give the most correct idea of their ornaments and decorations (See Plate 19).

Straight forward is the entrance into another chamber with two pillars. The wall of this place is outlined, ready for the sculptor to cut out his figure. It is here that we may plainly see the manner, in which the artist prepared the figure on the wall ready to be cut; and it is almost impossible to give a description of the various figures, which adorn the walls and pillars of this chamber. There are great varieties of symbolical figures of men, women, and animals, apparently intending to represent the different exploits of the hero, to whom the tomb was dedicated.

On going out of this chamber into the first hall is a staircase, which leads into a lower passage, the entrance into which is decorated with two figures, on each side, a male and a female, as large as life. The female appears to represent Isis, having, as usual, the horns and globe on her head. She seems ready to receive the hero, who is about to enter the regions of immortality. The garments of this figure are so well preserved, that nothing which has yet been brought before the public can give a more correct idea of Egyptian customs. The figure of the hero is covered with a veil, or transparent linen, folded over his shoulder, and covering his whole body, which gives him a very graceful appearance. Isis is apparently covered with a net, every mesh of which contains some hieroglyphic, serving to embellish the dress of the goddess. The necklace, bracelets, belt, and other ornaments, are so well arranged, that they produce the most pleasing effect, particularly by the artificial lights, all being intended to conduce to this purpose (See Plate 18).

On the wall to the left, on entering this passage, is a sitting figure of the size of life: it is the hero himself on his throne, having the sceptre in his right hand, while the left is stretched over an altar, on which are twenty divisions, as will be seen in Plate 1. A plate in the form of an Egyptian temple is hung to his neck by a string. It contains an obelisk and two deities—one on each side of it. Plates of this kind have been much sought after, as they appear to have been the decoration or breastplate of the kings of Egypt. Few have been found, and I have seen only two,—one is in the British Museum, and the other I was fortunate enough to procure from an Arab, who discovered it in one of the tombs of the kings in Beban el Malook. It is of black basalt, much larger and superior in workmanship to the other, which proves, that they were of various sizes, and more or less finished. It has the scarabæus or beetle in alto relievo on a small boat with a deity on each side of it, and on the reverse is the usual inscription. Over the head of this figure is the eagle with extended wings, as if protecting the king. On the upper part of each side of the walls of the passage is the history of the hero divided into several small compartments nearly two feet square, containing groups of figures eighteen inches high. The hero is to be seen every where standing on a heap of corn, receiving offerings from his soldiers or companions in war. Farther on is a small staircase leading into a short passage, where the procession still continues, and the sacrifice of a bull is to be seen, as in Plate 13. The walls of both passages are covered with hieroglyphics in separate divisions. From this short passage there is an entrance into another much wider than the rest. The charming sight of this place made us give it the name of the Room of Beauties. All the figures are in such perfection, that the smallest part of their ornaments can be clearly distinguished. The sides of the doors are most beautifully adorned with female deities, surrounded with hieroglyphics, and the lotus is to be seen both in bud and in full bloom, with the serpent on a half globe over it (See Plate 17). Farther on is the great hall with six pillars, containing on each side of it, two figures as large as life. The walls are adorned with the procession and other symbolical figures. Over the door, in the inside, is the figure of a female with extended wings, as in Plate 8. At each side of this hall is a small cell; that on the left containing various mummies and other figures, and that on the right a cow of half the natural size, with a number of figures under it, which form a very curious group. The walls also are covered with hieroglyphics. In the large hall close to the door are a number of men carrying a long slender pole, at each end of which is a cow's head, and on the pole, two bulls, as in Plate 15. Still farther, the hall opens into the large vaulted chamber. It would be impossible to give any description of the numerous figures, which adorn the wall of this place. It was here that the body of the king was deposited, as I found in its centre the beautiful sarcophagus. This is sculptured within and without with small figures in intaglio, coloured with a dark blue, and, when a light is put into the inside of it, it is quite transparent. The ceiling of the vault itself is painted blue, with a procession of figures and other groups relating to the zodiac.

The next is a chamber with a projection like a side-board. It has two square pillars with two figures on every side, as represented in Plates 4 and 5. The walls in every part of this chamber are also beautifully adorned with symbolical figures, a specimen of which is given in Plate 2, which represents a compartment over the door within the chamber. It is useless to proceed any further in the description of this heavenly place, as I can assure the reader he can form but a very faint idea of it from the trifling account my pen is able to give; should I be so fortunate, however, as to succeed in erecting an exact model of this tomb in Europe, the beholder will acknowledge the impossibility of doing it justice in a description.

The Arabs made such reports of this discovery, that it came to the ears of Hamed Aga of Kenneh; and it was reported to him, that great treasure was found in it. On hearing this, he immediately set off with some of his soldiers to Thebes, generally a journey of two days, but such was his speed in travelling, that he arrived in the valley of Beban-el-Malook in thirty-six hours by land. Before his arrival some Arabs brought us intelligence, that they saw from the tops of the mountains a great many Turks on horseback entering the valley, and coming toward us. I could not conceive who they could be, as no Turks ever came near this place. Half an hour after they gave us the signal of their approach, by firing several guns. I thought an armed force was sent to storm the tombs and rocks, as no other object could bring the Turks there; at last, when this mighty power reached us, I found it to be the well-known Hamed Aga of Kenneh, for some time commander of the eastern side of Thebes, and his followers. Accordingly I was at a loss to conceive what he wanted there, as we were on the west, and under another ruler; but I suppose, in case of a treasure being discovered, the first that hears of it seizes it as a matter of privilege. He smiled, and saluted me very cordially; indeed more so than usual, I presume for the sake of the treasure I had discovered, of which he was in great expectation. I caused as many lights to be brought as we could muster, and we descended into the tomb. What was on the walls of this extraordinary place did not attract his attention in the least; all the striking figures and lively paintings were lost on him; his views were directed to the treasure alone; and his numerous followers were like hounds, searching in every hole and corner. Nothing, however, being found to satisfy their master or themselves, after a long and minute survey, the Aga at last ordered the soldiers to retire, and said to me, " Pray where have you put the treasure?" " What treasure?" " The treasure you found in this place." I could not help smiling at his question, which confirmed him in his supposition. I told him that we had found no treasure there. At this he laughed, and still continued to entreat, that I would show it him. " I have been told," he added, " by a person to whom I can give credit, that you have found in this place a large golden cock, filled with diamonds and pearls. I must see it. Where is it?" I could scarcely keep myself from laughing, while I assured him that nothing of the kind had been found there. Seeming quite disappointed, he seated himself before the sarcophagus, and I was afraid he would take it into his head, that this was the treasure, and break it to pieces, to see whether it contained any gold; for their notions of treasure are confined to gold and jewels. At last he gave up the idea of the riches to be expected, and rose to go out of the tomb. I asked him what he thought of the beautiful figures painted all around. He just gave a glance at them, quite unconcerned, and said, " This would be a good place for a harem, as the women would have something to look at." At length, though only half persuaded there was no treasure, he set off with an appearance of much vexation.

Every thing must come round, and be told in proper time. I shall now introduce what happened previous to this period. It will be recollected, on my first voyage up to Nubia I took possession, in the island of Philœ, of sixteen large blocks of stone, which formed a fine group of various figures in basso relievo; that I had them cut thinner, to be taken more easily down the Nile; and that the boat, which was engaged to carry them, returned without them, as the Reis did not intend to take the great head on board his boat. On our arrival at the island, on my second voyage, we found these stones had been mutilated, and written upon in the French language, " *operation manquée.*" The hand writing could not be ascertained, as it was done with charcoal; but we knew there had been only three French agents there, Mr. Caliud, Mr. Jaques, and the renegado Rosignana, all in the employ of Mr. Drouetti. Ignorant which of the three to point out as the perpetrator of this wanton and spiteful mischief, we contented ourselves with writing to the consul at Cairo, and nothing more was said. But by this time Mr. Jaques, who had parted from the others and was alone, came to us, and, by way of exculpating himself, said that Caliud was the man, who mutilated the figures with his little hammer, which he always carried with him to break stones. Mr. Caliud was now in Cairo, and Mr. Beechey wrote to the consul an account of what had passed. Mr. Caliud, afraid of being turned out of employment, assured the consul, that he would prove his innocence in the face of Mr. Jaques, when he arrived in Thebes. Sometime after Mr. Caliud reached Thebes with a letter from the consul, stating the promise he had made of clearing himself from the imputation of Mr. Jaques concerning the breaking of the stones; but instead of confronting Mr. Jaques, who was there, he contented himself with abusing the English consul for having spoken to him about the business while in Cairo, and did not choose to meet Mr. Jaques and us, or say whether the charge were true or false. After abusing the consul, who was now five hundred miles distant from him, Mr. Caliud meditated more mischief before his departure. He became the friend again of Mr. Jaques, who stated to the consul, that all that had been written to him by Mr. Beechey concerning Mr. Caliud was not true, and that he never told us any thing of the kind. On the arrival of the consul at Thebes, Mr. Jaques was questioned before us, whether he had not told us, that Caliud mutilated the stones in the island of Philœ. He again repeated to the consul before us, that Caliud did break the stones: and being questioned by the consul, why he afterwards wrote, that such was not the case, said with the greatest *sang froid*, that he merely contradicted it at the request of Caliud. One broke the stones; the other first betrayed him, then retracted, and lastly confirmed it again. These were the sort of honourable Monsieurs I had to guard against.

Twenty days after the tomb was opened, we heard by the boats which came up the Nile, that there were three maishes, or large boats, coming up, with Englishmen on board; and, a few days after, Earl Belmore and family, Mr. Salt the consul, Captain Cory, Dr. Richardson, and the Rev. Mr. Holt, arrived at Thebes.

In passing Kenneh they went to see Hamed Aga, who told them of the new discovery of the tomb. They were delighted when they saw it; and as his Lordship was anxious to find a tomb, I pointed out two likely spots of ground in the valley of Beban el Malook, but they turned out to be two small mummy pits. This proves, that small tombs were permitted to be dug out in that valley, where it was supposed, that none but the tombs of the kings of Egypt were to be found; and agrees with my former opinion, that it was not in this valley alone the tombs of the kings were excavated. During his stay, his Lordship made many researches, and was pleased to send down the Nile two of the lion-headed statues I discovered in Carnak. Thus, with what was found and brought by the Arabs, he accumulated a vast quantity of fragments, which, when in Europe, will form a pretty extensive cabinet of antiquities.

The consul was so enraptured with the sight of the tomb, and, I suppose, of the sarcophagus, that he also began making excavations in the valley of Beban el Malook, in order to find some more of the depositories of kings. He continued his research four months; and what he has found he will of course describe himself with more minuteness than I could do. Lord Belmore and his family proceeded to Nubia a few days after; and I prepared to descend the Nile, as I had business in Cairo. Such however was the impression made on me by that beautiful tomb, that I resolved to return to Thebes, and form a complete model of it, of which I shall speak hereafter. The three travellers were now come back from Nubia, but they passed on without stopping.

Having embarked all that was found this season, I left Thebes with another accumulation of antiquities, of which an account will be found at the end of this volume. I shall not describe this voyage, as I think it useless to repeat almost the same things over again. We arrived at Boolak on the twenty-first of December, after ten months absence. My business in Cairo detained me longer than I wished, as I was anxious to return to Thebes, for the sole purpose of taking models and impressions in wax of all the figures and hieroglyphics in the newly discovered tomb, first called that of Apis, but now of Psammethis. Finding I could not immediately despatch my little business there, I sent up the boat, with the intention of going myself by land. I had engaged Signor Ricci, a young man from Italy, who was very clever at drawing, and who with a little practice became quite perfect in his imitations of the hieroglyphics. He was to begin the drawings of the tomb on his arrival at Thebes. Mrs. Belzoni resolved to visit the Holy Land, and wait for me at Jerusalem, to which place I intended to go after finishing my model of the tomb. My purse was now pretty well exhausted; for all my former stock of money was spent, and very little remained of the present I received from Mr. Burckhardt and the consul after my first voyage with the colossal head. Mrs. Belzoni set out for Jerusalem, accompanied by James the Irish lad and a Janizary, who went to meet a traveller in Syria, to escort him to Egypt.

At this time the celebrated and veracious Count de Forbin arrived at Cairo. I then lodged at the consulate; and the Count visited the house, to see the collection I had just brought down with me, as well as what had been brought the year before. The Count was not a little confounded at the sight of so many valuable things; and being Director of the French Museum, they could not fail to be interesting to him. The colossal head, the altar with the six deities, the colossal arm, and the various statues, particularly attracted his attention.

I was then in possession of some statues, which I had brought from Thebes on my own account, according to an understanding with the consul. I intended to send them to my native town; for which purpose I had arranged for their embarkation at Alexandria. The Count made a proposal to purchase them; and being told they were destined for Europe immediately, he urgently requested that

I would dispose of them to him, saying he should be under great obligations to me if I would comply with his request. I recollected that I might find more, and accordingly consented to gratify him. What he paid me for them was not one fourth of their value; but I was fully satisfied, as I never was a dealer in statues in my life.

At this time I received several journals from Europe; and found, to my great surprise, that all my former discoveries and labours had been published in the names of other people, while mine was not even mentioned. I must confess, I was weak enough to be a little vexed at this; for, after such exertions as I had made in Upper Egypt, it was not pleasant to see the fruits and the credit of them ascribed to others, who had no more to do with them than the governor of Siberia, except as far as related to supplying me with money. Thinking all was not right, and that people were by some means misinformed, I drew up a statement of the facts. I gave this account of my operations in Egypt to the Count de Forbin in the shape of a letter, which he promised to have published in France; but it would have been better, if I had never entrusted it to him, as the use he made of it was quite the reverse of what was intended. Every thing was again thrown into confusion by the French journals, who confounded one thing with another, so that the public knew but little of the truth from that quarter; and some others of the European journals, which copied and extracted from them, were also misled. I had despaired of correcting these mis-statements; but the many travellers who afterwards visited that country, and were impartial spectators, wrote to Europe an account of what they saw and heard; and by these means the real facts in time came out.

At this period Major Moore arrived in Cairo with despatches from India; and, as he could not set off on the same day for Alexandria for want of a cangiar, he went with me to visit the pyramids inside and out. While on the top of the first pyramid, I descanted to him on the various opinions entertained concerning the second, and what a pity it was, that, in an intelligent age like the present, it had not been opened, so that the interior remained quite unknown. On Major Moore's departure for England, he took with him the account of my operations in Egypt, and some of the plans of the newly discovered places, which he faithfully delivered to Lord Aberdeen, president of the Society of Antiquaries, agreeably to my request; and this was one source by which the truth began to be known.

The Count de Forbin made much inquiry about Upper Egypt, and expressed his wish to see that country. I know not whether it were my persuasions, or his own inclinations, but he took the resolution to go up, though the whole of his journey, from his departure to his return, occupied only one month. Having done so, he gave an account of the country, the city of Thebes, its monuments, tombs, temples, colossi, scarabæi, Europeans, &c. But he said his enterprising spirit of penetrating into Africa failed him, when he saw European women walking about Luxor. A very pretty excuse for a traveller! At the time of Norden, European women could not go about in Alexandria as they can now in Thebes, yet Norden continued to make his way as far as Deir. If the Count wanted to signalize himself as a traveller, he should not have scorned to enter the extensive sandy ocean of Africa, merely because he saw a European family walking freely at Luxor in Egypt. If the Count look at the map of that unknown country, he will find, that the civilization of Egypt will diminish very little of the glory he seems to wish to acquire by penetrating into Africa.

The Count mentions having found a colossal arm in Thebes; and that I, by advice of the British consul, had it taken away, though it belonged to him. Such an arm never existed. But if the Count be ashamed to say, that he has been in Egypt without finding a single piece of antiquity, and returned without bringing any thing to France except the statues he obtained from me, I think he might have been more candid, and have confessed, that the attraction of a more easy life did not permit him to proceed any farther into Africa. The Count abuses almost every one who comes in his way, merely because he did not succeed in making any thing of Egypt himself; but I should not have mentioned his name, had he not impelled me to it by the falsehoods inserted against me in his journal. One thing more I must observe respecting the Count. On his return from Thebes I met him at Cairo, in the house of the Austrian consul. I had begun the task of opening the pyramids, and had already discovered the false passage. The Count requested in a kind of sarcastic manner, when I had succeeded in opening the pyramid, which no doubt he supposed would be never, that I would send him the plan of it, as he was about setting off for Alexandria the next day, and thence to France. I thought the best retaliation I could make was to send him the desired plan, and I did so, as soon as I opened the pyramid, which was in a few days after his departure. Would any one believe, that the noble Count, on his arrival in France, gave out, that he had succeeded in penetrating the second pyramid of Ghizeh, and brought the plan of it to Paris? Whether this be the fact or no will appear from the following paragraph, taken from a French paper now in my possession.

"On the 24th of April, Mr. Le Comte de Forbin, Director General of the Royal Museum of France, landed at the lazaretto of Marseilles. He came last from Alexandria, and his passage was very stormy. He has visited Greece, Syria, and Upper Egypt. By a happy chance, some days before his departure from Cairo, he succeeded in penetrating into the second pyramid of Ghizeh. Mr. Forbin brings the plan of that important discovery, as well as much information on the labours of Mr. Drouetti, at Carnak, and on those which Mr. Salt, the English consul, pursues with the greatest success in the valley of Beban el Malook, and in the plain of Medinet Aboo. The Museum of Paris is going to be enriched with some of the spoils of Thebes, which Mr. Forbin has collected in his travels." Was this written in ridicule of the Count de Forbin by some person in France? or is it an attempt to impose on the public by a tissue of falsehoods?

Having seen so many erroneous accounts in the journals of Europe, I thought it my duty to inform the public of the real facts. Before my departure for Thebes I visited the pyramids in company with two other persons from Europe. On our arrival at these monuments they went into the first pyramid, while I took a turn round the second. I seated myself in the shade of one of those stones on the east side, which form the part of the temple that stood before the pyramid in that direction. My eyes were fixed on that enormous mass, which for so many ages has baffled the conjectures of ancient and modern writers. Herodotus himself was deceived by the Egyptian priests, when told there were no chambers in it. The sight of the wonderful work before me astonished me as much, as the total obscurity in which we are of its origin, its interior, and its construction. In an intelligent age like the present, one of the greatest wonders of the world stood before us, without our knowing even whether it had any cavity in the interior, or if it were only one solid mass. The various attempts which have been made by numerous travellers to find an entrance into this pyramid, and particularly by the great body of French savans, were examples so weighty, that it seemed little short of madness, to think of renewing the enterprise. Indeed, the late researches made by Mr. Salt himself, and by Captain Cabilia, during four months, round these pyramids, were apparently sufficient to deter any one. A short time before this period the few Franks who resided in Egypt had some idea of obtaining permission from Mahomed Ali, and by the help of a subscription, which was to be made at the various Courts in Europe to the amount of at least £20,000, were to force their way into the centre of this pyramid by explosions, or any other means that could be suggested. Mr. Drouetti was to have had the superintendence of this work. Indeed it had created some difference among themselves who was to have had the direction of the whole concern. Was not this enough to show the difficulties I had to encounter, and to make me laugh at myself, if any thought of such an attempt should cross my mind? Besides, there was another obstacle to overcome. I had to consider, that in consequence of what I had the good fortune to do in Upper Egypt, and under the circumstances above mentioned, it was not likely that I should obtain permission to make such an attempt: for if it could be supposed, that there was any possibility of penetrating into the pyramid, the operation would certainly be given to people of higher influence than myself.

With all these thoughts in my mind I arose, and by a natural impulsion took my walk toward the south side of the pyramid. I examined every part, and almost every stone. I continued to do so on the west,—at last I came round to the north. Here the appearance of things became to my eye somewhat different from that at any of the other sides. The constant observations I made on the approach to the tombs at Thebes perhaps enabled me to see what other travellers did not: indeed, I think this ought to be considered as a standing proof, that in many cases practice goes farther than theory. Other travellers had been also in various places where I had been, and came often to the same spot where I was, but perhaps did not make the observations I did. I certainly must beg leave to say, that I often observed travellers, who, confident of their own knowledge, let slip opportunities of ascertaining whether they were correct in their notions; and if an observation was made to them by any one, who had not the good fortune of having received a classical education, they scorned to listen to it, or replied with a smile, if not a laugh of disapprobation, without investigating whether the observation were just or not. I had often the satisfaction of seeing such travellers mortified by the proof of being wrong in their conjecture. I do not mean to say, that a man, who has had a classical education, should think himself under a disadvantage in regard to knowing such things, compared with him who has not; but, that a man, who thinks himself well informed on a subject, often does not examine it with such precision as another, who is less confident in himself.

I observed on the north side of the pyramid three marks, which encouraged me to attempt searching there for the entrance into it. Still it is to be remarked, that the principal signs I discovered there were not deduced solely from the knowledge I had acquired among the tombs of the Egyptians at Thebes; for any traveller will acknowledge, that the pyramids have little in common with the tombs, either in their exterior appearance, or in any shape whatever:— they are two different things,—one is formed by a vast accumulation of large blocks of stones;—the other is entirely hewed out of the solid rock. My principal guide, I must own, was the calculation I made from the first pyramid, and such was my assurance on this point, that I then almost resolved to make the attempt. I had been at the pyramids various times before, but never with any intention of examining into the practicability of finding the entrance into them, which was deemed almost impossible. The case was now different,—I saw then what I had not seen before.—I observed, that just under the centre of the face of the pyramid the accumulation of materials, which had fallen from the coating of it, was higher than the entrance could be expected to be, if compared with the height of the entrance into the first pyramid, measuring from the basis. I could not conceive how the discovery of the entrance into the second pyramid could be considered as a matter to be despaired of, when no one had ever seen the spot, where it must naturally be presumed to exist, if there were any entrance at all. I farther observed, that the materials which had fallen exactly in the centre of the front were not so compact as those on the sides; and hence concluded, that the stones on that spot, had been removed after the falling of the coating. Consequently I perceived the probability of there being an entrance into the pyramid at that spot. Encouraged by these observations, I rejoined my companions in the first pyramid. We visited the great sphinx, and returned to Cairo the same evening.

I resolved to make a closer examination the next day, which I did accordingly, without communicating my intention to any one, as it would have excited great inquiry among the Franks at Cairo, and in all probability I should not have obtained permission to proceed in my design. The next day's examination encouraged me in the attempt. I was confident, that, if my purpose had been known to certain persons, who had influence at the court of the Bashaw, I should never succeed in obtaining permission. On the following day therefore I crossed the Nile to Embabe, as the Cacheff who commanded the province which includes the pyramids resided there. I introduced myself to him, and acquainted him with my intention to excavate the pyramids, if it met his approbation. His answer was, as I expected, that I must apply to the Bashaw, or to the Kakia Bey, for a firman, without which it was not in his power to grant me permission to excavate at the harrans, or pyramids. I asked him, whether he had any other objection, provided I obtained the firman from the Bashaw; he replied, "none whatever." I then went to the citadel, and as the Bashaw was not in Cairo, I presented myself to the Kakia Bey, who knew me from the time I was at Soubra, and who, on my request for permission to excavate at the pyramids, had no other objection, than that of not being certain, whether round the harrans there were any ploughed grounds, on which he could not grant permission to dig. He sent a message to the above Cacheff at Embabe, who assured him, that round the harrans there was no cultivated land, but that on the contrary it was solid rock.

With such an assurance I obtained a firman to the Cacheff, to furnish me with men to work at the pyramids. My undertaking was of no small importance: it consisted of an attempt to penetrate into one of the great pyramids of Egypt, one of the wonders of the world. I was confident, that a failure in such an attempt would have drawn on me the laughter of all the world for my presumption in undertaking such a task: but at the same time I considered, that I might be excused, since without attempting we should never accomplish any thing. However, I thought it best to keep my expedition as secret as possible; and I communicated it only to Mr. Walmas, a worthy Levantine merchant of Cairo, and partner in the house of Briggs. It is not to be understood, that I intended to conceal the attempt I wished to make on the pyramids, for the effects of my work would plainly show themselves; but being near the capital, where many Europeans resided, I could not prevent myself from being interrupted during my operations; and as I knew too well how far the influence and intrigues of my opponents could be carried, I was not certain, that the permission I had procured might not have been countermanded, so as to put an end to all my proceedings. Accordingly having provided myself with a small tent, and some provision, that I might not be under the necessity of repairing to Cairo, I set off for the pyramids.

My sudden departure from Cairo was supposed to be an expedition to the mountain of Mokatam, for a few days, as I had given out. At the pyramids I found the Arabs willing to work, and immediately set about the operation.

My purse was but light, for very little remained of what I received as a present from Mr. Burckhardt, and the consul; and though it had been a little strengthened by the two statues I lately disposed of to the Count de Forbin, who had paid me one third of the money on account, my whole stock did not amount to two hundred pounds, and if I did not succeed in penetrating the pyramid before this was exhausted, I should have been at a stand, before the accomplishment of my undertaking, and perhaps prepared the way for others stronger than myself in purse.

Two points principally excited my attention: the first was on the north side of the pyramids, and the second on the east. There is on the latter side part of a portico of the temple which stood before the pyramid, and which has a causeway descending straight towards the great sphinx. I thought, that by opening the ground between the portico and the pyramid I should necessarily come to the foundation of the temple, which in fact I did. I set eighty Arabs to work, forty on the above spot, and forty in the centre of the north side of the pyramid, where I observed the earth not so solid as on the east and west. The Arabs were paid daily one piastre each, which is sixpence English money. I had also several boys and girls to carry away the earth, to whom I gave only twenty paras, or three pence, a day. I contrived to gain their good will by trifles I gave as presents, and by pointing out to them the advantage they would gain, if we succeeded in penetrating into the pyramid, as many visitors would come to see it, and they would get bakshis from them. Nothing has so much influence on the mind of an Arab as reasoning with him about his own interest, and showing him the right way to benefit himself. Any thing else he seems not to understand.

I must confess, at the same time, that I found this mode of proceeding quite as efficacious in Europe.

The works on each side continued for several days without the smallest appearance of any thing. On the north side of the pyramid, the materials which were to be removed, consisting of what had fallen from the coating, notwithstanding the appearance of having been removed at a later period than the first, were so closely cemented together, that the men could scarcely proceed. The only instrument they had to work with was a kind of hatchet or spade, which being rather thin, and only fit to cut the soft ground, could not stand much work among stones and mortar, which latter I suppose, as it fell from the pyramid, had been moistened by the dew*, and gradually formed itself almost into one mass with the stones.

On the east side of the pyramid, we found the lower part of a large temple connected with the portico, and reaching within fifty feet of the basis of the pyramid. Its exterior walls were formed of enormous blocks of stone, as may now be seen. Some of the blocks in the porticoes are twenty-four feet high. The interior part of this temple was built with calcareous stones of various sizes, but many finely cut at the angles, and is probably much older than the exterior wall, which bears the appearance of as great antiquity as the pyramids. In order to find the basis of the pyramid on this side, and to ascertain whether there were any communication between it and the temple, I had to cut through all the material there accumulated, which rose above forty feet from the basis, and consisted of large blocks of stone and mortar, from the coating, as on the north side. At last we reached the basis, and I perceived a flat pavement cut out of the solid rock. I caused all that was before me to be cut in a right line from the basis of the pyramid to the temple,

---

* In spring and summer, very heavy dews fall at night.

and traced the pavement quite to the back of it, so that there was evidently a spacious pavement from the temple to the pyramid; and I do not hesitate to declare my opinion, that the same pavement goes all round the pyramid. It appeared to me, that the sphinx, the temple, and the pyramid, were all three erected at the same time, as they all appear to be in one line, and of equal antiquity. On the north side the work advanced towards the basis; a great number of large stones had been removed, and a great part of the face of the pyramid was uncovered, but still there was no appearance of any entrance, or the smallest mark to indicate that there ever had been one.

The Arabs had great confidence in the hopes I had excited among them, that if any entrance into the pyramid were found, I would give great bakshis, in addition to the advantage they would derive from other strangers. But after many vain expectations, and much hard labour in removing huge masses of stone, and cutting the mortar, which was so hard that their hatchets were nearly all broken, they began to flag in their prospect of finding any thing, and I was about to become an object of ridicule for making the attempt to penetrate a place, which appeared to them, as well as to more civilized people, a mass of solid stone. However, as long as I paid them they continued their work, though with much less zeal. My hopes did not forsake me, in spite of all the difficulties I saw, and the little appearance of making the discovery of an entrance into the pyramid. Still I observed, as we went on with our work, that the stones on that spot were not so consolidated as those on the sides of them, and this circumstance made me determine to proceed, till I should be persuaded that I was wrong in my conjecture. At last, on the 18th of February, after sixteen days of fruitless labour, one of the Arabian workmen perceived a small chink between two stones of the pyramid. At this he was greatly rejoiced, thinking we had found the entrance so eagerly sought for. I perceived the aperture was small, but I thrust a long palm-stick into it upwards of two yards. Encouraged by this circumstance, the Arabs resumed their vigour on the work, and great hopes were entertained among them. Thus it served my purpose, as the work now went on briskly. I was aware, that the entrance to the pyramid could not be between two stones in this manner; but I was in hopes, that the aperture would furnish some clew by which the right entrance would be discovered. Proceeding farther, I perceived, that one of the stones, apparently fixed in the pyramid, was in fact loose. I had it removed the same day, and found an opening leading to the interior. This sort of rough entrance was not more than three feet wide, and was choked up with smaller stones and sand, which being removed, it proved to be much wider within. A second and third day were employed in clearing this place; but the farther we advanced, the more materials we found. On the fourth day I observed, that sand and stones were falling from the upper part of this cavity, which surprised me not a little. At last I found, that there was a passage from the outside of the pyramid by a higher aperture, which apparently was thought to have had no communication with any cavity. When all the rubbish was taken out, and the place cleared, I continued the work in the lower part beneath our feet; and in two days more we came to an opening inward. Having made it wide enough, I took a candle in my hand, and, looking in, perceived a spacious cavity, of which I could not form any conjecture. Having caused the entrance to be cleared of the sand and stones, I found a tolerably spacious place, bending its course towards the centre. It is evidently a forced passage, executed by some powerful hand, and appears intended to find a way to the centre of the pyramid. Some of the stones, which are of an enormous size, are cut through, some have been taken out, and others are on the point of falling from their old places for want of support. Incredible must have been the labour in making such a cavity, and it is evident, that it was continued farther on towards the centre; but the upper part had fallen in, and filled up the cavity to such a degree, that it was impossible for us to proceed any farther than a hundred feet. Half this distance from the entrance is another cavity, which descends forty feet (See Plate 11), in an irregular manner, but still turns towards the centre, which no doubt was the point intended by the persons who made the excavation. To introduce many men to work in this place was dangerous, for several of the stones above our heads were on the point of falling; some were suspended only by their corners, which stuck between other stones, and with the least touch would have fallen, and crushed any one that happened to be under them. I set a few men to work, but was soon convinced of the impossibility of advancing any farther in that excavation. In one of the passages below, one of the men narrowly escaped being crushed to pieces. A large block of stone, no less than six feet long and four wide, fell from the top, while the man was digging under it; but fortunately it rested on two other stones, one on each side of him, higher than himself, as he was sitting at his work. The man was so incarcerated, that we had some difficulty in getting him out; yet, happily, he received no other injury than a slight bruise on his back. The falling of this stone moved many others in this passage: indeed, they were so situated, that I thought it prudent to retreat out of the pyramid, or we might have reason to repent when too late; for the danger was not only from what might fall upon us, but also from what might fall in our way, close up the passage, and thus bury us alive. My expectation in this passage was not great, as I perceived from the beginning it could not be the true entrance into the pyramid, though I had strong hopes that it would lead to some clew for the discovery of the real entrance; but, alas! it gave me none, and I remained as ignorant of it as I was before I began.

Having spent so many days at the pyramids without being discovered by any of the people at Cairo, I did not expect, that my retreat could be concealed much longer, as there were constantly Franks from Cairo making a Sunday's excursion to the pyramids, or travellers, who, of course, made it a point to see these wonders on their first arrival at the metropolis. In fact, the very day I was to have quitted this work, I perceived, in the afternoon, some people on the top of the first pyramid. I had no doubt they were Europeans, as the Arabs or Turks never go up, unless to accompany somebody, to gain money. They saw part of my men at work at the second pyramid, and concluded that none but Europeans could be conducting such an operation. They fired a pistol as a signal, and I returned another. They then descended the angle which led towards us; and on their arrival proved to be Monsieur L'Abbé de Forbin, who had accompanied his cousin, the celebrated Count, into Egypt, but did not proceed higher. With him were the father superior of the convent of Terra Santa, Mr. Costa, an engineer, and Mr. Gaspard, vice-consul of France, by whom I was introduced to the Abbé. They all entered into the newly discovered passage; but it gave the Abbé less pleasure than a cup of coffee, which he honoured me by accepting in my humble tent. Naturally, after such a visit, all the Franks in Cairo knew what I was doing; and not a day passed without my having some visitors.

I was determined to proceed still farther with my researches, the recent disappointment making me rather more obstinate than I was before. I had given a day's rest to the Arabs, which I dedicated to a closer inspection of the pyramid. It often happens, that a man is so much ingulfed in the pursuit of his views, as to be in danger of losing himself, if he do not quickly find the means either of an honourable retreat, or of attaining the accomplishment of his intended purpose. Such was my case. The success of my discovery of the false passage was considered as a failure. I cared little what was thought of it, but I was provoked at having been deceived by those marks, which led me to the forced passage, with the loss of so much time and labour. However, I did not despair. I strictly noticed the situation of the entrance into the first pyramid, and plainly saw, that it was not in the centre of the pyramid. I observed that the passage ran in a straight line from the outside of the pyramid to the east side of the king's chamber; and this chamber being nearly in the centre of the pyramid, the entrance consequently must be as far from the middle of the face as the distance from the centre of the chamber to the east side of it.

Having made this clear and simple observation, I found, that, if there were any chamber at all in the second pyramid, the entrance or passage could not be on the spot where I had excavated, which was in the centre, but calculating by the passage in the first pyramid, the entrance into the second would be near thirty feet to the east.

Satisfied with this calculation, I repaired to the second pyramid to examine the mass of rubbish. There I was not a little astonished when I perceived the same marks, which I had seen on the other spot in the centre, about thirty feet distant from where I stood. This gave me no little delight, and hope returned to cherish my pyramidical brains. I observed in this spot also, that the stones and mortar were not so compact as on the east side, which mark had given me so much encouragement to proceed in the first attempt; but what increased my hopes was an observation I made on the exterior of the front where the forced passage is. I observed the stones had been removed several feet from the surface of the pyramid, which I ascertained by drawing a line with the coating above to the basis below, and found the concavity was inclined to be deeper towards the spot where I intended to make my new attempt. Any traveller, who shall hereafter visit the pyramids, may plainly perceive this concavity above the true entrance. Such has been the effect of two different hints; first my old guide from Thebes, I mean the spots where the stony matter is not so compact as the surrounding mass; and, secondly, the concavity of the pyramid over the place where the entrance might have been expected to be found, according to the distance of the entrance into the first pyramid from its centre.

I immediately summoned the Arabs to work the next day. They were pleased at my recommencing the task, not in hopes of finding the entrance into the pyramid, but for the continuation of the pay they of course were to receive. As to expectation that the entrance might be found, they had none; and I often heard them utter, in a low voice, the word "*magnoon*," in plain English, madman. I pointed out to the Arabs the spot where they had to dig, and such was my measurement, that I was right within two feet, in a straight direction, as to the entrance into the first passage, as will be seen from Plates 9 and 10; and I have the pleasure of reckoning this day as fortunate, being that on which I discovered the entrance into the great tomb of Psammethis at Thebes. The Arabs began their work, and the rubbish proved to be as hard as that of the first excavation, with this addition, that we found larger blocks of stone in our way, which had belonged to the pyramid, besides the falling of the coating. The stones increased in size as we went on.

A few days after the visit of the Abbé de Forbin I was surprised by the appearance of another European traveller. It was the Chevalier Frediani, who, on his return from the second cataract of the Nile, came to visit the great pyramids. I had known him at

Thebes on his ascending the Nile, and was much pleased to see him, as I thought he might be an impartial spectator of the event of my operations, which in fact he was. He greatly approved of my undertaking, but after being two days with me was ready to take his departure. I suppose he had as much expectation, that I should open the pyramid, as the Arabs who named me the *magnoon*. It happened, that on the very day he was to set off for Cairo, I perceived in the excavation a large block of granite, inclining downward at the same angle as the passage into the first pyramid, and pointing towards the centre. I requested the Chevalier to stay till the morrow, thinking perhaps he might have the pleasure of being one of the first who saw the entrance into the pyramid. He consented, and I was pleased to have a countryman of my own to be a witness of what passed on this important occasion. The discovery of the first granite stone occurred on the 28th of February, and on the 1st of March we uncovered three large blocks of granite, two on each side, and one on the top, all in an inclined direction towards the centre. My expectation and hope increased, as to all appearance, this must prove to be the object of my search. I was not mistaken, for on the next day, the 2d of March, at noon, we came at last to the right entrance into the pyramid. The Arabs, whose expectation had also increased at the appearance of the three stones, were delighted at having found something new to show to the visitors, and get bakshis from them. Having cleared the front of the three stones, the entrance proved to be a passage four feet high, three feet six inches wide, formed of large blocks of granite, which descended towards the centre for a hundred and four feet five inches at an angle of twenty-six degrees. Nearly all this passage was filled up with large stones, which had fallen from the upper part, and as the passage is inclined downwards, they slid on till some larger than the rest stopped the way.

I had much ado to have all the stones drawn out of the passage, which was filled up to the entrance of the chamber. It took the remainder of this day and part of the next to clear it, and at last we reached a portcullis. At first sight it appeared to be a fixed block of stone, which stared me in the face, and said *ne plus ultra*, putting an end to all my projects as I thought; for it made a close joint with the groove at each side, and on the top it seemed as firm as those which formed the passage itself. On a close inspection however I perceived, that, at the bottom, it was raised about eight inches from the lower part of the groove, which is cut beneath to receive it; and I found, by this circumstance, that the large block before me was no more than a portcullis of granite, one foot three inches thick.

Having observed a small aperture at the upper part of the portcullis, I thrust a long piece of barley straw into it, and it entered upwards of three feet; which convinced me, that there was a vacuum ready to receive the portcullis. The raising of it was a work of no small consideration. The passage is only four feet high, and three feet six inches wide. When two men are in it abreast of each other they cannot move, and it required several men to raise a piece of granite not less than six feet high, five feet wide, and one foot three inches thick. The levers could not be very long, otherwise there was not space in the four feet height to work with them; and if they were short, I could not employ men enough to raise the portcullis. The only method to be taken was, to raise it a little at a time; and by putting some stones in the grooves on each side, to support the portcullis while changing the fulcrum of the levers, it was raised high enough for a man to pass. An Arab then entered with a candle, and returned saying, that the place within was very fine. I continued to raise the portcullis, and at last made the entrance large enough to squeeze myself in; and after thirty days exertion I had the pleasure of finding myself in the way to the central chamber of one of the two great pyramids of Egypt, which have long been the admiration of beholders. The Chevalier Frediani followed me, and after passing under the portcullis we entered a passage not higher or wider than the first. It is twenty-two feet seven inches long, and the works including the portcullis occupy six feet eleven inches in all. Where the granite work finishes at the end of this passage, there is a perpendicular shaft of fifteen feet, and at each side of the passage, an excavation in the solid rock, one of which, on the right as you enter, runs thirty feet in an upward direction, approaching the end of the lower part of the forced passage, as will be seen in Plates 9 and 10. Before us we had a long passage running in a horizontal direction toward the centre. We descended the shaft by means of a rope. At the bottom of it I perceived another passage running downward at the same angle of 26° as that above, and toward the north. As my first object was the centre of the pyramid, I advanced that way, and ascended an inclined passage, which brought me to a horizontal one, that led toward the centre. I observed, that after we entered within the portcullis, the passages were all cut out of the solid rock. The passage leading toward the centre is five feet eleven inches high, and three feet six inches wide.

As we advanced farther on we found the sides of this passage covered with arborizations of nitre; some projecting in ropes, some not unlike the skin of a white lamb, and others so long as to resemble an endive-leaf. I reached the door at the centre of a large chamber. (See Plate 12.) I walked slowly two or three paces, and then stood still to contemplate the place were I was. Whatever it might be, I certainly considered myself in the centre of that pyramid, which from time immemorial had been the subject of the obscure conjectures of many hundred travellers, both ancient and modern. My torch, formed of a few wax candles, gave but a faint light; I could, however, clearly distinguish the principal objects. I naturally turned my eyes to the west end of the chamber, looking for the sarcophagus, which I strongly expected to see in the same situation as that in the first pyramid; but I was disappointed when I saw nothing there. The chamber has a painted ceiling; and many of the stones had been removed from their places, evidently by some one in search of treasure. On my advancing toward the west end, I was agreeably surprised to find, that there was a sarcophagus buried on a level with the floor.

By this time the Chevalier Frediani had entered also; and we took a general survey of the chamber, which I found to be forty-six feet three inches long, sixteen feet three inches wide, and twenty-three feet six inches high. It is cut out of the solid rock from the floor to the roof, which is composed of large blocks of calcareous stone, meeting in the centre, and forming a roof of the same slope as the pyramid itself. The sarcophagus is eight feet long, three feet six inches wide, and two feet three inches deep in the inside. It is surrounded by large blocks of granite, apparently to prevent its removal, which could not be effected without great labour. The lid had been broken at the side, so that the sarcophagus was half open. It is of the finest granite; but, like the other in the first pyramid, there is not one hieroglyphic on it.

Looking at the inside, I perceived a great quantity of earth and stones, but did not observe the bones among the rubbish till the next day, as my attention was principally bent in search of some inscription that would throw light on the subject of this pyramid. We examined every part of the walls, and observed many scrawls executed with charcoal, but in unknown characters, and nearly imperceptible. They rubbed off into dust at the slightest touch;

and on the wall at the west end of the chamber I perceived an inscription in Arabic, as follows:

$$\text{ونعمهم العلم احمد لجبار وذلك العلم}$$

$$\text{عثمان حضر والملك علي محمد اولاً ولغلاك}$$

and the various interpretations given of it compel me to explain some points, which will perhaps lead to a satisfactory explanation. It appears to me, that all the difficulty lies in the last letters of the inscription, which are supposed to be obscure. This indeed is the fact; but I must say, that these letters were so blotted on the wall, that they were scarcely visible. The transcriber was a Copt, whom I had brought from Cairo for the purpose, as I would not trust to my own pen; and not being satisfied of his protestations of accuracy, though it was copied under my own eyes, I invited many other persons, who were considered as the best skilled in the Arabic language of any in Cairo, and requested them to compare the copy with the original on the wall. They found it perfectly correct, except the concluding word, which indeed appeared obscure; but if it be considered how much that word resembles the right one, we shall find a correct sense, and the whole inscription made out.

Translation of the Inscription by Mr. Salame.

" The Master Mohammed Ahmed, lapicide, has opened them; and the Master Othman attended this (*opening*); and the King Alij Mohammed at first (*from the beginning*) to the closing up." *

* The Arabic to which I gave the meaning of these last words, "*to the closing up,*"

I must add, that the circumstance of the pyramid having been again closed up agrees with what I have said of my finding it so.

On several parts of the wall the nitre had formed many beautiful arborizations like those in the passage, but much larger and stronger. Some were six inches long, resembling in shape a large endive leaf, as I mentioned before. Under one of the blocks that had been removed, I found something like the thick part of a hatchet, but so rusty, that it had lost its shape. At the north and south sides are two holes, which run in an horizontal direction, like those that are seen in the first pyramid, but higher up.

Returning out of this chamber we reached the passage below. At the bottom of the perpendicular shaft were so many stones as nearly to choke up its entrance, and after removing these we found the passage running to the north, at the same inclination as above, an angle of 26°, as is to be seen in Plate 10. This passage is forty-eight feet six inches in length, when it joins an horizontal passage of fifty-five feet still running north. Half-way up this passage on the right is a recess eleven feet long and six feet deep. On the left, opposite to it, is another passage, running twenty-two feet with a descent of 26° towards the west. Before we proceeded any farther toward the north, we descended this passage, and entered a chamber thirty-two feet long, nine feet nine inches wide, and eight feet six inches high. This chamber contains many small blocks of stone, some not more than two feet in length. It has a pointed roof like that before mentioned, though it is cut out of the solid

is not spelled correctly in the paper I saw, a fault which I attribute to the transcriber from the stone. It ought to be وللغلاق instead of اولغلاك the latter word not being to be found in the Arabic language.

The words between the parentheses in the translation are not in the original.

A. S.

rock; for it is to be understood, as I before observed, that, after we entered through the portcullis, all the passages, and the large chamber, as high as the roof, are cut out of the solid rock of calcareous stone. On the walls and roof of this chamber are several unknown inscriptions, as there are in the upper chamber. They are perhaps Coptic. Reascending into the horizontal passage, at the end of it we found grooves for a portcullis like the former; but the stone of granite which served for this purpose had been taken down, and is to be seen under the rubbish and stones near the place. Passing the portcullis we entered into a passage, which ascended in a direction parallel with that above, as in Plate 10. This passage runs up forty-seven feet six inches. Here we found a large block of stone, placed there from the upper part; and by calculation I found, that this passage ran out of the pyramid at its basis, as, from the upper part of this square block, I could perceive other stones, which filled up the passage to the entrance, so that this pyramid has two entrances to it. Half-way up the horizontal passage, which leads into the large chamber, is some mason's work; but I believe it to be only the filling up of a natural cavity in the rock.

Having made all my observations, we came out of the pyramid with no small degree of satisfaction; and I was highly gratified with the result of my labour, of very little more than a month, the expense of which did not amount in all to £150, though I had accomplished a task, which was supposed would have required several thousands.

The Chevalier Frediani went to Cairo the same day, and the news of the opening of the pyramid soon brought the Franks to visit its interior. As I had no fear that the Arabian women would break the pyramid, I left the entrance open (*pro bono publico*); and in that place where the perpendicular descent, just inside the portcullis, is, I made a stone step for the accommodation of visitors, leaving half of the passage to enter into the lower chamber.

A young man of the name of Pieri, employed in the counting house of Briggs and Walmas in Cairo, came the next day to visit the pyramid, and, having rummaged the rubbish inside of the sarcophagus, found a piece of bone, which we supposed to belong to a human skeleton. On searching farther, we found several pieces, which, having been sent to London, proved to be the bones of a bull. Some consequential persons, however, who would not scruple to sacrifice a point in history, rather than lose a *bon mot*, thought themselves mighty clever in baptizing the said bones those of a cow, merely to raise a joke. So much for their taste for antiquity. It has been stated also, that it might be supposed these large sarcophagi were made to contain the bones of bulls, as the sarcophagus which we found in the tombs of the kings at Thebes was of enormous size, and more fit for a bull than a human body. I cannot agree in this opinion, however, for if the person who made the observation had an opportunity of seeing and examining the cases and sarcophagi in which the Egyptians were buried, he would find, that the better classes of people had cases within cases, some nearly double the size requisite to contain one person; and it is natural therefore to suppose, that the kings of Egypt had more cases than one or two, consequently the sarcophagus, which was the outer case, must have been much larger than the rest, to contain them all.

Outside of the pyramid I observed the rock surrounding it on the north and west sides to be on a level with the upper part of the chamber; and, as the rock is evidently cut all round, it appeared to me, that the stones taken from it must have been applied to the erection of the pyramid. Accordingly I am of opinion, that the stones which seem to form these enormous edifices were not all taken from the east side of the Nile, as is supposed and mentioned by ancient writers. I cannot conceive why the Egyptians should be thought so simple, as to fetch stones at seven or eight miles distance, and across the Nile, when they could have them from much nearer points; indeed from the very spot where the pyramids stand. It is evident, that stones of an enormous size have been cut out of the very rocks around the pyramids; and for what purpose were these stones extracted? It might as well be asserted, that they were cut to build old Babylon of Egypt, or to fill up the vacancies in the quarries of the Mokattam. If any traveller will go within less than half a mile of the pyramids, particularly on the east and south sides, he may see many places, where the rock has been formerly quarried to a great length; and he will find that there is stone enough to build many other pyramids if required. It is true, that Herodotus says, the stones to erect the pyramids were brought from quarries on the other side of the Nile; but I firmly believe he was misinformed on this subject, unless what he asserts is to be understood of the granite alone. And as to the causeways in front of the pyramids, said to have been made to convey the stones for the erection of these masses, I believe they were intended for the accommodation of visitors, particularly at the time of high Nile; for if they were only to convey stones, the labour of making them must have been nearly equal to the erection of the pyramids.

So much has been already said about the pyramids, that very little is left to observe respecting them. Their great appearance of antiquity certainly leads us to suppose, that they must have been constructed at an earlier period than any other edifices to be seen in Egypt. It is somewhat singular, that Homer does not mention them; but this is no proof, that they did not exist in his time; on the contrary, it may be supposed they were so generally known, that he thought it useless to speak of them. It appears, that in the time of Herodotus as little was known of the second pyramid as before the late opening, with this exception, that in his time the second pyramid was nearly in the state in which it was left when closed by the builders, who must have covered the entrance with the coating, so that it might not be perceived. But at the time I was fortunate enough to find my way into it, the entrance was concealed by the rubbish of the coating, which must have been nearly perfect at the time of Herodotus: notwithstanding this we were as much in the dark in this present age, as he was in his. We know, however, now, that it has been opened by some of the rulers or chiefs of Egypt; a fact that affords no small satisfaction to the inquirer on the subject of these monuments. Some persons, who would rather let this circumstance remain in obscurity, regretted, that I should have found the inscription on the wall, which proved it to have been opened at so late a period, as very little more than a thousand years ago; but I beg them to recollect, that the present opening has not only made known this very interesting circumstance, but has thrown much light on the manner in which these enormous masses were erected, as well as explained the occasion of them.

The circumstance of having chambers and a sarcophagus (which undoubtedly contained the remains of some great personage), so uniform with those in the other pyramid, I think leaves very little question, but that they were erected as sepulchres; and I really wonder, that any doubt has ever existed, considering what could be learned from the first pyramid, which has been so long open. This contains a spacious chamber with a sarcophagus; the passages are of such dimensions as to admit nothing larger than the sarcophagus; they had been closely shut up by large blocks of granite from within, evidently to prevent the removal of that relic. Ancient authors are pretty well agreed in asserting, that these monuments were erected to contain the remains of two brothers, Cheops and Cephren, kings of Egypt. They are surrounded by other smaller pyramids intermixed with mausoleums on burial-grounds. Many mummy-pits have been continually found there; yet with all these proofs, it has been asserted, that they were erected for many other purposes than the true one, and nearly as absurd as that they served for granaries.

Some consider them as built for astronomical purposes, but there is nothing in their construction to favour this supposition. Others maintain, that they were meant for the performance of holy ceremonies by the Egyptian priests. Any thing in short for the sake of contradiction, or to have something new to say, finds its advocate. If the ancient authors had advanced, that they were erected for treasuries, the moderns would have agreed perhaps more in conformity with the truth, that they were made for sepulchres; and they would not have failed to see plainly those circumstances, which clearly prove the facts, and which are not noticed as they ought to be. I will agree with others thus far, that the Egyptians, in erecting these enormous masses, did not fail to make their sides due north and south, and consequently, as they are square, due east and west. Their inclination too is such as to give light to the north side at the time of the solstice. But even all this does not prove in the least, that they were erected for astronomical purposes; though it is to be observed, that the Egyptians connected astronomy with their religious ceremonies, as we found various zodiacs, not only among the temples, but in their tombs also.

By the measurement I took of the second pyramid I found it to be as follows.

	Feet.
The basis	684
Apotome or central line down the front, from the top to the basis	568
Perpendicular	456
Coating from the top to the place where it ends	140

The circumstance of not finding hieroglyphics in or out of it makes it appear, that they were erected before this mode of writing was invented; for, strange as it may seem, not a single hieroglyphic is found in all these enormous masses. Yet I must beg leave to remark a circumstance, which perhaps will lead to the conjecture, that it might not have been the custom of the Egyptians in that part of the country, who might perhaps be even of a different religion from their countrymen, to put hieroglyphics on their monuments; for there are many mausoleums round the pyramids, and some of them very extensive, without an hieroglyphic to be seen within or without them; and I observed, that those which contain chambers with hieroglyphics are evidently of a later date than the former. All this would seem to prove, that till a certain period subsequent to the building of the pyramids hieroglyphics were not known. But what can be said when I assure the reader, that in one of these mausoleums, which stands on the west of the first pyramid, and which is so decayed that it has fallen in, and is in a very ruinous state, I saw and made others observe some hieroglyphics and figures reversed in one of the blocks, which formed that mausoleum; and the hieroglyphics so preserved within, as if they were to be hidden from the view? It certainly must be concluded, that this stone had been employed in a building, which was adorned with hieroglyphics, and consequently proves, that they were known previous to the erection of these mausoleums, though they were without any of these ornaments or inscriptions. This being the case, it may be supposed, that the people, who built the pyramids, were of the same way of thinking as those, who built the mausoleums; consequently nothing can be inferred respecting the age of the pyramids from the circumstance of their not having any hieroglyphics.

It has been supposed, that the first pyramid, or that of Cheops, was not coated. I must agree in this opinion, for there is not the slightest mark remaining of any coating. As to the coating of the second pyramid, I had an opportunity of investigating this subject in the excavation I made on the east side of it, where I found the lower part as rough as any of the upper, below the remaining coating, which confirms the account of Herodotus in this respect, who says, that the coating was begun from above; and I believe myself that it never was quite finished to the basis, for if it had, I should have met with some below, as the accumulation of rubbish over the basis would have kept the stones in their places, or at least enough of them to show there was a coating, as was the case in the third pyramid, of which I shall have to speak presently.

It is supposed, that the inundation of the Nile surrounded the pyramids, so that they remained like islands. I cannot say that it was not so, for the situation of the pyramids is like an island of rocks, separated from those on the west only by a valley of sand, which might naturally have been accumulated by the wind in the course of so many centuries. I think we cannot have a stronger proof of this than the sphinx itself, the basis of which is so much below the present surface, that if all the sand around the pyramids were on a level with it, I have no doubt the Nile must have run round them, which probably was the case in the early ages.

Having thus finished my operation on the second pyramid, I felt a great inclination to have a cursory view of the third. I observed, that some one had made an attempt to penetrate it by excavations on the east side. I commenced my labours on the north side, and, after removing a great quantity of materials, found a considerable accumulation of enormous blocks of granite, which had evidently formed the coating.—Proceeding yet lower, as I cleared away the rubbish I found, that part of the coating still remained in its place down to the bases. The removal of these blocks would evidently have brought me to the entrance into the pyramid, but it required more money and time than I could spare.

By this time the consul, who was at Thebes, hearing of the opening of the pyramid, wrote to me, that he was coming down the Nile; and at the same time Lord Belmore and family arrived at Cairo. It is somewhat singular, and I mention it with much satisfaction, that his Lordship arrived at Thebes one month after my discovery of the celebrated tomb of Psammethis, and was the first British traveller who entered it. On his return from Nubia, he arrived at Cairo a little more than a month after my opening the second pyramid, and was the first British traveller who entered this also. His Lordship and family had been at Thebes for some time, and had accumulated no small collection of antiquities; indeed, I esteem it the largest ever made by any occasional traveller. Dr. Richardson had taken the opportunity of observing the ruins of ancient Thebes at leisure; and I believe, by his minute remarks, he must have made himself well acquainted with many interesting points not yet explained, and I have no doub this account will be highly interesting.

The Earl and family set off for Jerusalem by way of the Desert; and I prepared for my departure for Thebes, my old residence, which I knew better than any other place in Egypt. A few days after, the consul arrived, and, in half an hour after him, Colonel Fitzclarence, with despatches from India for England. The consul, Mr. Salt, would have been kind enough to have paid all the expenses I had incurred in opening the pyramid; but this I positively refused, as I thought it would not be fair and right that he should pay for what he had nothing to do with.

I had the pleasure of accompanying the Colonel in a visit to the pyramid, as described by himself in his account of his journey from India to England through Egypt. He had suffered many hardships on his journey, but did not appear fatigued in the least. His short stay in Cairo did not permit me to write a full account of my labours; but at night I made a hasty sketch as well as I could, and addressed it to the Antiquarian Society of London, which he was kind enough to take to England for me. Mr. Salt, the consul, took the same opportunity of sending an official account of my operations in Egypt and Nubia to the ministers in England, I suppose because he had no opportunity of sending any correct account before that time.

My next and principal object was to make a small collection on my own account, and to take drawings of the tomb of Psammethis, with impressions in wax of all the figures, emblems, and hieroglyphics, the whole of which are in basso relievo; noting the colours exactly as in the originals, so as to enable me to erect a facsimile in any part of Europe. This project deserved my serious consideration, not only in calculating the time that it would require to complete it, but the expense I must incur. However, though I was only in Cairo, I did not want means of finding supplies for what I intended to execute, and in a few days all was ready for my departure on my third voyage up the Nile; when, having arranged my affairs with the consul, I set off for my old habitation among the tombs of Thebes.

END OF THE SECOND JOURNEY.

RESEARCHES AND OPERATIONS
IN
EGYPT, NUBIA, &c.

THIRD JOURNEY.

In the narrative of this my third journey to Thebes, I shall not detain the reader with an account of my stopping here or setting off there, as it would be no more than a repetition of what has been said before;—but shall remark only the principal things worthy of notice. I made an extraordinary quick voyage from Cairo to Melawi, which place we reached in two days and a half, though it occupied eighteen days in our second voyage. I stopped two days at Mr. Brine's, the sugar-baker, as it was a calm, and in two days more arrived at Siout. The next morning I went to see the Bey, that worthy fellow and dear friend to the English. He was about a mile out of town, exercising his soldiers and young Mamelukes in gunnery and horsemanship. The cannon exercise was with balls against the rocks; and, I must say, there were better marksmen than I expected to find among soldiers without discipline. He fired himself at the same mark with two balls in one barrel of an English gun, of which some one in Cairo had made him a present. He liked it extremely; and observed, " These guns may become offensive to their makers some day or other." I told him, if ever such a period should arrive, the English would still be superior in their weapons, as by that time they would have invented some guns of another construction, much superior to the most effective of the present day, as they are continually studying something new. I saw he was not pleased with my answer; but I said it, and would have said it again. After the cannon exercise, they began to fire at an earthen pot placed on a kind of pedestal of about six feet high. They commence their course at two hundred feet from it; ride towards it at full gallop; at the distance of fifty feet drop the bridle, take their gun, and fire at the pot while at full speed. The horse is so accustomed to this, that, before he reaches the stand on which the pot is, he wheels to the right, to make room for the next in the course. It is a very difficult matter to hit a small pot about a foot high, while the horse is running with all speed. In about two hundred shots I saw only six pots broken: the favourite Mameluke of the Bey, a lad of twelve years old, broke three. He had the best horse belonging to the Bey, and went as near the pot as the length of a gun and a half. Two other Mamelukes broke one each at a good distance, and one was broken by the Bey himself, for which he received of course great praise from all his subjects. The gold and silver on the riders gave them quite a theatrical appearance. When the exercise was ended, the Bey seated himself under a tree, and was very curious to know the particulars of my opening the pyramid, as he had heard of it, and desired to see a plan. As I was to visit him in the afternoon, I promised he should then see one.

At four o'clock I went to his palace. He was sitting on a very high armed chair, a fashion not common among Turks; though he did not sit like an European, but in the Turkish manner, with his legs up. Here I had an opportunity of being present at a trial upon life or death. The case was this: a soldier belonging to the Bey had been found dead upon the road near the village of Acmin, with his throat cut, and several marks of violence upon his body. He was on his return from Mecca, where he had been on a pilgrimage. His camel was found dead near the door of a peasant, and it was supposed that he had a great deal of money about him. He was seen in the house of the peasant, near which the camel was found, in company with seven other men, among whom was a Bedoween. The soldiers of the village, who took the prisoners into custody, asserted, that the prisoners had assisted the Bedoween in making his escape; and the Sheik of the same village affirmed, that one of them said he knew where to find him at any time. Several witnesses were examined, but no one gave any evidence that could bring the facts home to the supposed culprits.

One point, however, was very much against one of them, and this was, his countenance did not please the Bey; for no sooner did the Bey set his eyes on the poor fellow, than he exclaimed, " O ho! the case is evident! I see plainly who is the murderer; look at that man; can there be any doubt but it was he who committed the crime? So own at once that you did it, for denial will be useless; I see it in your face!" I must confess, I never saw more appearance of the assassin in a countenance in my life; but God forbid, that our courts of justice should adopt such a method of proceeding, and condemn people merely because the expression of their features is against them. Several witnesses came forward to prove, that the peasant, in whose house the soldier was, could have had nothing to do with it, as he was not in the town at the time. I have reason to believe, that witnesses in that country are rather more exact in their depositions than those of Europe, for they do not get off so easily as in our country. To make them impartial they generally get so severe a bastinado on the soles of their feet, that all the flesh is off to the bones, and they are unable to walk for a long time after. A thousand blows is reckoned a moderate number for a witness to receive. The business ended this day with beating and sending to prison again. I heard afterwards, however, that several of those supposed to be concerned in the murder had their heads cut off; but for this I have no further authority than my own interpreter.

After the trial the Bey sent to me, as if he were desirous of some conversation. I took the interpreter with me, as the Bey will speak no language but the Turkish, and seated myself on the bench near his chair. He began to talk again about the pyramids, and wondered we could not tell when they were built. He wished to be made acquainted with things, but in such a manner that his ignorance might not be perceived, asking questions as if he were already informed of what he was most anxious to learn. I showed him the plan of the second pyramid. He understood it immediately, as he said, taking a general view of it without inquiring into a single circumstance. As I knew he passed for an architect among the Turks, I took a pair of compasses, and showed him the scale of English feet, by which the plan was made. The word scale was mistaken for the Italian *scala*, and he asked me where a person mounted with that scale; and the interpreter, who was as curious as himself, asked nearly the same question. I could not help smiling, and turned the discourse to the forced passage, on which he rightly observed, that they who made it must have been in search of gold, or else they would not have given themselves so much trouble, with some similar remarks. I quitted him that evening, as it was rather late, being half an hour after sunset, and went to him to take my leave the next morning. I had a firman for him to renew, and to my surprise he did it without hesitation. He seemed to be pleased when he was told, that I was going to make a collection for myself, for which reason, as he said, he had given me the firman with full power to dig wherever I pleased, right and left of the Nile. I answered, that I felt much obliged to him, but that I hoped he would consider what I did for myself would be still for the English party. He made no reply to this, but I could easily see, that he felt a kind of displeasure at my returning to search as connected with the English. I wish Mr. Salt had been there incog, as he would have seen the difference of this man when behind his back, from what it had been before his face. He introduced the little story of the pipe made by Caliud, and sold as an antique to Mr. Salt; laughed much, and wondered how a person so full of knowledge could suffer himself to be so easily deceived by a Frenchman. I told him, that any one might well be deceived, as we bought many things from the peasants, good and bad together in lots, without even looking to see what they were, till they were brought home; consequently this pipe might have been bought in that manner. He asked me many curious questions, and among them, whether I should shave my beard when I returned to Europe, supposing my answer would be, that I should not do any such thing; for my beard appeared the finest of all that were before him at that moment, even superior to his own. I told him, to his astonishment, that no sooner should I reach the shore of my dear Europe, than I should rid myself of it as a great burden. He saw he had got himself into a scrape, by exposing the sanctity of the beard, to be despised before so many of his bearded countrymen, by asking such questions of a Christian; and thinking to mend the matter, as some of the French told him that in France many wear their beards, he said he knew that in France many people wore them, but did not know whether it was so in England. I replied, that neither in France, England, nor in any part of Europe, except by a few of the Russians, were beards ever worn. This sort of disrespect for beards did not appear to meet the approbation of the assembly, and he was glad to turn the discourse upon horses, &c.

Having received my firman, I left Siout the same day, and on the next arrived at Tacta. This I recollected was the residence of my old acquaintance Soliman Cacheff of Erments, who played me so many tricks; but as in the latter part of his command in that province he became our friend, at least in appearance, I thought proper to pay him a friendly visit, as, according to the way of thinking of the Turks, an injury is not easily forgotten, and sometimes revenge is taken, when the offender is in disgrace or in misfortune. I do not know whether this man were pleased at seeing me in his hut, as perhaps he might be mortified at the supposition, that I must recollect his prejudice, and the trouble he had given me: certain however it is, that he received me with all the marks of cordiality, that can be expected from a Turk. He gave me to understand, that as the deficiency found in his account with the Bashaw was nearly made good out of his monthly pay, his employ would be soon ended, when he should be a free man, and could go where he pleased; and if the Bashaw did not come to good terms with him, he would go to a place above Ibrim. Knowing he meant to Dongola, to the Mamelukes, I told him, that his highness the Bashaw was a worthy man, and if some friends of his in Cairo were to speak to him, all would end well. He said he expected, that the French consul would have done something for him, from his friendly professions, but he was disappointed; and added many other things, but all of trivial importance. At a moment when we remained alone however, even without the interpreter, he told me, in the Arabic language, that he should be under great obligations to our consul, if he would speak to the Bashaw in his favour; and that he might be assured he would gladly come to an understanding with him, as he had made great improvements in the lands, from which the Bashaw derived considerable advantages; but above all, as his debt was paid with the khasna or treasury. I promised I would do all I could for him; and sometime after I wrote all the particulars to Mr. Salt, acquainting him, that, if he could succeed in getting this man restored to his situation at Erments, he might depend on having a good friend in the commander of Thebes. I could scarcely get away from him; he sent his horses and soldiers to accompany me to the water-side; and on board our cangiar I found the customary provision of bread, a sheep, &c.

Proceeding on my voyage, the next day at about a league before we reached Acmin, on the 5th of May, 1818, at eight o'clock in the morning, I saw the finest eclipse I ever beheld. The moon at its full passed completely before the sun. The eclipse lasted about three-quarters of an hour. I saw the full moon in the centre of the sun, which formed a disc or ring; the moon appeared to me in the proportion of about half the size of the sun.

On the 10th of May I arrived at Thebes, and immediately proceeded to take the drawings of the tombs and impressions, as I stated before.

In the arrangement I had made with Mr. Salt previously to my re-ascending the Nile this time, it was agreed, that I should make researches on my own account: but on my arrival at Thebes I found, that all the grounds on each side of the Nile were taken, partly by Mr. Drouetti's agents, and partly by Mr. Salt himself, who marked the grounds before his return to Cairo this last time. Seeing that there was no chance of making any researches on my own account, without incurring the risk of some difference either

P P

with the French party or the English, I retired to my tomb, and devoted my whole time to taking models of it.

It is somewhat singular, and by no means pleasing to my recollection, that at this time I was at Thebes on my own account, and at my own expense, yet with less chance of finding any thing, than a perfect stranger who had never been in that country. A stranger might come, fix on a spot of ground, and take his chance, whether good or ill. My case was different; for if I pointed out any spot in any place whatever, one of the parties, I mean the agents of Mr. Drouetti or those of Mr. Salt, would consider it as valuable ground, and protest that it was taken by them long before. I verily believe, if I had pointed out one of the sand banks or the solid rocks, they would have said they just intended to have broken into it the next day: being however in the midst of Thebes, a place which was become to me quite familiar, and accustomed as I had been to continual researches, I could scarcely keep myself from doing something. I had already tried on an exhausted ground, known to have been originally opened by me, so that no one could say it was taken by them; but I soon perceived, that it was a hopeless attempt to proceed on spots which I considered as exhausted.

Between the Memnonium and Medinet Aboo, it is well known there are several fragments of enormous statues; particularly behind the two colossi. I had long before marked this ground, and Mr. Drouetti first opened near these fragments; but finding nothing except broken pieces of lion-headed statues, he quitted it. Sometime after Mr. Salt began to excavate in this ground while I was in Cairo, and found it to be the site of an extensive temple. There are pedestals of many columns of very large diameter and in great numbers. I counted about thirty, but it appears they are not half uncovered, and among them Mr. Salt found several colossal fragments of breccia and calcareous stone, but all so mutilated, that none were worth taking away. He proceeded in his work for a long time, but left the spot at last, I believe, as unworthy of farther labour. On mentioning my wish to proceed in my researches in the same place to Mr. Beechey, he informed me, that it was reserved for the consul, as it had been dug before on his account and under his own inspection. But such was my hope of discovering something of importance, that I determined to proceed, whether for my advantage or that of the consul.

I accordingly commenced my operations, and having observed, that the part where the sekos and cella must be was not touched, I set the men to work there. It was perhaps fortune that would have it so; but the fact is, that on the very second day of my researches we came to a large statue, which proved to be the finest of the kind I had yet found. It is a sitting figure of a man, in all points resembling the great colossus of Memnon. On the side of its chair are the same hieroglyphics, which are to be seen on the chair of the Memnon. It is nearly ten feet high, and of the most beautiful Egyptian workmanship. The stone is gray granite, and has the peculiarity of having particles in it of a colour not unlike that of the substance generally known by the name of Dutch metal. This and a lion-headed statue are the only ones of the kind I ever saw. Part of its chin and beard have been knocked off, but all the rest is quite perfect. In the same ground I found several lion-headed statues, like those I found in Carnak, some sitting and some standing.

I know not what to say about this temple, as I do not pretend to give an absolute decision on any subject; but as every one may have an opinion of his own, I shall venture to make a few remarks, or rather put some questions. Why may not this be deemed the great temple of Memnon, with as much, or perhaps more reason, than what is now named the Memnonium? It is to be observed, that the name was given to those ruins on the supposition that the great colossal statue now lying on the ground within the space included was that of Memnon; but now, when every one agrees that the statue of Memnon cannot be any other than that which is to the north of the two in the plain between Medinet Aboo and the Memnonium, I think that the temple, which stood in a direct line with these colossi, might with more probability be named the Memnonium. That the northernmost statue of the two in the plain of Gournou was that from which the sound proceeded I believe is beyond doubt, from the combination of numerous circumstances, but in particular from the testimony of the many visitors, who have verified it by their inscriptions on its leg. If the said statue were intended to represent the Great Memnon, I think the temple with which it was connected was the Memnonium. The magnificence of this edifice has never been described, because it never was seen or known to exist. Between the two colossal statues and the portico of the temple is an enormous colossus, thrown down and buried, all but the back of its chair, which is broken in two about the middle. I cannot conceive how this colossus escaped the notice of travellers. It was one of my principal objects to uncover it, but I never had an opportunity. I have no doubt some interesting points may be solved, and perhaps pieces of antiquity may be found in it; and I hope this opinion of mine will induce some of the travellers or other antiquaries in Egypt to excavate the interesting spot round the colossus. Among the columns of the portico were found a great many fragments of colossal statues of granite, breccia, and calcareous stones; and from the great number of fragments of smaller dimensions, and of standing and sitting lion-headed statues, I can boldly state, that these ruins appear to me to have belonged to the most magnificent temple of any on the west side of Thebes. It is my humble opinion, that the entrance into this temple was guarded by the two colossi, one of which is supposed to have represented the Great Memnon; and that on advancing farther there were other colossal statues in inner courts, the fragments of which are still to be seen, as I have just mentioned, in a line with the temple and the two colossi. In the front of the portico are other colossi, of smaller size, which appear as if adorning the entrance into it. The whole combined induces me to think, that an extensive temple stood on this ground. To explore it would require an excavation of no small extent; but I believe it well worth attention, and I am persuaded it would not prove a disadvantageous speculation to the adventurer. The base of the above columns stood much higher than the bases of the two colossi, consequently there must be an ascent from the colossi to the temple. If we take as an example the temple called the Memnonium, we shall find the same to be the case, and that the ascent into the temple was by steps. On my removing the colossal statue from the ruins last mentioned, I found that the pavement of the place where it lay was much lower than the interior of the temple; whence we may conclude that the former temple was erected on the same principle; and if it were so, the front of this temple is not uncovered; and I do not hesitate to say, that some interesting pieces of antiquity might be found there, beside perhaps giving farther elucidation of the real seat of Memnon. It is also to be observed, that the regular inundation of the Nile over that very ground has raised the soil to such a height, that it discourages a traveller from making researches; but without perseverance nothing can be effected. My occupation at the tomb did not permit me to advance farther in these researches, and I quitted them with the intention of recommencing, when I should have had an interview with Mr. Salt; for, as he had marked all this ground to be kept for his own excavation, I did not wish to encroach on his Thebean territory.

The works at the tomb went on uncommonly well. By this time I had taken many impressions of the principal figures in basso relievo to my entire satisfaction. The wax alone I found would not stand, as the climate did not permit it; but with wax, resin, and fine dust, I made an excellent composition. The greatest difficulty was to take the impression of the figure without injuring the colours of it. The figures as large as life I found to be in all a hundred and eighty-two: those of a smaller size, from one to three feet, I did not count, but they cannot be less than eight hundred. The hieroglyphics in this tomb are nearly five hundred, of which I took a faithful copy, with their colours; but they are of four different sizes, from one to six inches; so that I have been obliged to take one of each size, which makes nearly two thousand in all. Some wax I procured in the small towns of the country, but in such small quantities, that I was obliged to send down the Nile to Kenneh, Farshiout, and Girgeh.

At the latter end of June we had a visit from Mr. Briggs, on his return from India. He brought with him from that country the pine-apple and the mango, some of which he had planted in the garden of the Aga at Kenneh, and some he tried to cultivate at Thebes. The mango at Kenneh I believe turned out very well; but those which were planted in Thebes died, I imagine from want of care, as we had no gardener.

By this time I had ceased all sort of researches. As I could not dig on the grounds I wished, I contented myself with collecting what the peasants of Gournou used to bring to me; and I must say, that in consequence of having so many acquaintances among these mummy plunderers, I have been able to make a little collection of my own, in which I can boast of having a few good articles, particularly in manuscript, &c.

During this time, I attempted to make an excavation among the ruins of the temple at Erments, but I was soon convinced it would be to no purpose, and withdrew. This temple is very interesting, for it differs from almost every other in its plan and construction. The drawing, Plate 37, is as correct a representation as I could take of it. On the back of this temple is the figure of the camelopard, which is of such very rare occurrence among the hieroglyphics, that this, and that which I mentioned in the sekos of the Memnonium, are the only instances I can point out in Egypt.

MOTIVE OF MY JOURNEY TO THE RED SEA.

Some time prior to this, the Bashaw of Egypt was informed by two Copts, who landed on the coast of the Red Sea from Arabia, that they had seen some sulphur mines in the mountains near that shore, several days journey above Cosseir. On the report of these two men, the Bashaw sent an order to the Cacheff of Esne to enter the desert in search of those mines. He set off with an escort of soldiers, and sixty camels to load with sulphur, but on their arrival, they found only several pieces scattered about here and there, and having collected them all, they were not sufficient to load twenty camels. Among the soldiers of that escort was one of the Mameluke renegadoes, who stated, that he saw several mines and temples on the road to the coast of the Red Sea.

This little success did not discourage Mahomed Ali, who was always ready to persevere in any enterprise. He was advised to send some Europeans to examine these places, and see whether it were worth while to proceed in the discovery of sulphur. Mr.

Drouetti recommended to the Bashaw Mr. Caliud, a silversmith, who had been employed by him some time in the collection of antiquities. Mr. Caliud set off for that place, accompanied by an escort of soldiers and miners from Syria, and found the mines as steril as they had been described; but on his return he did not fail to visit the emerald mountains, according to the instructions he received from Mr. Drouetti, who evidently had seen the work of Bruce, where he mentions having visited these mines. On his arrival at the place, Mr. Caliud found several caves or mines, which had been evidently left by the ancients, and probably had never been touched by any one since. From the exterior of some of them he collected several pieces of the matrix of the emeralds; and when these were produced to the Bashaw, they were deemed sufficient to prove, that there were mines in the country, and to persuade Mahomed Ali to pursue his researches. Mr. Caliud in his pursuit of mines in this country happened to reach Sakial-Minor, situated in a valley, a few miles from the mountain of Zabara, and about twenty-five from the sea (See Plate 35).

It is a valley surrounded by high rocks. On each side of the rocks, at some little distance, are the remains of a few very small houses, built of rough stones, and all except one or two without mortar. The rocks of this place resemble an amphitheatre in form, not more than two hundred and fifty yards in length. The upper part of the rocks contains several mines of the ancients, and at one side there is a small chapel cut out of the rock, thirty feet deep, and less than twenty wide (See Plate 33, Nos. 6 and 7). The houses in all, as we counted them on our visiting that place, are eighty-seven, one only of which can be considered as the residence of a person distinguished from the rest. I do not know how it happened, but it appears, that the enthusiasm with which Monsieur Caliud gave the account of this place, seemed to impress on the minds of the antiquaries in Egypt the notion that it must have been the ancient Berenice, especially when he reported it to have eight hundred houses and several temples, and seemed to him in appearance like the ruins of Pompeia, &c. He asserted also, that it was near the coast, and that the communication with the sea was quite easy. At the same time he produced a Greek inscription, which we also found on the top of a niche: we copied it with the greatest care, and it will be inserted hereafter. This was quite enough. The ancient Berenice had at last been visited, and it was known where it was. Indeed, in a few points it did not quite agree with the situation described by the ancients; but these obstacles were soon removed, for I saw a modern geographer, a man of classical education, and a great traveller, take the pen in his hand, and, in order to make the newly discovered Berenice fall on the spot where it ought to be, and accord with the description of the ancient geographer, scratch out a large cape that incumbered him, being on the south of the supposed Berenice, and with the same coolness as if it had been a piece at draughts or chess, place it on the north; affirming that the bay was erroneously laid down by the ancient geographers, who made the chart of the Red Sea.

In the description of the mines Mr. Caliud was pretty correct, but it would have been more to his credit, if he had contented himself with an exact account of the new Berenice, as it was named. In consequence of all these reports Mahomed Ali engaged a Mahomedan Aga, a Syrian miner, and, with two hundred men, set off accompanied by Mr. Caliud, to show him where he found the ancient mines. Some time after, Mr. Caliud, finding that the mines would not be so productive as it was expected, quitted the place and returned to Egypt, leaving the Syrian miner to look out for the emeralds.

From the time of these reports I conceived the idea of making an excursion into these deserts on a visit to the new Berenice, and only waited the opportunity of a proper time, to execute my intended journey.

It happened, that near the end of September, one of the miners, who was sent from the mountains to the Nile for provision, had to come down from Edfu to Esne, and was returning to the desert, when he fell sick. Hearing from some of the Arabs, that a christian physician was at Beban el Malook, he came to beg the doctor would prescribe something to cure him. Of course I had good and clear information of all I wished from this man, who promised to show me the way through the desert, if I wished to go. I made up my mind at once, and set about preparing for my departure. Having communicated my intention to Mr. Beechey, he resolved to go also, and as the doctor would have been useful in drawing, I proposed that he should accompany us.

At this time we had a large boat loaded with antiquities of various kinds, among which I embarked the fine colossal statue I had discovered in the ruins of the temple, which I should name the Memnonium. The boat being ready, a servant of Mr. Drouetti requested Mr. Beechey to be permitted to take his passage on board to Cairo, which was of course granted. The boat set off. By the information I received from the miner, it appeared to me clear, that the place could not agree with the description given of its situation by Herodotus and Pliny; and that the direction of the road Monsieur Caliud had taken could not bring him so far south, as the town of Berenice was marked by the geographer D'Anville, who I had reason to believe was correct, having found him so on other occasions. At last, two days after the boat set off for Cairo, we hired a smaller one from Luxor, to take us up to Edfu, where we were to enter the desert. We embarked near the temple of Gournou, as the water reached quite to that place.

Accordingly we set sail on the 16th of September, 1818. Our company consisted of Mr. Beechey, the doctor, and myself, two Greek servants, the miner, and two boys from Gournou, whom we hired to take care of our luggage in the desert.

It so happened, that we were to witness one of the greatest calamities that have occurred in Egypt in the recollection of any one living. The Nile rose this season three feet and a half above the highest mark left by the former inundation, with uncommon rapidity, and carried off several villages and some hundreds of their inhabitants.

I never saw any picture that could give a more correct idea of a deluge than the valley of the Nile in this season. The Arabs had expected an extraordinary inundation this year, in consequence of the scarcity of water the preceding season; but they did not apprehend it would rise to such a height. They generally erect fences of earth and reeds around their villages, to keep the water from their houses; but the force of this inundation baffled all their efforts. Their cottages, being built of earth, could not stand one instant against the current, and no sooner did the water reach them, than it levelled them with the ground. The rapid stream carried off all that was before it; men, women, children, cattle, corn, every thing was washed away in an instant, and left the place where the village stood without any thing to indicate that there had ever been a house on the spot. It is not the case, as is generally supposed, that all the villages of Egypt are raised so high above the general level of the ground, that the water cannot reach them; on the contrary, most of those in Upper Egypt are little if any thing higher than the rest of the ground, and the only way they have to keep off the water on the rise of the Nile, is by artificial fences made of earth and reeds. It appeared to me to be in the midst of a vast lake containing various islands and magnificent edifices. On our right we had the high rocks and the temples of Gournou, the Memnonium, the extensive buildings of Medinet Aboo, and the two colossal statues, which arose out of the water like the lighthouses on some of the coasts of Europe. On our left we had the vast ruins of Carnak and Luxor; to the east of which, at a distance of eight miles, ran the Mokattam chain of mountains, forming the boundaries of this vast lake as it appeared from our boat.

The first village we came to was Agalta, whither we went not merely to see the place but to desire the Caimakan to send a soldier to guard the tombs, in addition to the Arabs, and some of our people, whom we had left there. I thought this necessary, notwithstanding the strong door I had caused to be made at its entrance. He appeared immediately on our approaching the village, and greatly lamented his situation, as he expected to be washed away by the Nile. There was no boat in the village; and should the water break down their weak fences, the only chance of escape was by climbing the palm-trees, till Providence sent some one to their relief. All the boats were employed in carrying away the corn from villages that were in danger. Both in Upper and Lower Egypt the men, women, and children are left to be the last assisted, as their lives are not so valuable as corn, which brings money to the Bashaw. As this village was then four feet below the water, the poor Fellahs were on the watch day and night round their fences. They employed their skin machines or bags to throw the water out again which rose from under the ground; but if their fences should be broken down all was lost. We offered to take the Caimakan with us in our boat, but he could not quit the place which he was ordered to guard. When we left this village there was but little wind, so we did not proceed much farther, and in the evening made fast our boat to some high ground between Agalta and Erments.

On the 17th we saw several villages in great danger of being destroyed. The rapid stream had carried away the fences, and their unfortunate inhabitants were obliged to escape to higher grounds, where it was possible, with what they could save from the water. The distress of these people was great. Some of them had only a few feet of land, and the water was to rise twelve days more, and after that to remain twelve days at its height, according to the usual term of the inundation. Fortunate was he who could reach a high ground. Some crossed the water on pieces of wood, some on buffaloes or cows, and others with reeds tied up in large bundles. The small spots of high ground, that stood above the water, formed so many sanctuaries for these poor refugees, and were crowded with people and beasts (See Plate 26). The scanty stock of provision they could save was the only subsistence they could expect. In some parts the water had left scarcely any dry ground, and no relief could be hoped till four and twenty days had elapsed. The Cacheffs and Caimakans of the country did all they could to assist the villages with their little boats, but they were so small in proportion to what was wanted, that they could not relieve the greater part of the unfortunate people. It was distressing to behold these poor wretches in such a situation. To approach them in our little boat would have been dangerous both to them and to us, for so many would enter it at once, that the boat would sink, and we along with them, to increase the number. On our arrival at Erments, where fortunately the land is very high, we found many of the neighbouring people collected. We landed immediately, and employed our boat to fetch the people from an opposite village. The Caimakan set off himself with another boat, and in the course of an hour he returned with several men and boys. He sent the boats again, and they returned loaded with men, corn, and cattle. The third trip brought still more corn, buffaloes, sheep, goats, asses, and dogs. I remarked, that there were no women in that village; but we were soon convinced of the regard paid to the fair sex in that country. The fourth voyage was employed in fetching over the women, as the last and most insignificant of their property, whose loss would have been less regretted than that of the cattle. I hope this circumstance will convince the European fair sex of our superiority over the Turks and Arabs, at least in point of due respect to them.

These people say, that women have no souls; and indeed, by the brutal manner in which they are treated, we cannot expect such poor creatures to have any.

On the 18th we arrived in Esne. Khalil Bey was gone to Cairo, to take the command of the province of Benesouef; and Ibrahim Bey was now governor of Esne. He received us with uncommon civility, and furnished us with a firman to the Cacheff who commanded the province of Edfu. On our return on board we found some bread, greens, and a sheep, sent by the Bey, for which we returned a fine English gun and some powder. At our desire, he sent us a soldier, to accompany us wherever we went, but he gave strict orders that we should not take any of the emeralds from the mines; for, though he was the most civilized Turk I ever knew, he could not help supposing, that we did not go into these deserts merely to see the mountains and the sand. He imagined, that, if we came where the mines were, we should naturally help ourselves to emeralds, which he thought would be worthy our notice. We set off on the next day, and arrived at the island of Hovasee before Edfu.

It was rather late in the evening; and on our approach to the fences which surrounded the village to keep off the water, we alarmed the Fellahs so much, that they all came to the spot where we were, made us proceed up to a place where there was no danger of injuring the fence, and kept strict watch over us all night. They were certainly right; for if our boat had struck against the fence, it would have inevitably made a breach, and, of course, inundated the village and the rest of the land.

On the 21st, in the morning, we all went to the Cacheff, who did what he could to procure us every thing necessary. He sent for the Sheik of the tribe that inhabited the deserts we had to pass. His name was Abada; and he was a hostage for the security of the people that worked at the mines near the Red Sea. We made our arrangements about the camels and drivers, and found the terms very reasonable; for we paid only one piastre a day for every camel, and twenty paras for every man; out of which they were to provide food both for themselves and their beasts. It was agreed, that we should keep the camels as long as we pleased, and go wherever we thought proper. We crossed part of the island with the boat, as there were four feet water above the banks, and went on shore on the east side of the main land. On our arrival we met with Mohammed Aga, the chief of the miners, who had just arrived from the emerald mountains, and was repairing to Esne. He seemed to be much concerned at our going thither, and would fain have persuaded us to wait till he returned, that he might accompany us, as no one could go to the place without him. We told him not to be alarmed, for we were not in search of precious stones, but of antiquities. This did not appear to satisfy him, and he said he would soon be back again. We remained the rest of the day, waiting while the drivers prepared bread for their journey.

In the morning of the 22d there was no appearance of departure. I had observed a sudden change in the Sheik since he saw the chief miner, and began to suppose, that his influence still prevailed on the Sheik to detain us at least as much as he could. The miner himself had proposed, that we should wait at the ruins of a temple, about two days on our journey, till his return; to which proposal of course we did not agree. I saw clearly he was not a little alarmed at our going, for fear we should make some discovery among the minerals; and all our assertions to the contrary had little effect. We insisted on setting off that day, and we did so the same evening.

Our party was increased by the soldier from Esne, four camel-drivers, and a Sheik to guide us, making in all twelve men. We had sixteen camels, six of which were laden with provisions, water, culinary utensils, &c. We halted at the foot of a hill three hours distance.

In the morning of the 23d we set off very early, and arrived at the first well in three hours. Here the camel-drivers informed us, that we could not advance till Sheik Ibrahim joined us, as he had to bring us more food for the camels. We had been waiting the whole day with impatience, but without seeing any body. The valley we entered afforded a good level road, till we came to the foot of the mountain, about fifteen miles from the Nile. We were seated under a dry sunt tree, at a little distance from a small well. Hot winds, that raised the sand, blew the whole day. Several of the Ababde came to water their cattle at the well, but kept at a distance from us. They live scattered about in the rocks and little valleys among the mountains, but occasionally assemble together in a few minutes. To pass this place without a good understanding with their Sheik for security would be imprudent and dangerous. Finding that the guide did not arrive in the evening, we sent one of the drivers to the Sheik, requesting him to send the man immediately, otherwise, if he were not with us at sunrise, we should return, and complain to the Cacheff.

At length, on the next morning, the 24th, he appeared, and we set off pretty early. The valley we now entered afforded a very level and good road. There are in it several sunt and sycamore trees, and in various places the thorny plant called basillah, represented in Plate 36. This is the plant on which the camels feed. It is of a green colour at a certain season of the year, I believe in the spring; but it soon becomes dry, and, of course, of a straw colour. It bears a small fruit of the size of a pea, but hollow inside. The stalk is of a similar substance with that of rushes, and it never grows higher than three feet. As we advanced, the valley became narrow, and the trees thicker in some places; but they gradually diminished, and at last we entirely lost them. On the right of the valley as we went up I observed the remains of a settlement, which I considered as a station for the ancient caravans from the Nile to Berenice, of which we afterwards found many others on the road, placed at proper distances for the caravans to halt at night. At some of them it is evident there were wells of good water, but they are now quite filled up. Advancing farther, the mountains approach till the valley becomes little else than a wide road; and after passing a narrow and high defile we entered an open plain. Here the mountains on the right run towards the south, and after a long circuit return to form a valley with those on the left. At the entrance of this valley stands a high rock, on the left of which is a small Egyptian temple. To this we now directed our course, and arrived at it six hours after setting off from the well in the morning.

On our approaching it we were not a little pleased at the sight. It is of small magnitude, as will be seen in Plate 20. The plan of it is given in Plate 33, No. 3. The portico, which is built projecting from the rock, has four columns, two in front and two in the centre. It is adorned with Egyptian figures in intaglio relievato, and some retain their colour pretty well. They are as large as life, and not of the worst execution. In the sekos, which is cut out of

R R

the rock, are four pilasters. At the end of it are three small chambers; and there are two others, one at each side, in the corners of the lateral walls, on which are to be seen figures and hieroglyphics in a pretty good style. On one of the columns we observed a Greek inscription, which I did not copy, as Mr. Beechey took the trouble himself*. I made the drawing of the exterior view of the temple stone by stone. The two front columns are joined to the sides of the portico by a wall nearly two thirds of their height. Near the temple are the remains of an enclosure, which no doubt was a station for the caravans; but it is totally different from any other that we met with on that road as far as Berenice. It consists of a wall, the form and extent of which may be seen in Plate 33, No. 4. It was built by the Greeks, is twelve feet high, and contained several houses within it for the accommodation of travellers. In the centre was a well, which is now filled up with sand. All round the well there is a platform or gallery, raised six feet high, on which a guard of soldiers might walk all round. On the upper part of the wall are holes for discharging arrows, similar to those we see formed in our ancient buildings for the same purpose. The sides of the gateways are built of calcareous stones, and the wall is of bricks. By this time I was convinced, that this must have been a road to some place of consequence, as it was obvious, that there was a frequent passage of caravans this way. The place is named Wady el Meeah. The fort, I think, must have been built by some of the Ptolemies, to protect the caravans, at the time when the trade with India, by the way of Berenice and the Red Sea, flourished.

At three o'clock in the morning of the 25th, we continued our

* The inscription taken by Mr. Beechey cannot be inserted, as, when that gentleman returned to London, he unfortunately doubted whether he had copied it correctly enough to be published.

journey. No vegetation of any sort was to be seen any where. Sometimes we passed over wide and level plains, and sometimes crossed rugged hills, till two hours before sunset, when we entered the valley called Beezak by the Arabs. This valley runs from south to north, and has several sunt trees scattered about in it, and the usual thorn. Here we halted for the night, and while our cook prepared our supper, Mr. Beechey and I went to see a granite rock at some distance, as the Ababde had informed us, that there was a magical stone there. We entered the valley toward the north, and observed, that it must have been an ancient road, as the usual marks of camels' feet were clearly impressed on the ground. There is seldom any sand on these roads; on the contrary they are covered with small pebbles, and where the passage of camels was frequent, they formed a strong impression, which is to be seen to this day, and may be traced to great length through those valleys till they reach the sandy country. When we arrived at the rock, we found it to be of fine granite in very large masses. On one side of it are several figures cut on the stone, which cannot be taken for any other than imitations of the Egyptian. They are meanly scrawled, without shape or form, but, united with the circumstance of the camels' paths, they are sufficient to indicate, that the valley was a high road, which, by the direction it takes, must have been that from Coptos to Berenice, so well described by D'Anville. At this place Mr. Ricci, the doctor, was attacked with a violent disorder, and it was decided, that he should return the next morning, as it would increase if he advanced farther in the desert.

On the 26th, in the morning, our caravan was divided into three different detachments. We sent the luggage and provision on the way toward the east, which we intended to take; the doctor returned toward the Nile on the west; Mr. Beechey and myself went in a south-east direction, to see something that the Ababde mentioned, though we could not make out what they meant. We entered a sandy valley with rocks on each side nearly perpendicular, of white and calcareous grit-stone, with some veins of white marble intermixed. After some hours' march we reached a place named Samount; here we found the remains of an ancient settlement or station, which appears, by its situation, to have been on the road from Berenice to Coptos.

It has several pieces of walls, which are the only remains, and evidently a well in the centre (See Plate 33, No. 5). The walls are built of rough stones without mortar.

We took the road to the east through several beautiful and romantic valleys, if so they may be called. The soil was sandy and stony, but there are thorny plants to feed cattle, and so many sunt trees, as to form a complete forest in some parts. The rocks on each side are of divers colours, exhibiting the most beautiful and solitary scenes. One who wishes to retire from the world might find a charming retreat in these wilds, were it not for the want of water and all that is necessary to the subsistence of human life, beside the intense heat of the sun, which on calm days is so great in these valleys, as to be almost insupportable. Advancing onward, in three hours we reached a summit, whence we saw at some distance what appeared to be the walls of a large and extensive town, surrounded by high rocks, as if by a fortification. On our approach we saw it was an extensive sandy plain, with several granite eminences. The rocks rose at some distance from each other, and appeared like so many little islands. If the sand had been water, I could not have distinguished this spot from the centre of the cataract, I mean from above Syene to the island of Philœ. This place seemed to me as if I were passing the cataract, with the difference only, that I had a camel instead of a boat, and the granite appeared to be of a finer quality than that of the cataract, approaching to porphyry. If the ancients did not make any use of it, it was no doubt in consequence of the difficulty of conveying it to the Nile.

From this place we travelled to the left toward the valley where it was intended we should halt. Our caravan had reached the place an hour before us, though we proceeded very fast on our march. Here we found two wells, one of salt water, and the other quite putrid and brackish. There are few waters in the world better than that of the Nile; and now to have to drink the worst was such a change in one day, that we could not help feeling the consequences of it. Mr. Beechey was taken very ill, from drinking at the first well, and we had great apprehension of the next, which was worse. We had provision for a month, but our fresh meat was gone, and it was with difficulty we could procure a very lean goat. The tribe of this country are all Ababde, and extend from the confines of Suez to the tribe of Bisharein, on the coast of the Red Sea, below the latitude of 23°. The manners of this race show them to be lovers of freedom: they prefer living among these solitary rocks and deserts, where they eat nothing but dhourra and drink water, before submission to the command of any government on earth. It is a great feast among them when they take the resolution of killing a lean goat, but they eat it without fearing, that any rapacious hands should take it from them. A man of this stamp, accustomed to liberty and independence, would naturally find himself as in a prison, if under the control of even the best of governments. Their greatest care is for their camels, which are their support. They breed them up to a certain growth, and then send them to be exchanged for dhourra, which constitutes their food. The camels, as well as other animals, live upon the common thorn plant, which is the most abundant to be found in the country. Some of the most industrious of the Ababde cut wood, and make charcoal with it, which they send to the Nile on camels, and barter it for dhourra, tallow, and tent cloth. Few, however, undergo such a labour, for they like to live at their ease. A pipe of tobacco is a luxury, and a piece of a fat ram quite raw a great dainty. They are all nearly naked, badly made, and of small stature. They have fine eyes, in particular the women, as far as we could see of those that came to the wells. The married women are covered, the rest uncovered. Their head-dresses are very curious. Some are proud of having hair long enough to reach below their ears, and there formed into curls which are so entangled, that it would be impossible to pass a comb through them, therefore the women never use such an instrument. When they kill a sheep that has any fat, which is very seldom, they grease their heads all over, and leave the fat in small pieces to be melted by the sun, which makes them appear as if they had powder on their heads; and this lasts for several days, till the sun melts the whole, and produces an exquisite odour for those who have a good nose. As their hair is very crispy, their heads remain dressed for a long time; and that they may not derange their coiffure when their heads itch, they have a piece of wood something like a packing needle, with which they scratch themselves with great ease without disordering their head-dress, of which they are very proud. Their complexions are naturally of a dark chocolate; their hair quite black; their teeth fine and white, protuberant, and very large.

The spot where the well at which we halted is situated is an amphitheatre of rocks, with trees in the centre. In the winter all the scattered Ababde in the mountains assemble together here, and if any marriage takes place, it is at this time. It is always performed with due ceremony. The lover first sends a camel to the father of the girl. If this be accepted, he applies personally to herself, in the presence of one man as a witness. If she consent, the day of marriage is appointed, before which the lover does not see his bride for seven days. On the eighth, she is presented to him in the tent of her father. This day is celebrated by killing some of their lean sheep, and by camel races. The next day the happy couple retire to the tent of the bridegroom. If the man become tired of his wife, he sends her back with the same camel which he sent to her father, as this is her own from the time of the marriage. The mother of the bride must not speak a word to the bridegroom as long as she lives; a regulation intended to prevent her from making mischief between the young couple; and which might perhaps be adopted with advantage in some countries of Europe.

It was now three years since they had had any rain, whence there was a scarcity of thorns; which was the cause, as they said, that their sheep were so meagre. To make some arrangements for our proceeding, and to purchase some sheep, we were obliged to stop all this day at the well. Having contrived to boil a quantity of the water, it became a little sweeter, and we were told, that the water of the next well was not so good as this. The Nile water we brought with us became bad two days after. We had put it into skins called hudry.

Before taking leave of this place, I shall give some farther account of the manners and customs of the people. When a child is born, the next day the father kills a sheep, and gives the child a name. When they are sick, they say *hulla kerim*, and lie down till they are better, or till they die. I saw old men that did not know or could not tell their age, as they keep no account of such things; but by appearance they must have been ninety years old. When any one dies, they dig a hole in the ground, and put the corpse into it, and very often on the spot where the person died, and then remove their tents a little farther on. They never intermarry with any but their own people. A girl had been refused in marriage to a Turkish Cacheff, though she was as poor as any of her tribe. The Cacheff attempted to use force, and the consequence was, that they assembled to the number of above three hundred, and he prudently retired, leaving his intended bride to be married to her cousin. They have shown, that they are sensible of their wild manner of living, but continue in it for the sake of liberty; for they wrote to the Bey at Esne, that they were content to live in that wild state, as all their forefathers had done, to remain free from tyranny and despotism; and that they would be quiet, if they were left so; but on the contrary, they would sooner perish than lose their liberty.

Some of these wild people, as they are called, came to the well in the course of the day, and as they saw us quiet and peaceful, they ventured, at the persuasion of our drivers, to approach us. A few of them had been as far as the Nile to purchase dhourra, and these were accounted men of knowledge, but the greater part had never quitted their mountains. One of them seeing a piece of lemon-peel lying on the ground, wondered what it was; and another, who had been to the Nile, to show his great knowledge of things, took it up, and ate it with an air of self-sufficiency. We gave them a piece of loaf-sugar, and when they had eaten it, they declared, that our valley must be better than their own, as it produces such good and sweet bread. When they buy dhourra they generally get it ground with the usual hand millstone in the village where they buy it, and carry the flour into the desert. Their bread is baked under the ashes, and is in the form of a large cake, without leaven or salt. Their great enemies were the tribe of El Mahasa and Banousy, which dwell from between Suez to the interior of Arabia and the confines of Syria. With these tribes they had had many battles, but it appeared, that neither one or the other advanced beyond their old possessions. They had also been at variance with the Bishareines on the south, but were now at peace with them all.

Their arms are chiefly spears, and swords or sabres of very old fashion, narrow at the hilt and broad at the point. They have very few firearms, and those they have are with matchlocks. Their constant hard way of life made them accustomed to eat raw meat, and to suffer the inconveniences of a desert with the greatest indifference. I have seen them for near four and twenty hours without drinking, and walking the whole day and night in the hottest season. They are not so religious as the Arabs of the Nile. I scarcely ever saw them saying their prayers. By the great caution I observed in our guide as we advanced in the desert, I perceived it was necessary, that he should acquaint them of the protection we had from their Sheik, by whose permission we ventured among them thus alone and without any escort. It appeared to me, that they were much exasperated toward the soldiers, who had lately been sent into their mountains in search of emeralds; and had it not been for the danger of their Sheik, whose property and life were in the hands of the Turks, they would soon have turned these people out of the mountains, particularly as the miners were a set of desperate fellows, who behaved very ill, often assailed their tents, committed depredations, and insulted their women, of which the Ababdes complained very much.

On the 28th, early in the morning, we set off, and passed through many rocky valleys. The road was not quite so level as before, but good enough for any horse to trot along. There was nothing interesting, except large plains of sand, and high mountains before us. We arrived in the evening at a spot named Gerf.

On the 29th we traversed several pleasing valleys. The mountains that surrounded them were all of hard stones, and beautifully variegated with different coloured marble.

About two in the afternoon we saw the Red Sea at a great distance, and having entered a range of mountains, stopped at a place called Owell, or place of the dragon.

On the 30th we set off early, bent our course to the south-

south-west, and passed through several valleys, towards a very high mountain called Zubara, a name given to it in consequence of the emeralds which have been found there. At the foot of this mountain about fifty men were encamped, and at work in the old mines of the ancients, in hopes of finding some of the precious stones: but it appeared, that their predecessors had searched pretty well before they quitted their works. These unfortunate wretches received a supply of provision from the Nile, but sometimes it did not arrive in due time, and great famine of course prevailed among them. There were two small wells, not more than half a day's journey distant, and one of them had a tolerably good quantity of water. Their work had commenced about six months before, but had been attended with no success. The mines or excavations of the ancients were all choked up with the rubbish of the upper part that had fallen in, and the labour to remove this rubbish was great, for the holes were very small, scarcely capable of containing the body of a man, crawling like a cameleon. They were all thoroughly tired of their situation, and cursed the being who had caused them to be sacrificed in these deserts, destitute of all the common necessaries of life. They rose several times against their leaders, and in one instance two of them were killed. On the day we were there one of the poor wretches nearly fell a victim to the avaricious caprice of their powerful employer. As he was penetrating into one of the holes, part of the roof fell down upon him, and not only cut off his retreat, but nearly killed him on the spot. He was fortunately taken out alive, but it did not give much encouragement to the rest. We contrived to acquire all the information we could about our expedition, and received very favourable accounts of it, with some additional hopes respecting the old town in question, which, according to these people, was only six hours distant south from us, and at six hours more there was a fountain of water. The sea was only six hours distant from the town, of which we hoped to have a fine view before night. We went to see the entrance into the mines. They were something like the common tombs at Gournou cut in the rock; but I observed, that the cavities were made so as to follow the veins of mica and marble, and had been carried to a great distance into the bowels of the mountain, till they found the emeralds.

There are a great number of mines all over this mountain; and the rubbish taken out of them, which is scattered about, gives an idea of the amazing works of the ancients.

The excavations are not carried on in any regular direction. Sometimes they are in an inclined plane of various angles, at other times they are perpendicular, or horizontal, as the mica runs. I was told by the miners, that, as they advanced towards the centre, and at great distances from the entrance, the two strata of marble, which inclose the mica, approach each other, till at last they join, and there is the most chance of finding the emeralds. Where the rocks form separate hills, I observed, that the veins of marble and the mica take their course towards the centre, and, by the distance they run inward from their entrance, it appears to me, that the place where the emeralds are found must be pretty near the centre of the hill; I mean under the highest point of that elevation, which distinguishes one hill from another. I was not fortunate enough to see any emeralds, as these people had not met with any in all their researches. Indeed their leader showed us some few specimens of a very inferior kind, and what was found till that period was only the matrix. He was determined, however, to persevere; and I heard some months after, that he had succeeded in finding some, but in small quantity. I believe too they are of a secondary quality, by what I have seen of them. The people who live there are in a dreadful situation. The nearest habitation is on the Nile, which cannot be reached in less than seven days by a caravan. They depend entirely on the supply of provision sent them from Esne, which is sometimes very scanty, though only bread, rice, and lentils: and according to their account it happens very often, that their supply is delayed merely by the negligence of the purveyors, who are directed to furnish them with it. Besides, they have another source of apprehension. They consider, and with good reason, that the Ababde are not pleased to see them in the deserts; and much less since some of the miners behaved very brutally to them, surprising them in their tents, and insulting their women, as before stated; and they were alarmed for the consequences.

Their great fear was, that the Ababde would assail the caravan of provision on its way from the Nile: for as they had no stock with them, before another supply could arrive, which would require at least fourteen days, they would all perish with hunger. These considerations rendered the people unwilling to work, and the operations were going on very slowly when we were there.

Having procured an old man from among the natives to guide us to the ruins of the anticipated Berenice, we sought all the information we could from the people, and some of the miners who had been at the very place when Monsieur Caliud was there. Their account of it indeed was not in conformity with that of Monsieur Caliud; but we considered, that these people went only in search of mines, and little regarded the beauties of ancient architecture, or the magnificence of edifices, which according to our expectations must be stupendous at least.

We prepared for our departure on the next morning, the 1st of October; and when we had gone about half a mile we perceived, that we were without our guides. Both he who had brought us from the Nile, and the old man who was to conduct us all over the country, to see the town and other places, were missing. We were consequently obliged to return in search of them, and found them hidden behind a rock, conversing secretly with each other. They professed to have been in search of a sheep, which was stolen in the night, and we had nothing else to live upon; but as they said they could not find it, we set off for the so much desired ancient city of Berenice.

Our road was now among the high rocks, and in very narrow valleys, but in which there were a great number of trees. Sometimes the mountains diverged into wide circles one or two miles wide. In such places the wood is abundant, and it is from these that the miners get the timber for their use. The most common plants among them are the sunt and the usual thorn. On the ground among the sandy spots I observed the coloquintida and other shrubs. Our direction was toward the south-west, and gradually to the west, till we reached the south side of the mountain of Zubara, which is the highest of the emerald mountains. Here we were led by the old man in various directions through wild and craggy places for seven hours. He told us, the place we wanted to see was near, but we had a high pass to go over the mountain named Arraie. We continued our journey and ascended a kind of gully, at the side of which was something like an ancient road or rather path. On the summit of the mountain above we observed a large wall, so situated, that it appeared to look over the path on both sides of the mountain. When we reached the top of the road, our camels were exhausted; some of them had fallen on the way, and were unloaded to enable them to ascend, and the strongest camels had to return to fetch the loads of the others. I never saw the camels suffer so much on any occasion as on this. A steep and craggy road over a mountain is no more adapted to a camel, than the deep sand of the desert to a horse.

From this summit we began to look out for the desired Berenice, but alas! in vain. Our imagination was so raised by the account of

Monsieur Caliud, that I, for my part, expected to distinguish the town by the lofty columns and architecture of some magnificent edifice, or the remains of some high tower, which was to serve me as a guide to the spot, to which I intended to run on the first view of it. Mr. Beechey was not less anxious than myself, and in equal expectation of grandeur. We had made our arrangements how to proceed when we arrived. We considered, that, as our provision was scanty, we could stop there but a few days, and we had already distributed our time accordingly. He was to take drawings of all the beautiful edifices, monuments, figures, paintings, if any, sculptures, statues, columns, &c. I was to run all over the vast ruins like a pointer, as fast as I could, to observe where any thing was to be found or discovered, to take measures of all the beautiful monuments, and plans of every stone in that great city. Such was our imagination; now to the fact. From the summit where we now were, I expected to have a distant view not only of the sea, but of a wide plain, as it was natural to suppose that a town like Pompeii could not have been built among these savage mountains without one foot of cultivated land about it. The non-appearance of any wide space I attributed to the situation where we were, and presumed, that we should be agreeably surprised on turning some of the rocks before us; so that my expectation was not diminished in the least. On our descent the old man told us, that we should soon see the *ballet*. He had already said, that, previous to our reaching the town we should see some grottoes in the mountains, which, according to our Quixotic imagination, we concluded were the tombs of the inhabitants of that vast city. We advanced insensibly, I continually keeping my eyes on the points of some rocks which stood before me, with the expectation, that on turning the next angle, I should have the glorious sight; and indeed the scattered and ruined walls of some ancient enclosures announced to us, that we should soon see some habitation. I observed a square hole in the rock, which had evidently been cut by some of the miners in form of a chapel, as before mentioned (See Plate 33, No. 7).

I now began to congratulate myself that we had nearly arrived, and while I was thus thinking, all at once the old man, who was at the head serving us as a guide, made a sign to halt. The drivers gave the signal to the camels, and the camels, who were already exhausted by passing over the mountains, did not wait for its repetition, but with all the baggage were quickly crouched on the ground, before I could perceive the reason why. I told the drivers, that we did not intend to stop there, but would advance farther into the town where the houses were to be seen; when to our no small astonishment we were told by the old man, that this was the place where the other Christian was before. I must confess, that my stupidity would not allow me at once to conjecture, that the report of Monsieur Caliud could be so exaggerated, as to lead us to suppose we should find another Pompeii instead of the place at which we had just arrived; and reproached the old man for his stopping there, and not advancing to the town, which, according to his own account, could not be far off. He again protested, that this was the place, and that there was no other with houses in any part of these deserts or mountains. I was still deeper in perplexity, and continued to urge him to take us farther. As to Mr. Beechey, he was in the same predicament as myself. Resolved not to submit to what I thought the imposition of the old man any longer, as it now wanted four hours to sunset, I mounted my camel again, which would much rather have remained where he was than have gone in search of old Berenice. I set off immediately; Mr. Beechey did the same, and consequently all the rest of the caravan followed at a distance. We entered a long valley, which ran toward the south, and filled with the hopes of seeing the said Berenice on turning every corner of the valley in succession, we went on incessantly for four hours, till it was nearly dark, without perceiving the smallest appearance of any habitation. At last we reached another valley, more spacious, and covered with the trees which the Ababde call egley, and other plants. The valley runs from south-east to north-west, and having lost all hopes of finding Berenice that night, we halted to rest under a beautiful rock on a clean bed of sand, instead of sleeping among the magnificent temples of the great city. By this time we were without water, and though in the proximity of a great town, according to Monsieur Caliud, no water could be had at less than fifteen miles distance. The camels, though more than tired, were obliged to set off immediately to the spring, not only to drink themselves, but to fetch water for us, as we were much in want.

Many were the conjectures we made on the cause, that could induce the old man not to show us the place described by Monsieur Caliud. I sometimes fancied that our drivers had received instructions from the leader of the miners, when we met him at the Nile, that we might not see any of the mines in or near the town of Berenice; but on the other hand we could not believe that the drivers would all with one consent deceive us, merely to oblige a man who had no influence over them. Thus we did not know what to think. Our provision at this time began to make us cautious. We had biscuit for twenty days yet; but the loss of the sheep in the mountain made it worse. Our little stock of water also was quite putrid. Still we were easily satisfied, so that we did but reach the desired emporium of the commerce formerly carried on by the nations of Europe with India; but alas! this much sought for town vanished, or rather never appeared, like the desired island of the squire of the astonishing champion of La Mancha. We contented ourselves with biscuit, and a piece of mutton killed three days before, which by the by gave me reason to congratulate myself on not possessing the sense of smell.

Early in the morning of the 2d, we perceived a high mountain on the south-east of the valley, about four or five miles distant. The valley we were told was named Wady el Gimall. It was quite full of that beautiful tree the egley, and as we had to wait the return of the camels, I thought we might ascend the mountain to have a view of the country, or of the remains of Berenice. Accordingly we set off, and on our way observed several flocks of antelopes, from which we were in hopes to obtain a repast for our empty stomachs, but with all our caution we never could get near enough to shoot at them. They were pretty fat, and we were extremely hungry, but for all this we were not able to approach them. The valley continued very beautiful, adorned with several groves of suvaroe and debbo trees, in addition to a profusion of the egley. The rocks on each side afforded many pleasing recesses to admit the traveller to rest and solitude. Perhaps no one had been in this valley for many centuries, and very likely no one will pass through it for many more to come. On our reaching the summit of the mountain, we took a view all round us. We had the map of the coast of the Red Sea by D'Anville, and a small perspective glass. The peak on which we stood commanded a prospect of many miles all around; but no place was to be seen, where the city could have stood. All that we saw was the summits of other lower mountains, and at last we began to be persuaded, that no such town existed, and that Monsieur Caliud had seen the great city only in his own imagination. It was rather provoking, to have taken such a journey in consequence of such a fabricated description; and I hope this circumstance will serve as a warning to travellers, to take care to what reports they listen, and from whom they receive their information. From the accounts of persons who are so given to exaggeration you cannot venture on a journey without running the risk of being led astray and disappointed, as we were in our search after the said town with its eight hundred houses, and much like Pompeii.

Having observed all the adjacent country and the mountains near us, I took a distant view where the opening between the mountains permitted, and observed, that the valley from which we ascended the mountain continued its course toward the east; and it appeared by the gullies, that the water of the rainy seasons discharged itself in that direction. On the south-east I saw some high mountains, which we were told by the old man, who had followed us all the way, were near the sea. Taking a minute view in that direction, on the north-east from the place where we stood, I perceived the motion of the water under the sun at a great distance, and we concluded, that the valley must conduct us to the sea-coast. Accordingly we made up our minds to pursue that course; and, as we had been disappointed in seeing the extensive ruins of Berenice, we proposed to ourselves to try whether we could reach the spot where D'Anville lays down the Berenice Trogloditica. We therefore descended the mountain, and returned to the place where we had passed the preceding night, to wait the return of the camels with a fresh supply of water; of which we had so little by this time, that a single zemzabie (a leathern bag containing nearly three quarts) only remained. Our thirst was great, and we felt in some degree the dreadful calamity of being in a desert without water. Hunger is painful to endure, but thirst is by far more intolerable. We often hear to what extremities a man can be reduced by hunger, because water is always at hand; but, if this element were to be deficient, we should see still more dreadful effects. At last, three hours after, the camels appeared in sight at the head of the valley on the west, and we rejoiced much at their arrival. The poor drivers were excessively fatigued;

but we had no time to lose in debates. When we told them, that we intended to go farther on to the south, they were all in consternation, and we had much ado to persuade them to agree to it. Indeed, it was not without promises and threats that we prevailed on them. At length we set off toward the sea in a north-east direction.

After travelling six hours we arrived in a valley, the rocks on each side of which were nearly perpendicular. They were composed of calcareous stone, intermixed with strata of white marble, as well as of red granite. During this time we proceeded without knowing in the least where our journey would end, our only hope arising from the sight I had of the sea in the morning. At sunset we came to a place where there was an opening in the mountains not unlike a breach. It is called by the Ababde *Sharm el Gemaal* (the rent of the camels), and appears as if the rocks had been separated by art; for each side is so perpendicular, that it might be supposed to have been cut for the purpose of making a way through it. After we had passed this, we entered a more spacious valley. The hills were small; and the sandy banks made us expect to reach the sea every moment. We went on till a late hour, and at last halted on a spot where we thought the sand would afford us a pretty comfortable bed. Fortunate for me that it was so; for the camel was so weary, that no sooner did we reach the sand, than, supposing I intended to go still farther, he completely threw me off his back, left me there, saddle and all, and, without delay, set out to feed among the thorns. Mr. Beechey and myself, anxious for the result of our journey, and in hopes of seeing the sea, which we thought not far off, walked to the summit of one of the small hills; but, on reaching it, we could scarcely perceive any distant object, as it was nearly dark. I was fully convinced of the non-existence of the imaginary Berenice, and felt the necessity of being on friendly terms with our guides, who I found were pretty correct in the information they had given to us. But no one could have supposed that a man, who found only a few desolate ruins of the miserable residence of poor miners, could fabricate a report, that he had discovered the city of Berenice, the emporium of the commerce between India, Africa, and Europe.

Early on the next day we resumed our journey. The valley still continued in the same direction, but to my amazement the hills, instead of diminishing, increased in size, which made us fearful, that we were yet far from the sea. At length, about noon, the valley opened all at once, and at the distance of five miles we saw the Arabian gulf. The sight of an open horizon, after the contracted view of a long and narrow valley, was much welcomed by us. On our reaching the shore, we plunged into the sea like the crocodiles into the Nile, and found, that a bath after a long journey was very refreshing; we had no time to lose, as our biscuit, as we calculated, would last only seventeen days, and not an hour longer.

Directly opposite us we saw the island of Jambo. It appeared at first sight only a sand bank; but on narrower inspection we perceived, that it had some high rocks on the south side. It was pretty high in the centre, and gradually sloped toward the north. The Ababde call it Gasira el Gimal, I suppose because it is just before the valley of this name. All the shore, as far as we could see, was composed of a mass of petrifactions of various kinds. I do not know whether I give the right name to this sort of composition, but it is a mixture of sea-weeds, madrepores, corals, roots and shells of many sorts, all formed into a solid mass like a rock, which extends from the bank of sand that forms the boundary of the tide, and runs into the sea for a great length. In some places there are beds of sand, but there is not a spot any where for a boat to land without the risk of being staved against the rock. We now resolved without loss of time to take the road toward the south along the coast, as far as till we might suppose we had passed the spot, where our maps place the ruins of Berenice, which, according to D'Anville, who is considered as best skilled in ancient geography, is immediately after the Cape Lepte extrema, a little beyond the 24th degree of latitude. We communicated our intention to our drivers, who were thunderstruck with fear on hearing such a project. They positively refused to accompany us any farther, and though we were very urgent with them, it was all to little purpose. They remonstrated, that we ran a great risk; our stock of biscuit was very scanty, there was no water to be found on that road, and we might meet the Bisharein, whose country we proposed to approach. But being determined to proceed in our design, we took that method, which persuades every one to act even against his own will: we told them, that we meant to go whether they would or not; and that, as we were superior in number, we would compel them. They soon saw, that it was in vain to resist; and at length it was concluded, that the camels should go with two drivers to the nearest spring, to take as much water as they could; that on their return we should set off to proceed as far as El Galahen, to which place we made them understand we must go; and thence take the road across to the well of running water. On a calculation we found, that with great economy in using the water we could do very well.

Accordingly on the 4th the camels set off for the well, and we had to wait two days till their return. During this interval Mr. Beechey and myself made an excursion along the coast toward the north, to examine a small bay, which we observed in the chart. We went along the sea-shore, and on our arrival at the spot where the bay ought to have been, we found that it did not exist. The coast was every where the same with respect to the petrifactions, and the plain, which extends from the mountains to the sea, was covered in many places with woods of sycamore and ciall trees; which confirms the account of Bruce, for undoubtedly this must have been the place where he landed, when he went to visit the emerald mines. The distance, in a right line, from the mines to the sea, is about twenty-five miles, and it may be thirty or thirty-two by the two valleys, which are the only passable roads. I do not see any reason why Mr. Bruce's assertion of having visited these mountains should be doubted. Neither the distance he had to walk from the sea, nor the danger of falling a victim to the rapacity of the natives, are any arguments against it; for we have instances enough to prove, that he was capable of overcoming greater difficulties than these; and I will venture to assert, that the only reason why such doubts could have been started, as well as many others respecting his work, was the spirit of contradiction excited by the illiberality of travellers, and those who were no travellers; the former, because they have not power to resist jealousy, which, in spite of all their efforts to conceal it, shows itself through the veil of their pretended liberality and impartiality; and the latter, because they are unable to control their bad propensity to dispute, and condemn every thing that they have no knowledge of.

In some rocks that lay at the foot of the mountains facing the sea, we saw several mines of sulphur, but I doubt whether their produce would be advantageous, owing to their situation. They are near the sea, but the conveyance by land to the Nile would prevent any benefit from the speculation. Being persuaded, that no vessel could be loaded on that coast, we returned to the place where we had left our caravan: hunger was not, I believe, visible on our faces, for we contrived to make some repasts out of some shell-fish, which abound in great quantities along the coast, and I cherished the idea, that as long as I could find some of them I should not perish. The large periwinkles are excellent, and, when young, are very tender and delicious, particularly to a hungry man.

We had some of them which weighed half a pound, and part of the tail quite delicate, though the white, or upper part, is rather tough.

On our return we found that the guide had met with an acquaintance of his who lived by catching fish, not far from where we were. His only habitation consisted of a tent four feet high, and five feet wide; and his wife, a daughter, and a young man, her husband, formed the whole family. We contrived to persuade the old man to go out and fish, and, though he was living in those deserts, he knew the worth of money, for he said that there were people among them who went yearly on the Nile and purchased dhourra, which they carried on camels all round those deserts, and sold it to the inhabitants, for which they took in exchange either camels or money; consequently we easily persuaded the old fisher to go out and catch fish for us; in fact, he set off to sea, accompanied by his son-in-law. Their mode of fishing is somewhat strange; they throw in the water a part of the trunk of the doomt tree, perhaps ten or twelve feet long, at each end of which is a piece of wood attached in an horizontal direction, so as to prevent the tree from turning round; at one of the ends a small pole is stuck upright to serve as a mast, on the top of which there is a piece of wood horizontally fastened as that below. A woollen shawl thrown over it, and fastened at each end, and to the piece of wood horizontally fixed below, forms a kind of sail, and the two fishermen mount on the large trunk as on horseback, and by way of cord, attached to the middle of the sail, take the wind more or less as is required. But it is only when the wind blows either from north or south that such a contrivance can serve; for if it blows from the east they cannot set off their boat from the shore, or if it blows from the west it will blow them too far out at sea. When the fishermen are thus at some distance from the shore, I do not know by what means the rest of the operation is executed; but from what I could see they darted their long thin spear at the fish when they happened to see any, and by these means they procured their subsistence. On their return they brought us four fish, each of about six pounds weight, and one foot six inches long; they were of a strong blue silvered colour; their fins, head, and tail red; and their teeth, which are only four, are quite flat and out of their mouths. They had very large scales, and their form not unlike the benne of the Nile. I am certain the Egyptians must have had a knowledge of this fish, as it is so clearly seen in their hieroglyphics, and in the new tomb of Psamethis I saw some painted exactly as they are in reality. They are exceedingly good, have very few bones, and very large galls.

On the 5th, in the morning, I ascended a high mountain to view the coast as far as I could, and I saw that it ran straight towards the south-east. The spot which we occupied is marked No. 16 on the map, to which I cannot give a better name than the mouth of Wady el Gemal, as it is precisely opposite the entrance into the valley of that name. I observed also that the southern point of the island of Gambe was in a right line with the rising sun at sea, and myself. It will be seen on the map, supposing the place I stood upon to be on the top of the mountain nearest to the above No. 16. By the help of a small compass, we contrived to take the direction of the northern coast as far as we had been the day before; our maps being so small, we did not find them so correct as we wished. Early on the 6th, the camels returned with a load of fresh water, and it was well they did so, for our thirst was increased, not only from the scarcity of water, but by the shell-fish which we had found and eaten abundantly; an inconvenience which the fishermen had not to contend with, being accustomed to the bitter water of a well not so far off. We now divided our caravan into two parties; we sent all the luggage, culinary utensils, the soldier, my Greek servant, and the best part of the camels, to a spring of running water in the mountains of Amusue, there to wait till our return. For ourselves, we took with us as much water as we could, and formed a party, consisting of Mr. Beechey and myself, a Greek servant, four drivers, and the two Arabian boys we had brought from Gournou, with five camels in all.

We set off in the forenoon, and went along the coast till we arrived at El Whady Abghsoon, near the mines of El Kebrite, or sulphur, and on the south-west were the mountains of Hamata. I observed the coast all the way, and took its direction. On our road we met some fishermen, like the former ones. When they saw us at a distance, they left their tents and marched off towards the mountains; all our signs to them to stop were to no purpose. We arrived at their tents, and found some excellent fish just roasted, which, no doubt, these people had made ready for their supper. We partook of their meal, and left some money in payment, on the top of a water jar, and continued our journey. For two days we had been troubled with the winds from the east, blowing strong and resembling the siroccos of Italy, so that all our nerves were relaxed. During this time, every thing we touched felt as if it had just been taken out of the water, and at night there was an excessive heat, and the atmosphere quite covered with clouds, which I had not seen for three years and a half: fortunately it changed after two days, and the north wind dissipated all. Had it lasted longer we could not have proceeded on our journey. At night we stopped at a well of bitter water. On the 7th, we set off early to see the mines of El Kebrite, or sulphur, as they were not out of our road. They never were productive; but what little they may have afforded, it appeared that the ancients had carried entirely away, so that they left them exhausted like those of the emeralds. Towards the evening we saw the island of Suarif, and we arrived at night at the Cape el Golahen. It was here that we began to feel short allowance of water. We calculated, and found that without great care we should be without it; therefore, our thirst was not satisfied. The 8th, early in the morning, we set off and continued our road to the south. Two hours after, we saw the sea at a distance, and went over a very extensive plain. At about noon we approached the sea, very thirsty, and regaled ourselves with a little water; and at one o'clock we arrived on the shore. We did not expect to arrive at any ruins, for, as yet, it did not agree exactly with the situation laid down by D'Anville; but, to our agreeable surprise, we found ourselves all at once on one of those moles of ruins which show the spot of ancient towns, so often seen in Egypt. We entered, and at once we saw the regular situations of the houses; the main streets, their construction, and in the centre, a small Egyptian temple, nearly covered by the sand, as well as the insides of the houses; and our wonder increased on examining the materials with which the houses were built. We could see nothing but coral, roots, madrepore, and several petrifactions of sea-weeds, &c.

The temple is built of a kind of soft, calcareous, and sandy stone, but decayed much by the air of the sea. The situation of this town is delightful (See Plate 34). The open sea before it is on the east, and from the southern coast to the point of the cape is like an amphitheatre of mountains, except an opening on the north-west plain, where we came from. The Cape el Galahen extends its point nearly opposite the town on the east, and forms a shelter for large ships from the north and north-west winds. Right opposite the town there is a very fine harbour entirely made by nature; its entrance is on the north, it is guarded on the east by a neck of incrusted rock, on the south by the land, and on the west by the town; the north side, as I said before, being covered by the range of mountains which forms the cape, protects the harbour also. Its entrance has been deep enough for small vessels, such as the ancients had at those times, but no doubt was deeper. It has at present a bar of sand across, so that nothing could enter at low water; but a passage could be easily cut, and the harbour rendered useful. We concluded this to be the Berenice described by Pliny and Herodotus, laid down by D'Anville, and it nearly agreed with the situation where it is marked on the map; but in order to ascertain with more accuracy, we resolved to venture by going half a day higher towards the south, and then we should be certain that we should pass the spot where D'Anville has put down the said Berenice. I measured the town, which is in breadth, from north to south, 1600 feet, and in length, from east to west, 2000 feet. I took the plan of the temple, which seems to be in construction according to the Egyptian style, and we imagined that the Greeks had taken their plans from this ancient people, as they had done in many other things (See Plate 32). It is one hundred and two feet long, and forty-three feet wide; it contains four chambers, two on each side of the sekos and cella, and two in the great hall in the front. Our difficulty now was about the water; it became very scarce, and we could not, positively, stay there the whole of the next day. The Ababdes nearly lost their patience with our researches, for they had not a drop of water for themselves; we could not spare any of ours, and the nearest well was supposed to be a day's journey distant. They had drank but little the day before. Notwithstanding all this, we were determined not to leave any thing undone as far as we could. We promised them that we would set off on the next day at twelve o'clock, and fortunately being moonlight, we employed part of the night to scrutinize the place.

It was now three days since we had eaten any thing but dry biscuit and water, except the fish we found at the fishermen's hut. We were contented ourselves with eating biscuit; but our thirst increased, and our hudry diminished. We persuaded the Sheik Ibrahim, our guide, to go with us towards the south on the next morning, and leave the rest of the people at the town. He agreed with reluctance, and said, that he feared his camels and people could not start without water. However, on the morning of the 9th, before the sun rose, we set the little Mussa to digging. He was one of the Arab boys we brought with us from Gournou. I made him dig in the temple. He had no spade; but with a shell or caquille he worked very well, as it was only soft sand. We set off along the beach, and made straight towards the southern point before us. We passed the fore part of the day in calculating that the spot where D'Anville marked the town could not be farther south. We saw nothing before us but an extensive plain to the foot of the mountain that formed the cape on the south. We had glasses, and could see all the ground, but no sort of elevation, or any other indication that could give a supposition of any remains of habitations.

We returned to the town, and found that the boy had excavated about four feet of sand close to the north-east corner of the cella; and, to our surprise, we saw that the temple was Egyptian. The part of the wall which was discovered was adorned with Egyptian sculpture in basso relievo, and well executed. We could see three figures, two feet three inches high, of which I took drawings as well as I could (See Plate 33, No. 1). The remaining part of the wall was covered with hieroglyphics, &c. I observed the upper part of the door which leads into the inner chamber; and in the same sandy hole the boy found part of an Egyptian tablet covered with hieroglyphics and figures (See Plate 16.) It is of a kind of reddish pudding-stone or breccia, not belonging to the rocks near that place. We took it away, as a memorandum of having seen an Egyptian temple on the coast of the Red Sea; a circumstance that, as yet, no antiquarian has had any idea of. The plain that surrounds this town is very extensive: the nearest point to the mountains which form the crescent is about five miles on the west of it. On the north, the mountain is about twelve miles distant, and on the south fifteen. All the plain is inclined to vegetation, such as a sandy soil can produce; but, in particular, the lower part of it towards the sea is perpetually moist, and would produce, if cultivated, pasture for camels, sheep, and other animals. This moisture is naturally produced by the damp of the sea, which is very strong when it happens. The upper part of the plain is not so damp, and, I believe, would be perhaps more productive of dry plants. I do not know whether grain for bread could be brought to any perfection, as the soil is of a sandy nature, with but a small portion of clay, impregnated with salt incrustations. It is full of small plants of sunt and suvaroes. This last plant I observed along the coast, growing close to the salt water, and generally out of the rocks, some quite under water, particularly at high tides. It is a small tree, generally no higher than eight feet: its leaves are of a substance like the laurel. Its form will be seen in Plate 36. This makes very good firewood; and, with the sunt-tree, I have no doubt that the town was well provided with that article. Water is the commodity of most importance in such a spot, for though there are three wells, they are so bitter, that the human palate cannot taste it without increasing the thirst. Camels and other beasts can drink it very well. As to good water, it is supposed that such a town could not be without a great supply of it. I observed, that the nearest mountain is only five miles distant. There must have been some wells in those rocks, which are now either choked up or are unknown. What I can assert is, that, at only one day's journey, there is a well of tolerably good water; and, at one and a half, an excellent spring runs out of the rocks of granite: and as the ancients had such facilities in transporting any thing from a great distance by camels, so this town may have been supplied with water at one day's journey distance. But I am inclined to think, that they had it from the nearest mountains; as, by their situation, they must afford wells, &c. As to greens and other necessaries, they might easily have been supplied by the soil, or from the Nile, as Cassara is at this very day. At a small distance from the city I saw several groups of ruins. It appears that they were houses situated out of the town in different directions.

The calculation I made about the houses and population compels me to observe, that the houses were not so extensive as they are built at this day. It was the custom of those people to live close to each other. I observed that the largest houses were about forty feet in length, and twenty in breadth; some were smaller; but I made the calculation at the rate of twenty by forty, and I found that the square of 2000 by 1600 feet would contain 4000 houses; but, as there were spaces of ground without buildings, which may be reckoned half of the town, I counted them to be only 2000, that I might not be mistaken for another Caliud. Those people had no need of great sheds to put coaches, chariots, or any such luxurious lumber. Their cattle and camels lay always in the open air, as they still do in all these countries: nor had they extensive manufactories. The only massy buildings for their commerce could be but a few store-houses, nor could the narrow lanes, which were in use in those times, occupy much of the ground. I calculated that, with the houses out of town, which are scattered about in groups here and there, the population of that port must have exceeded 10,000 inhabitants; a town which even to this day would be reckoned of consequence, if situated on that coast, as a port for commerce with India. I observed also some of the tombs dug in the nearest lower rocks, of a kind of soft or calcareous stone, which are the only ones on the plain near the town on the western side. We left the spot before the evening of the same day, in consequence of the want of water; and, as our camel-drivers had nearly lost their patience, we gave them half a pint each, and continued our road towards the mountain on the north-west, with the firm intention of returning prepared to scrutinize the whole of those ruins.

At about twelve miles from the sea we entered a vale, on the north-west of the town, in the mountain which forms the crescent round it.

We continued the best part of the night by moonlight, and fortunately arrived at the well at Aharatret at midnight, a mountainous place, where the water was good enough to drink. We were agreeably surprised to find the well, but much more so when we saw a few sheep around it. There never was a more welcome sight. We thought we might have something to refresh us. We proposed to purchase one, and eat it as soon as it could be half cooked. We approached, but the guardian of the flock beat a forced march into the mountain, and drove the intended repast away from us. We began to think we would not continue to be deprived of what we could purchase, and sent some of our drivers to follow the flock, which they heartily did, as they were not less hungry than ourselves. The fugitives were pursued and stopped. We reached the flock, and found that its guardians were two beautiful damsels of the deserts. The chocolate nymphs were surprised at the fountain by their pursuers, and took refuge on the mountains; but, with some few good words from their countrymen, they were soon persuaded to return, and trust themselves near us. We were gallant with them, for the sake of devouring some of their lambs. They became gradually more familiar, and scrupled not to let us see their chocolate faces by the moonlight; but the sheep prevailed above all, and took our chief attention.

Those poor girls had no other way to show themselves but at the well; that is the only place they have a chance to see or be seen. At last we purchased the sheep, and devoured it; the nymphs watered their flocks, filled their skins, and set off at daylight. On this road we observed camels' paths, and pieces of broken pottery, which indicated this to have been a principal way to the town; and half way between this well and Haboo Grey, we met with a station like the one which we saw before on the road to Coptos. I inquired and found that this valley communicated with the same I have mentioned; which gave us reason to believe, that the great road from Coptos to Berenice was directed to this place, which agreed with the opinion and maps of D'Anville.

Early in the morning of the 10th we set off again toward the mountain Zabara, with the intention to examine Sakiet Minor, as we had not well seen it before.

The valley we were in continued to the north-west, and we followed the sea. At about one o'clock we arrived at Khefeiri, a well of excellent water. Here we rested the remaining part of the afternoon, and succeeded in procuring another sheep, but no better than the first. The entrails were the best part of it; and on all the rest it may have had about one pound of pure flesh. No sheep has more in this country, unless of an extraordinary size.

We set off on the 11th, and passed through a valley surrounded by granite rocks. In the afternoon we arrived at a running spring, rising out of a granite chasm—a singular thing in this country, as no such abundance of water is to be found any where. It affords water enough to make a jet of about one inch diameter, and the water is excellent. This place is called Amusuè, and is only at one day's journey from Sakiet. Here we found the rest of the caravan, which we had sent from the sea-side, waiting for us.

On the morning of the 12th we sent our Greek interpreter to

Zabara, requesting Mahomet Aga, the leader of the miners, to send us two of those Greeks who saw the Frenchman measure the place in the mountains, or the ancient town; and we arranged to meet them at Sakiet, on the next night.

The spot where we were this day formed a cataract, which descended from an upper valley, connected with others still higher, and so on to the tops of the mountains.

On the 13th, we rested at this place all day, as we were all tired; and on the 14th we set off for Sakiet. On our arrival there, we heard from my servant, that Mahomet Aga was not returned from the Nile to the mines. We might have waited for him at the first temple long enough.

By this time we were pretty well convinced that no other place was to be seen; but, to satisfy ourselves, we set off on the 15th, for the coast again, through the valley from Sakiet to the sea, on the same road Mr. Caliud passed. I took all the directions possible with compasses and calculations. We arrived at the sea in the evening, a journey much longer than Caliud had said, as he reported it was only three hours' walk, but we found it required nine, and that by the best mode of travelling in these deserts. We had left part of our water skins at Sakiet, on purpose to facilitate our march. We arrived about a mile on the north of the valley Ell Gimàl, the spot which we had visited before.

The 16th.—We occupied ourselves with a long examination of this coast, and were convinced that there could be no landing on that shore. It happens that D'Anville's map is not correct on this point, for it marks a bay here, which, according to him, would form a fine harbour; but, on the contrary, there is not such a bay, and the coast is one continued rocky shore, so that a small vessel could not approach, nor is there any shelter for ships against any wind, or any appearance of a road leading to the inland places. The road we passed from Sakiet is the very way which Caliud took to the seaside, if a road it can be called. It is a vale which leads to the sea from the pass in the mountains; but it has not the least appearance of having been a road at any time. The inconvenience for camels to pass over this mountain, when loaded, would make the transport impracticable; besides, if they had to build a town for commercial purposes, they would never have built it on this spot. It is one day's journey from the nearest point of the mountains towards the east to the sea, situated among craggy rocks, in a dry and sterile valley.

On the 17th, we returned to Sakiet. I can but conclude of this spot, that it could never have been a place of commerce, or the habitation of any sort of commercial people; but I really believe that these few scattered houses may have been built for miners, who worked in the mountains in search of emeralds in the adjacent places, and that here was their chief residence. We arrived at this place late at night, and found that the man we left there to guard our water was gone. He had taken the skins with him, and did not leave us a drop of water. Fortunately the well was at only six hours' journey distance from us, so we sent the camels to water, and likewise to bring some to us.

The following are the Greek inscriptions, which Dr. Young has translated for me, and which I copied from a niche in the rocks. If the antiquarians, by these inscriptions, can make out that the above place is one of the Berenices, still it is certain that the Greeks did not build a great town under that name.

To face page 3

A.　　　ΥΝΤΟΙΣΤ ΕΚΝΟΙΣΚΑΚΑΙΚΑΤΟΙΕ ΣΥΝ ΕΜΟΣ
　　　　ΕΡΥΑΖΟΜΕΝ Τ
　　　　ΑΡΤΟΙ ΗΣΑΣΙΔΑΩΝΑΡΤΥΤ ΟΥΜΤΤΑΡΑΩ Ο
　　Ι ΑΙ　　　ΤΤιιΑΤΗΚΥΡΙΛΥΣ́ ΔΙΤΗΣΕΝΣΚΕΙΤ

B.　ΟΜΟΙΩΣ ΦΙΑΛΗΝΑΤΓΥΡΑΝΑΒ͝Υ ΤΑΥΤΑΠΑΝΤΑ
　　ΕΚΤΩΝΕΜΩΝ ΩΡΥ
　　ΚΑΝΤΙΟΝΕΥΧΗΣΤΗΣΑΣΤΟ͞Υ ΣΑΡΑΠΙΑΙΤΩΜ ΝΙΕ͞
　　ΤΟΝΑΛΚΚΟΝ ➤ Η ΥΟΣ ΠΑΥΝΙ ΚΑ ⊦
　　　　　　　　　ΣΑ͞ΟΤ═ΜΚΧΕΧΖΤΟΙΕΡ\Ο
　　　　　　　　　　　ΝΕΠΣΙΗΣΔ

C.　ΠΟ ΥΡΑΛΙΟΣ ΚΔΙΤΟΥΤΡΣ
　　ΩΔΙΗΝ°Υ ΜΕΧΚΙΡ Κ͞Ζ

D.　ΡΩΝΙΟΥΕΥΧΑΡΙΕΤΜΣΑΣ ΤΩ
　　ΚΔΙΤΗΙΣΙΔΙΚΑΙΩΔΠΟΜΩΝΙΚΑΙ
　　ΝΔΟΙΣΘΕΟΙΣΠΑΣΙΕΠΟΙΗΕΝΡΟΙΕΡΟΝ

E.　ΡΕΡΕΝΕΙΚΗΣ ΚΑΙΤΟΖΩΔΙΟΝΧΛΙΟΡΥΖΔΣ
　　ρε ΥΜΔΤΟΣΑΠΟΘΕΜΕΛΙΟΥΚΙ⊦
　　ΜΔΤΩΝΑΝΕ ΘΗΚΔΕΠΑΓΔΘΩ

F.　ΠΑΚΥΒⳊΣΤΙ⌐ ΤΗΣ
　　ΠΕΤΟΣΙΡΙΣ ΕΠΟ ΦΛΥΑΠΤ ΚΘ

　　ΠΡΟΗ ΤΗΣ
　　ΤΗΣΤΣΙΔΙ
　　ΤΟΣ ⨆Α ΚΘ/

Perhaps we should read,

A. Σὺν τοῖς τέκνοις καὶ τοῖς σὺν ἐμοὶ
ἐργαζομένοις
καὶ ποιήσασι καὶ μαρτυρουμ. παρὰ τῳ θεῷ.
καὶ παρὰ τῇ κυρίᾳ Ὑ'σιδι τῇ Σενσκείτῃ.

B. Ὁμοίως φιάλην ἀπύραν Λ β'. ταῦτα πάντα
ἐκ τῶν ἐμῶν χρη-
μάτων, εὐχαριστήσας τῷ Σαράπι καὶ τῷ Μνίει, 3δ.
τὸν λάκκον ⊳ η Κ.ος Παϋνι κα.
Σαράπ.. Μνίει.. τὸ ἱερὸ-
ν ἐποίησα.

C. ..πο.. υράλιος καὶ τοῦ Τρ... ς
..ωδιήνου Μεχεὶρ κζ'

D. ... ρωνίου εὐχαριστήσας τῷ ...
καὶ τῇ Ἰ'σιδι καὶ τῷ Απολλωνι [τοῖς συν-]
νάοις θεοῖς πᾶσι ἐποίησα πὸ ἱερόν.

E. ... Βερενείκης καὶ τὸ ζῴδιον καὶ ὀρύξας
ρεύματος ἀπὸ θεμελίου καὶ [ἐκ τῶν ἰδίων χρη-]
μάτων ἀνέθηκε· ἐπ' ἀγαθῷ.

F. Πακυβίστις τῆς..
Πετόσιρις... ἐπο... " Φωαπι" κθ'

Προήτης
τῆς Ἰσίδι
τος Πα.. κθ'.

The translation will be nearly thus:

A. [The homage of] . . . . with my sons, and those who have laboured with me, and have done this, and have testified to the god . . and to our lady Isis of Senscis.

B. . . . Likewise a phial untouched by fire of two pounds weight: all these things at my own expense: having presented to Sarapis and to Mneuis four drachms: the cistern half a drachm. The eighth year of Cæsar; the 21 of Payni.
      To Sarapis . . to Mneuis? I have made the temple.

C. Under Aurelius and Trajan ? . . .
 Of Herodian? Mechir 27th.

D. [Of Semp]ronius: doing honour to . . and to Isis, and to Apollo, and to all the other gods enshrined with them, I have made the temple.

E. . . Of Berenice, and the sculptured animal; and having dug [the channel] of the river from the foundation; and [at his own ex]pense has dedicated them: with good fortune.

F. Pacybistis the . . .
 Petosiris . . made . . Phaophi 29th.
 Proëtes the son of Isideïs. Pa[yni] 29th.

Here is no water nearer than one day's journey, either for man or beast, nor soil for any verdure: the spot is sheltered from the winds, so that it receives the full power of the sun in all points. Besides all the circumstances before mentioned, the small niche where this inscription was found is situated on the road to Berenice; and I cannot persuade myself that such a place as this can be one of those of that name. On the 18th, we searched for some hours all the neighbouring mountains, and found several mines at about half an hour's walk distant, in the valley that leads to the pass towards Zabora, and three others near this place.

The 19th.—Early in the morning we took our course to the

south, and at about two P. M. we reached the point where the road takes its course to the west. In this spot we found one of the stations, as before mentioned; it is called Kafafeet. We continued till the evening, and arrived at Habookady, near a mountain in form of a bell, in the valley of Wady el Gimal: we saw abundance of the trees *egley*, and the plant like rushes, called *murk*.

The 20th, early, we set off, and passed through a wide plain. As we left the mountain, and arrived at Habookroog, a place that appears to be at the entrance of the chain of mountains that leads to the Nile, our camels were so tired they could hardly crawl: we had lost three on the road, and one we expected would not last long. It is difficult to form a correct idea of a desert without having been in one; it is an endless plain of sand and stones, sometimes intermixed with mountains of all sizes and heights, without roads or shelter, without any sort of produce for food. The few scattered trees and shrubs of thorns, that only appear when the rainy season leaves some moisture, barely serve to feed wild animals, and a few birds. Every thing is left to nature; the wandering inhabitants do not care to cultivate even these few plants, and when there is no more of them in one place, they go to another. When the trees become old, and lose their vegetation in such climates as these, the sun, which constantly beams upon them, burns and reduces them to ashes. I have seen many of them entirely burnt. The other smaller plants have no sooner risen out of the earth than they are dried up, and all take the colour of straw, with the exception of the plant *harack;* this falls off before it is dry. Speaking in general of a desert, there are few springs of water, some of them at the distance of four, six, and eight days' journey from one another, and not all of sweet water; on the contrary, it is generally salt or bitter, so that if the thirsty traveller drinks of it, it increases his thirst, and he suffers more than before; but when the dreadful calamity happens that the next well, which is so anxiously sought for, is found dry, the misery of such a situation cannot be well described. The camels, which afford the only means of escape, are so thirsty that they cannot proceed to another well; and if the travellers kill them to extract the little liquid which remains in their stomachs, they themselves cannot advance any farther. The situation must be dreadful, and admits of no resource. I must not omit what I have been told happens in such cases.

Many perish victims of the most horrible thirst. It is then that the value of a cup of water is really felt. He that has a *zenzabia* of it is the richest of all. In such a case there is no distinction; if the master has none, the servant will not give it to him, for very few are the instances where a man will voluntarily lose his life to save that of another, particularly in a caravan in the desert, where people are strangers to each other. What a situation for a man, though a rich one, perhaps the owner of all the caravans! He is dying for a cup of water—no one gives it to him—he offers all he possesses—no one hears him—they are all dying—though by walking a few hours farther they might be saved,—the camels are lying down, and cannot be made to rise—no one has strength to walk—only he that has a glass of that precious liquor lives to walk a mile farther, and perhaps dies too. If the voyages on seas are dangerous, so are those in the deserts: at sea, the provisions very often fail; in the desert it is worse: at sea, storms are met with; in the desert there cannot be a greater storm than to find a dry well: at sea, one meets with pirates—we escape—we surrender—we die; in the desert they rob the traveller of all his property and water; they let him live perhaps—but what a life! to die the most barbarous and agonising death. In short, to be thirsty in a desert, without water, exposed to the burning sun, without shelter, and no hopes of finding either, is the most terrible situation that a man can be placed in; and, I believe, one of the greatest sufferings that a human being can sustain: the eyes grow inflamed, the tongue and lips swell: a hollow sound is heard in the ears, which brings on deafness, and the brains appear to grow thick and inflamed:—all these feelings arise from the want of a little water. In the midst of all this misery, the deceitful morasses appear before the traveller at no great distance, something like a lake or river of clear fresh water. The deception of this phenomenon is well known, as I mentioned before; but it does not fail to invite the longing traveller towards that element, and to put him in remembrance of the happiness of being on such a spot. If perchance a traveller is not undeceived, he hastens his pace to reach it sooner; the more he advances towards it, the more it goes from him, till at last it vanishes entirely, and the deluded passenger often asks where is the water he saw at no great distance: he can scarcely believe that he was so deceived; he protests that he saw the waves running before the wind, and the reflection of the high rocks in the water.

If, unfortunately, any one falls sick on the road, there is no alternative; he must endure the fatigue of travelling on a camel, which is troublesome even to healthy people, or he must be left behind on the sand, without any assistance, and remain so till a slow death come to relieve him. What horror! What a brutal proceeding to an unfortunate sick man! No one remains with him, not even his old and faithful servant; no one will stay and die with him; all pity his fate, but no one will be his companion. Why not stop the whole caravan till he is better, or do what they can for the best till he dies? No, this delay cannot be; it will put all in danger of perishing of thirst if they do not reach the next well in such a time; besides, they are all different parties generally of merchants or travellers, who will not only refuse to put themselves in danger, but will not even wait a few hours to save the life of an individual, whether they know him or not.

In contrast to the evil, there is the luxury of the desert, and also its sport, which is generally at the well; there one enjoys all the delight of drinking as much water as one likes, which tastes not unlike cordials or other precious liquors, with the others in that situation. The beasts, mixed with birds, drink together close to the well. There is a kind of basin made of clay which is filled up by the drivers, from the well, where the thirsty animals all drink together, camels, sheep, dogs, donkeys, and birds, as it is the only time they can partake of that liquid; for if it is not drawn up from the well, they cannot reach it. I only saw four species of birds, viz. the vulture, crow, wild pigeon, and partridge; of this last we eat some, and found them exceedingly good: the crows are the most numerous; they tease the camels by picking their wounds, if they have any. The other and most pleasing diversion is the beautiful damsels who come as shepherdesses to water their flocks, who, after being assured that there is no danger in approaching strangers, become more sociable. On such occasions, our observing their gestures afforded us great amusement: but, our water skins filled, and the camels loaded, we were obliged to quit these dear spots, with the hope of meeting another like it in a few days, and so on till we reached the blessed Nile; but the journey was pleasant enough this day, as we had a well only within a few hours. We set off at two in the morning of the 20th, and, before noon, reached the well at Hamesh, containing very good water. Here we lost another camel; he could not go any farther. We set off again in the afternoon, and arrived at a place at the foot of a mountain of granite. Early on the 21st, we set off again, and soon entered the ravine of granite rocks, that reminded us of the cataract which we saw on our passing before. After this, we arrived at the station of Samout, which we also saw before at the same time. We arrived at night at Dangos, where the mountains are not very high, and of calcareous stone. From the cataract, and nearly down to this place, we found the track of an old road, which continued in the direction of south-east and north-west, and I have very little doubt but that it is the same we saw at Bezack on our passing before, and which takes its course in a right line from Coptos to Berenice. On the 22d, we continued our route at one in the morning, and arrived at Wady el Medah at sunset. We took a measurement of the fort, which I mentioned before; and, early on the 23d, proceeded, and arrived at the first well: the water of this place tasted to us very bad on our going up, but it appeared pretty good on our return. In the night we arrived at the Nile, and our having been long deprived of good water made us sensible of the superiority of that of the river over the wells we had been accustomed to.

Certainly, I am of opinion that there are few waters, if any, in Europe that can be compared with that of the Nile. It answers all purposes; it has the freshness of spring, and the softness of river water; it is excellent to drink, and serves all other purposes. Plate 38 is a topographical map which I made of the above journey, as correct as I could.

We went on board our little boat the same night. On the 24th, the Sheik of the Ababdy came to us, and we presented him with a gun, and some powder and balls. We complained of the badness of the camels with which he had provided us; he assured us that no one of the Ababdy had ever undertaken such a journey as we had, and that the camels were not accustomed to such forced marches. We gave a gun, a shawl, and money, to our guide, who behaved uncommonly well. We talked of repeating our journey, and they assured us, that if we returned they would furnish us with camels that would take us any where we pleased, and as long as we would stay. We sent a pair of pocket pistols to the Cacheff in the island, thanking him for his goodness and attention.

The place we now reached on the Nile was a few miles north of that where we had entered in the desert opposite Elfou, and a little south of Eleithias. The road which I observed all along the valley undoubtedly was a communication between that town and Berenice, and on the east to the emerald mines. It is not to be wondered at that the town of Eleithias must have been of some consequence, as there is all the probability of commerce having been carried on there: there is still a landing-place, which evidently proves the loading and unloading of boats for that purpose; and I am of opinion that this place must have been more frequented by the caravans from the sea than Coptos, as it is a somewhat shorter journey to the Nile.

We set off for Esne. On our way down it was pleasing to see the difference of the country: all the lands that were under water before were now not only dried up, but were already sown; the muddy villages carried off by the rapid current were all rebuilt; the fences opened; the Fellahs at work in the fields, and all wore a different aspect. It was only fifteen days since the water had retired, and in that period it decreased more than eight feet. It is not so every year: when the Nile increases slowly, it decreases also in the same manner; this is in consequence of the abundance or scarcity of rain which falls during the rainy season in Abyssinia.

The natives rather prefer the rapid rising of the Nile, for it covers more space of land, so that it be not too much, as was the case this year; and if the water remain eight days over it, it does as much good as if it continued twenty. By this time the drowned people were forgotten, and the only calamity remaining was the scarcity of provisions among the Fellahs. The Nile had taken away their stock, and the Cacheffs were only busied in procuring grain for seed. In all such cases the poor labourer is the last thought of.

We arrived at Esne on the morning of the 25th, and visited the Bey, who received us very politely: he inquired about the mines, and was very anxious to know the result. We told him that nothing could be known on the subject till they were cleared of all the materials with which they were choked up. We made him a present of a fine English gun: he was much pleased, and offered to give us all his assistance in any thing that he could. We set off, and arrived at Gournou on the same night, after forty days' absence, which I hope were not uselessly employed.

ACCOUNT OF THE TAKING THE OBELISK FROM THE ISLAND OF PHILŒ TO ALEXANDRIA.

Having made arrangements for accomplishing the models of the tombs, I set off for Esne, with the intention of inquiring into the possibility of obtaining camels to go to the Great Oasis, which lies due west from that place. When I had obtained all the information I desired, I returned to Thebes to prepare for another sally into the western desert. On my arrival in Gournou, I found the consul, Mr. Salt, Mr. Bankes, and Baron Sack, had arrived from Cairo. Having convinced Mr. Salt of the impossibility of making a collection on my own account, according to our understanding, in consequence of his having taken possession of the grounds in Thebes, he proposed a new arrangement to be made between us, which was, that I might be at liberty to dig on either side of Thebes, on any ground I thought proper, taking for my exertion a certain share of what might be found in the intended researches. Having agreed to this proposition, I had to recommence my operations. I was fully satisfied with the above arrangement, as I supposed that I should have an opportunity of making a collection of antiques out of the share which would be allotted to me. About this time Mr. Drouetti arrived in Thebes, and, by the medium of Mr. Bankes, made an offer to purchase the celebrated sarcophagus of alabaster, but his offer was not accepted*. At this period Mr. Bankes solicited me to ascend the Nile as far as the island of Philœ, to remove the obelisk I had taken possession of before in the name of the British consul. The consul then informed me, that he had ceded the said obelisk to Mr. Bankes, who intended to send it to England on his own account. I gladly accepted the undertaking, as I was pleased to have the opportunity of seeing another piece of antiquity on its way to England, and of obliging a gentleman for whom I had great regard. Two days previous to our departure, the consul and myself crossed the Nile to Carnak, to point out the various spots of ground which had been previously taken by himself. On our landing at Luxor we met Mr. Drouetti, who offered to accompany us to Carnak, to be witness of the various spots of ground which were to be allotted to me for excavation. On the way, Mr. Drouetti told us a pleasant story of a man who was dressed like myself, and who was hidden among the ruins of the temple; whom he, Mr. Drouetti, had great

* One evening that the whole party were assembled, Mr. Drouetti happened to be there. The consul and he had some few words about a circumstance which I cannot avoid mentioning. It will be recollected that, previous to our departure for the Red Sea, a man from the opposite party desired to have a passage on board of our boat to Cairo, which was granted. At Girgeh, six days' sail below Thebes, this unfortunate man was drowned, by falling overboard, as was stated by all the crew, and some of our people who were on board when the boat arrived at Cairo. The report was made to the consul, Mr. Salt, of the accident; and, though Mr. Drouetti was there at the time, he did not signify that any investigation should take place on this affair. Now that Mr. Drouetti was in Thebes, and the consul also, Mr. Drouetti complained much that he did not take into consideration the death of that man. The consul replied, that he never heard of any occasion to investigate the matter: to which Mr. Drouetti replied, that he ought to have done it. The consul then told him, that, as the man was in Mr. Drouetti's employ, he was surprised that he did not make an application while in Cairo. Mr. D. said, that he did not for delicacy's sake; which answer was received with general laughter. Nothing was left undone by our opponents to slander out insinuations.

reasons to believe was a person who wished to do him some injury; and that he had already acquainted the Caimakan of that place of the circumstance. I begged him to tell me what reason that man could have for assuming my appearance. He said, that it was done to deceive him, and if he (the impostor) had done any thing bad, it was to make the people believe that it was myself who had done it. The consul laughed at the story, and observed that I could not be so easily imitated. The conclusion of all this was, that, if I had happened to go among the ruins, which it was my constant practice to do, and some one had sent a ball at me, they could have said after, that they mistook me for the person who had assumed my appearance in dress and figure. I informed Mr. Drouetti that I hoped he would tell his European people to inquire before they should fire at the supposed person representing me, whether it was the real or the sham Belzoni, as it would not be quite so pleasant or satisfactory to me if the mistake had been found out after. He replied, that that person was sent away from Thebes, and would not return again. We went all over the ruins, and marked out the various spots of land which had been taken by us previous to Mr. Drouetti's agent's arrival in Thebes; so all was well understood, and all was so arranged that it was hoped that no further differences should arise from any party. Now, my reader, read it and judge.

It is not agreeable to my wishes to insert in this volume these matters, which perhaps may cause a supposition of my inclination to expose; but such is the case that I cannot avoid mentioning it, as I have done many others; for if I was to conceal from the public what happened at that period, an advantage might be taken, and matters brought before them in any light but that of truth.

After having now gone over the various places where I had to excavate, Mr. Drouetti, with all the complaisance possible, invited the consul and myself into his habitation among the ruins of Carnak. We were regaled with sherbet and lemonade, and talked of our late journey to Berenice. The discourse turned on our next expedition to the Isle of Philœ; when I happened to say, that, as I had to take the obelisk from that island down the cataract, I feared it was too late in the season, as the water would not serve at the cataract to float and launch down a boat adequate to support such a weight. On hearing this, Mr. Drouetti said, that those rogues at the Shellal, meaning at Assouan, had deceived him; that they promised many times to bring down the said obelisk for him, but that they only promised to do it, to extort money from him. I then informed Mr. Drouetti that those people knew they could not take away that obelisk; as, since my first voyage up the Nile, I took possession of it in consequence of a firman which the consul, Mr. Salt, who was there present, had obtained from the Bashaw. The consul informed Mr. Drouetti that he had ceded the said obelisk to Mr. Bankes, who intended to have it removed to England. On hearing this, Mr. Drouetti said, that he was not aware we had taken possession of it, and inquired if any money was spent in that affair on our side; and having been answered that we paid money to keep a guard over the obelisk, and that it was well understood with the Aga of Assouan that we were again to carry it away on the first opportunity, he replied, that those people had deceived him, to exact money from his agents, &c.; but notwithstanding all this, as the obelisk was intended for Mr. Bankes, he would not say a word about it, and voluntarily ceded it to him. This was not in compliment to our consul, who was present. I thought this was another present, made to Mr. Bankes like the cover of the sarcophagus made to me, which was so far buried among the rocks of Gournou, that all their efforts could not prevail to take it out. Mr. Drouetti inquired when we should set off, and the consul told him on the day after to-morrow.

Accordingly, on the 16th of November, we left Thebes for the first cataract of the Nile. The party was numerous—Mr. Bankes, Mr. Salt, Baron Sack, a Prussian traveller and a celebrated naturalist, Mr. Beechey, Mr. Linon, a draftsman, Doctor Ricci, and myself: a large boat was taken for the consul, a cangiar for Mr. Bankes, a small boat for the Baron, and a canoe for the sheep, goats, fowls, geese, ducks, pigeons, turkeys, and donkeys, which occasionally joined the chorus with the rest of the tribes, and accompanied the fleet with a perpetual concert. As to provisions, we were pretty well supplied, I believe; for, as their boats came lately from Cairo, they brought full stores: yet it was arduous travelling, living in that manner, destitute of every commodity of life; for even at table we had not ice to cool ourselves after the hot repast, which was concluded with fruits, and only two sorts of wine. In short, our lives were a burthen to us from the fatigue and dangerous mode of travelling. We were not like travellers who live on the best of every thing they can get, and write at home the hard life they undergo. O, no! O, no! we would scorn to travel in such an effeminate manner. To be sure, some travellers will say, Why should I starve myself, while I am in a plentiful country? O! then, but you should not make the world believe you are starving, while you live like Sir John Falstaff.

On our passing Eleithias, we stopped there part of a day, and nearly the whole of the next. As I have nothing to add to the description of that place, I shall not enter into any further description of it.

On the 21st, we visited Edfu, and took a minute survey of these truly magnificent ruins, which are so covered with a profusion of objects, that if a traveller was to repeat his visits every day of his life, he might still find something new to be observed. This place was at that time under the researches of Mr. Drouetti's agents; one of whom, we understood, had received a despatch from his master, by an extra courier, and had immediately set off for the island of Philœ.

We continued our voyage, and before we arrived at Silsili, or the Chain of Mountains, we met a small boat, in which was Mr. Lebulo, the said agent and countryman of Mr. Drouetti, a Piedmontese: he was hailed, but would not stop to speak. We stopped at this place at night, and early in the morning we were all scattered about these quarries, not in search of partridges, but in search of sepulchres, ancient stones, Greek inscriptions, sphinxes, or any sort of Egyptian wonder. Indeed, I must say, that this place deserves more of the attention of the scientific traveller than has hitherto been bestowed upon it. There are several interesting burial-places among the quarries of the rocks; and it is evident, that the famous sphinxes with the ram's head, which are to be seen in Carnak, have been taken from this spot, as one of the same kind is to be seen cut out in the rough, and partly removed from the rocks to the Nile, and another, like it, is nearly cut out of the quarry. As to the old story, that these two mountains were chained, I can but say, that I have my objection as to the fact of it; for if the ancients wanted to prevent the passing of boats, it may be supposed that Assouan was a more suitable place for that purpose, as the passage from the island of Elephantine to the rocks of old Assouan is much narrower than that of the Silsili mountains, and the cataract itself would form as good a barrier as any that could be constructed on the Nile. There is a stone on the west side of the said mountain, which is supposed to be that to which the chain was attached; but, for my part, I could not see any marks where this chain was fixed, nor does the stone seem to have been suited to such purposes; and I am rather inclined to think, that the name of the Chained Mountains is derived from the position of the mountain itself; it runs in a chain from east to west, and stretches over the Nile at each side, so that it forms the narrowest passage in that river, from the cataract to the sea; from which circumstance it is possible that the ancients had given it that name, for I do not believe that their commerce was so flourishing as to oblige them to put an iron chain across the Nile, to stop the boats at night, at a time when iron was reckoned a most valuable article, and was employed for better purposes.

We reached Ombos on the next day; and as the party had to stop there one day longer, I was anxious to reach Assouan, as I expected no good from the early journey of Lebulo, the agent of Mr. Drouetti. Accordingly, I set off for that place in a cangiar, which had come to meet us, to take the consul up to Nubia. I took with me a young Scotchman, who had been brought into Egypt at the time of the last English invasion of that country: he was taken prisoner, and some years after entered into the service of the Bashaw of Egypt, and assumed the name of Osman. He became acquainted with Sheik Burckhardt; and, in consequence of his honesty and attachment to him, the Sheik rewarded him in his will. He was the only and the last person who closed the eyes of that lamented traveller, and I had much conversation with him on the subject.

On my arrival at Assouan, I found that the said Lebulo had suggested to the Aga of Assouan, and to the natives of the island of Philœ, not to let the English party, who were coming up, carry away the obelisk. The Aga remonstrated with him, that the obelisk had been taken possession of by me three years before, and a guard had been paid for it on that account. In consequence of this refusal, Mr. Lebulo proceeded to the island of Philœ; and having heard from all the natives that I had taken possession so long before, he adopted the method of a trick to seduce those simple people: he pretended he could read the hieroglyphics on the obelisk, and said it was written, that the obelisk belonged to Mr. Drouetti's ancestors; consequently he had a right to it. The people believed him, and he gave them some trifling presents, and brought them to the Cady, or justice, to hear their testimony that the obelisk was the property of Mr. Drouetti. The Cady received a present, and wrote a sort of certificate, on the evidence of these people. Having done all this, Mr. Lebulo wrote a note, which he left with one of the Sheiks in the island to give it to us when we arrived, and set off immediately, as he thought his face could not be impudent enough to meet us.

On my arrival at Assouan, I heard of the difficulties this agent had thrown in our way; but I remonstrated with the Aga, that he must recollect that it was well understood, that I took possession of that obelisk ever since my first voyage, and that the money I paid for a guard was given to him by the medium of one of the Bashaw's Janizaries, who was ready to testify the case, and that he, the Aga himself, made a contract to receive three hundred piastres (thirty dollars) on the removal of the obelisk. He acknowledged all this, and said, that the other party would have taken the obelisk away several times, but they could not succeed; and that lately they tried again, but the water of the cataract was too low, so that they could not effect the passage through for this season. This last observation concerned me more than all the rest of his discourse; for it was entirely on the possibility of effecting the passage down the cataract this year that depended the success of exporting the obelisk. Next day the party arrived at Assouan, and I went to the island of Philœ to take a view of the bank where I was to embark the obelisk, and have it conveyed to the cataract where it was to be launched. On my arrival there, an old Sheik immediately presented to me the following note:

" Le chargé d'affaire de Mr. Drouetti prie Messieurs les Voyageurs Européens de respecter le porteur du présent billet gardant l'obelisque, qui est dans l'île de Philœ, appartenant à Mr. Drouetti.

" LEBULO."

" Philœ, le 22 Sep^{bre}. 1818."

The people of the island then informed me of the means which Mr. Lebulo had taken to persuade them to testify that the obelisk belonged to his party. By the date of the note I perceived that this was done only eight days before; and as we had been fifteen days on our voyage from Thebes to Assouan, they had time to do all this underhand work at their leisure.

On my return to Assouan I acquainted the consul and Mr. Bankes of what passed, and suggested to them, that the only mode of proceeding was to have an interview with the Aga himself, and from him to hear who was the first to take possession of the obelisk. Accordingly the Aga was requested to come on board, and, in the presence of the consul, he declared, that I was the first person of all who took possession of the obelisk. Accordingly I set the men to work. I procured a boat for that purpose, which by chance was in Assouan. The greatest difficulty was to persuade the Reis, or captain of the shallal, to undertake to launch the boat down the cataract with the obelisk on board. The water was very low at that time; and what was more against the undertaking of the operation was, that the opposite party had applied to him two months before, when the water was much higher, and he refused on the score that it was not high enough. However, the promise of a good present, and half of the money in his hands, mollified the captain, and he promised that he would accomplish the undertaking. To the Aga I made a present of a gold watch, worth one hundred and fifty piastres (fifteen dollars), in the name of Mr. Bankes; the Sheiks of the Moraida, and other places round, were to be gained to our side, that they might provide men to work. This was done, of course, by way of giving a trifle more than to the rest of the labourers, and promising more if they behaved well. I had some little difficulty to procure a few sticks, or small poles, at Assouan, as there is no wood in those places except what they procure from Cairo, merely to repair their boats. I had also some difficulty at first in removing the said obelisk from its original station; but once put on its way, it soon came to the water-side. The pedestal was rather more troublesome; owing to its square form, it was almost buried under the rubbish; and as we had no tackle whatsoever, and very little wood, it retarded the work one or two days longer. At this time the Aga of Assouan came to the island, and presented a letter he had received from Mr. Drouetti himself, sealed with his own seal, which the Aga knew well, ordering the Aga not to permit any one to take away the obelisk. The letter was translated by the Scotch Osman, from whom we had no doubt of the correctness of its contents. The consul begged the Aga to send back his compliments to Mr. Drouetti, and to tell him that we were going to remove the obelisk. At this time, Mr. Baley, Mr. Godfrey, and two other gentlemen, arrived in the island, from their tour through Greece, &c.

Our party prepared for their voyage to the second cataract. The obelisk was now ready to be embarked, when the following accident happened, which was entirely owing to my own neglect, by trusting a single manoeuvre to some who speak more than they can execute. I had left the care to others of making a sort of temporary pier of large blocks of stones, while I had to go to examine a certain passage in the cataract where the boat was to be taken up empty, and launched down when loaded. On my return, the pier appeared quite strong enough to bear at least forty times the weight it had to support; but, alas! when the obelisk came gradually on from the sloping bank, and all the weight rested on it, the pier, with the obelisk, and some of the men, took a slow movement, and majestically descended into the river, wishing us better success. I was not three yards off when this happened, and for some minutes, I must confess, I remained as stiff as a post. The first thing that came into my head, was the loss of such a piece of antiquity; the second was, the exultation of our opponents, after so much questioning to what party it belonged; and, lastly, the blame of all the antiquarian republic in the world. It happens very often, that after a vase slips through the hands and breaks on the ground, it is by a natural impulse that one turns himself to look at the pieces; so did I: I fixed my eyes on the place where the pier set off by itself into the Nile, and observed that the stones which were to serve as a foundation on a sloping bank had been only laid on the surface of it, so that naturally the weight of the obelisk must have carried it, or rather pressed down into the Nile. The obelisk was still peeping a little out of the water: the labourers were of various humours; some were sorry, not for the obelisk, which was no loss to them, but for the loss of what they might have gained in future operations in passing it down the cataract, and others were laughing, I suppose, at seeing the evident disappointment expressed on my countenance; some went one way, some another, and I remained alone, seated on the bank, to contemplate the little part which projected out of the water, and the eddies made by the current on that spot in consequence of the obelisk below. The effects of surprise did not last long; I began to reflect, and saw the possibility of taking the obelisk up again. Unfortunately I had not a single machine to help the undertaking, and even our ropes, which were of palm leaves, were broken and half rotten, and scarcely any wood at all suited to employ to that purpose. The obelisk is one single piece of granite of twenty-two feet in length, and two in breadth at the basis. It is not smaller in height than that in St. George's Fields, but of a stone of a much heavier quality. I had, however, in my favour the people, who are excellent watermen, and who could stay in the water the whole day without the least difficulty.

Having made up my mind to have the obelisk taken up, I found that the loss would be only two or three days work. Accordingly I ordered the men to come the next morning, and sent to Assouan that evening to fetch some ropes if possible. Mr. Bankes was not there when this happened, as he had crossed the Nile that afternoon; but the labourers who returned home after the obelisk had fallen in the water, informed him of what had happened. I believe he was not less displeased than myself when I saw the accident, and on his arrival he said, that such things would happen sometimes; but I saw he was not in a careful humour himself, so I informed him that the obelisk was not lost, and that in two or three days it would be on board. The two next days were employed in this operation, which was done as follows:

I caused a great quantity of stones to be brought to the waterside. I then desired several men to enter the water, and to make a heap of stones on the side of the obelisk opposite to the shore, and to form a solid bed for the levers to rest upon. I accordingly placed the levers under the obelisk, one at the basis, and the other near the leaning point, so that by the pressure of the levers, the obelisk must turn round upon its axis: the men could not put down the lever under water as they do on shore, but by seating themselves on the extremity of the levers, the pressure of their own weight produced the effect. Two ropes were passed under the obelisk: that end which was from under it was fastened to some date-trees, which happened to be on the bank, and to the ends which came from above I put as many men to pull as I thought were sufficient. At the side where the levers were I put some good divers, who were ready to put large stones under the obelisk when it rose, so that it might not return back to its former situation. Having set the men at the rope to pull, and those of the divers to mount on the extremities of the levers, the obelisk rose on the side opposite the bank; and when the levers were to be removed, the obelisk was propped by stones under it. It was risen so that its own weight caused it to move round at each turn of it, when we gained nearly the space of its own breadth, and so on till it came quite on dry ground, which was effected in less than two days; the party then set off for the second cataract. Previous to the taking on board the obelisk, I thought it better to export from the island the pedestal of it, as I could not use the boat for both. I embarked and took it at the Marada, in a good situation, that it might be easily embarked. At this moment, an agent of Mr. Drouetti came to Assouan, and put the whole town in an uproar. He brought the Aga to the island of Philœ, to speak to me, and to persuade me for my best advantage to leave the obelisk there. I asked the Aga what he had to say on this affair; that if he thought proper I should leave the obelisk where it was, ready for embarkation, for Mr. Drouetti. The Aga seeing me smile, replied that he had nothing to say on the subject; that Mr. Drouetti had written to the Defterdar Bey at Siout, and that the Defterdar Bey had written to him, the Aga, not to meddle with either party. The agent abused the Aga, but to no purpose, as all his proceedings would not interrupt my work. He then attempted to convince the Sheiks that they might stop the men from working, offering to pay them for their loss of time without any trouble. Such offers, made even to the labourers, were rejected by them with disgust. I continued my operation, and put the obelisk on board, by means of a bridge of palm-trees, thrown from across the boat to the land under the obelisk, which was now turned on the bridge, and entered on board: when in the centre of the boat, I removed the trees from under it; and no sooner was this done than we set off with the obelisk for the Marada, to have it ready to be launched down the cataract on the next morning.

The Reis of the Shalal, or cataract, continued firm on my side, and I continued to keep him so. He had half of the money. He now came to receive the other half previous to his undertaking. I did not think it prudent to disappoint him in his expectation, so I paid him the other half, which was twenty-five dollars, on condition that he would make a promise, before two of my people, to maintain his word; and, on the contrary, if he failed, that I should appeal to Mahomet Ali, the Bashaw at Cairo. He was satisfied; and, having made the arrangement for the number of men who were to be employed the next day, he set off on his business. On the same evening I took a walk among the granite rocks of the cataract, where we had to pass. The next day an object of attention came in my way, which I often thought to speak of. There are many of these rocks with hieroglyphics and figures cut on them, which evidently were done only by scholars, who, perhaps, were practising the science of sculpture on those masses. The observation I made was, that a calculation of ages might be made by the various colours which the rocks have taken from their original, and from the time it has been cut; for instance, we have to suppose that, when nature first formed the mass of granite, it was as white as it may be seen now when newly cut. We next must fix on an epoch for the time when the hieroglyphics on those rocks were engraved, and by that we may calculate the degree of the three colours, which are in view; for instance, the part which has never been touched is dark brown; that which has been cut, supposed about three thousand years ago, is light brown; and some sculptured in later ages is still lighter. That which has been cut only one hour before may be supposed to be as it was on the day of its creation as above: so, by the proportion of the various colours on the rocks, a calculation of the age may be formed, and by that means we may find the age of the creation.

I beg my readers to pardon my thus speculating on a point which, in my humble capacity, can afford but little instruction; however, as the idea struck me, I lay it before the public.

Next morning all was ready for the dangerous operation of passing the cataract with the obelisk. I have mentioned before that this is the greatest fall, or rather descent, of water in the cataract. When the inundation is half high in the Nile, it is a column of water of about three hundred yards in length, which falls in an angle of twenty and twenty-five degrees among rocks and stones, which project out in various directions. The boat was brought to the margin of the cascade; a strong rope, or rather a small cable, was attached to a large tree, the end of which was passed through the beams of the boat, so as to be slackened or stopped at pleasure. In the boat there were only five men; and on the rocks, on each side of the cascade, a number of others in various places, with ropes attached to the boat, so as to put it either on one side or the other, as it required, to prevent its running against the stones; for if it should be touched in the smallest degree, with such a weight on board, and in such a rapid stream, the boat could not escape being dashed to pieces. The cable, which I borrowed from a merchant-boat in Assouan, was pretty strong, but not sufficient to stop the boat in its course, in case it should be in danger of running against a rock. It was only sufficient to check its course down; nor could the boat have been stopped in such a situation, for in that case the water would run over the boat, and sink it instantly. Under these circumstances, all depended on the dexterity of the men who were posted in various parts to pull or slacken according as necessity required. I did not fail to use all the persuasion possible, and promises of bakshis, to the wild people, as they are called, but who on this occasion were as steady as so many pilots. The Reis, of whom I had hired the boat, was almost out of his senses, thinking it would be certainly lost. The poor fellow had engaged his vessel merely because it happened that his trade failed; and he was in Assouan for some time without hope of getting a cargo, and had incurred debts, which confined him there, and he would have been glad of any freight to get out; but when he saw the danger his boat was in, he cried like a child, and begged I would relinquish my project, and return his boat safe to him. But when he saw the vessel on the point of being launched, he threw himself with his face to the ground, and did not rise till all was out of danger. Having seen that all was ready, I gave the signal to slacken the cable. It was one of the greatest sights I have seen. The boat took a course which may be reckoned at the rate of twelve miles an hour. Accordingly, the men on land slackened the rope; and at the distance of one hundred yards the boat came in contact with an eddy, which, beating against a rock, returned towards the vessel, and that helped much to stop its course. The men on the side pulled the boat out of the direction of that rock, and it continued its course, gradually diminishing its rate, till it reached the bottom of the cataract; and I was not a little pleased to see it out of danger. The labourers altogether seemed pleased at the good success of the attempt, even independently, I believe, of the interest they might derive from it; and it is not very often that such feelings enter the bosoms of these people. The Reis of the boat came to me with joy expressed in his countenance, as may easily be imagined.

Having set all to rights to pass the other parts of the cataract, I went on board, and we continued the course of the current. We had only two or three places of little danger to pass; but, thank God, we arrived safe at Assouan on the same day. I beg it to be observed, that this is not the passage where small boats are taken up or down the cataract; for there are other smaller columns of water, which are deep enough to float small boats, but not such as that one with the obelisk.

Immediately after my arrival there, I prepared to depart for Thebes, and having satisfied the Aga according to our promise, I departed. Previous to my arrival there, I quitted the boat, as the wind was against us, and went by land. I took up my old residence at the tombs, in Beban el Malook. There I found Mrs. Belzoni, who had returned from Jerusalem, as I had written to her that I could not go into Syria. It was then Christmas, and we passed the solemnity of that blessed day in the solitude of those recesses, undisturbed by the folly of mankind; and only a few inoffensive Arabs, who guarded the new tombs, were there; but it was not to last long so. I must now enter into new contests with evil beings; and in spite of all the study I made to avoid bringing before the public the foul deeds of malice, I find that I cannot avoid inserting them in this volume. The following circumstances have induced me to quit Egypt; and any one who will kindly read and attend to the catastrophe, will agree with me in saying, that it was high time to do so. It happened at this period that a certain person, whose name, for compassion's sake, I do not wish to mention, but who was neither English nor French, came into

Upper Egypt, not to see antiquities, but to purchase some if he could. He came from one of the capitals of Europe, and was to return. He offered to do any thing for me in Europe if I wished; he was on friendly terms, and I believe sincere, till the diabolical spirit of interest got into his breast, and then he suffered himself to be led by it. As I happened to know him before, I took the opportunity of his return to that very place where I was in want of a person to transact some business for me. The business was, that, as he was on his return to Europe, he would take four of the sphinxes, or lion-headed statues, which were allotted me for my share, to the very metropolis where he was going, and there make an offer, as a present, to a certain high personage in my name, which he undertook to do with great pleasure; and it was so arranged that I should give him an order on the British consul in Alexandria, to receive the aforesaid statues, which were lodged in the charge of the British agent in Rosetta. It happened that, at the same time, this man became acquainted with the people of our opposite party, and, as he must come in in the following account, I shall call him the "*stranger*."

On the eve of Christmas, the boat with the obelisk on board arrived, and stopped at Luxor, waiting for a few small articles to be loaded, and then to proceed to Rosetta.

It will be recollected that, previous to our last departure for the cataract, I entered into an arrangement with Mr. Salt, settling where I was to excavate on several spots among the ruins of Carnak. On St. Stephen's day I passed the Nile to that place, with the intention of examining the spots of ground which were allotted to our party, according to the arrangement made by Messrs. Salt and Drouetti. At Luxor I was mounted on a very high donkey, the only mode of travelling short journeys in those countries, as horses are scarce, and it is too inconvenient to mount a camel for a small distance. I was followed by my Greek servant and two Arabian drivers. I was unarmed; my servant had two pistols as usual. Our opponents, with their commander, Mr. Drouetti, were lodged in some mud houses among the ruins of Carnak. The boat with the obelisk which I had just brought down and put up at Luxor, was rather too close under their noses, as they expressed themselves; and it irritated them to such a degree, that they premeditated the mode of revenge by, as they said, only abusing and insulting Belzoni; but this could not have been done without some danger of retaliation, and perhaps with interest equivalent to the merit of the operation. The only way this was to be done was by taking the advantage of a pretext, and by raising some differences against me in some way or other; the plan was well laid. The first piece of ground I had to examine among these ruins, was occupied by the labourers of Mr. Drouetti; consequently, it was expected that I should take notice of it, that some altercation would ensue, and then would be the time to satiate their revenge. Previous to my arrival at the above ground, I was warned by an Arab not to go where the other Europeans were; but I took no notice of what he said, as sometimes those people make much out of nothing. I continued my route till I arrived on the above ground, and the first thing I saw was a number of men working on a spot too well known to be of our lot according to the arrangement. I then perceived what these gentlemen wanted; so I took no notice, and actually passed on without stopping to look at them. None of the Europeans were there, and my servant observing to me, that that ground was of our share, I told him not to meddle himself about it, and we passed on. The above working ground was close to the small lakes, and these gentlemen were living in the window of the great propylæon, which is at least a good quarter of a mile distant from the above ground. We passed quietly before them, and continued on our way straight to the north side of the ruins as far as their extremity, another quarter of a mile from where they were. I remained some time there in examining some grounds, and on my return towards the great propylæon where we had to pass on our return to Luxor, we met an Arab running towards us, crying, from having received a severe beating from our opponents, merely because he served, and was faithful to us, as far as an Arab can be. This would have been another motive to create some altercation, but it had no effect; I took no notice of it, and was going on straight to Luxor. I was at about three hundred yards from the great propylæon, when I saw a group of people running towards us; they were about thirty Arabs, headed by two Europeans, agents of Mr. Drouetti. On their approaching, Mr. Lebulo was first, and the renegado Rossignano second, both Piedmontese, and countrymen of Mr. Drouetti. Lebulo began his address to me, by asking, what business I had to take away an obelisk that did not belong to me; and that I had done so many things of this kind to him, that I should not do any more. Meanwhile he seized the bridle of my donkey with one hand, and with the other he laid hold of my waistcoat, and stopped me from proceeding any farther: he had also a large stick hung to his wrist by a string. By this time my servant was assailed by a number of Arabs, two of whom were constantly in the service of Mr. Drouetti. At the same moment, the renegado Rossignano reached within four yards of me, and with all the rage of a ruffian, levelled a double-barrelled gun at my breast, loading me with all the imprecations that a villain could invent; by this time my servant was disarmed, and overpowered by numbers, and in spite of his efforts, took his pistols from his belt. The two gallant knights before me, I mean Lebulo and Rossignano, escorted by the two other Arabian servants of Mr. Drouetti, both armed with pistols, and many others armed with sticks, continued their clamorous imprecations against me, and the brave Rossignano still keeping the gun pointed at my breast, said, that it was time that I should pay for all I had done to them. The courageous Lebulo said, with all the emphasis of an enraged man, that he was to have one-third of the profit derived from the selling of that obelisk, when in Europe, according to a promise from Mr. Drouetti, had I not stolen it from the island of Philœ. My situation was not pleasant, surrounded by a band of ruffians like those, and I have no doubt that if I had attempted to dismount, the cowards would have despatched me on the ground, and said that they did it in defence of their lives, as I had been the aggressor. I thought the best way was to keep on my donkey, and look at the villains with contempt. Lebulo said, that another of their party had been drowned at Girgeh, on board of the English boat, and that they had no redress for it, meaning, I suppose, the poor man that fell overboard at Girgeh on his passage to Cairo. I told Lebulo to let me proceed on my way, and that if I had done any thing wrong, I should be ready to account for it; but all was to no purpose. Their rage had blinded them out of their senses.

While this was going on, I observed another band of Arabs running towards us. When they came nearer, I saw Mr. Drouetti himself among them, and close to him a servant of his, armed with pistols. On his arrival before me, Mr. Drouetti demanded, in a tone not inferior to that of his disciples, what reason or authority I had to stop his people from working. I told him that I knew nothing of what he meant, and that I found myself extremely ill used by his own people, and that he must answer for their conduct. In an authoritative tone he desired I should dismount, which I refused to do. At this moment a pistol was fired behind me, but I could not tell by whom. I was determined to bear much, sooner than come to blows with such people, who did not blush to assail me all in a mass; but when I heard the pistol fired behind my back, I thought it was high time to sell my life as dear as I could. I dismounted, but then the kind Mr. Drouetti assured me that I was not in danger while he was there; and Mr. Lebulo, who had before acted the part of a ruffian, now contrived to play that of a neutral gentleman. By this time many other Arabs of the village of Carnak had reached this place, and seeing me thus surrounded, would any one suppose it! for the honour of Christendom and civilization, those wild Arabs, as we call them, were disgusted at the conduct of Europeans, and interfered in my behalf. They surrounded the renegado Rossignano, whose conduct they thought most outrageous and base, not for an European, but even for the worst of Arabs. What ideas must have been formed in the minds of those people of the civilization of Europe, by the conduct of such villains! I was now informed that an European stranger was in the place of residence of Mr. Drouetti. I sent an Arab to beg he would come where we were, as I thought I might have a witness to what might afterwards take place, though the affray was almost over. Mr. Drouetti, who was now very mild, said, that he never had given any order to his people to work on any grounds belonging to us; that I should have made application to him, and he would have put them right; but that I should not stop the people from their work. I repeated that I did not know what he meant, and that all this was a combination of traps put together by his agents. He said that an Arab came to his lodging, and informed him that I ordered the people away from their work. I persisted that the Arab should be brought before me; but he was not to be found; he was called every where, but did not answer. One of the two Arabs from Gournou, who followed me as a driver, recognised the said Arab, who all this time was close to Mr. Drouetti, who had called to him in vain, and who, though he had seen him a few minutes before, did not recognise him again. Being before me, I stared in the man's face, and ordered him to repeat what he had said of me to Mr. Drouetti. He replied, that he did not say to Mr. Drouetti that I stopped the men from working, but that my servant did, though I was totally confident of the contrary, as he was not two yards from me when we passed that way. It was useless for me to contest that point, as I saw it was brought forward merely to cover the true cause for which they attacked me, which was shown by their first words to me about the obelisk. I insisted that Mr. Drouetti should come where the men were at work, that I might point out to him that his people were the aggressors, by encroaching on our lot of ground, of which he was forcibly convinced. As we went on, the assailant Rossignano continued at a distance behind me. The stranger arrived where I was, and proved to be the person alluded to before, by whom I had to send the four statues to Europe. On his arrival, I informed him of what had passed; but Mr. Drouetti told him that we had only had a few words, and that was all. The stranger observed to him, that he saw those people take up arms, while he was in their house or habitation, and run out, and remembered Mr. Drouetti himself said, he must run after them, for fear they should do some mischief, and that they did wrong to act so. To which Mr. Drouetti replied, that he could not help what these people did; to which observation the stranger replied, that he should not keep them in his service. Mr. Drouetti made a long lamentation on the taking away the obelisk. I reminded him that he must have known it was taken possession of long before any of his agents reached the island of Philœ; and that he did wrong to send his agents to that place to prevent my taking it, after he knew we had set off for that purpose. He said, this was owing to Mr. Bankes not calling on him previous to his departure for that place, and conversing with him on the subject. The fact is, that Mr. Bankes did not think proper to put himself under an unnecessary obligation to Mr. Drouetti. I then informed Mr. Drouetti, that I had resisted many and various sorts of attacks by his agents, but I did not expect they would come to such a pitch, and that it was high time for me to quit the country; so I returned to Beban el Malook, and immediately commenced my preparations to depart for Europe, as I could not live any longer in a country where I had become the object of revenge, of a set of people who could take the basest means to accomplish their purpose; and notwithstanding the advantages I might have derived in the continuation of my researches, the conditions of which with the consul were now more advantageous to me than any I had hitherto obtained, I was so totally disgusted, that I took the above resolution accordingly.

I had written the particulars of what had happened, to the consul, adding, that by the time he received my letter I should be on my way to Alexandria, as I was determined to proceed to Europe by the first opportunity. As to any redress, I did not ask for it, as I could not expect to have any in that country; and as the boat with the obelisk was not set off, I availed myself of the opportunity of descending the Nile in it.

Having finished all the models, drawings, &c. of the tomb, and put on board all that I had accumulated on my own account, I began the operation of taking the sarcophagus out of the tombs. I must lament the unfortunate fate of some of the figures within this place. It will be recollected, as I mentioned before, that the entrance into the tombs was situated under a small torrent of water, which, when it happens to rain, runs over into the valley. I was then making a canal to turn the course of the water, that it might not run into the tomb in case of rain; but, on the arrival of the consul, all was put an end to. The consequence was, that while I was absent up the Nile it happened to rain; the water, finding the entrance open, ran into the tomb, and though not much, was enough to occasion some damage to some of the figures. The dryness of the calcareous stone, which is more like lime itself than raw stone, absorbed the dampness, and consequently cracked in many places, particularly in the angles of the pillars on the doorways, &c.; and in one of the rooms there was a piece of stone detached, containing the upper part of three figures; and in another chamber, was a figure, which fortunately fell without much injury; though broken in three pieces, I saved it from farther destruction. I was not a little vexed to see such a thing happen. The damage done at that time was inconsiderable in a place of such an extent; but I fear, that in the course of a few years it will become much worse; and I am persuaded, that the damp in the rainy days has caused as much damage in the tombs as has been occasioned in any other way. It is worthy of observation, that the atmosphere must be much changed since the time of Herodotus, when he mentions a circumstance of some rain having fallen in Thebes as an extraordinary case or a phenomenon, for at present it rains in Thebes every year. I do not mean to say that it rains in a manner similar to what we are accustomed to in Europe, but enough to say it does rain; for instance, two or three days in the winter, and in these two or three days perhaps only half an hour at a time. It appears also, that at moments the water drops are pretty large, and wet the traveller, who, not being prepared, feels it strange to be thus served; but the great body of water, as I mentioned before, comes from the desert, through the valleys into the Nile. It is curious also to remark, the great difference in the climates only in the short distance of little more than two hundred miles to the south of Thebes, where it very seldom rains; indeed, some years pass without any, and it is owing to this circumstance, with the combination of this place being under the tropic of Cancer, that it may be calculated to be the driest and hottest spot on earth: I mean that track of land which extends from the first to the second cataract of the Nile, named Lower Nubia. It includes the tropic of Cancer, consequently these countries receive greater heat from the sun than any other on this side of the equinoctial line, as it passes vertically over it twice in the course of a few days, at the time of the solstice. This circumstance, united with the phenomenon that it never rains, for it never can be said to do so, unless a few drops, perhaps, in the course of five years, or more, can be reckoned as rain, cause the rocks to be so perpetually hot, that the heat rises in higher degrees than any other part on earth. It will be recollected, as I mentioned before, that in the beginning of June, in the island of Philœ, we had the thermometer at 124° of Fahrenheit in the shade; but it is to be observed, that the thermometer did not show us to what degree the heat arose, as it only marked 124°, consequently the mercury might mount higher if the glass had permitted. But now to our departure from Thebes.

Having put all things in readiness, and all the models of the tombs being embarked, I took out the celebrated sarcophagus, which gave me something to do (in consequence of its being so very slender and thin), lest it might break at the smallest touch of any thing: however, it was safely got out of the tomb and put in a strong case. The valley it had to pass to reach the Nile is rather uneven for more than two miles, and one mile of good soft sand and small pebbles. I had it conveyed on rollers all the way, and safely put on board. By this time Mr. Wright and Mr. Fisher arrived in Thebes, on their return from Nubia. I had the pleasure to walk over the remains of old Thebes with these gentlemen, and I must confess, that I felt no small degree of sorrow to quit a place which was become so familiar to me, and where, in no other part of the world, I could find so many objects of inquiry so congenial to my inclination. I must say, that I felt more in leaving Thebes, than any other place in my life. It was on the 27th of January, 1819, when we left these truly magnificent ruins, and we arrived in Cairo on the 18th of February.

After passing Benisouef we saw a small boat, and, by its appearance, concluded there must be some Europeans in it. They called to us, as they, too, saw we were Europeans. We went to shore: it was Mr. Fuller, who ascended the Nile,—a gentleman of most excellent good manners, and whom I had the pleasure to know after in Cairo. He was accompanied by a person who ascended the Nile to distribute the Arabic Bibles for the society. It was pity that he was not well informed of some particular places in Egypt, and in the province of Faioum, where many christian Copts are residing, and would have been happy to have had a Bible amongst them. In the above boat I saw a person of a strange appearance, which caused my inquiring who he was. I was agreeably surprised when I found him to be Mr. Pearce, who resided in Abyssinia for several years, and was left there by Lord Valentia, now the Earl of Mountnorris. Our acquaintance was soon made, but I was sorry I should have met him on such an occasion, as we could be together but so short a time. To the inquiries I wished to make of him concerning those countries, he answered in a manner that convinced me he was an enterprising man, much accustomed to fatigue: the life and hardships he underwent in Abyssinia would be most interesting to the public. At Cairo we only stopped a few days, and continued our voyage to Rosetta: there we landed the various pieces of antiquity, the obelisk, the sarcophagus found in one of the king's tombs, and the cover of another sarcophagus, which is the best piece

I accumulated on my own account. It had been thrown from its sarcophagus when it was forced open, and being reversed it remained buried by the stones, and unnoticed by any visitor. I cleared off all the stones, and on examination of the under part, found that it was a fine figure, larger than life, in alto relievo, and, except the foot, all the rest was quite perfect. On turning the stone, I found that, besides the said figure, which is in the centre of the cover, there are two others at each side in basso relievo, and, also, excepting the feet, are quite perfect: its preservation is owing to its being reversed. Having reimbarked all those articles again on board of a djerm, we came to Alexandria with a firm intention to set off with the first opportunity; for though I felt much regret in quitting the very country in which I wished to remain undisturbed a little longer, yet under the circumstances of such a persecution I could not help hastening my departure. But the time was not yet arrived. At Alexandria I found letters from the consul and from Mr. Bankes, in answer to mine from Baban el Malook. The letters had been sent by an Arab as far as Cairo, and from thence to Alexandria. The consul advised me to stop till I could receive a certain answer from England, and to have redress of the outrageous behaviour of those gentry: this was the last thing that I could wish for, for I knew enough of the country to know how that affair would end; I knew the influence of their master, who I was certain would do all in his power to prevent any justice being done, so I did not find my inclination to remain, particularly as it happened to be the time of the plague; but Mr. Lee, the vice-consul in Alexandria, acquainted me that he had already made a deposition of the deeds in Thebes, and presented to the French consul, Mr. Rousell. I was glad to see that my cause had been taken up, but I was in very little hopes to have any redress, as no such a thing ever happened in those countries, in particular against such people.

Mr. Drouetti, who was by this time in Alexandria, took to himself the defence of his agents, and made a protest against Mr. Salt, the British consul, who, he said, was his accuser; and it was agreed that the matter should be left alone till Mr. Salt's return from Upper Egypt, so my departure was postponed till that period. At this time I had the pleasure of becoming more acquainted with Mr. Briggs, a gentleman who was on the eve of setting off for Europe: he was the person who suggested to the Bashaw of Egypt to cut the canal from Foua to Alexandria, to facilitate the exportation of the products of the country on board of the European vessels in the harbour, which sometimes were obliged to wait six months for their cargoes, owing to the difficulty of passing the bogazo, or bar, that crosses the mouth of the river, and often kept the djerms loaded for three months without effecting the passage. This cut is forty miles in length, and cost above three hundred thousand pounds to finish it; but it is a great accommodation in the exportation, and of course useful to the commerce of Egypt in general.

Before this time the stranger, to whom I have before alluded, had arrived in Alexandria, and was quite changed in his conduct as a witness: he had already signed his name to a deposition written by Lebulo himself, which of course was not against the party; and when he was called to give evidence, had forgotten that he saw those people take up arms and run towards the spot where I was: whatever points or words I could clearly put in remembrance, and repeat to him, he had forgotten all, and did not scruple to say, before the consul, Mr. Lee, that if I had been the first to apply to him, or to make my own deposition, he would have signed his name for me as he did for the other people. Now having proved him contradictory to his deposition, he came into the office of the consul, and, with the greatest indifference, actually made a deposition to contradict what he had asserted in favour of the assailants. He had stated previously, that he was present at the dispute or altercation, as the gentlemen of our opponents'. party would have it called; but he now said, that he only heard by Mr. Drouetti and his agents that an altercation of words had taken place. Such were the preparations for this defence; and now to end the affair with the stranger. No sooner did he communicate to my opponents the intention I had to make an offer of the four statues above mentioned, as a present to a certain court of Europe, than they immediately entered into a league with each other, and every thing was carried on in great secresy. Some statues of their own were put on board a vessel for Europe, and a collection of antiquities was made up to be offered for sale to the above court, and this was to be done previous to my offer being made; and when I thought my statues were to be embarked, and conveyed to Europe to be presented as above, I found that the stranger had set off with what he had procured from my opponents, leaving me and my statues to learn how to know him better.

I do not mean to blame any one for endeavouring to do any thing to their advantage, so that it is done in an honourable manner; but I cannot help observing, that whatever speculation he could have made, with what he has brought into Europe for our opponents, was obtained by a very wrong proceeding.

Seeing that some time would elapse before the consul returned, I did not know how to employ myself in the interval: I thought of making some researches in Lower Egypt, but I doubted not I should encounter some difficulty there also, as the fountain head of our opponents was not far off; but idle I could not stay. For a long time I had a wish to make a small excursion into the western desert. I had observed that the temple of Jupiter Ammon had been an object of search for a long time, and by more than one traveller, but that the true spot where it existed had not been fixed. I considered that the Faioum was a province as yet little explored, and that I might make an excursion in it perhaps undisturbed, and from thence proceed to the western desert. I should have no difficulty in obtaining a firman, but as I could not have it without letting every one know where I was going, I preferred to go without, as I hoped to make my way in some manner or other. An English merchant, who resided in Alexandria, lent me a small house in Rosetta, near the British agency, where I left Mrs. Belzoni. Accordingly I took a small boat, and set off for the Faioum.

JOURNEY TO THE OASIS OF AMMON.

I LEFT Rosetta on the 20th, and arrived at Benisouef on the 29th of April, 1819. I took with me a Sicilian servant, whom I hired in Alexandria, as my Irish lad had taken the opportunity of returning to England from Jerusalem with Mr. Legh. I took with me, also, a Moorish Hadge, who was on his return from Mecca, and begged to be taken on board our boat at Gene. I thought, as he was a Hadge, or pilgrim, his company would be of some service to me; and he proved very useful. At Benisouef we procured some donkeys to take us and a little provision as far as the lake Mœris.

On the 29th we set off, and directed our course through a vast plain of cultivated land, of corn and other products of the country. This plain is all under water at the time of the inundation, excepting the scattered villages, which stand elevated, and appear like so many islands during that time. About fifteen miles from the Nile, the chain of mountains on the west are but low. They open and form a valley into the Faioum; and it was at this entrance that we arrived on the first night of our journey. The Bahr Yousef passes into the centre of this valley, and enters, in various serpentine directions, into the Faioum. We took our station under some date-trees near the water, about two miles from the first pyramid. Here, after a slight repast, I went to sleep on my usual bed, a mattress, thin enough to serve as a saddle when folded up, but, when laid on a mat or on the ground, affording as good a bed as any traveller ought to expect. The Sicilian servant, the Moorish Hadge, and the donkey-drivers, kept watch in their turn; and I arranged so, that this system should be observed during the whole of our journey.

On the 30th, we set off before sunrise, and soon arrived at the pyramid. It is composed of sun-burnt bricks, and stands on a high ground at the foot of the hill on the northern side of the valley. Its basis is covered round with sand and stones, out of which it rises sixty feet, but its original height must have been above seventy, as the top has been thrown down. The basis above the sand is eighty feet. I observed several large blocks of stone intermixed with brickwork, so disposed as to support and strengthen the whole of the mass. The bricks are twelve, fourteen, and sixteen inches long, and five or six inches wide. I ascended the pyramid, and from the top could see the whole valley, and the entrance into the Faioum. On the west, at only two hours' walk distance, I could see the other pyramid, situated on a lower ground; consequently it appeared less high. Further to the west, I saw Medinet El Faioum, which stands on the ruins of ancient Arsinoe, and has a respectable appearance at a distance. From this pyramid I descended towards the canal again, and crossed a strong bridge on the west side of the valley. We then continued along the foot of these hills, till we reached the other pyramid. We forded the river on donkeys to come to the west, and pass over another branch of the same river, which was nearly dried up at that season. We entered a place 600 feet square, surrounded by high earthen dikes, apparently to protect the above ground from the inundation of the canal. This spot had no doubt been the seat of some ancient town, of which nothing remained but a few blocks of stone, and the appearance of some brick-work. We advanced towards the pyramid, and, after passing a small canal, which had been cut by some of the late rulers of Egypt, came to the foot of the pyramid. I found that the basis of it is only thirty feet above the level of the water of the canal, and nearly of the same size as the first. It is surrounded by smaller tombs; and, on the south side, there are the remains of an Egyptian temple, which must have been most magnificent. Of this there are to be seen only some fragments, of the colours of granite, and I must observe that it is the only column of that stone I had seen any where; and that, in all the temples known in the valley of the Nile, there are none that can boast of such grandeur. There are several tombs, quite in the Egyptian style, cut under ground. We quitted this place, and arrived at Medinet El Faioum on the same evening. The whole country is very fertile, and interspersed with plantations of fruit-trees and roses. This place is celebrated for making rose-water, which is sold in Cairo, and all over Egypt, for the use of the great people, who continually keep their divans and other places sprinkled with it, and present it also to any stranger who visits them. On our approaching the town, I agreed to call at the house of Husuff Bey, the governor of the province of Faioum, but found he was gone to Cairo. However, on application to his Kakia Bey, I obtained a firman and a guide, which was all I wanted, and was also accommodated with a lodging in one of the rooms of the house.

On the morning of the 31st, a soldier was given to me as a guide to the Lake Mœris. I set off the same day by the road leading to the northward, and passed the extensive ruins of Arsinoe, which I reserved for inspection till my return, as I intended to come back by the same route. The country continued very fine and well cultivated. At noon we arrived at El Cassar, the ruins of an ancient temple, and site of a town, where nothing remained but part of the walls. The temple was not very extensive, as may be seen by what is left of the foundation; and two parts of the wall, the only remains of which are composed of large blocks of stone, without hieroglyphics. At night we arrived at Senures, a village situated about 10 miles from Lake Mœris.

On the morning of the 1st of May, we proceeded on our journey, and, after passing several groves of palm trees and other plantations as before, the view opened all at once on a wild country, which gradually sloped to the edge of the lake. The water extended from north-east to south-west, and the mountains opposite formed an awful and sterile appearance. At noon we reached the lake, but could observe no trace of any living being. The guide conducted us along the shore, till we arrived at a small habitation, or rather a fisherman's hut, situated near the place where the canal, or Bahar Yousef, discharges into the lake, where only a small rotten boat was seen.

The hut was inhabited by a few fishermen and a soldier, who formerly received the duties on the fish they caught; but now, the fishermen have only a share of the fish they catch, and the remainder is sold at Medinet el Faioum, of which the Bashaw receives the profit. Our guide bespoke a boat, which was sent for at some distance up the canal, and when it arrived I never saw any thing that could be better compared to old Baris*, or boat of Charon: it was entirely out of shape. The outer shell or hulk was composed of rough pieces of wood scarcely joined, and fastened by four other pieces, wrapped together by four more across,

---

* The boat in which the Egyptians carried their dead to the grave.

which formed the deck: no tar, no pitch either inside or out, and the only preventive against the water coming in was a kind of weed moistened, which had settled in the joints of the wood. Having made an agreement with the owner of the boat, who might have been named Old Charon himself, we put on board some provisions, and made towards the west, where the famous Labyrinth is supposed to have been situated. The water of the lake was good enough to drink, but a little saltish: it was only this year that it could be tasted at all, owing to the extraordinary overflow of the Nile, which surmounted all the high lands, and, in addition to the Bahr Yousef, came in such torrents into the lake, that it raised the water twelve feet higher than ever it had been remembered by the oldest fisherman among them. We advanced with old Baris, or Charon's boat, towards the west, and at sunset saw the shore quite deserted, and nothing to look at but the lake and the mountains on the north side of it. Old Charon, the pilot, lighted a fire, while the other went to fish with a net, and soon returned with a supper of fish.

The land we were now in had anciently been cultivated, as there appeared many stumps of palm and other trees, nearly petrified. I also observed the vine in great plenty. The scene here was beautiful—the silence of the night, the beams of the radiant moon shining on the still water of the lake, the solitude of the place, the sight of our boat, the group of fishermen, the temple, which bears the name of Old Charon, a little way off, put me in mind of the Lake Acheron, the boat Baris, and the old ferryman of the Styx. I perceived this was the very spot where the poets originated the fable of the passage of the souls over the river of Oblivion. Nothing could be more pleasing to my imagination than being so near the Elysium, perhaps on the very Elysium itself. I thought that the plants, which appeared nearly petrified, have been the very ones when the souls were enjoying the happiness of their purity. I was thus strolling along the banks of the lake in solitary musing, not unlike one of these wandering souls waiting its turn to cross the Styx, while my old Charon with his semi-demons were preparing supper. I wish that I had been a poet, that I might sing in verse the beautiful ideas and sensations I felt on that occasion. I thought that night one of the happiest in my life, and myself out of the reach of evil mortals. Happy in the Elysian Fields, I feared not the malice and treacherous arts of envy, jealousy, spite, revenge, nor the thousand other snares of man. I nearly forgot I was living: and I suppose, that had I continued in my ecstacy, I should have verified that these waters had the power of oblivion.

On the 2d, before sunrise, we entered the old Baris, and steered towards the west till we arrived near the end of the lake, which, according to these fishermen, extended further this year than ever they remembered it, in consequence of the above extraordinary inundation. We landed here, and I took two of the boatmen and set off for the temple, named Cassar el Haron, about three miles from the lake, standing in the midst of the ruins of a town, of which there is still a track of the wall to be seen, and the foundations of several houses and other small temples. There are fragments of columns, and blocks of stone of a middling size. The temple is in pretty good preservation, excepting in the upper part: it is of a singular construction, and differs somewhat from the Egyptian; but I believe it has been altered, or rather rebuilt, and divided into various small apartments, as may be seen in the plan, Plate No. 32. There are no hieroglyphics either inside or out, and only two figures on the wall of the western side of the upper apartments, one of which I took for Osiris, and the other for Jupiter Ammon. In the front of this temple there is a semicircular pilaster at each side of the door, and two pilasters attached to the wall; but the exterior workmanship is evidently of a later date than the temple. Part of the town is covered with sand. On the east side of it there is something like a gateway, in an octangular form, and at a little distance there is a Greek chapel, elevated on a platform, with cellars under it.

After having taken a proper view of the temple and of the town, I went to see the small Greek chapel, accompanied by the two boatmen; and as there was no appearance of any danger, I left my gun and pistols in the temple, but had nearly suffered for my temerity; for just as I was mounting the few steps that lead to the platform of the small chapel, a large hyena rushed from the apartments beneath the chapel, and had I not been on the first step it could not have avoided attacking me, as there was no other way by which it could come out. The animal stopped three or four yards from me, and then turned round as if determined to attack me; but it appeared on second thoughts to have relinquished its intent, and after having shown me its pretty teeth, gave a hideous roar, and set off galloping as fast as it could. At the moment I regretted I had no arms with me, but was happy to see it gone. I attributed its flight to the noise made by the two boatmen, who being near me thought the hyena would swallow them alive.

This little chapel was evidently built in a later age than the rest of those works of which but very little now remain. On the west of the temple there are parts of other gates connected with the wall. I observed several pieces of marble and white granite. The granite has given me reason to think that there must have been some building of considerable importance in this town, for they must have had more trouble to convey it hence than to any other place in Egypt, in consequence of the distance. But whatever remains of beauty might be seen in this town, it does not appear that this was the place of the famous Labyrinth, nor any thing like it; for, according to Herodotus, Pliny, &c. there is not the smallest appearance which can warrant the supposition that any such edifice was there. The Labyrinth was a building of 3,000 chambers, one half above and one half below. The construction of such an immense edifice, and the enormous quantity of materials which must have been accumulated, would have yet left specimens enough to have seen where it had been erected, but not the smallest trace of any such thing is any where to be seen. The town was about a mile in circumference, with the temple in its centre, so that I could not see how the Labyrinth could be placed in this situation. I accordingly left the place, and on my return towards the lake passed a tract of land which had once been cultivated, and saw a great many stumps of plants almost burnt. On my arrival at the lake a high wind arose from the south-west, which swelled the lake very much, drifted the sand in the air, and drove our boat on shore. At the above place we gathered plenty of wood, made a fire, and passed the night under shelter of a mat hung over two sticks planted in the ground.

Before morning of the 3d the wind ceased, and the lake soon became smooth. We re-embarked, and shaped our course towards the north side, coastwise the whole day. At the foot of the mountain, which bounds the lake on that side, I perceived nothing worthy of remark. There are a few spots near the water's edge where great quantities of weeds grow from under the water; and great quantities of game are always found among these plants. The pelican is as common on this lake as it is on the Nile. There are many wild ducks and a kind of large snipe. Towards evening we arrived at the shore opposite to where we embarked, and the boatmen made up their minds to cross the lake the next morning, and take us back to our former place of embarkation; but as I recollected, that in some of the descriptions of that lake I had seen a town marked not far from the spot where we then were, on the morning of the 4th, instead of going on board, I took my route towards the mountains. The soldier and the boatmen ran after me, to persuade me there was nothing to be seen there; but I told them I must ascend the mountains to see the lake and the whole country round. One of them happened to say unguardedly that there was nothing to be seen except a few houses in ruins, and a high wall. That was enough for me; and having secured the man by promises and threats, I insisted that he should show me the above place. I accordingly set off with my whole crew, and had scarcely reached the summit of the lower range of the mountains, when I perceived the ruins of a town not far distant. On my arrival, I found it to be a Greek town, (vide Plate 23.) and it cannot be any other than the city of Bacchus, which I have observed in some of the maps of ancient authors. There are a great number of houses, half tumbled down, and a high wall of sun-burnt bricks, which incloses the ruins of a temple. The houses are not united, nor built in any regularity as streets, but only divided by narrow lanes, not more than three or four feet wide, and all built of sun-burnt bricks. There is a causeway, or road, made of large stones, which runs through the town to the temple, which faces the south. In the centre of the city I observed several houses, or rather cellars, underground, as they appeared from their tops, which were covered with strong pieces of wood, over which there were some cane, and then above that a layer of bricks, on a level with the surface, so that one might walk over without perceiving that he was treading on the top of a house. As the fishermen had brought their hatchets, I caused two or three of these houses to be uncovered. After removing the layer of bricks, we found a layer of clay, then a layer of canes, which were nearly burnt, and lastly, under the canes some rafters of wood, forming the ceiling. The wood was in good preservation, and of a hard quality. The inside of the hut, or cellar, was filled up with rubbish; but they had evidently been habitations, as we saw a fire-place in every one of them. They were not more than ten or twelve feet square, and the communication to each house was by a narrow lane, not more than three feet wide, which was also covered. I cannot conceive the reason why these people lived in such places. Certain it is that they did not live there to be out of the heat; on the contrary, they must have had all the force of the sun shining upon them, without the slightest chance of a breath of wind. The houses above ground were constructed in a manner somewhat different from any I had seen before. There were few which had a second floor, and those which were higher than the rest were very narrow, so that they were more like the form of towers than common houses; but now there is scarcely one to be seen entire. As to the temple, it is fallen, but appears to have been pretty extensive. The blocks of stone are of the largest size, some eight and nine feet long. The ruins are in such confusion, that it is impossible to form an idea of its plan or foundation. I am almost certain, by what I could see, that the falling of this temple was caused by violence, as it appears to me that it never could have been so dilapidated by the slow hand of time. Among these blocks I saw the fragments of statues, of breccia and other stones of Grecian sculpture, but no granite; and I observed the fragment of one which appeared to me not unlike part of an Apollo. There were also fragments of lions of grey stone, not belonging to these mountains. The town, from what I could see, might have consisted of 500 houses, the largest of which was not more than forty feet square. The area of the wall which surrounds the temple is 150 feet square, thirty feet high, and eight feet thick. On the north side of this town is a valley, which appears to have been once cultivated, but at present is covered with sand. On inquiry, I found this town was known to the Arabs of the lake under the name of Denay. We returned to the boat and crossed to the island of El Hear, which is entirely barren, and no trace of any habitation any where to be seen. We then crossed the lake to the east, and saw several fragments of pillars and ruins nearly under water, and arrived in the evening at the same shore where we embarked. I took up my station for the night to the eastward of the small hut, and made an excellent supper of fresh fish and a piece of pelican. The soldier who lived there happened to kill one of these birds, which was devoured by the fishermen as soon as it was boiled: its flesh is not unlike mutton in substance and appearance, but it tasted much like game, and was upon the whole very tender, and pleasant to the palate. It must have weighed at least forty pounds; the fat was rancid, and as yellow as saffron.

On the morning of the 5th, I took the road on the west side of the lake, and saw the site of another town, named El Haman, of which nothing now remains but scattered pieces of brick and part of a bath. This place is situated full forty feet above the lake, and the ground all round was covered with small shells, such as cockles, small conchilies, and others not unlike periwinkles. We returned afterwards on the east on the same day, and passed several ancient villages, built of sun-burnt bricks. At a place named Terza I observed several blocks of white stone and red granite, which evidently must have been taken from edifices of greater magnitude than what had ever stood there. Reflecting on the description of Pliny of the situation of the Labyrinth, which he says was on the west side of the Lake Mœris, I made diligent researches on that subject in particular, on the ground where I then stood. I could not see the smallest appearance of an edifice, either on the ground, or any appearance from under it; but I observed all through that part of the country a great number of stones and columns of beautiful colours, of white marble and of granite. I saw the above pieces of antiquity scattered about for the space of several miles, some on the road, and some in the houses of the Arabs, and others put to various uses in the erection of huts, &c. I have no doubt, that by tracing the source of these materials, the seat of the Labyrinth could be discovered, which must be most magnificent even in its ruined state; but I fear it is rather too late for such researches, for the cause of its disappearing might be, that it was not an edifice of great height, the lower apartments being under ground. It may have been buried by the earth which is yearly brought there by the water of the Nile; or it is not impossible that the Labyrinth stood in such a situation as to be covered entirely by the water, as we may see other remains of antiquities on the east side of the lake, which are nearly all under water. It is certain, that the yearly discharge of the Nile into the lake brings with it a great quantity of earth or clay, and leaves it there, consequently the lake must have risen from its original bed and spread so much over the land, as to induce one to suppose that the said lake was made for a reservoir to retain the water at high Nile, and to make a kind of second inundation: it is evident that it is made by nature and not by art; but that it might have served as a reservoir for the above purpose, does not appear to me to be at all impossible. This second inundation could not extend out of the Faioum; the water might be retained in the lake at the time of high Nile, by a bar across the canal, at the entrance into the lake; and at low water it might be let out: but the canal must be stopped at the entrance into the Faioum on the east, otherwise the water would again return into the Nile by the said Bahr Yousef, consequently a second inundation could not take place in any other part but the Faioum, which being surrounded by mountains on the north, and high grounds on the other side, would form a lake of itself.

We continued our journey, in a direction parallel with the lake, through several villages, woods of palm and other fruit-trees, and well cultivated lands, and at sunset arrived at Fedmin el Kunois, which means the Place of Churches: it stands on a high mound of earth and rubbish, and has evidently been rebuilt on other ruins. It is divided into two parts by a small canal from the Bahr Yousef. One side of the town is inhabited by Christian Copts, and the other by Mahomedans; and though the two religions officiated almost in sight of each other, they never interfered on each other's rights. The poor Copts were destitute of the principal means of educating their children; and the only reference they had to the rites of the Christian religion was an old book of manuscripts, copied from the Bible: but even this was kept as the only relic they had. If, by chance, I had had an Arabic Bible or Testament, I might indeed have become a great man among them; and I wonder that the Missionaries of the Bible Society, who lately visited Egypt, omitted this place, being a noted Christian town; but I suppose the magnificent works of old Pharaoh made them forget Moses, his followers, and all those who wish to know any thing about him. But I must do justice to truth. A young man, of the name of Burckhardt, cousin to my good friend the celebrated traveller of that name, came, unprotected, into Egypt for the purpose of distributing Bibles, consequently was persecuted, and obliged to fly in great haste. He went into Syria, but with over fatigue, or perhaps from the effects of the climate, he was unable to proceed higher than Aleppo, where he died; and, I am sorry to say, that others who succeeded him, and went up the Nile with protection and all their leisure, made their journey to very little purpose.

The tradition of the town of Fedmin el Hanaiser is, that in ancient times there were on that spot three hundred churches, which were allowed to fall in ruins by the old inhabitants of the place, and that when the Mahomedans succeeded to the country, they built the present town on these very three hundred churches; for which reason the town is named Fidmin of the Churches. The story is somewhat strange, and may afford grounds for a modern traveller to place the Egyptian Labyrinth in this spot; for, by conceiving that the three hundred churches were the three hundred cellars of the Labyrinth, as mentioned by Herodotus, or by supposing that the father of history meant to say three hundred instead of three thousand, the above churches could have been nothing less than the old Egyptian Labyrinth itself. All this might pass off well enough among the wanderers; but, unfortunately, there is proof to the contrary, which will do away with any such supposition. The above branch of the Bahr Yousef passes through the town, cut not above two centuries ago; and none of the said churches appeared in the progress of the excavation through the town, which must have been the case had it been built on the said three hundred churches. However, I must conclude, that, notwithstanding the little probability there is of the Labyrinth being in this place, I cannot help repeating my observation, that it must have been at no great distance from the lake, as the great quantity of materials which is scattered about the country has evidently belonged to some extensive and splendid building.

We left Fidmin on the 6th; and, after traversing a most beautiful country, arrived at night at Medinet el Faioum.

On the morning of the 7th I went to see the ruins of the ancient Arsinoe. It had been a very large city; but nothing of it remained, except high mounds of all sorts of rubbish. The chief materials appear to have been burnt bricks. There were many stone edifices, and a great quantity of wrought granite. In the present town of Medinet I observed several fragments of granite columns, and other pieces of sculpture, of a most magnificent taste.

It is certainly strange that granite columns are only to be seen in this place and near the pyramids, six miles distant. Among the ruins at Arsinoe I also observed various fragments of statues of granite, well executed, but much mutilated; and it is my opinion, that this town has been destroyed by violence and fire. Among the rubbish there are pieces of stones and glass, which have evidently been nearly melted by fire. It is clearly seen, that the new town of Medinet is built out of the old materials of Arsinoe, as the fragments are to be met with in every part of the town. The large blocks of stone have been diminished in their sides, but enough is left to show the purposes for which they originally served. About the centre of these ruins I made an excavation in an ancient reservoir, which I found to be as deep as the bottom of the Bahr Yousef, and which was no doubt filled at the time of the inundation for the accommodation of the town. There are other similar wells in these ruins, which proves that this was the only mode they had of keeping water near them, as the river is at some distance from the town. Among these mounds I found several specimens of glass of Grecian manufacture and Egyptian workmanship; and it appears to me, that this town must have been one of the first note in Egypt.

Having seen all I wished in that place, I visited the obelisk, which is too well known to require any more said about it. I then prepared for my journey into the oasis on the west. Accordingly I went to see Hussuff Bey, who by this time had returned from Cairo. He was a native of Circassia, and bought at the usual market as a slave, by the Bashaw of Egypt, who, after many years' servitude, made him Bey, or governor, of the finest province of that country. He was uncommonly civil, and eager to know any thing with which he was unacquainted; but, on my application for a Bedoween guide to conduct me through the desert, he said that the Bedoweens were all encamped in that part of the province which was subject to Khalil Bey at Benisoeuf. I was happy to hear that my old friend Khalil Bey was the person to whom I had to make my request, and immediately inquired where the Bedoweens were encamped, and on being told that they were about ten miles distant, on the morning of the 10th, I set off, and reached the camp before noon; but none of these people could inform me about the oasis on the west. They all pointed towards the south, indicating that the oasis were in that direction. I saw that they meant the oasis of Siout and Maloni, which are known by the name of the Great Oasis. At last, after much ado, an old man told me that there was an Eloah on the west of the Lake Mœris, the very place I wished to go to, but that none of the Bedoweens would go there. I inquired if any of them knew the road; he said that he knew a Sheik of theirs, who lived in a camp at eight miles distant, who had a daughter married to one of the Sheiks of the Eloah. I was not a little pleased with this discovery, and flattered myself that I would be able to persuade the said Sheik to accompany me thither. We remained all night at the camp, and, on the morning of the 12th, set off for the Nile again. We passed through several plantations of fruit trees, and a great quantity of roses, with which, as I mentioned before, they make the rose-water. The cotton-plant is quite abundant; and figs are in such plenty, that they dry them in the sun, and send them to Cairo. It was quite night before we arrived at the banks of the Nile; and, as no business could be done that evening, I caused my saddle to be prepared for my bed, and went to sleep. I do not know to what cause it is to be attributed, but I certainly slept more soundly on the banks of the Nile, or on the sands of the desert, than I ever did in any other place, and particularly under a roof.

Early in the morning of the 13th I was awoke by the Moorish Hadge, who told me, with an air of surprise, that a strange person was coming towards us: he mistook him by fear, and supposed that some thief was at hand. I took up my arms, but was soon undeceived when I saw an European, who turned out to be the Reverend Mr. Slowman, a gentleman sixty-two years of age, who for a walk had alighted from his canjiar, and, in spite of his years, followed the tracks of celebrated travellers, but who did not boast to his friends in England of his arduous task, and consequently did not pass for a courageous and gallant adventurer. This old reverend divine had the courage to go through all the lands in Syria, which travellers fancy wonderful difficult. He never had an interpreter, nor did he know a single word of Arabic. He encountered and overcame every difficulty. He suffered much, but never complained, except of the ill treatment he received from other travellers, who were ashamed that a venerable old man of sixty-two should silently follow all their steps, and think nothing of what he had undergone, nor did he care whether any one ever knew any thing about his journey. He was then on his way to the second cataract; and some time afterwards I had the pleasure of seeing him, safe and well, on his return from that place. He was laughed at, and even ill-treated, by some person who deserves to be mentioned, and who wished to be alone in travelling; but, as I said before, I will not now enter into the particulars of the proceedings of some travellers in Egypt, as I mean to explain the whole facts in another volume. The Rev. Mr. Slowman proceeded on his journey, and I went to see my good old friend Khalil Bey of Esne, who was now commander of the province of Benesouef. It happened to be after dinner when I called. He was much pleased to see me, and glad he had it in his power to serve me. Having informed him that I wished to penetrate into the western Oasis, he immediately sent, agreeably to my request, for the Sheik of the Bedoweens. He inquired after many things, and in particular about the sulphur and emerald mines, as he thought them extremely interesting to the treasury of the Bashaw. I remained with him the rest of the evening, and promised to see him again the next day, when I should see the Sheik of the Bedoweens.

I went accordingly on the 14th, but the Sheik did not arrive, and I spent the whole day in the laborious task of idleness. As the Bey entered his harem after a certain hour, I went to the coffee-house in the bazar of the town, the only place of amusement, and in such cases one cannot help wishing for something to occupy the time. These places are only frequented by the Turkish soldiers, for though a cup of coffee is only five paras, little more than a halfpenny, yet it is more than an Arab can afford to pay, as his general pay for a day's labour is only twenty paras, threepence, so that it is very seldom an Arab is to be seen in these spendthrift places. It is somewhat singular to observe, that while these soldiers are drinking their coffee, they assume the same airs and consequence as their Beys. A beenbashe, who is only in rank with a serjeant, issues to the corporal the order he received from the Cacheff, in the same tone as it was delivered to him; the corporal does so to the soldier, who occasionally passes it to an Arab in the same manner.

On the 15th the Sheik arrived, and protested he was unable to show me the road to the place I wished to visit. The Bey insisted that he should find some one in his camp who knew the way, which he of course promised to do. It was agreed that I should meet the Sheik at a village at the foot of the desert where I was to meet Sheik Grumar, who would conduct me to the Oasis. I proposed to the Sheik that I should have a firman from the Bey for the Sheiks of the Oasis, but he said it was unnecessary, and made me understand that it was better to go without one, as I should be accompanied by a man sent from the Bey.

Accordingly, on the morning of the 16th, we set off for the appointed village, named Sedmin el Djabel, at the foot of the desert, where the Bedoweens were encamped. I need not describe the ground we went over, as it is pretty much like the rest of the Faioum. On my arrival I went to see the Cacheff of the village, where I also found the Sheik of the Bedoweens, and Sheik Grumar, waiting for us. I had some little difficulty in persuading them to take only six camels, as they feared we should not be able to carry enough of water; but the great difficulty was, that Sheik Grumar, who was to accompany us, was afraid of ill consequences by taking us to the Oasis, as he assured me that no European had yet been there, and that even very few of the Bedoweens themselves travel to these places at all, excepting when they go to purchase rice and dates; but having surmounted all these little difficulties, it was arranged that we should wait three days at the camp, for the purpose of making provision for our journey, &c.

The camp of the Bedoweens was situated at the foot of the range of low mountains which form the skirt of the desert (See Plate 25). The chief had a large tent, higher than the rest, and was as great as a king among his own people. I took up my residence directly before his tent, and my Moorish Hadge, with two shawls, contrived to make a tent for me. The mode of living of these people has been so often described, that I conceive every one to be acquainted with it; but as there may be some peculiarity in one tribe more than in another, I shall insert what I have seen in that of Sheik Grumar. He was a tall stout man, six feet three inches high, with a countenance that bespoke a resolute mind, and great eagerness after gain. He preserved an air of superiority over his subalterns, and what he ordered was instantly done without any hesitation. He had two wives, who agreed pretty well with each other, and an old black slave, by whom he had two fine children, and who in consequence had as much power as the other two, who were only somewhat fairer than herself. Their chief occupation was grinding corn and making butter. Their hand-mill was rather of a larger size than what is used by the Arabs of Egypt, which proves their superior strength. The flour is put into boiling water, and by stirring it with a stick they make a large pudding. It is then turned out upon a straw plate, when a hole is made in the top and filled with butter. This is their chief repast, which is called asceed. These people are now happier than they were a few years ago, as Mahomed Ali has given them liberty to rent lands on the borders of the desert. They do not trouble themselves about plowing the ground, for they find it more profitable to breed camels. Their greatest trouble is to break the straw to feed them when there is no pasture, and this is done by a machine of five or six irons, passing over the straw on the ground. Their horses are not in very good condition, but they are very strong. They often remove their camps into better situations, but always far from any habitation, at least a large village or town. The women are covered with a thick woollen cloth made on the Barbary coast, and sold in Cairo and other towns in Egypt. The men have generally a linen gown and a large woollen shawl, which covers the whole person from head to foot. They generally have a great many fleas, I believe owing to the quantity of thick cloth they wear, and even their tents are so infested, that it is impossible to approach them without being molested. During the time I was there, I never slept a moment. The first day of our arrival, the people were rather shy in entering into conversation with us, but when once they did begin, they were continually inquiring of many things concerning our country, and asking for trifling articles of little value. At last, after having provided bread for our journey, and provisions for the camels, we set off on the 19th, and entered the desert in a western direction, along the south side of the Faioum, and after two hours march, we passed near the ruins of an ancient village; and in another hour and a half we reached a place called Raweje Toton, the seat of a very extensive ancient town. I saw a great many blocks of calcareous stone with hieroglyphics and Egyptian figures very finely executed, and some pedestals of columns. The chief materials were burnt bricks; but I observed several pieces of granite, and from their extent, I have no doubt that this must have been a very large town. In another hour after this, we came to the ruins of another village, named Talet el Hagar. It is somewhat singular that this village is crowded with pedestals of columns, which evidently have been taken from the large town, and converted into millstones for grinding corn. At sunset we reached a place called El Kharak, a land quite detached from Faioum, and which is watered by a branch of the canal or Bahr Yousef. This place has a village of that name, with several pieces of well cultivated ground around it, which produce dhourra and clover in the proper season. The few people who live there are mostly of the labouring class, who rent the place from the Bey of the Faioum. Here we took in provision for the camels, and filled the skins with fresh water.

On the 20th, we advanced towards the west: here the face of the earth is entirely changed. We soon found ourselves among low rocks, sandy hills, and barren valleys. At a few miles distant from our last place, I observed the upper part of a very thick wall, evidently as if it had surrounded a large town, but entirely buried under the sand. I should have taken it for a wall inclosing some cultivated spots of land, had I not observed in the interior of it the upper part of other buildings, and very thick walls of sun-burnt bricks. On the exterior of the wall I perceived a great quantity of stumps of trees, and vines, nearly burnt to ashes, and which crumbled into dust as soon as touched. This place is named the same as the one we left in the morning, El Kharak.

We continued the remaining part of the forenoon through several valleys of rocks and banks of sand; and towards evening we arrived at a spot parallel with the eastern extremity of the lake Mœris. We passed the night at the bottom of a sand-bank, and at four o'clock on the morning of the 21st continued our route. The valley we were now in opened wider; and, in a few hours, we came in sight of a high rock at a great distance from us. We continued nearly the whole day in the said valley, among rocks and sand; and, towards evening, arrived at Rejen el Cassar, a place once populated, where there were several good spots of ground, which had been once cultivated, but now was nearly all covered up with sand. It is surrounded by high rocks, and its extent might have been about three miles square. There is a great abundance of sunt and date trees, which bear no fruit. Under the sand there is water to be found in great abundance; for, by only thrusting down a stick, the water springs up. There are the remains of the foundation of a small Egyptian temple, which has served as a burial-place to people of later ages. We passed the night very happily under the palm-trees; but, unfortunately, the water of this place was rather saltish, otherwise it might invite a hermit to pass his days out of the busy world.

On the 22d we continued our route toward the west, and had to pass over a very high bank of sand to leave Rejen el Cassar and reach a valley, in which we continued travelling in that direction till we came to an open plain, and a fine horizon before us. I observed at a distance a spacious plain of sand and stones, with several heaps above the rest. On our approach I found that they were tumuli, nearly in the form of a parallelogram, from twenty to thirty feet long. There were, I believe, nearly thirty, and some of them I calculated were large enough to contain a hundred corpses; and consequently, altogether, form a good number. I must beg leave to make one observation on these tumuli, which, perhaps, will give some idea to the learned, as I hope my humble opinion will meet the approbation of some of them. It will be recollected, that Cambyses, after having conquered Egypt, sent part of his army to the conquest of the Ammonii in the deserts of Lybia, which was betrayed by their guides, who were Egyptians, and left to perish in the desert, and nothing more was heard of them. It is the general opinion, that the Ammonii were in the western direction of the Nile; and it is well known that Alexander employed only nine days on his visit to that place from Alexandria. Consequently, it is pretty clear that the Ammonii were not in the southern Oasis, as it is supposed, merely because it is stated by Herodotus, that Cambyses sent his army into that place from Thebes; but, by all other accounts, it appears that they could not have been so far from the sea. And it is more probable that the army was sent from Memphis, and not from Thebes, which agrees with many other points in history; for instance, not only in the distance, but also in the description of the western Oasis and its temple. I am now laying before my readers my own ideas, which I formed in consequence of what I had seen, and of the little calculation I could make from ancient history on the subject. Recollecting that the said army of Cambyses had been lost in these deserts, I have no hesitation in supposing, that the above tumuli were made to cover the unfortunate wretches who perished, no doubt, from thirst. The direction from Memphis to these Elloah, either of Siwah or El Cassar, is westward. The situation where these people are stated to have perished is the desert of Lybia: the tumuli are situated between Memphis and the Elloah in the desert of Lybia, where there is no index to direct the stranger on his way, if he is left by his guide; nor even a stone or a shadow to shelter him from the sun.

A learned man wrote to me, that these people could not be Persians, merely because it was not their custom or religion to cover the dead bodies, but to leave them to the birds of prey; consequently, these could not be the army of Cambyses. But let this learned man recollect, that, independently of the points he has mentioned, these people could not have been buried by their countrymen at all; for it is natural to suppose that they did not know where they were, otherwise there would be reason to believe that we should know something more of what became of them than the dry account given by Herodotus, that they were left to perish in these deserts. It is, therefore, more reasonable to suppose that the remains of these wretches were accumulated by some other nation, perhaps by the Ammonii themselves, though they protested they knew nothing of them, and that the army never reached their country. At any rate, I should be happy to know who these people were, and by what cause they came there, if they are not the above people from the army of Cambyses.

The calculation of the number could not have been made with accuracy, in consequence of the different sizes of the tombs; besides, if these corpses were collected only when skeletons, they would of course occupy much less space than when in flesh; but, notwithstanding all this uncertainty, I have no hesitation in asserting that, in those tumuli I saw, there could have been buried 3000 people. Besides, from the information I received from the Bedoweens, I found that this was not the place where there were the greatest number, and that, at a little distance, there were a great many of the same, to which I could not persuade the Bedoweens to take me, as they were afraid that our supply of water would fall short.

On the 23d, we continued our journey to the west, over a plain, covered with pebbles of brown and black colours, and so flat that, in a few hours, we found an horizon all round, not unlike the sea. We continued so the whole day.

On the 24th we went on, and towards the evening reached Bahar Bela Me, where we saw high rocks on the west. This place is singular, and deserves the attention of the geographer, as it is a *dry river*, and has all the appearance of water having been in it: the bank and bottom are quite full of stones and sand. There are several islands in the centre; but the most remarkable circumstance is, that, at a certain height upon the bank, there is a mark, evidently as if the water had reached so high; the colour of the materials above that mark is also much lighter than those below. And what would almost determine that there has been water there, is, that the island has the same mark, and on the same level with that on the banks of the said dry river. I am a little at a loss to know how the course of this river is so little known, as I only found it marked near the Lakes Natron, taking a direction of north-west and south-east, which does not agree with its course here, which is from north to south; yet it has the same name, and runs north and south as far as I could see from the summit of a high rock on the west side of it. The Arabs assured me that it ran a great way in both directions, and that it is the same which passes near the Lakes Natron. If this is the case, it must pass right before the extremity of the Lake Mœris, at two or three days' journey distance, in a western direction. This is the place where several petrified stumps of trees are found, and many pebbles, with moving or quick water inside. I saw about half a dozen of a flinty substance, without veins of any sort.

On the morning of the 25th, we continued westward, and passed several isolated rocks and sand-banks. At noon we saw a high hill at a distance, and soon after the guide pointed out the Rocks of Elloah: in a few minutes after this we saw two crows, which appeared to have come to meet us,—a sure sign that water is not far off; for though these birds can travel both cheap and expeditious, they generally keep near the water in those deserts. In the afternoon we reached the brink of the Elloah, named El Cassar, a valley surrounded by high rocks, which form a spacious plain of twelve or fourteen miles long, and about six in breadth. There is only a small portion of the valley cultivated on the opposite side which we reached, and it can only be distinguished by the woods of palm-trees which cover it. The rest of the valley is wholly covered with tracts of sand, but it is evidently seen that it has once been cultivated every where. Many tracts of land are of a clayey substance, which could be brought into use even now. There are several small hills scattered about, some with a natural spring on the top, and covered with rushes and small plants. We advanced towards a forest of date-trees, and before evening we reached within a mile of a village, named Zaboo, all of us exceedingly thirsty: here we observed some cultivation, several beds of rice, and some sunt-trees, &c. Before the camels arrived they scented the water at some distance; and as they had not drank since they left Rejan, they set off at full gallop, and did not stop till they reached a rivulet, which was quite sweet, although the soil was almost impregnated with salt. I observed here a great many wild birds, particularly wild ducks, in greater abundance than any other. At this place we alighted for a moment, to allow our camels to drink; and I observed a certain uneasiness in the manner of Sheik Grumar, our guide, that I could not account for. He had often hinted to me whether I wished to pass for a Mahomedan or Christian, but I always told him I could see no reason for disguising myself. I went some distance from the camels to drink too; and after having watered our camels, we were about to proceed slowly towards the village; but no sooner were we mounted than we heard a voice hallooing at us, and at the same time a man rushed out of one of the bushes with a gun, and put himself in an attitude as if to fire upon us. His appearance was not very terrifying, nor did his garments bespeak him to be a person of any consequence in that land. He was not above four feet high, of a chocolate colour, most wretchedly ill made, and covered with a black woollen cloth. Sheik Grumar immediately dismounted, and advanced towards the man, speaking to him in a kind of Arabic dialect, which I found to be the dialect of the place. The man soon recognised him, and they approached each other in a friendly manner, which gave me hopes that all would go on well at that place. The man was anxious to learn who we were, when our guide at once told him that we were people in search of old stones, and that one of us was a Hadge, just returning from Mecca. This last assertion appeared to satisfy the man; but he replied, that no one ever came there to seek for old stones; and that he did not know what the Sheiks of Zaboo, the village, would think of our coming there, and that he was going to shoot me when I was drinking. Meanwhile we advanced towards the village, and our guide contrived to persuade him that we were harmless Franks, meaning me and my Sicilian servant. He did not know of what tribe the Franks were, but said that their Cady, who had been once in Cairo, must know them. All this was told us in Arabic by our guide, who continually kept inquiring about the health of such and such a Sheik, and, above all, of the Sheik Hebrims, his son-in-law. The man began to walk before us, and on our approaching the village, he ran off as fast as he could into the wood of palm-trees. We advanced, and entered a lane among these plants; and as we penetrated farther, we entered a most beautiful place, full of dates, intermixed with other trees, some in blossom, and others in fruit: there were apricots, figs, almonds, plums, and some grapes. The apricots were in greater abundance than the rest, and the figs were very fine. The soil was covered with verdure of grass and rice, and the whole formed a most pleasing recess, particularly after the barren scenes of the desert.

On our approaching a wide place the guide halted, and desired us to wait till he returned: he walked on, and I observed him go into a kind of habitation at some distance. Accordingly we waited there some time; but in about half an hour I thought it rather strange that he did not return. I inquired of the drivers where our guide had gone; they told me they did not know. At last, I became tired of waiting, and set off with my gun towards the place where I saw the guide enter; but before I reached the place I heard the voices of men, women, and children; and when I came nearer, I saw a wall inclosing a great many houses, and immediately within the gates there was a yard, in which were assembled all the chiefs of the village and many others, sitting on the ground, debating whether or not we should be admitted, and my guide very busy in persuading them that we were but harmless people, and only come there to look after old stones. On my arrival at the gate their whole attention was turned upon me, and a perfect silence ensued. I walked straight forward, when they all rose and stared at me; but from their countenances I saw they did not know what to say. I went in among them and inquired who was their Sheik, when my guide told me that three or four elders and a young man were the Sheiks of the place. I saluted them freely, and shook hands, which they do not unlike the English manner. I wished them prosperity. I saw by their manner on this occasion that they were divided in opinion. Some received me with good humour, and others retired murmuring something I could not learn at the moment. They inquired what I wanted. I told them I was a stranger, merely come to visit that place, as I expected to find some stones belonging to the holy mosque of my ancestors, and hoped we should be friends. At the same time, I sent my guide to fetch the camels, and on their arrival ordered coffee to be made. I had a good mat and a new carpet, which made a fine appearance. I spread them by the side of a wall, sat down, and invited the Sheiks to come and sit near me; at the same time, I asked if I could procure a sheep at a cheap rate. Some of them cheerfully seated themselves on my mat, but others kept at a distance, frowning upon me, which I pretended not to see. The son-in-law of my guide approached, and said he would sell me a sheep for a dollar, which I accepted, on condition that he would boil two large basins of rice in its broth. I knew that rice was very cheap there, and took that method, to let them suppose I had not plenty of money, but at the same time that I wished to make a feast with them. By this time, my Sicilian servant and the Hadge had made a large pot of coffee, and become quite free with some of them. In serving round the coffee, I gave the preference of the first cups to the Sheiks, and the sight of such a treat brought the other rusty fellows to sit down also and share the same dainty, as they could not resist the attraction of a cup of coffee, a luxury which they perhaps taste only once a year, on the first day of the arrival of the caravan of Bedoweens, who come there for the purpose of carrying dates to Cairo or Alexandria. By this means the wildest became more mild, and seeing my indifference whether they were friends or not, thought it would be more to their advantage to become social. By this time the rest of the village had assembled, cows, camels, sheep, donkeys, men, women, and children, all staring in a semicircle as if I had come from the moon. Some of them had seen Turks and other tribes of Arabs, but none had ever seen a Frank or a Christian before. I produced a little good tobacco, and having presented each of the Sheiks with a pipe, we commenced smoking, and talked of what I could see the next day. They told me I could see nothing there, but must go to the next Elloah, four days' journey north-west, where

I would see something I was in search of. No doubt they meant Siwah, which is also reckoned to be one of the Oasis of the Ammonii. There is a temple there, visited by Messrs. Brown, Horneman, and De Buden. My guide told them several stories during this time, wonderful indeed, but one in particular, that he and some of his companions had gone far to the south, and met with a tribe quite different from us, who walked like dogs, and that the women fought against the other tribes. These tribes, said my guide, are so far off, that their *bellad*, or village, is very near the skies, and that if I had time to walk to the top of a high hill, I might touch it with my own hands. The ideas of these people are, that the sky and the earth meet at the horizon.

While all this was going on, the other Sheiks held a consultation among themselves, and appeared much concerned about my expressing an intention of visiting the country all round, to see if I could meet with some old stones. At this time three men brought some large wooden bowls filled with rice, and having put one down to me, they set the rest before the other people. They all sat round theirs, and I remained with my large portion by myself. I immediately told them that unless all the Sheiks ate with me I would not taste it, at which they were all much pleased, and came to mess with me; even the most rough among them came and dipped in the same bowl. Soon after a man came and threw a basket on the ground, which raised such a dust, that it covered our rice like sugar on cream. As I could not conjecture, I was anxious to know what was in the basket, when one of the Sheiks opposite thrust his hand in and took out a piece of boiled mutton. I had seen dinner served up in many ways, but I never saw boiled mutton eaten out of a basket thrown on the ground in that manner. The pieces were distributed and devoured. We became more intimate after dinner, as I found that an empty stomach makes a man angry as well as hungry; but the fact is, that strangers in these countries, after having eaten together, lay aside all enmity, and sometimes become friends. There is treachery, it is true; but after a person has eaten with a stranger in public, he must at least play the part of a friend. We had some more coffee and pipes, and I again hinted about going to see the grounds the next morning, and the son-in-law of my guide promised to conduct me any where I chose. Our conversation was in bad Arabic as far as they liked to converse with me, but amongst themselves they talked in another language, in use in Siwah. It being rather dark by this time, a wax candle was lighted, which astonished them much, and was handed all round for every one to see it. I should not have mentioned this circumstance, had it not appeared almost incredible that these people, living only at the distance of a few days' journey from the Nile, should never have seen a candle. Coffee being ended, one of the Sheiks rose, when the rest followed, and, without saying a single word, walked off with the candle, leaving me in the dark, with my carpet and saddle to sleep on. The camel drivers had brought all our provisions, &c. quite close to us, and continued the old plan of keeping watch all night, of two hours each.

On the 26th, before sunrise, some of the natives came thither to see us, and for all my civilities to them on the preceding evening, they were quite rude in the morning. As the sun rose, the Sheiks came and held a consultation, whether I was to be permitted to see the ruins, or whether I was to be sent to the other village over the mountain. I was already informed, that on the west of the Elloah there are other and greater villages than this, and that there were several ruins among them; but as I had made an acquaintance here, I wished to see every thing before I proceeded elsewhere. Accordingly, when the Shieks were all in council, I went and told them I had not come there as their enemy, but their friend, and that I wished to be informed of their objection against my going to see the country. They replied, that they knew I wanted treasure, and not stones, and that a man would not cross the desert to procure stones in the Elloah, &c. In short, all I could do was to no purpose; they were persuaded that I wanted to go there for treasure, which is their constant story. I then adopted the ancient mode of persuading them to the contrary. I told them that if I found any gold I would give it to them, to which they all agreed, and said it was done, meaning that they should have the treasure. At last, off we set towards the east, and after passing through a thick wood of palm-trees, &c. as on the day before, we came to an open ground, the soil of which is in some places so covered with fine salt, that it appeared like snow. And what is more singular, there are several rivulets which run over that salt plain, and form a sediment of their own which does not incorporate in any way with the salt, and keeps quite sweet; and on advancing farther, we came to a place where there had evidently been an ancient town. A little farther there were several holes, not unlike the tombs of Egypt. On my approaching these cavities, I entered one, to the great astonishment of the natives, who never in their life ventured to penetrate any of them, as they supposed the devil was in them. I found it to be a tomb cut out of the rock, in the same manner as those in Egypt, and running downwards in various directions. On my coming out again, I underwent a minute scrutiny by the Sheiks, in order to discover if I had any treasure. It was well I had no money of my own, as they would have said that I found it there; and it is somewhat singular that their chief notion of coin is the Spanish dollar. The reason is, because the few Bedoweens who go there to buy dates and rice bring some of that money to pay for them, besides several articles for barter; and it sometimes happens that the caravan from Mecca to Fezan or Tripoli passes through the Oasis, and purchases rice, which is paid for in dollars. We advanced farther, and at last I was taken to see the ruins of an old edifice made only of sun-burnt bricks, and which perhaps might have served for a Christian church, but no signs of any thing now remained, and I only judged so from its form, which is somewhat inclined to that mode of building. We then took the route towards the village again, but in another direction. We passed over several pieces of ground which might have been cultivated, and I believe the only reason why it was not was merely because the inhabitants had enough for what they wished to cultivate. Their lands are watered from the running springs. On our way I was taken to see what they named the devil's habitation, made by himself in one night for his own use; it was a low rock, at one side of which there were several tombs, also in the Egyptian style; but as their entrance was somewhat different from the other, it bore the above title, and the natives never ventured near them. On my approaching the place, they all kept at a great distance, and even the Moorish Hadge, who had seen the tombs near the pyramid in the Faioum, began to be alarmed on their report that the devil was in these places. I took my Sicilian servant and a lighted candle, and entered a chasm in the rock, which in the interior led into various small apartments, and little chambers cut out as sepulchres in the Egyptian manner, but without any hieroglyphics. In an inner apartment we found several sarcophagi of burnt clay, in the form of a man, and generally of the usual size to contain one: they are two inches thick, and baked very strong; the lids are quite flat, and have a head of a man, woman, or animal, just above the head of the mummy. The sarcophagus being rather too heavy for a camel to carry through the desert, I took with me some of the men's heads on the lids, and one of a ram. They are most roughly made. On our coming out, we found the Sheiks and others in doubt, whether we could return from the habitation of

Pluto; but, notwithstanding this, they did not give up the supposition that we searched for money. We returned to the village, and after a slight repast, went to see a fountain of water, or rather a running spring. It is a rivulet of curious water, and very convenient for the people; for by putting their woollen cloth, if white, into it, for twenty-four hours, it is taken out as black as any dyer could make it. This is a great accommodation to the women and children, who are nearly all covered with gowns of that colour. The Sheiks and people of respectability are in white. They are of the Mahomedan religion, but very poor followers of it. In the village there was a young man who had been in Egypt, and had learned a little spelling, and was an oracle among them; and all his references were made to a few sheets of paper, with copies of texts of the Alcoran. What a precious article would an Arabic Bible have been in this place! Their mode of living was very simple; rice, of which they have great abundance, was their chief food; but it is of so inferior a sort, that they have but very little traffic in it, and what they have is only among a few Bedoweens who go there yearly to purchase dates, which are very fine. They have a few camels and donkeys, several cows, buffaloes, goats, and sheep, and altogether have no reason to complain. They could be happy in this Elysium, indeed, for this place has more to deserve that name than any other, as it is separated from the rest of mankind; but they are mortal, and they must have their evils. The greatest enemies they have are their own neighbours at the other village, named El Cassar, on the other side of a high rock, separated from them three hours' journey, and Siwah four days. They are continually in dispute, and often attack each other's party, and sometimes for very trifling causes. In the afternoon, I was taken to see another piece of antiquity not far from the town, and passed over some high hills of sand, and arrived at a wide plain which extended to the foot of the rock which divided the two villages. In the midst of this plain there is a small hill on which there were the ruins of a small temple, built of large bricks of sand-stone not unlike the Egyptian, but not one single hieroglyphic was to be seen on it. It has several scrawls in Greek letters, but so defaced that I could only trace one or two in different places. Round the temple there have been houses built of burnt brick. By this time the village of El Cassar were informed that a stranger had arrived in Zaboo, in search of treasure, which was to be found in the ruins under the village, and that he had ventured into the devil's house without fear. They were all in an uproar, and swore that he should never enter their village, or even come near it. A man who lived half way between the two villages, and occasionally reported what passed or was said from one to another, came to me while I was looking at the said temple, and said there was a very large temple in the other village, named El Cassar, and that there were holes under ground, directly under the village, where great treasure was to be found, but that the people had sworn that I should not enter the village at all. I inquired of him the names of the principal people, the great Sheik and the Cady, and having taken down their names, I asked him if he would take a message to them from me: at first he hesitated, but on promising that I would not tell them that he informed me about the treasure, he agreed to go to the village early next morning. The message was, my salutes to the great Sheik Salem, and to the Cady, or justice, Sheik Ibrahim, and to tell them that I came into the Elloah to visit them; that I was not a soldier, and that if they would appoint a place where I could meet them the next morning, I should be glad to see them any where they pleased. I returned to the village, and the man to his habitation. The evening was passed much in the same way as the preceding one, and the great talk was on the risk I had run in entering the devil's house without finding any money or gold in it. The Sheiks were laughing at each other, at the thought of their having approached near enough the place.

On the morning of the 27th, I was taken to see the seat of an old town in the south. The Sheiks were sure, that if I knew how to look I should find the treasure there; but all my endeavours to persuade them I was not in search of treasure were of no avail. We arrived at this place, which is not more than a mile and a half distant. There are several heaps of rubbish, and tombs cut out in the same manner as the rest, some of which were choked up with rubbish. I proposed to dig and open one of them, and they did not dislike my idea, as we might find some jewels in it; but after a faint trial they got tired, and left the tombs with the supposed treasure. We returned towards the village, but before we reached it, we were informed that the Great Sheik and the Cady of the other village were coming towards Zaboo. We hastened to meet them, but I observed that some of our Sheiks were not pleased with the intelligence. On our arrival at the village, we met the party coming towards us. The first was a good-natured looking man on horseback, dressed in linen cloth, striped blue, red turban, pistols, and a gun. I was informed he was the Great Sheik of the Elloah. The next was a complete rough looking fellow as ever I saw, dressed in green cloth and turban, pistols and gun. He was the Cady and Shiek, which means justice of peace and Sheik of the church. He was more conspicuous than the rest in his attire, with a turban of a Cashmere shawl, which he had procured when in Cairo. After these two personages came about twenty horsemen and as many foot, all well armed with pistols, guns, and swords. My guide by this time had drawn near me, and informed me that these two personages were the chief commanders of the Elloah. When Sheik Salem reached the walls which surround the village, he halted, dismounted, and looked round to see whom he knew. The Cady did the same; and the other people on horse and foot surrounded them. A few mats were brought and laid on the ground, under the little shade of a wall, ten feet high. The chiefs seated themselves there, and invited some of their attendants to sit with them. Meanwhile I observed the principal Sheiks of Zaboo had retired to another spot by themselves. I kept at some distance, till I saw they were all accommodated, and then went to them. After the usual salute of salame was over, I was requested to sit down between the two chiefs. I do not know what figure I cut in that place, but I certainly knew this, that to judge from appearance, the party round me, except the Sheik Salem, was not favourably inclined towards me. I then began to enter into conversation with the two great men, who were anxious to know my business in the Elloah, but did not like to be the first to inquire. At last, the Cady said plainly to me in Arabic, "Where are you going, and for what are you come here?" I replied, that I was a wandering traveller in search of old stones; that I only came there to see if any old buildings could be seen, that could give me any idea of the religion and writing of my ancestors, which was now lost. It appeared that this man had the same impression as Daud Cacheff in Nubia, for he made me the same answer, but rather more roughly. " You came here in search of treasure," said he, " and not for stones. What have you to do with stones?" I replied, that I wanted no treasure, but only to look at the stones; that I did not want to take them away unless it was agreeable to him; and, as a proof of my sincerity, I promised to give them whatever treasure I found. My proposal made the Cady consider, and the Sheik Salem said, that if I found any treasure, the Bashaw of Egypt would make war against them, and take it away. His reflection was very just, but I told him there was no danger of their running any risk in my finding money, for I had no thought of the kind. " But," said the Cady, " for what purpose then do you come into this country?" I again explained to them about the stones, and that I came only to look, if they would allow me, and if they did not, that I did not care; that to-morrow I should return to the Nile again, since they threw so many difficulties in the way of a stranger, who wished only to see a few stones. My apparent indifference had its desired effect, and the two Sheiks began to relax in their austerity. By this time some of my good coffee and tobacco came in, when we all smoked and drank. The Cady kept a secret conversation with some of the horsemen by his side, and one of them suddenly rose, and swore by Mahomet, that the stranger should never enter their village, for if he did, they should all fall sick and die. This was done at the instigation of the Cady, perhaps to see what impression it would make on me. I replied again, that if my going into the village was the cause of dispute, I would return, sooner than have the bad will of any of them. The Sheik Salem then said, that his people were afraid I would bring some evil disorder into the village. I then observed, that if I had the power of doing so, I certainly had not done it to the people of Zaboo, who were all well, although I had been there three days. There was much to do and say on this subject for about two hours. At last it was concluded that I should enter the village in the evening, but only on condition that I was not to write a single word; to touch or take any thing away; and that I should keep at a great distance from the ruins. I agreed to all these points; and as I had ordered a sheep to be killed, fortunately dinner was brought in. The armed men were fed by the Sheiks of the village Zaboo, and we were left to eat by ourselves. The Sheiks of Zaboo seeing that I would become friendly with the others, were more free with me than before; however, on my inviting them to eat, they refused, but at the request of the Cady they came, and we all ate out of the same dish, or wooden bowl, except Sheik Salem, who ate with none. I asked him several times to say what was the reason, but he refused, and smiled at me. I soon perceived that these people were not on friendly terms, and that he, as chief Sheik, could not eat with the people of Zaboo, for if he did, it would have made a general peace among them; but as I was perhaps not sure in my conjecture, I could not interfere in such an affair, which would have been dangerous in my case. No sooner had the rest finished their dinner, than a portion, reserved for that purpose, was brought to the Sheik himself. I was then invited to eat with him, which I contrived to do, as my first repast was not so abundant but that I could take another. After dinner and coffee, they all set off. Some time after we prepared to follow them, and the Sheiks of Zaboo made me promise that I would come there on my return. Three hours before sunset we set off, and passed over the sandy banks on the west of the village, crossed the plain, and ascended the rocks which separate the two villages. From the summits I had a fine view of the site of the Elloah, and on the side of El Cassar the country was most pleasant. A forest of palm-trees surrounded the village, and stretching over a wide circuit, which included a great space of cultivated lands. Farther on before us, there was the range of rocks which surrounds the Elloah, and opens to the west, forming an entrance into a valley which runs in that direction. We descended the rock, and gradually advanced towards the village, and on our approaching, we found the place we had to pass crowded with people; they knew the stranger was coming there to seek for treasure, and they were not pleased with our intrusion. It was well for me that I had had an interview with their Sheik and Cady, who had previously assured them that they would take care we should do no harm to them. The first we met came right before us, stopped the first camel, and would not let us proceed any farther; consequently we stopped where we were, at a quarter of a mile from the village, but he thought we had advanced far enough. I told my guide to speak to them, and to send one to the Sheik or to the Cady; but it was almost night, and there we remained. The people kept watch all night that we did not advance any farther.

Early in the morning of the 28th many of them came to look at us, but kept at a great distance. We wished to send some one to the Sheik, but no one would hear us. The guide told them, that the camels could not stay without provisions, consequently that they would die. The people replied, that we might die too as soon as we liked. All the forenoon was passed in this manner. The place we were in was a dry spot, without shelter from the sun, and no water near us; nor had we brought any provisions with us, as we did not expect such a reception. My guide and camel-drivers were determined to return to Zaboo as soon as the sun was declining, and I could not prevent them. Near this place I observed a quarry, from which large blocks of stone had been taken, which assured me that some building of the same must be in the village, or not far off. At last, towards evening, the Cady came to us, and said, that we could not enter on the night before, because the people were not consulted, and did not agree that we should enter till that moment—a difficulty which I afterwards learned was entirely owing to the Cady himself; for though the people were not pleased at our going into the village, they did not make more objection on the first night than the second.

At length, we marched slowly toward the village, and before we entered we dismounted. We passed under a gateway, which led into a spacious place. This was their market, the place where camels and other cattle were sold; in the midst of which we took up our abode. The principal difficulty was to obtain food for the camels, which they absolutely refused at first; but, on consideration that a Mahomedan would be at the loss of his beasts, they gave them some rice-straw. We made a fire, and prepared our utensils for coffee. The baggage was all put close to us, and we seated ourselves round it. The fragrant smell of the enticing coffee made these wild people stretch out their noses. By the time it was made, some of them came near us in soft conversation. I drank my coffee, and so did my guide. The people drew nearer still, till I could ask them if they wished to take any; to which they replied with a hearty affirmative. The sight of drinking coffee by these people drew many others nearer and round us. We began our conversation, and, after some time, the Cady appeared, and caused a large mat to be spread on the ground near me; and, to my great surprise, two large bowls of rice were brought before us. This was in return for what I had given to them on the morning before. After this, coffee was given again, and the great Sheik himself came to partake of it. I might with reason exclaim on the virtue of a cup of coffee. We talked of every thing but the subject of seeing the ruins. At last, as the night grew dark and late, the Sheik invited me to enter his house to pass the night. I would rather have remained where I was, but I could not venture to refuse him. I went, and, having laid my saddle on the ground, I thought I could sleep. The house of the Sheik was as usual made of mud; a few beams of palm-tree, laid across, formed the roof; on the top of which was thrown a great quantity of straw, with old mats over. It rains in this place sometimes, but not much. When we were alone, the Sheik told me, that all he could do for me he would; but that the Cady's father, being a merchant of dates, had received many dollars from the Bedoweens, who came there to market once a year, and that it was supposed that he hid them in the ruins; consequently he was alarmed, thinking that I would take them from under the ground by my magic. I assured the Sheik that I was not a magician, and that I did not care for treasure.

At last the old Sheik went to sleep, and so did I; but I hope my reader will not do the same.

On the morning of the 29th a great consultation took place, and the great difficulty was to persuade the father of the Cady to let me walk to the ruins. The debates were great; but at last it was concluded that he himself should accompany me, and no one else; that I should go no farther than where he led me; and that I should not write any thing down, or take any thing away. All the above conditions were of course agreed to, as I considered, that, if there should be much to see, I could not avoid observing it, and could put it in my memorandum-book at night; or, if any thing of consequence to examine, that I would find the means to see it again after my first visit. We set off with the old miser, and he took me through a lane where the houses were built upon the ruins of some great edifice. The blocks of stone project in several parts, and into the very path in the lane: but this was all seen in passing. At last, we descended on one side of the village, which is situated on an eminence, no doubt formed by the ruins. We went round part of the village, and on the north side of it I saw the remains of a Greek temple, consisting of a high wall with two lateral sides, and an arch in the centre. It is so situated, that it must have been built on the ruins of another of larger dimensions. This is not more than sixty feet in breadth, and, of course, it must have been long in proportion. The people were in crowds behind us, but kept at some distance; and it appeared to me that the influence of the old man was great. At about one hundred and fifty feet he stopped me from going any farther, and I could not persuade him that the distance was too great for me to be able to distinguish any thing. On the top of the wall there were many people looking outside at what I was going to do.

As I thought I might see some inscription on the wall, I took from my pocket a small telescope, which, when opened, was not more than two feet long. Having put it in a direction to the upper part of the wall, all the people that were there retired in great precipitation, and the others near us were on the point of doing the same. The old man stared at me and at the telescope, and wished to know what I was about. I thought it best to please the old man by letting him have a peep. He was shy at first, but he took it; and, after a long examination, I had some trouble to make him put it to his eyes. At last he caught the focus of the glasses, and was much astonished that the stones of the wall should come so near to him. He thought this was not fair, as I promised not to do any thing magical. I explained to him that it was not magic, but what the Europeans could make every day. I took a long observation on that wall, but could not discover any inscription, except four letters on the lateral wall on the east, and above the cornice, which are exactly as follow: E·P·H·S·

We reascended the ruins, and entered through a house into the interior of the temple; but there I could see nothing but the inner part of the above wall, which must have been the sanctuary. We returned to the house by the same road, and all I had observed was apparently to me the vast ruins of a great edifice, covered with the mud cottages which formed the village, and that the standing part of a temple was built by later nations, and that the materials of the former temple have been employed to erect the latter, but the stones had been diminished in size. The rest of the evening was passed in the house of the Sheik, to persuade him and the others of my honourable views, as by this first trial they must have found that I did no harm to any one. The telescope remained fixed in the mind of the old man; and he told the rest, that though I did not trespass farther than he permitted me to go, yet I had the mode to draw the wall of the Cassar, or ruin, near me, so that it was the same as if I had gone near. But all this was said in a pleasant manner by the old man, so that all the rest laughed.

At this time two negroes who lived in the Elloah brought in two pomkins of a liquor which they extract from the palm-tree, by cutting all the branches of it; they make a hole in the top of the tree, into which they thrust a pipe, attached to which is a pomkin flask; the liquor runs up the trees, and is discharged into the flask through the pipe. It is not unlike ale, but the natives cannot drink much of it without getting tipsy. I drank some, and ordered the blacks to bring more.

By this time the principal people of the village had arrived, and in consequence of my not having taken any treasure from the temple, they began to persuade themselves that I was not in search of gold. But, notwithstanding all this, the idea that a man should travel so many miles only to come to see the stones of that place could not enter into their heads. The telescope was what drew their attention at present, and it was handed from one to another; but unfortunately, after the first no one could see any thing; he protested that a branch of a date tree, which was at some distance, came so close to him that it touched his nose. All the rest were willing to see this wonder, but he unwarily had put the telescope off its focus, consequently the others could not see. When I put the focus right again, the first that could see exclaimed, that he was close to the tree. His pleasure of sight did not last long, for no sooner did he say that he saw something, than the glass was taken from him, and put out of its focus again. This created us sport for more than two hours, and I received my telescope back again without injury, which was more than I expected. They were so pleased with it and with their knowledge, that I proposed to take a tour round the village on the outside of it, and they all agreed to accompany me any where I pleased to go. I was on my legs immediately, and off we all set out of the village, with at least half of the people of it after me; for when the people saw that I had not brought any disorder among them, they became more free with us. I inquired from some of them, who seemed to be disposed to tell me any thing, if there were any places under ground any where: they seemed surprised how I should know of any places of the kind, and told me that there were many round the village. I took my course towards them; and on my arrival, I perceived several tombs cut out of the rock, like the others at Zaboo, and much in the same manner as the Egyptians. I entered with candle-light. I found three or four chambers, in each of which were several sarcophagi of burnt clay with the mummies inside, their folding not so rich or so fine, the linen of a coarse sort, and the corpses without asphaltum, consequently not so well preserved. They are in great quantity in each tomb. Many of the sarcophagi are still in good preservation, but I could not take any away, as it would have been too great a burthen for a camel.

After a long tour over these tombs, we returned towards the village. My next point was the well of warm and cold water which I heard talked of by my guide. Had I inquired for this fountain, I should have found perhaps some difficulty to be taken there; so I expressed a wish for bathing, and the said fountain was pointed to me. I returned to the house of the Sheik, and after all the crowd had dispersed, which must have been about three hundred people, I waited for an opportunity to set off unperceived, not to have such a crowd about me. I took my Sicilian servant, and the Hadge, who by this time had been to see the fountain, as he was more at liberty to go unnoticed than I was. I found it to be a well, eight feet square, and above sixty deep. When I first put my hands into this water I felt it warm; it was then after sunset: it springs from the bottom of the well, and overflows in a rivulet, which runs to irrigate some cultivated lands. This well is situated near the ruins, in the centre of a beautiful wood of palms and other trees. The water is blackish, but perhaps this is owing to the soil of the earth; it passes from the bottom to the top of the well. The next visit was to be made at midnight, to observe the difference of the temperature of the water. On our return to the Sheik's house, I found there the Sheiks of the village of Zaboo, who came to see me, as they said, but I rather think that these people were inclined to become friends again with those of El Cassar. Some rice was brought to us as usual, but no mutton. I observed that the great Sheik of Zaboo did not eat with the rest, as the other did on his visit to his village, and a portion had been brought to him as the other had also for himself. He invited me to eat, and of course I could not refuse, so I partook with him. Rice and fried eggs was the supper for him. Though it was rather late, they all set off to return to Zaboo again, and we went to rest for a while, but not to sleep, as I waited till midnight to visit the fountain. They all went to sleep, and I contrived by the light of a small lamp to write my little journal, of what passed on that day. At midnight, I took my servant and the Hadge, and went to the fountain. On our way we passed by several people, who sleep always about the lane which leads to the outer part of the village, and reached the fountain. We had to go over a wall to get at the place, as the door was closed at this time, but we soon overcame that difficulty. I found the water apparently much warmer than I had left it in the evening, and indeed I regretted I had broken my thermometer. We returned safely to the house, and went to sleep. Early in the morning, before the sun, we went to the fountain again, on pretext of bathing. I found the water as I left it at midnight, or rather less warm, but not so much as in the evening,

For instance, if we were to suppose the water to have been at 60° in the evening, it might be at 100° at midnight, and in the morning at about 80°; but when I returned at noon, it appeared quite cold, and it might be calculated in proportion to the other at 40°. These are, to my little observations, the various degrees of temperature which appeared in the water of that fountain, but I am well convinced, that it must have been the effect of the various degrees of heat in the atmosphere, and that water being so kept in a well of sixty feet deep by eight square, has not time to cool, so that it being constantly in one temperature, and that the effect of the apparent change, is caused by the change of the atmosphere itself, particularly as the water has proved to be pure, and free from any saline incorporation, as I had the analysis made since my arrival in London. But whatever may have been the causes of this apparent change of temperature, it does not signify, for the principal point is to prove the existence of the fountain itself, according to the description found in Herodotus, in Melpomene, where he says that there is a fountain near the temple of Jupiter Ammon, whose water changes its temperature, being cold at noon and midnight, and warm in the morning and evening. This does not altogether agree with my finding the water warm at midnight, but we have to recollect that Herodotus was only told of this phenomenon, for he never was himself in the deserts of Lybia, and that if the fountain was only apparently changed in its temperature, owing to the heat of the atmosphere, we have to consider that the simplicity of these people did not let them observe the true reason of the above change; but they naturally supposed it was the water that made this alteration. It is enough for me to remind my reader, that it is said that such a fountain was described to be near the temple of Jupiter Ammon, and that in the combination with other descriptions concerning the distance and situation of these ruins, we have reason to suppose that this may be the seat of Jupiter Ammon's temple; for my part, I shall leave others to conjecture, whether it is or it is not; in my simple opinion, I think that, with all this combination, we ought to consider that Siwah, which is another Elloah of the Ammonii, has as much right to be supposed the seat of the above temple of Jupiter Ammon; though, unfortunately, it is the opinion of many of the first literati, that it is not according to the description given by the travellers who have been there, particularly Mr. Horneman and Mr. Brown, who positively affirm, that the temple they saw in Siwah was not that of Jupiter Ammon. Still I beg to observe, that the Elloah of Siwah agrees with the account, in point of distance, as well as the Elloah el Cassar; and as it forms an angle with that place and Alexandria, and is at the same distance of nine days' journey from that port, I think that one place has as much claim as the other; the only objection I have against Siwah is, that the ruins in that place are surrounded by water, of which we have no account from the ancient authors, yet it might have formed a lake since that time; but what I will give as my firm opinion is, that no other places but these two Elloahs are meant by the old authors as the residence of the Ammonii, consequently the seat of its temple can but be within them, or not far off. Having seen all I could in this place, I made a proposal to pass to the other Elloah of Siwah; but for all my offers, promises, and entreaties, I could not persuade my guide, Grumar, to take me there: I then proposed to go to the Elloah el Haix, three days in a south-west direction, and found some little difficulty, but I overcame it by a small present to the Sheik and the Cady; and on the 31st, we set off through the valley on the west side of the Elloah. We continued our route south-west the whole day, and nothing of consequence to be described, as I saw only a few rocks, elevated above those which formed the valley. We went a good day's march, as the camels were fresh again; and the next day, the 1st of June, towards the evening, we saw another Elloah at a great distance. On the 2d we arrived there; it was a long tract of land, forming a crescent of more than twenty miles, from one point to the other. There are several good spots of ground to cultivate, and various springs of good water. The side where we entered was at one point of the crescent; there we found a few trees, some spots of ground with rice, a tomb of a Mahomedan saint, and no one to be seen any where. We advanced in search of water, and soon found it close to a large sycamore tree, which afforded a fine shelter from the sun; close to the tree we found a hut, made of four mats attached together; inside of it we saw a bowl of fresh milk, and in a bag attached to the hut we found some dates. One of the drivers was sent in search of the inhabitants of this hut, and it was some time before he could find one; at last a miserable-looking wretch was brought there, who was so frightened at the sight of strangers, that notwithstanding the good treatment he met from us, he could not get the better of it. He was a good-natured sort of being, living far from the wicked world, as I thought, and I almost envied him; but mankind are the wildest of all animals, particularly against each other. We took the usual accide, which we ate with the milk, and made the man partake with us: we gave him some dhourra and flour, and some grains of burnt coffee, which he tasted with delight. After eating he set off, and soon returned with another man, with an appearance even worse than his own: a sort of short ugly-looking fellow, turned up nose, long teeth out of his mouth, and uncommon thick lips; his eyes standing out of his forehead, and his hair resembling the serpents of Medusa. He was very sulky with us; and for all we tried to be friendly with him, he could not reconcile himself to us. I could not conceive what was the reason why this man was so totally different from the other; the fact was this,—that my guide happened to be recognised by him to be one of the assailants of part of his tribe at a place near the southern Elloah, and that he escaped from them by chance. All this was told by the good-natured man to my Hadge, in Arabic, who repeated it to me. I told it to the guide, and he immediately recognised the man. The guide then went up to him and talked in friendly terms, but he could not put him into good humour. I caused the Hadge to inquire how many people there were in the Elloah; he said a great many, but would not tell the number: probably, I thought, they were but few, only they wished to frighten us away. Notwithstanding all this, I thought it would be proper to keep a strict guard at night; but we soon found that we were not to sleep there. The ugly man disappeared half an hour before we perceived it, and by this time it was quite dark: we perceived great uneasiness in our guide, but he did not wish to show it either to us or to the other men of the place. Some time after the other man, on pretence of fetching water, set off, so that we remained by ourselves. Our guide was still more uneasy: at last I insisted to know what was the matter; he then told us plainly that he expected we should be attacked by a party on that night, and that he feared they would be too strong for us; he thought the best expedient was to load our camels, and set off as soon as we could. I thought there was no time to be lost; but notwithstanding I did not like to be frightened away merely on supposition: we concluded that we should load the camels, and change our position, till we saw what might happen. It was well that we did so, for soon after we perceived a number of men from various parts. Our camels were sent off with the luggage, and I remained not far from the place where we were before with the guide. Though it was pretty dark, we could see enough of their actions and of their disappointment at not finding us there; they were in greater numbers than we could have opposed. We made a forced march, or rather a hasty retreat, and with the same pace we kept on the whole night, till we reached the opposite point of this Elloah: here we were extremely tired; the camels could not stir any further without resting: at last, after a few hours, we entered this place in the morning of the 3d, which we found better cultivated than the other side of the crescent. It was owing to the necessity of wanting water that we came there to refresh our camels, otherwise we should not have passed that way, as it was not in our road back to the great Elloah. Here I found more verdure, and several trees of small sweet apples, which are also found in Egypt: there are dates, plants, and vegetation for the camels. At some distance I saw a high wall, which drew my attention. On my arrival there I found the site of a small ancient town, built of burnt bricks: the baths are the only buildings which remain in good preservation. They are cemented within with the same material which was in use by the Greeks and Romans for that purpose: it is a kind of reddish cement, made of ground bricks mixed with lime. The walls of the houses are to be seen; and close to the town stands the high wall which drew me there. It evidently enclosed an edifice, of which a very little portion now remains; no doubt the materials have been taken to erect other buildings, as at no great distance from this I saw another wall, and on my approaching it I found it to be a Greek Christian church, in a good state of preservation. The inside is built in the form of a cross, and has various divisions at each side; at the end there is the usual chapel, and two places for the lateral altars, which form the sides of the cross. It is about fifty feet long and twenty wide: the materials are of burnt and unburnt bricks. At some distance from this I came to another building, very massive; it was a square wall, without entrance. I contrived to ascend to the top of it, and found that it must have been a Copt convent. There were several cells separated from each other, and a very deep well of water in the centre, so that the inhabitants of the place were independent of the necessity of coming out to seek that element.

Having fed the camels, we advanced farther into this part of the Elloah, as we had to cross it to come on our road again. At some distance we saw a man, who no sooner perceived us than he set off like an antelope. Our guide ran after and succeeded in reaching him within the distance of a gun shot; he then hailed him, and he stopped; for when a man is within the reach of a gun, if he do not obey, he may expect a ball will reach him. Our guide then turned back, and the man followed him. When he came sufficiently near to allow me to speak to him, I found that he was nearly out of breath with fear. As it is time that I should state the reason why this man, as well as he, of the other part of this Elloah, were so frightened, I must inform my reader that my guide was no less than one of the Sheiks of these Bedoween tribes, who make their incursions into these places at a time when the rice or barley are up, and take away all they find; rob the poor inhabitants of the fruits of their labour, and often leave them to starve in the lone desert; and if any resistance is made, their lives are often the forfeit of this attempt to protect their property. Grumar was well known by all the people of the Elloah, but no one communicated this to me; but the Moorish Hadge came to the knowledge of it by other people, and he of course communicated it to me; and if we had staid a little longer in the place where we were the night before, we should have paid the forfeit for what Grumar had done before to these people. This was the reason why he would not take us to Siwah, for he was too well known there; and if we had gone to that place with such a man, we should have become the victims of revenge. We requested the poor man to show us some water, which he took us to in a few moments. We halted a while to refresh our camels, and make our accide, or flour pudding. We took our station under a large sunt tree, and set the camels to finish their repast. The country here forms a circle, with a running rivulet in the centre. The water is very sweet, and the land produces good rice and barley. The inhabitants are only six in number, four men and two women: they live entirely on the product of their own labour and water. It is not to be wondered at that they were afraid of my guide, as they knew his past tricks, when he visited them with all his tribe. Of these people we only saw two; the rest were absent far off at work, and would not return till night. We left this place, and arrived at a day's distance from our first Elloah, or El Cassar; and on the 4th, in the evening, we reached that spot again. It appeared that our Hadge had lost his purse on the road, with three or four dollars in it. He thought he could find it if he could procure a donkey to go back a few miles, but no one was willing to lend him one; and having informed themselves where he thought he might have lost it, they set off themselves and found the purse, which they of course claimed as their own.

We passed the forenoon of the 5th in the village: I inquired if any of them had any articles to dispose of, and told them that I would give them money in return: nothing was brought to me of any consequence, only a broken Grecian vase of bronze, about eight inches high, of a very curious shape; and a small cherub of Greek work, not more than three inches high. During the morning I was taken on one side by the Cady, who was uncommonly polite to me all this time, for which attention I could not account: he told me in a few words, that himself, the Sheik Salem, and his father, had made up their minds to offer me to remain there with them; that I should become a Mahomedan, and that a great feast would be made on my account on the day of the festival of that ceremony; that I should partake of part of their lands, and if I knew how to introduce some new produce, it would be all to my own advantage; and lastly, that I might choose four wives from among their own daughters, and that I should be happy there without going about so much after stones. I had not a little difficulty to get myself out of this scrape: I left the Cady with hopes that I would return soon, and then, perhaps, my mind might be more inclined to stop there and marry; but, for the present, I could not leave all the rest of my affairs at Cairo, which I left unsettled. My Sicilian servant was attacked also at the same time, but he got off in a more speedy way than myself: he told and promised them, that as soon as he had accompanied me to Cairo, he would return immediately, and stay there with them all the rest of his life.

At last, we set off in the afternoon for the village of Zaboo, and left all good friends at the village of El Cassar. To Sheik Salem I made a present of a string of very ordinary sort of corals, which he took with great pleasure, some pieces of soap, and a portion of coffee; to the Cady I gave equally the same. On our coming out of the village, the people saluted us very cordially, and said they expected us soon back again to stay with them. This day we began our journey very merrily, but it ended very badly. We ascended the rock we had to pass to come at the village of Zaboo, and on our descending, my camel slipt his foot on one side, and rolled down the rock the height of about twenty feet, taking me, of course, along with him. I did not get off so easily this time as I did when I fell on the sand in Wady el Gemal, for here they were all hard stones; fortunately, however, no other harm was done, as it appeared at the time, but a few bruises and a blow on my side. I was put on a donkey belonging to a man who followed us from the other village, and I was brought so to Zaboo, to the house of Sheik Ibrahim, the son-in-law of our guide. My saddle was my bed, as usual. Fortunately we had a few drops of brandy in our stock, and my bruises were rubbed with it, but my side did not permit me to stir without great pain. On our entering into the house, I saw a great number of people assembled, eating rice out of their usual bowls. I was accommodated in the passage which leads from the street door to the yard behind the house. My mattress, or saddle, occupied half of the space from one wall to the other, and in all there was not two feet left, for the men, women, children, cows, buffaloes, donkeys, sheep, goats, and dogs, to pass there. The passage was constantly crowded with people, who occasionally trod on my feet, or gave me a kick on the head. But this was not the worst of the thing; it happened often, that while the cows, buffaloes, or donkeys passed, I had reason to fear the consequence of my being thus situated. There was another thing which was not the least of all the rest. The feast of rice eating was kept in consequence of the death of a man related to Sheik Ibrahim, the landlord of the house where I was, and he was taken to be buried just before we arrived. No sooner was the eating ended, than the most tremendous noise issued from the outer doors; it was the widow of the deceased, who returned home, accompanied with all the rest of the matrons of the village, all in great uproar; they had all to pass by my side into the yard, where the house of the deceased was, and every half hour they had to repeat this lamentation all through the street before the house, so that the place where I lay was a continual passage. The pain in my side was not diminished, and the skin became rather black: I tried to move, but I could not.

On the morning of the 6th, I had many visits of the Sheiks. They all congratulated with me that I did not break my neck, for it might have been so by the fall I had. I spent the rest of the day in taking notes. Towards the evening of the second day, I was with the Moorish Hadge and my Sicilian servant, who were my physicians.

I felt my side was somewhat better, and I was in hopes to be able to bear the motion of the camel on the next day. After sunset, the widow who had buried her husband on the day before came and seated herself near to me, sobbing, I supposed, for the loss of her husband. My Sicilian servant tried to persuade her to bear the loss patiently; but she continued sobbing: at last she said, that none but me could restore her to happiness, and that she hoped that I would not refuse her the favour. I could not understand what the woman meant, and she sobbed again, while the Moorish Hadge was talking to quiet her, but in vain. She still continued there, and said, that none but me could cure her of all her trouble. At last I asked what she wanted of me. She said, that she saw me writing magic, and begged I would write two pieces of paper—one to get another husband, as soon as possible, and the other to make use of for the same purpose if he should die. We endeavoured to persuade her that I was not in possession of magic; but she would not be convinced, and went away much displeased with my harsh proceeding against her. I could not help reflecting, that if I had the art of procuring husbands to widows, I could have obtained employment enough in Europe, without travelling in strange lands for such a purpose.

On the 7th, I tried to mount the camel, but my side would not permit me. At last, on the 8th, in the afternoon, we set off. I felt much pain the two first days, but it appeared diminishing after. The above two days, the 8th and 9th, brought us to the flat desert of the horizon; and another day, the 10th, to the tumulus; the 11th to Rajan. There we were without water, and we had to drink some from that place, which was very salt; we, however, filled the hudris, and on the 12th, took the road towards the south-east by east, as I wanted to go to see a place named El Moele. We passed a great quantity of sand-banks this day, and slept on the summit of one of them.

On the 15th, after noon, we reached El Moele, hoping to find fresh water, but, alas! we were disappointed. The drivers made the accide with salt water, and we eat it. In this place I found the ruins of a small ancient village, and the remains of a very large Christian church and convent. Some of the paintings on the wall are very finely preserved, particularly the figures of the twelve apostles on the top of a niche, over an altar; the gold is still to be seen in several parts, and their faces are well preserved. This place is situated at the end of a long tract of land, which had been cultivated in former times, but it is now left for want of water. It extends more than ten miles from west to east towards the Nile. We went on as soon as we had refreshed ourselves with salt pudding and salt water; for as we were disappointed there, our next resource was the Nile, or at least some of its canals. We travelled till midnight, and arrived within twelve miles of that river. We suffered much from thirst this night: though we were so near the water, my mouth had formed a crust of salt within it, so that I could scarcely articulate a word, and for several hours I felt what it was to be truly thirsty. We were almost all in great distress. At last one of the drivers told us to stop, for there was sweet water near us. At the sound of these words, we were all agreeably surprised; but I could not conceive where the water could be, as we were in a flat plain, covered with small pebbles and stones. He had kept a small skin of water concealed in a sack all the way from the Elloah, as he said he expected this would happen. I do not know that in all my life I have tasted any thing more sweet and pleasant than that water, though it had been closed up in a skin for several days. At last, on the morning of the 14th, before the sun, we arrived in the valley of the Nile, at the Bahar Yousef: on the evening of the same day we reached Sedmin, the place where I engaged my guide; and on the 15th, we returned to Benesoeuf, where I embarked for Cairo.

3 K

The blow I received from the fall in the Elloah did not get better; it continued to pain me much, and the part became black, and swelled. I found the consul, Mr. Salt, had returned from Upper Egypt. The plague was very violent in Cairo at that time; but as I had business to transact with the consul, I went at night to the consulate, and having arranged my affairs with him, I returned to Rosetta, where I arrived on the 23d, in hopes to end the business of the attack in Carnak, as soon as I could, and set off for Europe. But I was totally mistaken, for the intrigue displayed in this affair is almost beyond the possibility of explaining. Mr. Drouetti, in defence of the two assailants, Lebulo and Rosignano, his compatriots, and in his service, said that Mr. Salt was the accuser; that in the account I sent to Mr. Salt I had declared that I did not seek for redress: and, in fact, I did not, as I was well aware of the intrigues which would have been displayed by my adversary; but as the affair had been brought forward, I made a formal declaration against the two assailants, Lebulo and Rosignano. Mr. Drouetti, availing himself of the influence he had with the new consul, Mr. Russel, made up a tissue of stories of his own fabrication, saying, that I went under his window to stop the people from working; and that it was a mere dispute, and not a premeditated attack. Mr. Russel wished to have this affair thrown aside, and that nothing more should be said; but we insisted it should be brought forward, and upon having the two assailants brought down from Thebes to Alexandria. Mr. Drouetti continued to put himself forward, saying, he was accused by Mr. Salt; but a declaration made by me, that my deposition was against the two assailants, put it out of his power to have any farther ground to prevent our proceeding against his agents, on the pretext that he was accused also.

By this time, the hurt I received from the fall in the Elloah turned out to be troublesome, and had confined me near a month to my bed in Rosetta. It happened that Mr. Russel, the French consul, was to return to France, and Mr. Tednar Divan, the vice-consul, succeeded him provisionally. This good sort of honest gentleman, a great honour to his country as a justice of peace, had been in Egypt for many years; he was one who cut a conspicuous figure in the days of the Revolution: he never was higher than Cairo, and had a great wish to go up to Thebes. He never had a better opportunity offered to him than the present, as he was to be judge in the above cause. He answered to our consuls, that if I wished to proceed, I must deposit immediately 1200 dollars, as a security to defray the expenses which would be incurred in the examination of this affair; that he must go up to Thebes accompanied with Lowjars, clerks, stewards, witnesses, boats, barges, canjars, &c. and all this at my expense, while I might only hope for redress. I was more than tired, and as I knew the people we had to deal with, and to what point they could carry their intrigues, I had no hopes of redress.

Be assured, my gentle reader, that in this simple sketch of this affair, you can but form a very small idea of what passed, for I cannot at present enter too far into the explanation of it. I shall only state how it ended.

The two assailants, Lebulo and the renegado Rosignano, Piedmontese, were obliged to come to Alexandria, to take their trials; and when they arrived, were so sure of getting off in some way or other, that they not only confirmed my deposition, but boasted of what they had done. Now to the conclusion. Their protector, Mr. Drouetti, knew very well how he should get out when the affair came to the extremity. I demanded an interview with him before the consul, and a number of other people, to have an explanation of the various wrongs he had done to me; but all to no purpose. I insisted, and at last it was arranged by Mr. Drouetti, that an interview should take place with only the British vice-consul, the French consul, him, and myself. This was not what I wanted; as I thought I might have the chance to expose his conduct publicly; but he took care not to consent that a public meeting should ever take place. Unfortunately, on my first landing in that country, I became under an obligation to him and another person, particularly by having had an apartment in his occaley for three weeks, during the time of the plague; and through the said obligation it was supposed and expected I should sacrifice my principles, which has been another cause of so much hatred against me. When I requested him to explain before the two consuls what cause I had given him to induce him to evince such animosity against me, I believe he was not on his guard at that moment; for the first word he expressed related to my wrong proceeding in taking the obelisk from the island of Philœ. I could scarcely believe that a man, who held a situation once as a consul, should forget himself, and show an open inveteracy against an individual, merely because he was fortunate in his undertakings. I must acknowledge, that it must have been provoking to a man like Drouetti, who did not search antiquity from the love of these relics, but merely for interest, and whose views were directed chiefly to the British and French Museums, to see a stranger accumulate in three years a greater and far superior collection than he had done in fifteen; and, as in consequence of this, his hopes on the British Museum were lost, he could not restrain his passion. The conclusion of all this affair was, that after a nine months' struggle to bring the two assailants to a trial, the French consul put an end to it in a few words, by only saying, that the two persons accused were not French subjects, but Piedmontese; and that if we wanted redress, we must go to Turin for it. Thus I received redress for that shameful outrage; but I was not surprised, as I fully expected it would end in such a manner.

I should not intrude such a narrative on the patience of my reader were it not that, even at Paris, I found the persecution of Mr. Drouetti had not ceased. On my arrival in that capital, I found his son-in-law busied with the public prints, who, only on the assurance of his assertion, and the prejudice already excited against me, for serving another nation, put before the public whatever he could persuade the censors to pass, and what he could not, he publicly asserted in a most atrocious manner. I had sent an answer to these publications to be inserted in the journals of Paris, but such were the intrigues carried on, that my reply was intercepted, and sent to Mr. Drouetti, in Alexandria; consequently it never reached the hands of the editors. At last, having put an end to all my affairs in Egypt, in the middle of September, 1819, we embarked, thank God! for Europe: not that I disliked the country I was in, for, on the contrary, I have reason to be grateful; nor do I complain of the Turks or Arabs in general, but of some Europeans who are in that country, whose conduct and mode of thinking are a disgrace to human nature.

After an absence of twenty years I returned into the bosom of my family, from whence I departed for England; and having been persuaded to put before the world the narrative of my researches and operations in these countries, I hope the English reader will pardon me for the many errors I have committed in this volume, particularly in the English phrases.

MRS. BELZONI'S TRIFLING ACCOUNT.

MRS. BELZONI'S TRIFLING ACCOUNT

OF THE

WOMEN OF EGYPT, NUBIA, AND SYRIA.

Having heard so much of Turks and Arabs, I took the opportunity, while in Egypt, to observe the manners of the women in that country. During my stay in Soubra, I had many occasions to remark them; but as it was my lot to ascend the Nile, I contrived to see the various modes of living among these half wild people. The first place we staid at for any length of time was Old Thebes; but I shall pass this, as I mean to speak of it hereafter.

On our arrival at Assouan I went to visit the women of the Aga of that place. I was met at the door by himself, his wife, his sister, her husband, two young children, three old women, uglier than Macbeth's witches, and an old negro slave. I entered into a small yard, and a deal chair was brought me. The Aga went out, and the women then stood round me, while the husband of the Aga's sister made coffee, and prepared a pipe, which he presented me, not allowing the women to touch it. He durst not trust them with any thing, as he knew of their monkeyish tricks whenever he turned his back. He seemed to pride himself much on his great knowledge of the world, by correcting the rough curiosity of the women when they attempted to examine my dress too rudely.

I made a sign I wished them to sit down, and in particular that the wife should take coffee with me: but he treated them very harshly, made me understand that coffee would be too good for them, and said water was good enough; at the same time he held the coffee-pot, pressing me to drink more: on my refusing, he locked it up in a small room, that the women might not drink it. By this time I had been so much among the women in Egypt, and compelled to smoke, that I could easily finish my half pipe. After having smoked for some time, I laid it down; one of the women took it up, and began to smoke: on seeing such a horrid profanation, the man took it from her with violence, and was going to beat her, which I naturally prevented: he filled it again, and offered it to me; but as I did not wish to smoke any more, he went and carefully locked it up, making me understand when I wanted it, it was at my service.

I must confess I felt hurt to see the distinction he made, but afterwards I saw the necessity of so doing. I could not help reflecting on the inconsistency I often met with from these men: they treat women with the greatest contempt, and yet they always behaved to me not only with respect, but even with humility; so that their roughness seems not directed towards women in general; and I have often heard them remark to me, that if they treated these women as I was treated, they would become quite unruly.

A short time afterwards the Aga came in, and inquiring if they had served me with coffee and a pipe, he went to his treasury and brought out some dirty bruised grapes, as a great treat, which he presented me, the poor women looking with wistful eyes towards the basket: in the impulse of the moment I took it and offered them to his wife, and then to the rest, who all refused; and though they did not dare to take any themselves, yet they pressed me to eat, and seemed astonished when on account of their dirt I only took a small bunch. I kept the grapes in my hands for some time before I could muster resolution to eat them. I began at last, one by one, trying to wipe them in an handkerchief without their perceiving it; but I was mistaken, for their eyes were fixed upon me very closely: an old woman saw what I was doing, and ran and fetched me a burdock of water. I did not ask for water at first, as, not knowing the customs of these people, I was afraid to do any thing to offend them.

I now gave my little present of beads and a looking-glass, which contained a drawer: the beads pleased them, and the glass, being the largest they had ever seen, and made to stand by itself, was to them a matter of astonishment. To describe the tricks the women played with it, tearing it from each other, and setting it in any way but the right, would be thought a caricature. I at first attempted to show them the right way to use it, but there is no other method with those women than letting them have their own way; and I believe it is pretty well so in more civilized countries, or I am much mistaken. When the wife perceived they had got the glass out of its frame, she put it in a little room, and locked it up with the beads: they then began their examination of my dress, as the man was not there, which I had reason to be sorry enough for. I was then in European clothes.

The first thing was my hat and hair; my neckerchief of black silk, which they coveted much; next the buttons of my coat: nothing could persuade them but money was hid in them. I opened one, to convince them of the contrary: this seemingly did not satisfy them, for, judging by their own tricks, they thought it was one put there purposely to deceive. I verily believe, if the man had not now come in, they would have been very troublesome. However I learnt sufficient in this my first visit to guide me in future, and to put on a greater degree of consequence with other women I might have to deal with; for by showing myself free with them, on account of my ignorance of their character, they would take advantage of it. On the man coming in, they began to prepare to cook the dinner for the Aga, which consisted of a dish of bamià boiled in mutton broth, poured over bread, with a little mutton, and some minced meat, mixed up with rice into balls: what other ingredients might be mixed shall by me be nameless; the cleanliness of this preparation I have not eloquence to describe: the horror I felt at the idea that I should be obliged to eat of it, was more than my English stomach could reconcile at that moment. They brought me all the dishes before they took them out to the Aga and Mr. B., who was to dine with him; the first was the bamià, which I refused, but I took a piece of the boiled mutton, as being the cleanest, with some bread: that would not do: the wife took some of the minced meat and rice in her hands, and insisted on my eating it, making me understand it was the best. At last all was carried to the Aga. I was then served with the customary coffee and pipe. The house, or rather stable, consisted of four walls, which had the sky for its ceiling, inclosing two small rooms; one in which the Aga used to keep his treasure locked, such as coffee, coffee-cups, tobacco, &c.; the other was the wife's, and contained all their great wardrobe, besides bread, onions, flour, dhourra, oil, and many other things of the kind. The furniture consisted of water jars, sieves to clean the corn and sift the flour, a few earthen pots to cook in, some wooden bowls to eat out of, an oven, and some burdocks for cooling water, a small coffee-pot, and old mats to lie on. I took my leave, giving the children and women a small present of money, promising to call and see them on my return.

Next morning another wife of the Aga sent me word she would be glad to see me. I felt little inclination to go, but not wishing to make any distinction between them, I went, and found, to my surprise, a very pretty young woman: she lived next door to the other, who got upon the walls to see what was passing between us. She had no coffee to give me, but instead presented me with some dates and dhourra in grain. She seemed much afraid of the other wife. Though pretty in my eyes, she was not thought so by her own people; the other, though old, was considered the greatest beauty in Assouan, on account of her being so extremely fat. Their hair was plaited after the Nubian custom, adorned with a few gold ornaments, with plenty of stinking raw fat, and a certain bark of a tree beat in powder to make it black besides, giving a horrid perfume, which they consider as a great improvement to their charms: it is not the same powder they use in blacking the eyebrows and eyelids. I made her a present of some beads, which she tried to hide, and I wished her farewell.

On our arrival at Ybsambul I did not go on shore. The wife of Davoud Cacheff having heard there was a Frank woman on board, sent a young negro girl on purpose to see what kind of animal I was: she was rather shy to come near me at first, but the men telling her if she came into the boat the setté would give her a bakshis, she came with reluctance. I gave her some beads, which instantly got the better of her fears, and she observed every thing on board minutely. Having kept her eyes fixed upon a half-pint basin, she jumped up and ran away; she returned in a few minutes, bringing me some dhourra bread and dates, telling me her mistress hoped I would not refuse to send her that beautiful basin, pointing to it: it was curious to see the anxiety the girl showed, for fear I should not give it to her: she made me understand her mistress had taken all the beads I had given her. I gave her some more, with the wonderful basin and a plate like it. The joy the poor thing felt on receiving it was such, that in her hurry to get out of the boat she had nearly broke them.

On our return from the Shallal we stopped at the village Eshke to transact some business with Hosseyn Cacheff. I remained on board while Mr. B. went to visit him; during which time the women of the village with their children came running towards the boat; but some men belonging to the Cacheff would not let them approach, and those who pressed forward they beat, and at the others flung stones: on my seeing this I made a sign to the women to approach, and seemed in a great passion with the men for beating them: those that could come near me kissed my hand, and seemed much gratified at my preventing the men from beating them; they were much pleased at the whiteness of my skin and the colour of my hair. To those that had but few ornaments I gave beads for themselves and children. What pleased me most was, they did not show any disposition to covetousness, or express any desire that I should give them any thing; they seemed perfectly content that I allowed them to see me, and imitated the action that I made to the men not to beat them. Those I gave beads to went away; I did not expect to see them again: they shortly after returned, bringing me some dhourra bread and dates, finer than I had ever seen before or since. I naturally concluded it was a demand for another bakshis. According to the custom of the Arab women, on my giving them some beads, they took out what I had before given them, and kissing my hands, begged me to accept their presents, which I did; they then sent for more dates. I made them understand I gave them the beads only as remembrances of me, and not for the sake of getting any thing in return. On seeing Mr. B. and some of the Cacheff's men at a distance, they set up a great shout, and made me understand they must go. I was very sorry to part so soon with those women: their manners were much more friendly than I have ever met with: they watched the boat at a distance till we left the shore.

On our return to Ybsambul I went to visit Davoud Cacheff's wife: she had been previously informed of my intended visit, and accordingly put herself and palace in order: by the look of the building outside, I certainly expected to have found something better inside; but it was much the same as that of Assouan. On entering, I found her sitting on black goats' skins sewed together; I perceived this was considered a mark of grandeur that was not used in common: she got up, and after saluting me took the said skin and placed it for me to sit on, and sat on the earth herself. I would, with much pleasure, have dispensed with the skin. She was dressed in a blue cotton gown of Lower Egypt, which is considered a very grand dress in Nubia. The coffee that was brought me was some we had given them on passing, as they can seldom have any: they use kerkadan, a small grain, the produce of the country, of which I have a few. Her young child was lying on a skin naked: it was twenty days old: but she scarcely took any notice of it. I gave her some different kinds of beads; she was surprised I did not wear any myself. I informed her as well as I could that I was dressed as a man; she then spoke softly to the little girl, the slave before mentioned, who came and sat down by me, and some other old hags she had sent for: the girl first untied my neckerchief, examined my coat, and showed as much curiosity about the buttons as my friends at Assouan; their remarks on my corsets, which I still wore, were extremely sensible. I made them understand they belonged to the female part of my dress, not knowing the custom that is come up since I left Europe: they kept crying *tayib, tayib,* (good) at every thing I showed them. The Nubian women in general I found more kind and civil, and did not show that invidious jealousy and covetousness the Arab women possess. After satisfying their curiosity about my clothes, she ordered the women, whom she had sent for on purpose, to dance, thinking to amuse me; but unfortunately I did not appreciate this mark of respect they thought they were paying me. Some time after I got up and bade her farewell, though she wished me to stay longer.

During my stay there a young woman came on board, begging me to give her some beads, showing me at the same time she had but very few, among which I saw she had two or three antique beads of cornelian, with a drop, which she exchanged with me for other beads, and went away very highly pleased. I was well content with my exchange, and was determined to go among the women at every place we might stop at. On our arrival at the isle of Philœ, I, according to custom, left Mr. B. and went in search of the women. The first I met was a pretty young female with a child on her shoulder, who saluted me in a very friendly way, and offered to show me about the place; in a few moments after we were joined by an old woman and her daughter, a very pretty girl; she did not seem pleased with the notice I took of the other young woman, to whose child I had given some beads; but I have reason to think they did not know I was a woman, for they had not seen any of the people of our boat, and as they had seen some Europeans some months before in the same kind of dress, it is possible they were mistaken. Seeing the other had got beads, she demanded some in a rough manner; however I gave her the same quantity I had given the other: she asked, in an importunate manner, for more, and made as if she would return those I had given her if I did not: on seeing this I took them from her, and gave them with some more to the first young woman. She got in a passion, and attempted to take them from her, which I prevented; she then begged me more civilly to give her some, but I would not give her any then, and made her understand I would not be compelled. After this we went to see the different temples; we were joined by other women belonging to the island. After seeing all the buildings, we came to a very small temple, wherein this same lady lived: it was closed by a door, but she offered to show it to me. She took me by the hand very kindly, and seemed to have forgot the little dispute about the beads, and was unlocking the door, when my good friend with the child gave me a squeeze on the right arm, which was next to her, and made me a sign not to go in: I concluded she had heard the other express some bad intention against me. I refused to go in. I could not conceive why the other did not wish me to enter: she seemed pleased I took the hint, and immediately showed me back to where Mr. B. was. I gave her and another good-natured old woman a small bakshis, and I passed the remainder of the day at the Morada, in exchanging beads with the women. Were I to mark down every thing that I saw, or that happened to me, it would be thought, perhaps, too trivial.

On our return to Assouan we had to procure a boat to take us to Luxor. The Aga wished me to go and stop with his beautiful fat wife till we got a boat, which I positively refused, preferring rather to rest under the palm-trees than run the risk of being more disagreeably accommodated. After fixing on a spot, we had all our luggage which we had brought with us, and likewise all that which we had left with the Aga, particularly a large mat, which I was happy to be in possession of: I had it immediately spread on the ground, one part for our mattresses, and the other part to eat off. I was flattering myself we should be very comfortable, and get a little rest from much fatigue, after being screwed up in a small boat for a month. After all was prepared for the night's lodging, the Aga made his appearance, followed by a servant, bringing a tray with a number of dishes, which he said he had prepared for us and himself. I am certain it was the first time the Aga in his life had dipped in the same dish, *sour sour*, together with a woman. After our feast was over he wished us good night. We tried to sleep, but to no purpose; we were much tormented, as we supposed, by ants from the trees.

The next morning early we went on board a little boat, scarcely large enough to hold us; there was no other, and we were in a great hurry to reach Tebes. The large mat I mentioned before, I had spread over the boat, covered with other small ones, to shade us from the sun: but woe unto us! the wicked Aga had, during our absence, used the mat all the time we were in Nubia, and on our return had it rolled up as we left it, and the very thing we had been guarding so perseveringly against befel us. What with being attacked with an intermitting fever, without medicine or tea, and not being able to lay my mattress straight, besides the dreadful situation the miserable mat had involved us in, made our condition very unpleasant indeed.

We at last reached Luxor. Still there was no rest for the soles of our feet. There was no boat to take the great colossal head on board; and, notwithstanding this poor accommodation, we were obliged to set off for Gheneh. We had no sooner arrived there than we were obliged to return, as there was a large boat pressed for the use of the bashaw, wherein some Franks had taken their passage as far as Assouan, which boat was promised to Mr. B. for the head. We tied our little boat to the large one. We had come down well enough with the stream with our miserable bark; but on going against it we had not set off twenty minutes when the Arabs began to cry out most dreadfully: in a moment we found the boat half full of water. Fortunately the large boat, perceiving our danger, ran to land immediately, and we went on board of it.

The next morning we arrived at the wished-for haven. Mr. B. had but just time to put me in a house, where he was informed there was a room on the top for me; he was then obliged to sail to Esne, to secure the boat.

This was the first time I had ever been left alone with the Arabs without an interpreter or an European, with about twenty Arab words in my mouth. What they denominated a room, consisted of four walls open to the sky, full of dates put to dry in the sun, an oven in one corner, a water jar, and a fire-place of three bricks for a pot to stand on, without a chimney; and this place not to myself, as it was the apartment of the women. I never in my life felt so isolated and miserable, in a violent fever, exposed to the burning sun; besides the torment to have all the women of the village coming out of curiosity to see me. At last I began seriously to think of inclosing one corner this place for myself: it fortunately happened to be market day; I sent to buy some mats, and with the help of the women (I was going to say), who did more harm than good, I made me a comfortable little room, inclosed and covered over: I had all my things taken in. Beside the pleasure to be by myself, I had the additional luxury of two ounces of tea, which I had received from Cairo by return of a courier. I felt more content at that moment than I now should in the first palace in Europe. The inmates of the other part were an old woman, four daughters, and a daughter-in-law, the wife of the master of the house. During this time I observed a woman bringing some meat: they made me understand it was for me; but on account of the fever I then laboured under, I did not mean to eat any: I made me some tea, and retired to my apartment, where I could see every thing that passed, and from whence I saw the daughter-in-law with the meat between her teeth, one hand holding it out, and the other with a bad knife, cutting or rather tearing it up till she made it small enough to her mind. I considered it very lucky I was not hungry or inclined to eat: when done, the poor woman brought it, and begged me to eat: I told her as well as I could, that after taking the tea I could not take any thing else. I pressed her to eat, which she did, no doubt to let me see there was not any thing in it to hurt me; I broke some bread with her and eat a little, to let her see I did not object to eat with her. I had just began to enjoy a little repose, when I had an attack of ophthalmia.

During the first ten days a virulent humour discharged from my eyes: I had not any thing to apply to them: I could not bear the light. I used to filter the water to wash them. Whenever the women saw me wash them with water they would all set up a cry, telling me it was very bad, and that it was my washing them every morning that had made them so. In Nubia they had the same idea.

During this time Mr. B. had to go several times backwards and forwards to Esne and Gheneh, which he could not avoid. I must do justice to the Arab women, Mahometans as well as Christians, for their kind treatment of me; there was not a day I was not visited by the women of Luxor, Carnak, and other villages near: the Christian women, in particular, used to burn certain herbs in a small earthen pot, repeating prayers, and making the sign of the cross over it; the Mahometan women waiting with great anxiety to get possession of the blessed ashes that might be left, thinking as those were done for a Christian it would have its full virtue, which, if done for them, would not have the same effect: for example, the last time I was at Luxor, and on the point of leaving it, I showed to some of the men by putting scorpions in oil they would have a remedy against the bite; I believe oil alone would be as efficacious. They looked at me and shook their heads, and said I had some other secret which I put into it. When I went in my little room, the second year I was there, scarcely a night passed I was not called up by people who had been bit; it was useless my sending out the oil to them, for unless I did it myself they took it in their heads it would have no effect. I make these remarks only to show the incredulity of the Arabs; the most simple things are by them kept as great secrets, which makes them pass for wise and learned men. Most villages have one of those great men of knowledge; therefore if a traveller is kind enough to tell them any thing to be serviceable, they will not believe but he keeps the great secret back, as they are accustomed to from the example of their own wise men.

To return to my eyes; they were determined not to be cured so easily: blest with the comforters of Job, the women told me in twenty days perhaps I might get better; but if not in that time, it would go on for forty days, and finished by crying *malash* (no matter). Instead of being better at the end of twenty days, I became totally blind. I cannot describe the agony I felt on the occasion: I thought I had lost my sight for ever. My situation was not an enviable one; the women still crying *malash*. The last stage of the disorder was truly dreadful; the eyelids lost their power, I could not lift them up: this was another blow. The women boiled garlic in water to steam my eyes over: it is possible it might have done some good, though I did not feel the effect immediately. I found their experience in this matter perfectly correct; the eyelids began to gain strength, and by degrees, at the end of forty days, I could see a little.

By this time Mr. B. had got the colossal head on board, when he was attacked with the same disorder. I have not the presumption to give a fixed opinion on what it proceeds from, I only remark how I came by it. I had been the night before standing sidewise by a hole, that served for a window, in the wall of my apartment; I felt at the time a draught of wind to my eyes, but took no notice of it. The same way Mr. B. got his; he received a blast of wind. It is in general supposed it proceeds from the great heat or sands, which the air is at times full of; it may be so; I speak from my own experience only. At this time we had been in Egypt and Nubia eighteen months, ten of which we resided at Subra, a short distance from Cairo, in front of the Nile, exposed to all winds. We had no glass windows, therefore if the hot winds affected the eyes, I think we should have not have escaped all this time, annoyed and exposed as we had been in Egypt and Nubia; at Soubra, in the time of the camseens, our shutters were not sufficient to keep the sands out. For hours the air has been full of hot sands, so as to render it troublesome to breathe, and obliged us to keep our eyes shut. During this time I expected every day we should be affected with this disorder; but nothing happened, except feeling my eyes a little uneasy in consequence of the hot winds. I used to wash them, which gave me instant relief. I found my sight much clearer at that period than I had it in Europe. The great perspiration, in my simple opinion, helps to clear the sight, provided it does not go into the eyes.

After getting well of this attack, I made it a rule to wash my eyes daily with water mixed with aqua vitæ, which strengthened them much: if ever I found them inclined to a relapse, I made the wash stronger, and kept washing them several times in the day: it never failed to cure them; though I have never had my eyes so strong as they were before.

On my second arrival at Philœ, on June the 5th, 1817, I found Mr. B. and some countrymen of mine preparing to depart for Ybsambul. Mr. B. felt very anxious to finish opening the temple, which he had began on our first visit the year before, when there was not one European with us. My wishes were to go also, but as we could not afford to incur the expenses of a boat expressly for that occasion, I was obliged to remain at the isle, to my great mortification, and left that country without seeing the inside of that interesting temple, which had occasioned us so much anxiety the preceding year. I still live in hopes. I cannot pass this over without dwelling a little on the partiality of some of my countrymen, who on their visiting Ybsambul, some time afterwards, gave the merit to others, and not to the right person; such is liberality and love of truth at the present day. Truth must be sacrificed by some travellers, because they are absolutely afraid of speaking, for fear of gaining the ill will of some of their colleagues.

I was informed by some one who was there, that the boatman, as well as the servants of Mr. Salt, who accompanied Mr. Beechey, had as much merit in assisting in the concern as the other gentlemen, but they were not English. Had I been there, I should have helped to remove the sand as well as them, as far as my strength would have allowed me on such an occasion, and claimed as much merit.

During Mr. B.'s absence, I took up my residence on the top of the temple of Osiris in that island, and with the help of some mud walls, I had inclosed two comfortable rooms. It was rumoured about there were thieves on the island opposite, though I rather think it was a trick to see what effect it might have on me. I thought it proper to guard even against those Barabras that had been engaged by Mr. B. to guard me. I had a servant with me at this time who had been with us some years: we kept the fire-arms always ready, and made our guards see we were not afraid, and that they might inform their friends we had plenty of powder and ammunition for their reception. It is well known that the people fear you when they know you do not fear them. They knew there was a deal of luggage left with me, and saw some silver spoons and forks which were brought up for the use of Mr. Beechey; and the servant used to let the Arabs and Nubians see and clean them. These people, when they see trunks or boxes belonging to Europeans, judge they are full of gold and silver, particularly after having seen such unnecessary things as spoons and forks of that metal. I was visited every day by the women inhabiting the different villages on the other side of the Nile; they used to cross on a ramouse, bringing sometimes one or two beads of cornelian antiques, or a little barley, some eggs and onions, getting in exchange glass beads or small looking-glasses. My old acquaintance from the first year came to see me, particularly the friendly Zara, with the good old woman, who hailed me affectionately, and continued so to the last. The old woman was the merriest and best natured simple creature I ever met with: she would not have disgraced England itself; she used to make many sensible remarks upon our customs. Her husband and two fine lads were killed in a battle with another tribe, mentioned by our much esteemed friend Burckhardt, page the 6th, account of Philœ. One day, on seeing some of our coarse cloth, she, in a very humble tone, asked me, if I had got an old piece of the same kind to put on her head, as she had not got any thing, she should be very happy. I told her I would look if I possessed such a thing, for I made it a rule, from dear bought experience, never to give any thing on the moment it was asked for: on the next day I gave her a piece. I cannot describe the joy she expressed on receiving this present; but after examining it some time, she said it was too clean, and would spoil her head, and she must make it dirty before she could use it. The reason she gave was, that being clean it would draw all the grease out of her hair, and particularly as all kind of fat, butter or oil, was very scarce and hard to be got: besides the beauty the glitter of the fat gives, it preserves the head against the burning heat of the sun. She wanted to go with me to my bellad, meaning my village or country (they knew of no other town besides Stambul or Mesr), telling me she would wear Franks clothes, or any thing I would give her, showing me by pantomime she would wash my feet and clothes, make my bread, cook for me, and any thing else I might want; the only stipulation she made was, that I must give her wheat bread, and not dhourra. If she could have spoken Arabic I should have taken her: they certainly have not the prejudice of the Arab women.

One day some of my people brought twelve fowls; a native told me to look at them, for they were not fit to eat, as they were full of vermin, and the skins sore, desiring me not to tell who told me. On finding what he said was true, I desired to know who they were brought from; but that was a secret none dared to tell me. All that I could find out was, that ten had been bought from a woman from the opposite island, and two from the she devil, as they style her, inhabiting the small temple, whom I had affronted on my first visit the year before: the women begged me not to have any thing to do with her, calling her a fright, and many other names; but as I had a reason to suppose the whole was brought from her, I was determined not to let such an imposition pass, as I had longer to stay in the island than they knew of. The women I could perceive did not give me the above advice in earnest, as she had made them all tremble at her. I made a boy, a native of the place, and who had been with us on our first voyage, pick out the two fowls and carry them back, and desire her to give me two better, or send the money back: the women laughed, and said I should never get one or the other; which made me more determined. The next day I went myself with the boy and an old man: the boy told me to take my pistols, or she might do something bad to me; I took them, and put them under my coat, not on account of her, but it was well for those who were with me to know I had such a thing. When she saw me coming she called her mother, thinking to frighten me; the other woman stood at a respectable distance, not daring to approach. I made the old man demand better fowls or money; the old woman abused me much, with her daughter; I thought it then time to speak in a commanding tone. I went up to them, and insisted they should speak no more. The mother, on seeing I was not to be frightened, began to cry out dreadfully, and beat herself, and fling dirt over her head, and exclaim they were lost. I left them, threatening vengeance against them if they did not send me the money or fowls. Seeing she could not succeed in mastering me, the next morning she sent me word she wished to be in peace with me, and that she would send me two better fowls. I sent her word she must bring them herself. She came with her mother with two better fowls, kissed my hands, and begged me not to think any more of it. I told her it was not the fowls or money I wanted, but that I would not let any one impose on me: I then made her a present of the two fowls she had brought, and gave her some beads. I then called in my friendly Zara, and gave her the other ten fowls: she had never been so rich in her life. She said the only food herself, her husband, and two children, had daily, was a small bowl of dhourra, boiled in the morning, with a little bread of that grain, and the same at night. She said she could clean the fowls by washing them in salt-water. Peace was once more restored in the island, to the no small gratification of the rest of the women, to see I had conquered the great devil. She used to beat their children whenever she could catch them, because she had none herself.

One thing I must observe, which I did not think to mention, till on reading in page 146 of Burckhardt's account of Nubia, of the dreadful death the Nubians give their wives. When the women used to recount me many particulars concerning this woman, I expressed my astonishment, as she used them so ill at times, that they did not tell her husband: the Arab women would have done so, besides exaggerating the facts. The answer a young Barabra gave me was this, that if they did, the husband would cut her to pieces and fling her in the Nile; besides, the husbands of the other women would beat them for so doing. My idea on the subject is, that it is not so much from humanity as from the dread of the consequences of such quarrels between the different tribes, that these women have learnt to be prudent.

The trifling anecdote of the fowls is, indeed, too insignificant to have been recounted; but as a countryman of mine has already made himself very liberal on this subject, whose merit lies in low buffoonery, caricaturing, and imitating, like a monkey, every one he has ever been in company with, no matter whether friends or foes, particularly against unprotected females and old men, without much regard to common decorum or delicacy, I take the present occasion of noticing his behaviour. I, indeed, pity, and feel contempt for men who daily amuse themselves by slandering any one whom their wanton malice may dislike: was my soul as illiberal as that of some of those kind of gentlemen, I have sufficient scope to return the compliment with interest. I shall say with the Arab Ma-lash, every thing will find its own level.

Mr. B. having returned from Ybsambul, we departed a few days afterwards for Luxor. On my return to that place I went to my old habitation, which they had inclosed with brick walls. Unfortunately the husband had taken another wife during my absence, and had built up an apartment for her, attached to the walls of our house, whose top was covered with mats. The first wife was first cousin to her husband, and his sister was married to her brother: on account of this double tie, she took those advantages that are not allowed to women in general. There was a continual disturbance every day; and when her husband used to threaten to send her home, her brother sent him word, if he sent back his wife, he would do the same by him. The old mother-in-law, who was her aunt, of course sided privately with her niece, not on account of any love for her, but to prevent her own daughter from being sent home: unfortunately all her hopes rested upon me. The Christians in the village had made much mischief, and had put her up to resist the other wife; and upon my arrival, she thought I would head the concern, and used to tell her husband when the cetté arrived, meaning me, that she would not allow him to keep his new wife: as she knew I was her friend, and as the Christian women imprudently meddled with Mahometan customs, she thought I should do the same. All I could or would do was to give her good advice, and point out to her she was acting wrong, and contrary to her laws; and according to these laws, a man may take four wives if he can support them, which her husband could, therefore he might marry two more: and if he did not send her home, as she had no children, at least as good as none, as she only had a female child of four years old, he might make her the last, and treat her as a slave. Though it is the custom from time immemorial to marry four wives, yet they hate each other most cordially. The sly, wicked tricks they play, and the hatred that grows up between the different children, continually employ their thoughts. The husband seldom knows of the tricks they play among themselves: they are obliged to show a good humour before him; that is, if he is a husband who knows how to govern his family properly. I had felt much friendship for this woman, on account of the attention I received from her the first year, when my eyes were bad, and out of kindness to her did not see the new wife, but tried all I could to make peace between them; and often when all the women of the village went out to any feast, and she was locked in, on account of quarrelling with her, I used to intercede with her husband that she might go out with his mother and sisters: when she got permission, she lamented and said she had got no money like the rest of the women: I would then give her some. When I tried to reconcile her to her situation, she would say, But your men have got but one wife. I told her our laws and religion did not permit them to have more.

It was customary with me every evening to ride to Carnak: I was certain on coming home to see the house in the greatest confusion. She had a great party in her favour, particularly all the Christian women, not out of love or friendship, but because the other wife was a native of Carnak. The people of Carnak and Luxor are never friendly. The sisters, who had instigated their brother originally to take another wife because of her arrogance to them, enjoyed the mortification she now suffered. One evening on coming home I found the yard full of people, and flinging stones, bricks, and any thing they could catch hold of, into the apartment of the new wife. On my entering they were in hopes I should interfere. She never would persuade herself but I would join her in so laudable a concern; but when she was convinced I would not head her party, as I told her the English never interfered with the laws or customs of others, she got outrageous against me in her heart, and did me all the petty tricks an Arab woman is capable of; such as coming up at night softly and spoiling the jar of water which was always prepared at night to clear for the next day, and then making a noise to prevent my sleeping. One night we saw her set fire to the mats that covered the house of the other wife. One morning I am certain she put something into the water she used to prepare for my breakfast, for I was seized with a violent sickness: I took some medicine, though it left me very weak for some days. At that moment I did not suspect her; but I soon had reason to observe the change in her conduct. About a fortnight afterwards I was served the same. After this time I took care she should not do any thing more for me, and we soon after went to reside at Beban el Malook, in the entrance of one of the tombs of the kings. When I mentioned the subject to Scotch Osman, he said he was certain she had given me something to injure my health, as he said they were full of those tricks to each other. Shortly after, we left this place, and departed for Cairo.

When we arrived there, I found it impossible to remain in that place; and go again to Thebes I would not. I persuaded Mr. B. to let me visit the Holy Land. It was that idea only that had brought me first into Egypt; and as I knew circumstances might prevent him from his intended visit to that place, and that I should be obliged likewise to depart without seeing it, I took this opportunity.

I accordingly left Cairo on the 5th of January, 1818, and arrived at Damietta on the 10th, where I was detained two months, through the negligence of our agent. One month I staid in his house, in the apartments of his mother, waiting with the utmost anxiety to hear if there was water enough to take the ships out of the Bogos, when, one day being on the top of the house, I saw a ship go out. It was vexatious to see myself detained there when other ships could go out. My passage had been taken on board of a ship the day after I had arrived there, with the promise of being the first to set off. I had then waited a month. I insisted on going on board, which I did that night; and, with the continual hopes of daily going, I was detained another month. At last we departed, and arrived in Jaffa on the 9th of March; and left there on the 11th for Rama, where we slept, and arrived in Jerusalem on the 12th of March. I shall never forget the effect the first sight of the walls of that memorable place had on me. I arrived just in time to witness the Catholic ceremony that took place the three last days of Passion week, inside of the building that covers the holy sepulchre. My much esteemed and respected countryman, Maundrell, has given so exact and minute an account, that I feel myself incapable of giving a better.

On the first of May I went to the Jordan. A Christian merchant of Jerusalem, a relation of our consul at Jaffa, provided me a mule and a driver he could depend upon, to accompany me. I set off some time before the governor who goes to protect the pilgrims: they were all on the sides of the road, waiting for the signal of departure, on my arrival at the boundaries, where none dare go beyond. A black man who was put as guard there, on seeing me ride on, galloped furiously up to me, gave my poor mule a blow, and desired me to stop. On his trying to take hold of the mule, I aimed a blow at him with a corbatch, which he avoided, brandishing his sword at me. The mule then stopped, and I slipt off, being determined to be as obstinate. I dared him to touch me, and walked on, leaving both mule and driver behind, who was much frightened at my insisting to go on. When outside of the boundaries I looked back, and, to my surprise, saw the man driving the mule after me.

My wish was to arrive in the valley of Jericho before the great concourse of pilgrims. As I had no one but myself to depend upon, I wished to procure a spot where I could be out of the crowd; and, without putting myself under obligation to any one, I just arrived in time to take possession of two bushes. I made the man cover them over with Arab shawls to shade me from the sun, and remained there till our departure for the Jordan. During the afternoon, an European traveller we had known in Egypt, in his strolling about encountered me, and politely offered to render me any services he could in that place; but in those journeys I made it an invariable rule to be independent of every one, that it might not be said, if it had not been for *me* or for *us*, she could not have gone on; and indeed as it was, I could not escape petty hints from a countryman of mine, who, " for his part, had no notion of people being so romantic as to travel about, who had no fortune to support it."

The European traveller whom I mentioned before informed the English party where I was, some of whom kindly condescended to visit me, and invited me to their tent, which I justly refused; and though the only European woman there, I was better where I was than expose myself to receive some polite insults, which some of the party were so well versed in towards women. Yet it is true I felt a little cowardly as the night drew on.

The gentleman who had engaged my servant, who wanted to return to England, was good enough to permit him to come and guard me till we should depart. I felt a little fear, though I took care no one should know it, particularly when the pilgrims were made to enter the camp, which I did not, as I had nowhere to go to. It is true I might have joined some Syrian women; but the next day I should have had no peace, for they would have spread it about among the pilgrims I was a woman. As I had now some one that could answer the guards as they passed, I had nothing more to fear; for I never could have got the poor driver that was with me to have courage enough to answer them. Some time before daylight I mounted my mule, as all the pilgrims were in motion. We all set off. I find it impossible to describe the scene. Camels, horses, mules, donkeys, mixed in confusion together; women and children, screaming and crying, hung at the sides of the camels in baskets. I was in danger of being knocked off my mule by their coming in contact with me. All my man did was to drive my mule, no matter for what was on it, sometimes in profound darkness, at other moments the glare from the fire-pots showed me the confusion of the scene, the negro guards flying about to keep us together.

We arrived at the Jordan by break of day. The principal part of the pilgrims were Greeks. They all took with them a new gown, in which they bathe in the Jordan: they immediately after fold it up, wet as it is; and on their return to the valley of Jericho, they open and dry it: when arrived at Jerusalem, they take some wax candles that were lighted at the holy fire that descended from Heaven into the Holy Sepulchre on a feast-day of theirs, and make the sign of the cross on the said gown with the wicks of the above candles: this gown is to be kept till they die, and in it they are to be buried. Hell has no power over those who are thus attired.

After resting some time on our return to the valley, we once more set off for Jerusalem, where we arrived late at night, all fatigued enough.

A noble family then at Jerusalem, from whom I received much politeness, hearing I meant to go to Nazareth some time before I quitted the Holy Land, as they were going there, kindly invited me to join their party; which opportunity I gladly embraced. Being a good many in number, they took the most interesting roads mentioned in Scripture, and which road is not always safe for two or three to pass. We left Jerusalem on the 8th of May, 1818, and arrived at Nazareth on the 14th, where I remained.

It was my intention to have remained there some time, but the Christian Arabs employed in the convent had reported in the village I was some great person in disguise. Accordingly, I never could go out without being followed by a concourse of women and children. Having seen every thing that was interesting in that place, I left them eight days after. The superior engaged a Christian Mokaro to go with me. I left Nazareth on Friday, 22nd of May, in the evening, with the intention of travelling all night, on account of the heat, and particularly as I was alone, to avoid meeting any Arab tribes. By the time the sun was hid we arrived at some long black tents belonging to the shepherds of the Bashaw of Acre: they, according to the custom of the world, judging me wrongly by my dress, took me into the tent of the men; that of the women joined this, but none dared to make their appearance. I was presented with coffee and fresh milk from the goats. They killed a kid. We eat with a friendly hospitality together, unknown in Europe. I am entirely indebted to the great cowardice of my Mokaro for keeping the secret of my being a woman. He begged of me to remain there till twelve o'clock, as being a safer hour to depart. Having consented, I put my portmanteau under my head, and covering myself up in my burnoose, I composed myself to sleep; but the fleas, to welcome my arrival, were determined I should not. Unfortunately for me, they did not prevent my Mokaro from sleeping. Having awoke him, I desired him to prepare for departure, which he positively refused; alleging, by way of excuse, that on our passing the different tents, though the people might be asleep, the dogs were not, and would fly out upon us, and a great many more lies. Finding I could not prevail, patience was my only remedy: with much persuasion, an hour before daybreak on the 23d, we departed. I never suffered in Egypt or Nubia such a dreadful unwholesome heat as on this day.

I could enter into many particulars; such as, at daybreak meeting with a camp of Arabs in their tents, all busily employed in preparing cheese, sour-milk, and gista, or clouted cream; women churning butter in the skins of goats, hung up in the middle of three poles, which they kept shaking. Going on, we met with a number of wild-looking Arabs; which not only frightened my poor Mokaro, but would have frightened Munchausen himself, had he been there; and I must confess, I did not feel very courageous myself. We arrived, in the evening, at the most wretched, miserable Turkish village I had ever met with. I would not go to the Shiek, which is customary, as I knew my Mokaro would have told him who I was. We went to an enclosed yard belonging to some poor miserable creatures, the most wretched in Egypt; where, a princess, compared to the people of this village, I fixed upon a spot, and was in hopes of resting a little after the miserable night and day I had passed. During the time I was eating some bread and cucumber, the only thing I could obtain, a number of men, women, and children came, and said I was passing that road to avoid paying the tribute that Christians are liable to. I had left my firman at Jerusalem, and I began to consider what to do, as the Europeans are exempted from paying. I was determined not to give any thing. On my desiring my Mokaro to tell the people to go away, that they had no right to demand any thing from me, instead of telling them so, he begged me to give the people something, or, he said, it would be bad for us. This made me nearly lose patience, and I saw into the trick. Having hinted them myself to go away, but still resisting, and being importunate, I got up in a threatening manner, and began to open my portmanteau. The Mokaro not knowing but that I might have pistols in it, began to tell them to disperse. I complained unjustly of the few fleas I had the preceding night at the shepherds' tent; for the horrid torture I suffered this night no words can express: they must have been in thousands. The very inmates, accustomed as they were to them, were far from sleeping sound, scratching and rubbing in a most miserable way, and at times getting up and shaking themselves, and walking about, but seemingly unconscious of what made them so miserable. Some time back I might have got a premium in Spain from the Holy Inquisition for such an invaluable addition of cruel torture.

We left this village of fleas on the 24th, two hours before day. The country we passed this day was finely cultivated, and the best I have seen since I left Europe. We saw immense quantities of Indian figs.

We arrived at the convent of Rama at one. I went to bed immediately, being too much fatigued to eat; not so much from the journey, as that was trifling, but from the dreadful nights I had passed. I rested in this quiet, peaceful retreat till the 27th. Its situation is beautiful: from the top there is a fine view of the country for miles. We departed for Jerusalem on Wednesday, where I went to remain till Mr. B. should come for me, which was his original intention. During this time I tried all means I possibly could to enter the temple of Solomon, but to no purpose, though often promised.

When the Turks want to repair any buildings, they send to Acre and other places for the poor Christian Arabs, who do all the labourers' work, though they allow no Christian to enter into the temple. Inconsistent as they are, they are glad enough to have them to repair or build their sacred places; and when finished, purify it from their contamination. Such was the case when I arrived at Jerusalem: the temples were undergoing a repair. The Christians employed in this work were nearly all Catholics. They were, of course, lodged in a quarter appropriated by the convent for pilgrims and Europeans; in which quarter I was, as women are not allowed to enter the convent. As I daily mixed among those people, it struck me, that by their means I might get into the temple. Some one put it into my head, after the men had given up all hopes of assisting me to enter; that it might be possible, if the men could procure permission for their wives to enter, as they had been allowed to go in when they first began to repair the temple, that by dressing myself like one of them, I might enter with them. It was a good plan; but the temple was nearly finished, and the Turks did not care to oblige them. They did not, however, tell me they could not get permission; but, on the contrary, said they had procured it, and I should go in with their women. According to the time appointed, they brought me the clothes. Being dressed, and my face comfortably smothered up in July, my feet cramped into boots with high heels, that were not large enough for me, but like the glass slipper, I would have suffered any thing rather than not go, off we went. I cannot describe the sensations I felt between hope and fear. After going down hill for some time, creeping like snails, as it is not the custom to walk fast, beside the misery I endured, from my toes being cut by being flung forwards by the high heels, we arrived at Mount Sion, where stands the Moska where our Blessed Saviour eat his last supper with his disciples, and where the tomb of David and Solomon is. As I had seen it on the outside on my first arrival, I knew I could enter at any time for a dollar. The women began to whisper among themselves, and called their husbands out, I thought for the purpose of accompanying us to the temple; but no one can imagine the cruel disappointment, when they told me this was the temple. Judging me like their own women, they thought they could pass this off as the Temple, and get the bakshis from me. I instantly saw their intention, when too late. What with the disappointment, and the imposition they had put upon me, and the state of my feet, and the shame I felt at having been deceived by those women, I refused to enter, and began to scold them for the trick they wanted to play me. Seeing I knew this place was not the temple, they seemed for a few moments quite stupefied; at last they began to excuse themselves, saying they had just heard they could not get permission for their wives to enter: but I was not in a humour to listen to those stories. They, thinking to pacify me, told me the Ramadan would begin in a few days, and that it would be easy enough to get me in then. I had lost all confidence, and was quite indifferent to all they could say. After venting my passion a little, I went into the Mòska. I returned properly mortified, and shut myself up in my room, and would not let any of the women come nigh me. They sent me all the excuses possible, with a thousand promises. After this I went to Bethlehem and to St. Giovanni, and to the desert where he preached, and to the valley where David killed Goliah. After my return, I began to prepare to depart for that sink of vice and wickedness, Grand Cairo, as I had received letters from Mr. B. that there was no chance of his being able to visit Syria, at least for some months. During my preparation for my voyage, the drogueman of Mr. Bankes arrived in Jerusalem to fetch the doctor of the convent, as he was ill in Jaffa. This man had been some time in Nubia with Mr. Belzoni. I took this opportunity, as I did not dare to trust the interpreter of the convent, to get this man to go to the head scrivan of the temple, telling him what I would give him if he could succeed in getting me in. The drogueman returned, telling me the man would give me an answer in the evening: it was only a trial, for I had no hopes. The drogueman told me the scrivan said, if I had been a man he could get me in. Of course, when he heard that, he thought of his master, who he knew wished much to enter two years before. A few days after this, having all my things ready, and my mules engaged, I took a little boy of nine years old, son of the porter, well known by travellers, and told him to show me the way to the door that leads into the grounds where the temple was. Leaving the boy at the gate, I walked slowly on. I had got half way towards the steps, when I saw a Turk at a distance; but being dressed as one, he took no notice of me. I had got black shoes on, which I had blacked for the Passion Week, to enter the Holy Sepulchre, and which I was determined to wear all the time in the Holy Land, and which I have now. The weeds prevented my shoes from being seen, otherwise I should have been known for a Christian. I at last got to the steps on the north, that lead up to the platform where the Holy of Holies stands. During the time I took to consider whether I should venture to go on, I found myself on the top. Here I had to consider again; but imperceptibly I walked on, and passed the door on the east, and came to that on the south, which has an inscription over it, and which looks towards steps opposite to those I came up. I passed and went towards that on the west, and then to the northern, and passed again the one on the east, and came again to the southern door, which I went up to, and looked in, and saw some pillars of marble or granite in the inside. I left it again with the intention of reconnoitring a little, to see if any Turks were in the way. I had got to the western door the second time, when I observed a man following me, but did not dare to look at him. He said to me, in Italian, when passing, "Follow me," and went on, as if not noticing me. I was surprised; but, on looking, I found it to be a Christian, with whose wife I was intimate, who lived in the same quarter, and who often said, if he had not been afraid of the other Christians, he would have taken me in. Unfortunately, the Christians are very treacherous, and betray each other to the Turks; which makes those people dislike and despise the Christians so much.

I naturally concluded he would take me into this same building; but as I could not speak to him, I followed in silence. We went down the southern steps, and passed a fountain of water which comes from Solomon's pools at Bethlehem. This water both Turks and Christians prize much; and during the time they were working there, each man was allowed to bring home a large pitcher every night for his own use; and the women used to give me some every day as a great treat. Having passed some cedar trees, we came to the great mosque, according to Ali Bey Ell Aksa, a large building. In the words of Ali Bey, page 215, no Mussulman governor dare permit an infidel to pass in the territory of Mecca, or into the temple of Jerusalem. A permission of this kind would be looked upon as a horrid sacrilege: it would not be respected by the people, and the infidel would become the victim of his imprudent boldness. This edifice forms the south-east corner of the city of Jerusalem, and occupies the site on which formerly stood the temple of Solomon.

When we consider the permission which Dr. Richardson had to enter, it may be observed there is some inconsistency in the above account of Ali Bey: but no, the Doctor had rendered the Capodi Verde a service in his medical capacity, which he knew not how to return in a manner sufficiently to gratify him, and to show the high estimation and gratitude he held the service he had received from him, but by granting him permission to enter the Holy Sanctuary: a permission the Emperor himself has not power to grant. It is true, he may give a firman to that effect; but when arrived in Jerusalem, and on their presenting it, they are told they do not refuse them to enter according to the firman, but it does not say any thing about coming out: therefore that he is welcome to go in if he likes, but remember, if he wishes to come out, he must embrace their religion, or suffer death in all its horrors, by being burnt alive. Such is the information I received in Jerusalem, and I have no reason to doubt the truth of it.

On entering it, the man took off his shoes, and put them under his arms. I slipt mine off; but, in the hurry on entering this building, I left them at the door, and went after the man. This place is full of large columns and pillars, some of granite, with different capitals, in the rude Turkish style, which I could scarcely look at, after what I had seen in Egypt. We entered a recess, wherein was a large window: there I found a Christian at work. He was well known, as he had his nose cut off by the Bashaw of Acre, a little time after the French were there. He told me this was the spot where St. Simon and St. Anne had taken our Saviour in their arms and prophesied. There are some small marble and granite pillars in this place. On walking to the end of this building, where are windows which look over Siloe, they showed me a place in the wall where, as they say, originally stood a door which our Saviour used to go out of; and on the spot was a stone on which they say is the impression of our Saviour's foot. Close by there is a small staircase to ascend, similar to our pulpits, where the priests, I suppose, preach or pray with the people. The men took me into two other little rooms, one on the right and the other on the left, which were undergoing a repair, and full of rubbish of stones and mortar. They told me they were holy on account of our Saviour: for what, I could not understand. I do not attempt to give an account of this place. I understood but very few words of Arabic, and Italian very imperfectly; and if I had, it would here have availed me nothing, for those men knew it not: that is to say, they had, when boys, and serving at mass, picked up a mixture of Italian, Portuguese, and Spanish. Therefore I saw without understanding, and had not the advantage of having every thing pointed out to me. Having seen all in that place, I expected to return the same way I came. The man, observing I had not my shoes, asked me what I had done with them: I recollected I had left them at the door on entering. On attempting to go after them, he stopped me, and said he would go for them himself. I remained in the recess before mentioned. He returned without my shoes. He said a Turk had seen them, and taken them as a witness against him that he had let a Christian enter. He seemed much frightened. Whether all this was true I know not. He gave me a pair of red shoes. I was now more vexed at the loss of my precious shoes than alarmed at the consequences, and told him positively, that he must get them, promising to give him a bakshis when he brought them to me; which he did the day after. He then took me out at a little door, thinking he was going to show me something more, when I found myself outside the building, in a wild kind of a place; and though I kept asking where we were going, he made no answer, making a sign not to speak; but, to my sorrow, I soon found out where I was, seeing we were near the Armenian convent. I had left the poor boy at the door, who knew not what had become of me. About a quarter of an hour after my return, he came into our quarter, crying and beating himself, saying that I was lost; that after he had waited some time at the door, he went in and ran all over the place to seek for me, but could not find me. This day turned out to be a day of strife; for, on my return, the carpenters, scrivans, and their wives, were quarrelling amongst themselves, because I had been in without them, and had lost the promised bakshis; each reproaching the other with having taken me in slily. The Padre Curato, a Spaniard, had been informed of the confusion in our quarter, though I had shut myself up very quietly in my room, without taking notice of the quarrelling in the yard below; indeed, I did not know it concerned me. On his coming into my room, the first word he said was, Is it true, Signora, you have been in the temple? I understood the poor father was alarmed for fear the Turks should come to be informed of it, and should come upon the convent for a sum of money, which they are accustomed to do very often, upon one frivolous pretext or other. I answered him I had been in a building, where I was informed our Saviour was presented, and had seen a stone with the impression of our Saviour's feet on it, which I had the satisfaction of kneeling down to kiss. He had evidently come into the room to scold me; but the pious father, on knowing what a good Christian I was, could not find in his heart to proceed, only saying, "Che corragio," and telling me that the oldest friar there had never dared to go into the street that leads to the temple, which I sincerely believe. In the evening, the Christian women of this quarter having satisfied themselves that no one had taken me into the Temple, came to my room, and sitting down around me, exclaimed every now and then, lifting up their hands, that it was God saved me. And when I expressed my sorrow that I did not go into the Holy of Holies on the platform, when I was on it, they would exclaim, in crossing themselves, that it was Christ and the Virgin Mary that protected me from going in, otherwise I must have been burnt, and a great many more things. But, however, I thought it prudent to leave Jerusalem the day but one after for Jaffa. On arriving at the house of our Levantine agent, I found Mr. Bankes, who was beginning to recover from a fever. I was obliged to wait some days before I could procure a passage for Damietta. During this time I understood from the Drogueman of Mr. B. that he was buying an Albanian dress for him, with the plea of going to Rama for few days on account of ill health, and to pass on quick to Jerusalem, and proceed straight into the temple. It was a good plan, and nothing more easy; for as Mahomet passed for an Albanian, he could pass Mr. B. off as his countryman, who could not speak any other language but his own, as it is not expected an Albanian should know either Arabic or Turkish; and having practised from his Drogueman the ceremony of the prayers, there was little doubt of his succeeding.

The domestic comfort of the Christian women I had the opportunity of mixing with in Jerusalem, Bethlehem, and Nazareth, was much greater, and they were much more respected by their husbands, than any I had seen since I left England; for the state of the Christian women and natives of Egypt is not better than the Mahometans. During a few months' residence in the Holy Land, particularly in Jerusalem, I used to go among them every day. In their houses they were particularly neat and clean; though they had neither chairs nor tables, yet, according to their customs, they were very proud to furnish their little place, such as having mattresses with good coverings, and quilts of printed cotton, which are things of some consideration in Syria, besides a handsome set of coffee-cups, and pictures on the walls: they are fond of ornaments in their houses, but every thing for use and comfort. The women in the quarters were the wives of the carpenters and scrivans employed in the temples, so that I used to see all their customs. They used to wash their clothes on Friday or Saturday, and mend and fold them up with the greatest neatness, and clean up all the house for the Sunday, which they passed in the most comfortable and amicable way: they had only to prepare their little dinner: husband and wife, father and mother, and children, always eat together, and sometimes invite a few friends to dine with them on a Sunday, or go and take a walk. The best part of the women I knew were very pretty, and some would even in England have been accounted beautiful. I knew one young married woman: according to my idea of female beauty she was very fair, without that sickly fairness which is so often seen in the East: I have seen no face to please me so much in any place I have been in since; something so extremely expressive in her countenance; large, full, light blue eyes, with an engaging simplicity seldom to be met with in those countries. In general their eyes are black, and, when expressive of modesty, are very pleasing; but then there are some that disgust you by too bold or forward a look, or extreme stupidity. I visited a family belonging to a Christian merchant—I do not mean merchants like ours; but however he was very well off: his house had every domestic comfort, and was provided even with what are considered luxuries, and would, in England, be thought so too. I took a lady, then in Jerusalem, to see this family. In Bethlehem the Turks are absolutely afraid of the Christians. I one day went to see the wife and family of the Drogueman. A poor Mahometan woman came in: I was astonished to see her humility. The Christian woman treated her like a slave. The Christians had massacred a great number of Turks about fifty years ago, and this woman was one belonging to some that had been murdered. By what I saw, the Christian women in those places are much superior to any others, both in regard to their household concerns, and the consideration they are treated with. In Egypt the Christians seldom eat with their wives.

The English agent had engaged a cabin for me on board a Turkish ship, and as it was not to go till the next day, he invited me to go and see a garden of his: we had scarcely arrived there, when some one came running after us, saying the ship was going to sail immediately: through this mistake I had not bought any provisions for the voyage. Fortunately for me there happened to be in Jaffa two Italians who had been on a pilgrimage to Jerusalem, one a worker in tin, and the other had served his time to the wax business in all its branches; a thing much wanted in Egypt. They wished to go to Alexandria straight forward, but not being able to procure an immediate passage, and having heard Mr.

B. was an Italian, they consented to go to Cairo with me; and though it is a short passage of two or three days, yet sometimes it is much longer. Had it not been for these two men, I believe I never should have reached Cairo alive, being continually troubled with bilious fever.

A Portuguese servant of Mr. Bankes, who was left in Jaffa, exerted himself with the other two men in sending my luggage to the water side, and in procuring what little provision they could get at that late hour in the evening. We went down to the water side, with the intent of going on board. On arriving at the port-gate, I was informed the governor was sitting in it, but that he would go in a few minutes. After waiting a good half hour, I asked the consul what I was made to wait for in that manner: he told me there was no other door to go out at, but that one where the governor was sitting, and that no one could go out of it till he left it. If they were all slaves to the Turks, I told them, I was not. As I knew none of these courageous gentlemen durst speak a word to the Turks, I began to complain in bad Italian, and still worse Arabic, of my being kept a prisoner by the Turks in Jaffa. A respectable Turk, formerly belonging to the Barbary coast, and who had been to England, that is Gibraltar, which they denominate so, spoke Italian very well: he said the governor would be gone in a short time, and begged me to have patience. I told him, in broken Arabic, the English were not slaves to the Turks, loud enough for the governor to hear me.

I certainly did not think my words would have any effect. This man went to the governor, and he immediately left the place. I was glad at his going. The English agent, a Levantine, thought proper to say the governor wanted to see me, having heard I was a woman. This is not true, and if it was so, I am indebted to him for telling the governor that I was a woman. It is the custom, when any English arrive there, for him to accompany them to the governor, and, to support his high notions of dignity, he thinks they cannot be too liberal in their presents, and cries up the greatness of the riches of my lord English; but understanding I was not a rich person, though as liberal in making remuneration in return for civilities or things received as others, no doubt had reported I was a person of no consequence, which the governor hearing, he thought, though he dare not show his consequence to Englishmen, he could display it to me: at any rate, if such was his idea, the words I used in the hearing of him and his people must have made him feel very little. We went on board the ship, which was under weigh. What was my distress on finding the cabin, which had been engaged for me for a hundred and thirty piastres, full of melons, and the deck full of Albanian soldiers, which alarmed me, on account of what I had seen in Egypt of them; and though taken ill immediately on getting on board, I insisted on being sent on shore to complain to the consul. The boat was still alongside us: the moment I insisted on going, and requested that my luggage should be put in the boat, they ordered it slily off, and all I could say was useless. The two poor men who were with me, and who knew very little of the customs of the Turks, and nothing of the language, begged me, for the love of the Virgin, not to say any thing to them, for we were in their power. Though extremely sick, I desired them not to show these people they were at all alarmed. I was still on deck: it was quite dark, and we were in great confusion, as is customary in Turkish ships, which have no regulation or compass but the stars, and pride themselves on being wiser than the Europeans. I insisted on having my cabin cleaned out, according to contract. After a great deal of talking, and trying every means they could to prevent the melons being taken out, as it was late, it was at last concluded a part should then be taken out, and the rest the next morning: my luggage was taken down, and I was accommodated as well as could be expected. The wind altered, and after three days of contrary weather we were obliged to put into Cyprus, where we stopped three days. We once more set sail for Damietta, and were much delayed by calms. At last, after thirteen days from the time we left Jaffa, we arrived in that port. I never suffered on the ocean what I suffered in this insignificant voyage. I must now once more mention with gratitude the respectable and decent conduct, added to the assistance these men rendered me, for I was ill the whole time I was on board. It is in these moments we see the soul of mankind, and sorry enough I was I could not show a greater liberality towards them than my limited purse would allow me. I should not have thought any sum too much for the assistance they had given me.

On arriving at Damietta I found, in the short space of six months, the mother of the consul and his sister, with whom I had lived a month in much friendship, both dead; the mother was only forty, and the sister twenty-eight, and left, I believe, a fond husband to deplore her loss, with four fine boys. I cannot help observing and thinking with the Arab, that, indeed, God was with me; for during the time I was in that house, a younger brother of the consul, about nine years old, came home one day in a high fever; the mother told me of it; I presented her with a little tea, which she made for him, and he perspired: the next day he was better, and my going on board the ship, vexed at being detained in Damietta so long, was what saved me; for although the boy got better, yet the disease lingered about him, and a few days after my departure he was seized with a violent malignant fever, which the mother caught from him. Her daughter caught it likewise, and both died. I could not put it in their heads to refrain from eating many things which I told them were bad; the only answer I received was, What can I do? I like it, and God is good. The women, shut up as they are, employ themselves in eating every trash they can get hold of to get fat; therefore it is no wonder they are always ill. Had I staid, I probably should have had the same fate, by catching the fever from them.

After resting five days at the house of a female relation of the consul's, we departed for Cairo, where I expected to have met Mr. B. I remained there two months, during which time Abdalla, the Wahabee chief, was brought in a prisoner by the Turks, to be sent to Constantinople to be beheaded. Having inquired the day he was to enter Cairo, I took a Mameluke who had run away from Dongola, and staid some time with Mr. B. at Ybsambul: he was now in Cairo, and I took the opportunity of having his escort about the town. We set off by break of day, and having rode in and out of that city till we were tired, each Arab giving us a different account of the road the chief was to enter, we at last heard he was arrived, and was gone up to the citadel: on our arriving there we found he was not yet come, but was expected. We went to a coffee-shop that commanded a full view of the gate, and after having waited about an hour, drinking coffee and smoking, we at last found out he was at the house of the Kakia Bay, where all the Turks were going to see him. I now gave up all hopes. We set off, however, once more in search of him, but on arriving at the Kakia Bey's house I stopped on seeing a number of Turks, and felt my courage give way, as they are very different to the Arabs, and was a little shy about entering. At last I asked the Mameluke what answer he would give in case any one should question him about who I was. He said that he would tell them I was an English Turk. I was dressed as a Mameluke, so I mustered all the consequence and courage I could assume, though, indeed, I felt a little unpleasant, fearing the Turks should recognise me to be a woman: let it not be mistaken—they would not molest me, but their curiosity would be excited.

I went through a large yard, and entered a little room where Abdallah the chief was seated, seemingly much fatigued: I understood he had been ill on the road. The Pashaw sent his carriage for him some part of the road, but they took care to put heavy irons on him. I judged him to be about twenty-eight or thirty, of a very expressive and interesting countenance; perhaps his situation made it appear more so to me: he spoke to no one. He had a brother with a vulgar Fellah countenance, talking with every one of the Turks, particularly those belonging to the church: he wanted to make them believe, though his brother had fought against them, he never had. After we had staid some time looking at him, they ordered all out, to make room for others. I passed out with more courage than I entered, and much pleased at having gratified my curiosity so easily.

After waiting two months in Cairo, and understanding it might be some time before Mr. B. could return, I determined on a third voyage to Thebes, taking the Mameluke before mentioned. I went to Boolak, and engaged a canja with two small cabins; one held my luggage, and the other my mattress, for which I paid 125 piastres. I left Cairo on November 27th, and arrived at Ackmim on the 11th December, at night. A heavy rain, accompanied with thunder and lightning, commenced an hour after sunset, and continued the whole of the night: it poured in torrents. My mattress and coverings were wet through, and were so for some days; and though the rain had ceased, yet it came pouring from the mountains through the lands into the Nile on each side for several days after. I arrived at Luxor on the 16th, and was informed Mr. B. was gone to the Isle of Philœ: I crossed the Nile, and took up my residence at Beban el Malook*. The men left to guard the tomb in Mr. B.'s absence informed

---

* I shall here take occasion to mention a little anecdote, which will give an idea how far revenge is carried by these people. Having no one to attend on me but men, I took for that

me of the heavy rain they had experienced on the night I mentioned, and, in spite of all their efforts, they could not prevent the water entering the tomb; it had carried in a great deal of mud, and, on account of the great heat, and the steam arising from the damp, made some of the walls crack, and some pieces had fallen. On hearing this I went into the tomb, and the only thing we could do was to order a number of boys to take the damp earth away, for while any damp remained the walls would still go on cracking. Mr. B. arrived two days before Christmas, and on St. Stephen's day he crossed to Carnak to review the various spots of earth he had to excavate, when an attempt was made to assassinate him. I had then a violent bilious fever, which, added to this fright, flung me into the yellow jaundice. Having sent a man to procure me some medicine from a doctor at Ackmeim, he returned after five days with about half an ounce of cream of tartar, and two teaspoonsful of rhubarb. Fortunately for me, two English gentlemen happened to arrive, on their return from Nubia for Cairo, and gave me some calomel, which was of great service to me, and which I remember with much gratitude.

We then bade adieu to Thebes, and embarked for Cairo. On our going down, the Mameluke informed me there was a large boat with four Turkish ladies, who had just returned from a pilgrimage to Mecca, and were now on their way to Constantinople. They had stopped two nights where we did: they had heard there was an Englishwoman in our boat, and expressed a wish to see me. When we halted for the night, I sent our Mameluke to them to say I should be happy to visit them. The man that was sent to accompany them came with the Mameluke to fetch me. On our going on board, he knocked at the door, and told them in Turkish that I was there. The door was opened enough to permit me to enter: it

---

purpose a young girl, the sister-in-law of the woman at Luxor who was so spiteful on my refusing to head her party against her husband's second wife, and whom I suspected to have on that account given me something to injure my health. I was very partial to this young girl, and some few days after my arrival, talking to her about her sister-in-law, I told her I knew what she had done to me. I saw the girl seemed frightened. The day after, she told me she wanted to go and see her mother, but she did not come back. I expressed my surprise on the occasion, when a Christian told me, that after what I had told her, the girl was afraid to stay with me, for fear I should revenge myself on her for what her sister-in-law had done to me, as they were accustomed to do among themselves.

was a maish, with two large rooms in it. On entering, I found the ladies sitting on fine cushions that were placed round the room. They received me with much politeness. Two female servants sat in front of the middle door to observe what was passing, and to be ready to hand the coffee, sherbet, and oranges; and though they knew not one word of Arabic, and myself not one word of Turkish, yet women are never at a loss to talk. My Mameluke stood on the outside of the door to tell me, in Arabic mixed with a few words of Italian, what the ladies said: by which means we contrived to keep up a conversation for some time. They began to tell me of the holy journey they had taken, and the fatigue they had undergone. They then began to inquire where I had been, as the Mameluke had informed their men that I was a Hadge, and that I had been on a pilgrimage to Jerusalem. They said how happy I was to have been there, as this place is considered by the Turks as a holy city, on account of its being one of the stairs to Mecca, as well as containing the tombs of Suleiman and Daoud. They expressed much admiration and surprise when I told them I had been to see their tombs. They were much surprised how the English should know any thing about David, and Solomon, and Jacob, and Joseph, as they belong to the Turks. I told them they belonged equally to us, and began to mention pretty well various names in the Old Testament, such as Adam and Eve, Cain and Abel, Abraham and Isaac, and Sarah, telling them that was my name, Moses and Aaron, and all I could think of at the moment; telling them Christ descended from David. They were the first to ask me about the Virgin Mary and our Saviour, and seemed much gratified. The Turks have a great respect for the Virgin Mary, and likewise for our Saviour. Those places are holy to them, but not the tomb of our Saviour. They laugh at our kneeling in the tomb, as they say Christ was a spirit, and as such could not have been crucified, and that a man in his form and figure was crucified in his stead. I do not wish to be thought presumptuous enough to attempt to contradict or to know better than any one else, for my knowledge is very limited; but, according to Ali Bey's account of the Turks, our Saviour left his likeness to Judas, who was crucified in his stead. How could that be? for in the 27th chapter of St. Matthew, verse 5th, he went and hung himself. The ladies lifted up their eyes and hands in wonder, and began asking me if I could read; and, as I knew all those belonging to them, how it was I did not know Mahomet. I told them he was a great man.

The only way to gain these people is by giving into their prejudices a little, if we wish to gain any advantage; for from my small experience, there is not an easier people than the Turks to be converted to christianity; and though I may be condemned for my opinion, there is no religion would suit them so well as the protestant church of England, on account of its simplicity; for they cannot bear any kind of figure or images. And though I am much against forcing our religion on any one, yet, as they have began to translate the blessed Scriptures in every language, I would to God our Prayer Book was translated, and joined to the Old and New Testament: it is not forcing it on any one, and those that would like to read it might or not, as they pleased. I mean those translated into the eastern languages.

They asked me if I had ever been at Stambul, or Constantinople. I told them I had not, but that I hoped I should. They began to praise it, telling me it was the finest place in the world, and said they hoped they should see me there.

All this time they had been anxious to know if I had any jewels on my head under my turban: to gain this information, they took off the kerchiefs of their head-dresses to show me theirs. I observed a great delicacy in their manners towards me, fearing to offend. I was not astonished at the sight of the pearls and diamonds, but that they should make a journey to Mecca and return without being robbed: though it is true Mahomet Ali had troops there at this time, the road is sometimes dangerous. I had now seen their jewels, which was a good way of asking me to show mine. It was useless for me to observe I had none, but I knew I could gratify their curiosity equally well. All the women are extremely fond of long hair, and for some reason or other they seldom attain it, and my hair was a little longer than they were accustomed to see. I told them, as I was obliged to travel in the dress of a Turk, I could not carry any thing belonging to women. They seemed to think it was perfectly right, and asked me if our women in England wore pearls, and diamonds, and ear-rings, and bracelets, and many other questions.

I took off my turban, and showed them my hair: they got up and felt it, to be certain it was my own, and had a long conversation among themselves about it.

Among the four ladies were a mother and daughter. The daughter had been married some years, and had no children, which occasioned her journey to the holy shrine of Mecca. They showed me many relics they had brought from thence. They told me their husbands were scrivans to the sultan, and that on their arrival in Cairo they should go to the house of the Khalil Bey till they proceeded to Alexandria; and hoped we should see each other every night if we should stop in the same place, if not in Cairo. We parted very friendly, hoping to meet again; and certainly if I ever should go to Constantinople, I shall remind them of their invitation. I sent them in some pieces of fine soap from Jerusalem, with which they were highly pleased. On arriving at Cairo I was too much occupied in preparing to leave that place for Alexandria, and could not visit them. The Mameluke saw them there, and they sent me a message, to say they were likewise going to Alexandria in a day or two, and hoped to meet me in that place.

On arriving at Rosetta I remained there for some time, therefore I lost the opportunity of meeting those ladies again. On Mr. B.'s making up his mind to go into Lybia, he settled me comfortably in a house in Rosetta, which belonged to an English merchant of Alexandria, who was kind enough to lend it to him: and having laid in those provisions that would have been dangerous for me to buy, as the plague was now beginning to show its horrid face, and engaged a man to call every day, to buy meat, bread, vegetables, &c. he departed for Lybia.

My prison companions were antelopes, sheep, goats, and fowls. I had collected a great number of cameleons, but I never could, in five months' trial, get them to live longer than two. The Arabs in Lower Egypt in catching them jump upon them, or fling stones, or strike them with sticks, which hurts them much. The Nubians lie down gently on the ground, and when they come down from the date-trees, they catch hold of the tail, and fix a string to it, therefore the body does not get injured.

I do not presume to give a description of the cameleon any farther than what observation I could make, having had those animals for several months with me. In the first place, they are very inveterate towards their own kind, and must not be shut up together, for they bite each others' tails and legs off. There are three species of cameleons, whose colours are peculiar to themselves: for instance, the commonest sort are those which are generally green, that is to say, the body all green, and when content, beautifully marked on each side regularly on the green with black and yellow, not in a confused manner, but as if drawn. This kind is in great plenty, and never have any other colour except a light green when they sleep, and when ill, a very pale yellow. Out of near forty I had the first year when in Nubia, I had but one, and that a very small one of the second sort, which had red marks. One cameleon lived with me eight months, and most of that time I had it fixed to the button of my coat: it used to rest on my shoulder or on my head. I have observed, when I have kept it shut up in a room for some time, that on bringing it out in the air it would begin drawing the air in, and on putting it on some marjorum it has had a wonderful effect on it immediately: its colour became most brilliant. I believe it will puzzle a good many to say what cause it proceeds from. If they did not change when shut up in a house, but only on taking them in a garden, it might be supposed the change of the colours was in consequence of the smell of the plants; but when in a house, if it is watched, it will change every ten minutes: some moments a plain green, at others all its beautiful colours will come out, and when in a passion it becomes of a deep black, and will swell itself up like a balloon, and, from being one of the most beautiful animals, it becomes one of the most ugly. It is true they are extremely fond of the fresh air, and on taking them to a window when there is nothing to be seen, it is easy to observe the pleasure they certainly take in it: they begin to gulp down the air, and their colour becomes brighter. I think it proceeds in a great degree from the temper they are in: a little thing will put them in a bad humour: if in crossing a table, for instance, you stop them, and attempt to turn them another road, they will not stir, and are extremely obstinate: on opening the mouth at them it will set them in a passion: they begin to arm themselves by swelling and turning black, and will sometimes hiss a little, but not much. The third I brought from Jerusalem was the most singular of all the cameleons I ever had: its temper, if it can be so called, was extremely sagacious and cunning. This one was not of the order of the green kind, but a disagreeable drab, and it never once varied in its colour in two months. On my arrival in Cairo I used to let it crawl about the room, on the furniture. Sometimes it would get down, if it could, and hide itself away from me, but in a place where it could see me; and sometimes, on my leaving the room and on entering it, would draw itself so thin as to make itself nearly on a level with whatever it might be on, so that I might not see it. It had often deceived me so. One day having missed it for some time, I concluded it was hid about the room; after looking for it in vain, I thought it had got out of the room and made its escape: in the course of the evening, after the candle was lighted, I went to a basket that had got an handle across it: I saw my cameleon, but its colour entirely changed, and different to any I ever had seen before: the whole body, head and tail, a brown with black spots, and beautiful deep orange-coloured spots round the black. I certainly was much gratified: on being disturbed, its colours vanished, unlike the others; but after this I used to observe it the first thing in the morning, when it would have the same colours. Some time after, it made its escape out of my room, and I suppose got into a garden close by. I was much vexed, and would have given twenty dollars to have recovered it again, though it only cost me threepence, knowing I could not get another like it; for afterwards being in Rosetta, I had between fifty and sixty; but all those were green, yellow, and black; and the Arabs in catching them had bruised them so much, that after a month or six weeks they died. It is an animal extremely hard to die. I had prepared two cages with separate divisions, with the intention of bringing them to England; but though I desired the Arabs that used to get them for me to catch them by the tail, they used to hurt them much with their hands; and if once the body is squeezed, it will never live longer than two months. When they used to sleep at night, it was easy to see where they had been bruised; for being of a very light colour when sleeping, the part that had been bruised, either on the body or the head, which was bone, was extremely black, though when green it would not show itself so clear. Their chief food was flies: the fly does not die immediately on being swallowed, for upon taking the cameleon up in my hands it was easy to feel the fly buzzing, chiefly on account of the air they draw in their inside: they swell much, and particularly when they want to fling themselves off a great height, by filling themselves up like a balloon: on falling, they get no hurt, except on the mouth, which they bruise a little, as that comes first to the ground. Sometimes they will not drink for three or four days, and when they begin they are about half an hour drinking. I have held a glass in one hand while the cameleon rested its two fore paws on the edge of it, the two hind ones resting on my other hand. It stood upright while drinking, holding its head up like a fowl. By flinging its tongue out of its mouth the length of its body, and instantaneously catching the fly, it would go back like a spring. They will drink mutton broth: how I came to know this was one day having a plate of broth and rice on the table where it was: it went to the plate and got half into it, and began drinking, and trying to take up some of the rice, by pushing it with its mouth towards the side of the plate, which kept it from moving, and in a very awkward way taking it in its mouth.

When in Italy, a gentleman, a professor of natural history, had two sent him from the coast of Barbary, but they did not live long; he dissected them, and his idea on the change of colour is, that he found they had four skins extremely fine, which occasioned the different colours. He means to publish his opinion soon. It may be so, but of this I am positively certain, whatever it may proceed from, they have their different colours peculiar, distinct, and independent of each other and of themselves. I could make many more remarks, but wanting capacity to explain them, I thus finish my little description of these animals.

Having occasion to change the man who used to buy my provision, another was recommended to me, who was a Jew. I thought if I could procure some Bibles from the British consul at Alexandria, through the means of this man, I might distribute some, by promising him a profit: it is well known those people will not refuse money if they possibly can help it. I wrote to Alexandria for some, and as I was entirely ignorant in what manner the society wished them to be disposed of, I requested Mr. Lee to inform me of it. The answer was, that "as to the money, it was of the least consequence," leaving it to me. I ordered the Jew to go to all the Christians, and inform them what books I had got. The plague was at this time raging abroad: it was no easy task to find a way to dispose of the Bibles without risk of catching the infection, as paper is susceptible. The first Christian who came for one desired to see it: it is a matter of much consideration when a man comes to the determination of spending so large a sum as thirty piastres, three dollars. I sat on the top of the stairs: he ascended some steps, and stood near enough to read while I turned over the leaves: he bought it after much wrangling, and making little of it, in hopes to get it cheaper, as is customary in those parts when buying or selling. I recommended to this young man to let his friends know where there were more to be had; but so much for Christians' love among themselves, instead of doing so, the pride of being the only one to be in possession of so fine a book would have frustrated my plan, if it had not been for the Jew, to whom I had promised, on selling all, to give a bakshis. The next who came was the scrivan, or overseer of the linen fabric, who took five. I was much satisfied at my success; this was six out of eight. The same day this man took his own Bible to the gate of the governor's house, where the governor was then sitting, as is the custom there, and seeing him read this fine book, desired to know what it was about, and asked to see it. He told him to read some of it; and I suppose he read those parts in the Old Testament he knew the Turks were acquainted with. He inquired where he had got it: the man telling him from some English in Rosetta, he sent to Signor Lenzza, our agent there, desiring him to get one for him, sending the thirty piastres for it. The other I had left I sold to another Copt. Had it concerned any other cause, I should not have had patience to have passed over the disagreeable affronts one is subject to in selling things to those people, who naturally think you sell them from interested views. The very last person I sold to affronted me grossly; but on such an occasion I was indifferent to it. They all informed me that some friends of theirs had bought them for two dollars in Alexandria; but, as I saw they were anxious to possess them, in spite of all their chattering, I was obliged to keep to my first demand of thirty piastres. Being English, I made it a rule to show the Arabs with whom I had any dealings that we had but one word; and when they know people to be particular on that point, they have more respect and confidence in any future dealing with them.

Having sold all the books, I sent to Mr. Lee for more, informing him what I had disposed of them for, when he sent me the following answer: "The cost of the Bibles is from forty-five to fifty piastres; but as the principal point is the circulation of them, they can be distributed for thirty, if more cannot be procured: there are some people who can afford to give more than others." Now I will appeal to those who really know the Arabs or Copts, whether such a thing can take place in that country, as to make one pay more than another. Why not have given me this information in the first letter, when I requested it? I own I was at that moment vexed. To tell an Arab Christian that Europeans distribute those books out of humanity and brotherly love, that they may have the word of God, and that we give them for less than they cost, out of christian love, is a point very difficult to make them comprehend; and let any one preach such a doctrine to an Arab richer than another, that, on account of our selling the books to the poor Arabs for less than they cost, they must for that reason pay more, it would be preaching to the wind, and would possibly prevent, in a great measure, the distribution of the Bibles, as these people would think we wished to impose upon them. If indeed we could establish schools upon the same principle as in India, where the morals are attended to, then we might reap the benefit of the translation of the blessed Scriptures. But the state of the native Christians in Egypt is unfortunately very immoral, and I see no chance of their being much better while under the Turks, as bad examples are the worst of evils.

Mr. Lee sent me more Bibles; but as I was confident I could not get more than thirty piastres, as they had never been sold for so much before, my enthusiasm began to give way. I sold only two more, which I had promised: the rest I returned.

The oshour plant, mentioned by Norden, and lastly by Sheik Ibrahim, on our first voyage to Nubia, in August, 1816, was then in full bearing. On examination, it struck me the silky texture in the inside, by being properly cultivated, might be rendered serviceable. The fruit is of different sizes: I have seen some as large as an ostrich egg or more; the outside rind is full of a thick milky juice; the pod that contains the silk is in the centre, and detached from the outside rind by fibrous strings, which are puffed up and hollow over it. By cutting a branch off, the juice runs out in great quantities. It has never been cultivated. By the little experiment I have been able to make, I am certain it will spin well. I have some of the silk and some of the inside pods. I felt much interested in this plant, and particularly so, as the Mameluke I have mentioned before, seeing me very anxious about it, told me, that in Dongola they made all their ropes from the branches of this plant, and were much stronger than those made from the palm or date tree; and, by his description, it was prepared in the same manner we do hemp. This plant is to be met with in Syria, in the Lower and Upper Egypt, and Nubia; and very possibly in Greece. I think it would thrive well in Malta, as it does not seem to require good earth: I have observed it grow near mountains and in sandy soils, where it is supplied with plenty of fresh water. Though I have not been in the Ionian Islands, I have reason to think it would do well there. It produces in its wild state much more than the cotton plant. The juice is of an astringent quality. I think the plant should not be gathered before it is perfectly dry, as it must give a greater strength to the silk. It requires some process after being taken out of the pod, as the least air disturbs it, and it gets into the eyes.

THE END.

LONDON:
PRINTED BY THOMAS DAVISON, WHITEFRIARS.

A) couverture

Appendix au voyage de Belzoni

l'atlas est in f°

N.a la carte du cours du nil est placée dans l'atlas in

Ⓒ

APPENDIX,

CONTAINING

AN EXPLANATION

OF SOME OF THE

PRINCIPAL HIEROGLYPHICS:

EXTRACTED FROM THE ARTICLE EGYPT, IN THE SUPPLEMENT OF THE ENCYCLOPÆDIA BRITANNICA: WITH ADDITIONAL NOTES.

(par le D.r Young)

APPENDIX.

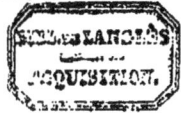

Explanation of some of the principal Hieroglyphics, extracted from the Article Egypt in the Supplement of the Encyclopædia Britannica; with additional Notes.

In the midst of all the zeal and activity displayed by our countrymen who have travelled, or who are resident, in Egypt, it is greatly to be desired that their attention has not yet been turned to an object, which is paramount to all the rest in its importance, for the substantial advancement of our acquaintance with the ancient history and literature of the country; this is, the recovery of the lost fragments or of some of the duplicates of the "trilinguar," or rather trigrammatic STONE of ROSETTA; a monument which has already enabled us to obtain a general idea of the nature and object of any given hieroglyphical inscription, by pursuing the investigation already carried to an unexpected extent by an anonymous author, whose interpretation was communicated to the Antiquarian Society by Sir ROUSE BOUGHTON, together with copies of some fragments of manuscripts which this gentleman had brought from Egypt. *Archæologia,* Vol. XVIII. p. 61. *Museum Criticum,* No. VI. and VII.) Mr. de SACY, and more especially Mr. AKERBLAD, had made some progress in identifying the sense of the several parts of the second inscription of the stone; but they had scarcely at all considered the sacred characters, and it was left

APPENDIX.

An Explanation of some of the principal Hieroglyphics, extracted from the Article Egypt in the Supplement of the Encyclopædia Britannica; with additional Notes.

In the midst of all the zeal and activity displayed by our countrymen who have travelled, or who are resident, in Egypt, it is greatly to be deplored that their attention has not yet been turned to an object, which is paramount to all the rest in its importance, for the substantial advancement of our acquaintance with the ancient history and literature of the country; that is, the recovery of the lost fragments or of some of the duplicates of the "trilinguar," or rather trigrammatic STONE of ROSETTA; a monument which has already enabled us to obtain a general idea of the nature and subject of any given hieroglyphical inscription, by pursuing the investigations already carried to an unexpected extent by an anonymous author, whose interpretation was communicated to the Antiquarian Society by Mr. ROUSE BOUGHTON, together with copies of some fragments of manuscripts which this gentleman had brought from Egypt. *Archæologia*, Vol. XVIII. p. 61. *Museum Criticum*, No. VI. and VII.) Mr. de SACY, and more especially Mr. AKERBLAD, had made some progress in identifying the sense of the several parts of the second inscription of the stone; but they had scarcely at all considered the sacred characters, and it was left for British industry, to convert to permanent profit a monument, which had before been a useless, though a glorious trophy of British valour...

The block or pillar of black basalt, found by the French in digging up some ground at Rosetta, and now placed in the British Museum, exhibits the remains of three distinct inscriptions: and the last, which is in Greek, ends with the information, that the decree, which it contains, was ordered to be engraved in three different characters, the sacred letters, the letters of the country, and the Greek. Unfortunately a considerable part of the first inscription is wanting: the beginning of the second, and the end of the third, are also mutilated; so that we have no precise points of coincidence from which we can set out, in our attempts to decipher the unknown characters. The second inscription, which it will be safest to distinguish by the Greek name *enchorial*, signifying merely the characters "of the country," notwithstanding its deficiencies near the beginning, is still sufficiently perfect to allow us to compare its different parts with each other, and with the Greek, by the same method that we should employ if it were entire. Thus, if we examine the parts corresponding, in their relative situation, to two passages of the Greek inscription in which *Alexander* and *Alexandria* occur, we soon recognise two well marked groups of characters resembling each other, which we may therefore consider as representing these names; a remark which was first made by Mr. de Sacy, in his Letter relating to this inscription. A small group of characters, occurring very often in almost every line, might be either some termination, or some very common particle: it must, therefore, be reserved till it is found in some decisive situation, after some other words have been identified, and it will then easily be shown to mean *and*. The next remarkable collection of characters is repeated twenty-nine or thirty times in the enchorial inscription: and we find nothing that occurs so often in the Greek, except the word *king*, with its compounds, which is found about thirty-seven times. A fourth assemblage of characters is found fourteen times in the enchorial inscription, agreeing sufficiently well in frequency with the name of *Ptolemy*, which occurs eleven times in the Greek, and generally in passages corresponding to those of the enchorial text in their relative situation: and, by a similar comparison, the name of Egypt is identified, although it occurs much more frequently in the enchorial inscription than in the Greek, which often substitutes for it country only, or omits it entirely. Having thus obtained a sufficient number of common points of subdivision, we may next proceed to write the Greek text over the enchorial, in such a manner that the passages ascertained may all coincide as nearly as possible; and it is obvious that the intermediate parts of each inscription will then stand very near to the corresponding passages of the other.

In this process, it will be necessary to observe that the lines of the enchorial inscription are written from right to left, as, Herodotus tells us, was the custom of the Egyptians; the division of several words and phrases plainly indicating the direction in which they are to be read. It is well known that the distinct hieroglyphical inscriptions, engraved on different monuments, differ in the direction of the corresponding characters: they always face the right or the left of the spectator accordingly as the principal personages of the tablets, to which they belong, are looking in the one or the other direction; where, however, there are no tablets, they almost always look towards the right; and it is easily demonstrable that they must always have been read beginning from the front, and proceeding to the rear of each rank. But the Egyptians seem never to have written alternately backwards and forwards, as the most ancient Greeks occasionally did. In both cases, however, the whole of the characters thus employed were completely reversed in the two different modes of using them, as if they were seen in a glass, or printed off like the impression of a seal.

By pursuing the comparison of the inscriptions, thus arranged, we ultimately discover the signification of the greater part of the individual enchorial words; and the result of the investigation leads us to observe some slight differences in the form and order of some parts of the different inscriptions, which are indicated in the "conjectural translation," published in the *Archæologia* and in the *Museum Criticum*...

It might naturally have been expected that the final characters of the enchorial inscription, of which the sense is thus determined with tolerable certainty, although the corresponding part of the Greek is wanting, would have immediately led us to a knowledge of the concluding phrase of the distinct hieroglyphical characters, which remains unimpaired. But the agreement between the two conclusions is by no means precise; and the difficulty can only be removed by supposing the king to be expressly named in the one, while he is only designated by his titles in the other.

3 R

With this slight variation, and with the knowledge of the singular accident, that the name of Ptolemy occurs three times in a passage of the enchorial inscription, where the Greek has it but twice, we proceed to identify this name among the sacred characters, in a form sufficiently conspicuous, to have been recognised upon the most superficial examination of the inscriptions, if this total disagreement of the frequency of occurrence had not imposed the condition of a long and laborious investigation, as an indispensable requisite for the solution of so much of the enigma: this step, however, being made good, we obtain from it a tolerably correct scale for the comparative extent of the sacred characters, of which it now appears that almost half of the lines are entirely wanting, those which remain being also much mutilated. Such a scale may also be obtained in a different manner, by marking, on a straight ruler, the places in which the most characteristic words, such as *god, king, priest,* and *shrine* occur, in the latter parts of the other inscriptions, at distances proportional to the actual distances from the end; and then trying to find corresponding characters among the hieroglyphics of the first inscription, by varying the obliquity of the ruler, so as to correspond to all possible lengths which that inscription can be supposed to have occupied, allowing always a certain latitude for the variations of the comparative lengths of the different phrases and expressions. By these steps it is not very difficult to assure ourselves, that a *shrine* and a *priest* are denoted by representations which must have been intended for pictures of the objects denoted by them; and this appears to be the precise point of the investigation at which it becomes completely demonstrative, and promises a substantial foundation for further inferences. The other terms, *god* and *king,* are still more easily ascertained, from their situation near the name of Ptolemy...

A. DEITIES.

1, 2. The word GOD is always represented in the inscription of Rosetta, and often in many others, by a character resembling a particular kind of hatchet, which is delineated repeatedly at Medinet Abou, as a weapon in the hands of warriors, and is even found among the modern weapons engraved by Denon. This character is frequently exchanged, in parallel passages of different manuscripts, or of the same, for a figure sitting or standing without distinct arms or feet, either with a human head or a hawk's head; or sometimes, by a deviation from the correct nature of an abstract or general term, with the heads of different animals, according to the character of the deity to whom it is applied. But in the inscription of Rosetta, this symbol appears to be exclusively appropriated to the gods in their JUDICIAL capacity; and it occurs several times in the term meaning *lawful*, n. 151. This interpretation is also fully justified by the testimony of Plutarch, that "the figures of *judges* were represented without hands."

3. A GODDESS is denoted by the hatchet or sitting figure, with the addition of the female characteristic, generally as a termination; but sometimes the simple character is applied to gods and goddesses indifferently. The semicircle and oblique oval, distinguishing the feminine gender, are observable in almost all well marked names of females found in different tablets, and the crooked line, which corresponds to them, in the enchorial character of the stone of Rosetta, may be distinguished at the end of each of the five names of females that occur in the inscription. Occasionally the characteristic is prefixed, and this position agrees better with the Coptic TI, which distinguishes a female: nor must we omit to observe, that a semicircle seems to answer to the T in some other cases, and is always expressed in the running hand by the character which Mr. Akerblad calls T or D, and which is also exactly the Syriac T. The asp or basilisc standing erect is a symbol of divinity, which occurs on the green sarcophagus, called the tomb of Alexander, and elsewhere, instead of the more ordinary character. In a few instances, the semicircle is found without the oblique oval.

4. The plural, GODS, is formed by repeating the character three times, or by placing three dashes after, or sometimes before it. In the enchorial inscription, the dashes are united into a crooked line, and are placed in this instance both before and after the principal character; but, in general, the second line is straighter than the first. The dual is expressed by a double character only.

5. A winged globe, sometimes flattened, as if intended for an egg, but often coloured red, is very commonly represented as hovering over a hero, and generally occupies the lintel of some of the doors of a temple. A globe nearly similar is also sometimes connected with the head and

tail of a serpent, bearing the symbol of *life*, which is the common characteristic of a deity. There can, therefore, be no objection to considering these representations as belonging to the *Agathodæmon*, or *Chnuphis* of the Greek authors; and the same symbol is sometimes found in the text of an inscription, in the neighbourhood of the pictural representation; so that its sense may be considered as tolerably well ascertained. [The proper hieroglyphic character of this deity seems, however, to be a hand with a bent bar]...

6. The symbol, often called the *Hieralpha*, or sacred A, corresponds, in the inscription of Rosetta, to PHTHAH, or Vulcan, one of the principal deities of the Egyptians; a multitude of other sculptures sufficiently prove, that the object intended to be delineated was a plough or hoe; and we are informed by Eusebius, from Plato, that the Egyptian Vulcan was considered as the inventor of instruments of war and of husbandry. In many other inscriptions, the pedestal or pulley is used indifferently for the plough. Horapollo tells us, that Vulcan was denoted by a beetle; and the Monticœlian obelisc of Kircher has the plough on three sides, and the beetle on the fourth: Horapollo, however, is seldom perfectly correct; and the names of different divinities are frequently exchanged on the banners of the same obelisc; nor is there any clear instance of such an exchange of the plough for the beetle as occurs perpetually in the case of the pedestal. The beetle is frequently used for the name of a deity, whose head either bears a beetle, or is itself in the form of a beetle; and in other instances the beetle has clearly a reference to generation or reproduction, which is a sense attributed to this symbol by all antiquity; so that it may possibly sometimes have been used as a synonym for Phthah, as the father of the gods. The plough is very rarely found as the name of a personage actually represented, and it is difficult to say under what form the Egyptian Vulcan was chiefly worshipped; but on the tablet of a Horus of bad workmanship, belonging to the Borgian Museum, he is exhibited with a hawk's head, holding a spear; while in the great ritual of the *Déscription de l' Egypte*, Ant. II. Pl. 72. Col. 104, he seems to be represented by a figure with a human head; an exchange, however, which is very common in some other cases, with respect to these two personifications, though it does not extend to the substitution of the heads of different animals for each other.

7. Ammon, the Egyptian Jupiter, is sufficiently identified by a combination of evidence of various kinds, although no single link of the chain extends very far. A figure with a ram's head is denoted, both on the green sarcophagus, and on the temple at Elephantine, by a water jar, sometimes, but not always, accompanied by a bird: now a water jar of this form is constantly converted, in the running hand of the manuscripts, into a character like a z; and this character, in the enchorial text of Rosetta, is made to express the name of Jupiter; a fact which confirms the testimony of the Greek authors, who considered the Egyptian Jupiter as having been represented with a ram's head. A similar figure is found at Edfou, or Apollinopolis Magna, and at Esne, or Latopolis: the temple at Edfou seems to have been dedicated by Amenophis or Memnon; and he appears to be called *lover of Ammon*, that is, Miamun, which is not unlike the name Memnon.

8. The common astronomical diagram for the sun, ☉, seems to have been adopted by the Latin astrologers from their masters in Egypt; since it is not very probable that both should have employed a point in the centre of the circle, without some communication with each other; the circle alone having been mentioned by some of the Greek authors, who say, that it was the symbol of the sun. The deity Re or Phre is indicated by this character followed by an upright bar; and the circle is often enveloped in the coil of the body of a serpent; an oval and an arm also often follow the circle. The enchorial name of the sun is extremely like that which corresponds in the manuscripts to this hieroglyphic: and a similar circle, with rays diverging from it, though seldom exactly in straight lines (N. 160), is used in the sense of "enlightening," or "rendering illustrious;" and it has also been observed by some of the French, who have been in Egypt, to stand in several inscriptions with a manifest reference to light...

9. The name of Rhea may, without impropriety, be assigned to a female personage very commonly accompanying the sun, and distinguished by many of his attributes; although the evidence would have been somewhat more conclusive, if the name had been found attached to the figure of the mother in the tablet of the birth of Isis. On the coffins of the mummies, this personage is generally represented with outstretched wings; in other tablets without wings: but she carries in both cases a

circle on her head, emblematic of the sun. If we considered the analogy of the hieroglyphic name only, we should be disposed to interpret it as meaning the wife or sister of Ammon.

10. Ioh, the Moon, is not a deity of very frequent occurrence; but the character is easily interpreted, both from its form, and from its being found, in a different position, as a part of the word month. (No. 179.) At Dendera, this character is accompanied by the epithet God, and without any female termination, as well as in several passages of an epistolographic manuscript sent home by Mr. Bankes; a circumstance which is favourable to the opinion that Ioh was considered by the Egyptians as masculine in mythology as well as in grammar. It is well known that Men or Lunus was sometimes made masculine by the Greeks and Romans, even though the name of the planet was feminine; the fact, however, is not absolutely decisive of this question, since the character is not accompanied in the manuscripts by the delineation of any personification of the deity.

11. The historical description of the god Thoth, or Hermes, as the scribe, or secretary of Osiris, and the inventor of writing, sufficiently identifies him with the person who is perpetually represented standing before Osiris, and writing with a quill or a style on a square or oblong tablet. He has always the head of an ibis, and this bird, standing on a perch, constitutes his hieroglyphical name, as the ibis is known to have been the emblem of Thoth; the hieroglyphic for letters, N. 103, is also frequently found among his titles; and all these circumstances abundantly confirm the opinion of his true character, which Zoega and others have already advanced from conjecture only. The enchorial name is much disfigured, but the manuscripts exhibit a character which may serve to supply the connecting link, and another abridgment of the name which deviates still more widely from the original, being simply the common substitute for a feather, which here seems to stand for the whole bird, or perhaps merely for a feather which is often found projecting from the end of the perch. Next to Osiris, we find that Thoth is of more frequent occurrence than any other deity in the great ritual; and it is probable that the mummies of the ibis, which are so commonly found, were preserved in honour of him. The semicircle with two oblique dashes, under the perch, seems to correspond to the epithet "great and great" of the Rosetta inscription; this character being generally significative of a

THE PRINCIPAL HIEROGLYPHICS.

dual. The scale, with eight dashes, and two other characters, is also very frequently employed as an epithet, and sometimes as a synonym of Thoth: it seems to mean "dispenser of the eight treasures or laws, of the country;" for Diodorus informs us that the principal laws of Egypt were contained in eight books.

12. The name of OSIRIS is found, with the epithet "divine," in a great majority of all the mythological inscriptions that have yet been discovered; so that this circumstance alone is sufficient to show that it must have been that of the principal deity of Egypt. The enchorial character of the inscription of Rosetta is readily identified, and it agrees perfectly well with that of the manuscripts, answering to the eye and the throne; so that the manuscripts here completely supply the want of that part of the stone which contained the name in the sacred character. This name is also universally annexed to the great figure which is found at the end of almost all the manuscripts, and on the coffins of mummies, holding a hook and whip or fan, and of which the small detached images are also extremely common. In the sculptured inscriptions, the eye generally precedes the throne; in the running hand of the manuscripts, and on the coffins of some mummies apparently of later date, the eye sometimes follows. Plutarch had perhaps been rightly informed respecting this character, but by a mistake, which was easily committed from a want of perfect recollection, he has called it "an eye and a sceptre;" and this combination has not been recognised as the name of a deity, though a symbol something like it occurs in some of the tablets. The pictured delineation of Osiris has indifferently a human head or that of a hawk; but never that of any other animal. The tear, N. 100, seems also sometimes to have been used as an emblem of Osiris, as well as of Apis and Mneuis, who were considered as representations of him. The name is found perpetually on monuments of all kinds as an epithet of a departed person; and this is one great reason of the frequency of its occurrence.

13. ARUERIS, the Apollo of the Egyptian mythology, is sufficiently identified by the comparison of various inscriptions with the fragment of Hermapion, preserved by Ammianus Marcellinus, as the translation of the inscription on a particular obelisc, with which, however, it does not exactly

beginning of almost all the obeliscs in existence, supposing only the hawk to be part of the name of Arueris; which is, besides, an inference extremely probable, from the tablets of several of the obeliscs, representing a deity characterized by a hawk with two bars, and styled the son of another personage who seems to be the sun, as Apollo is called by Hermapion, and Arueris by Plutarch.

14. ISIS, the sister and wife of Osiris, is very naturally denoted by the throne with the female termination: and, in more than one instance, the female figures, which have been long recognised as representations of Isis by other attributes, are distinguished by bearing the throne on the head, which is a common mode of characterizing the different personages of the tablets. The manuscripts, again, enable us to discover the connecting link between the sacred and enchorial characters, and to supply the defects of the stone of Rosetta; though the resemblance is somewhat too imperfect to have satisfied us without their assistance. The goddess, thus distinguished, is very generally represented as standing at the head or feet of a corpse, with another female figure opposite to her; and we find the same personages at the opposite ends of several of the sarcophagi; so that the analogy of Isis to Proserpine, and her character as the guardian of the remains of the dead, are sufficiently consistent with these representations. On a scarabæus, brought from Egypt by Mr. Legh, and in a hieroglyphic inscription at Philae, she appears to be called the offspring of Phthah. She often bears in her hand a sceptre forked at the foot, with a lotus for its head, while Osiris has more commonly a similar sceptre with the head of an animal; but these attributes are sometimes assigned to other deities. In one of the boats on the green sarcophagus, and on Letheuillier's mummy, both in the British Museum, she is personified as a basilisc. Mr. Hamilton has published some Greek inscriptions from Philae, and from the small temple at Dendera, which show that Isis was the principal deity of these temples; and the hieroglyphics, as far as they have been copied, are precisely of the same import.

15. The constant companion of Isis can be no other than NEPHTHE; her name somewhat resembles that of Isis, with a scale or basin annexed to it, but the square surrounding the throne is completed, and the scale is sometimes detached from it, with a circle interposed; and, in this form, the name comprehends one of the characters denoting a temple. (No. 87.)

It seems also to be a head of Nephthe that is found at Dendera and elsewhere, supporting a little temple or shrine, in the place of the capital of a column; nor is it improbable that the great temple at Dendera was dedicated to Nephthe; for the Greek inscription has Aphrodite, which is mentioned by Plutarch as a synonym of Nephthe. It is true that the birth of Isis is represented on one of the ceilings; but it does not, therefore, follow that Isis was the principal goddess of the temple. A head bearing a shrine is not an uncommon ornament of a sistrum; and this agrees perfectly with the remark of Plutarch, that the head of Nephthe, as well as that of Isis, was sometimes represented on these instruments.

16. The emblem of a bird in a cage, which is often found in the manuscripts, accompanied by the figure of a child, seems to indicate the character of a *nurse*, and may without inconvenience be interpreted as relating to the goddess *Buto*, the nurse of Horus and Bubastis. On the sarcophagus called the Lover's Fountain, in the British Museum, she is delineated with a hawk's head; in the western temple at Philae she has a human head with a horned head dress, and she sits near Isis and Horus; a circumstance which strongly confirms the propriety of the denomination.

17. The enchorial name of HORUS seems to be derived from the figure of a hawk followed by the character denoting Isis; an arrangement which agrees very well with the supposition that his usual denomination was HORSIESI. The figure of the infant (N. 133), the chain, and the knot, clearly form a part of the name on a Horus engraved by Montfaucon *Ant. Expl.* II. p. 602), and on an obelisc from Bosc in the Supplement of the same work. In some cases a feather, following the infant, seems to supply the place of the bird, as in Caylus, Recueil, IV. Pl. 13.

18. PAAMYLES, mentioned by several authors as the Priapus of Egypt, is sufficiently distinguishable by his usual attributes. He is often figured with one hand only, which is elevated towards the angle of a kind of whip or fan, suspended above him...

B. KINGS.

33, 34. We are informed by Pliny, that the *Alexandrian* obelisc was erected by Mesphres or Mestires, the reading of the different manuscripts being different; and since no king of the name Mestires is mentioned by other authors, we may consider this *Mesphres* as the Mephres or Mesphris who succeeded his mother Amersis about 1700 B. C., or perhaps a century or two later. The hieroglyphical name of his father contains that of the god Thoth, and may therefore possibly have been intended for the *Thuthmosis* of the chronologers, who is said to have been the grandfather of Mesphres. The obelisc at Alexandria, now called Cleopatra's Needle, like almost all others which contain three lines on each side, exhibits different names in the middle and the outer lines: from this circumstance, as well as from the great depth of the sculptures, which is generally observable in the middle line, there is reason to suppose that this line stood at first alone, and that the two on each side were added by a later monarch. The *Lateran* obelisc, however, is remarkable for exhibiting the name of Mesphres on all the lines of the different sides. The *Constantinopolitan* obelisc has only one line on each side, with the name of Mesphres the son of Thuthmosis.

35. The *Isean* obelisc of Kircher has a " son of Mesphres, favoured by Phthah;" we must therefore distinguish the king by the name *Misphragmuthosis*, who is recorded as the son and successor of Mesphres.

37—39. A multitude of ancient Greek inscriptions identify the statue of Memnon, celebrated by all antiquity for its musical powers, which, Strabo says, he witnessed in person, though he could not very positively decide that the sound proceeded from the statue, rather than from some of the bystanders. In one of the inscriptions we find the word *Phamenoth*, not as a date, but as a synonym of Memnon, which must be considered as identical with the Phamenoph given by Pausanias as his Egyptian name, and with the Ammenoph or Amenophis of Manetho or others, which differs from it only as wanting the article. There is, however, some doubt to which Amenophis this statue properly belongs. Manetho makes Memnon the eighth king of the eighteenth dynasty, who may be called Amenophis the Second; but Marsham brings him down to the Ammenephthes of Manetho, or Amenophis the Fourth, and principally because he thinks that only a successor of Sesostris could have been well known in Asia; and he even supposes him to have been later than Homer, who, he says, never mentions him, though Hesiod calls him the son of Tithonus and Aurora. But, in fact, the name of Memnon does occur in the Odyssey, where Ulysses alludes to his beauty in a conversation with the shade of Achilles;

and Hesiod could scarcely have mentioned a king as descended from a deity, that was not considerably earlier than his own time; so that the tradition of Manetho seems to be preferable to the mere conjecture of Marsham. At the same time, we cannot well call him Memnon the son of Thuthmosis, the name of the father not agreeing with that of this king; and there is another circumstance which seems to lead us to the third Amenophis, intermediate between those two extremes, who was the son of Ramesses Miamun, or Ramesses the lover of Ammon; which is, that Amenophis himself appears to have built a temple to Ammon in the isle of Elephantine, and is called Miamun in several hieroglyphical inscriptions still existing there; so that there is little doubt that the name Memnon must have been derived from Miamun. Besides the different statues of the Memnonium, we find monuments of the same personage in almost every part of Egypt, though they are much more frequent at Thebes and in its neighbourhood. The name is marked on all the lion headed goddesses of black granite which are now in the British Museum, and on some others which are in possession of Mr. Bankes. The first of this series having been purchased, as Bruce informs us, for a large price, by Donati, for the King of Sardinia, the inhabitants were induced to take some pains in digging the others out of the sand. The building, called by the French the tomb of Osymandyas, bears also the name of Memnon, and it is remarked by Strabo, that Memnon and Ismendes may probably have been the same person. The name is also found in the grottos at Byban El Molouk, on some statues representing Osiris, and in some inscriptions at Ombos, as well as on a seal of Denon, Pl. 98. Mr. Bullock has presented to the British Museum a scarabæus of very hard stone, on which we find the name of Memnon, together with that of his father and mother, whom we may call, in order to preserve the mythological analogy, *Tithous and Eoa*, although without asserting that this Tithous was the builder of the labyrinth, which some authors have attributed to a king named Tithoes, and others to Ismendes. The mother's name occurs also alone, as "the goddess mother," on the back of a beetle in Gordon's Mummies, Plate 22; a circumstance which removes the doubt, that might otherwise arise, from the want of the female termination in the name; the father's is found on a square seal, in the possession of Mr. Legh. There is another copy of the inscription of Mr. Bullock's scarabæus, on a scarabæus belonging to Mr. Palin, which had long been used by a Greek priest at Athens, for stamping the paschal bread. (*Dubois*, Pierres Gravées, Par. 1817, Pl. V. N. 5.) The beautiful head, lately brought from the Memnonium to the British Museum, has only a part of the father's name remaining, which does not appear to be that of the father of Memnon, though the first three characters are the same; but the fourth is the pedestal representing Phthah; and a similar name is found on some other colossal statues and obeliscs remaining in Egypt, as well as on a smaller figure of red granite, brought by Mr. Hamilton from Elephantine.

40, 41. The obelisc at *Heliopolis* has every mark of considerable antiquity, and the shortness and simplicity of its inscription is appropriate to a remote period. Pliny says, that Mitres or Mestires first erected obeliscs at Heliopolis; he also mentions Sothis, and apparently Ramesses, as having left similar monuments of their magnificence in the same place. The principal name on the obelisc now remaining at Matareah may also be observed in several other inscriptions, but with the substitution of two other names for that of the father; so that the name of the son must probably have belonged to many different individuals; a circumstance which, as well as the sounds belonging to the different characters, agrees very well with Ramesses, for we have RE, "the sun," MES, "a birth," and SHESH, "a pair;" so that we may venture to call it *Remesses;* and we may take *Heron* for the father of the first Remesses, from Hermapion, though it is possible that he may be the Armais of Manetho; but we have scarcely sufficient evidence to appropriate to him that name. Another Remesses seems to have been a son of Sesostris; a third Ramesses follows Ammenephthes in Manetho, and agrees with the Rhampsinitus of Herodotus, and the Remphis of Diodorus, who is mentioned as the successor of Proteus; and this may, perhaps, have been the Remesses of the frizes of Montagu and Ficoroni (Hierogl. 7 Ou. 9 If), who seems, from the resemblance of the different parts of the work, to have been nearly contemporary with Sesostris. (Hierogl. 7 H. I.) There is also another Remesses on the Lions at the fountain of Aqua Felice, near the baths of Diocletian at Rome, the name of whose father is a little like the name supposed to belong to Arsinoe, N. 60.

42, 43. The obelisc, erected by Augustus in the *Campus Martius*, is said, by Pliny, to have been the work of Sesostris; and there are sufficient documents of its identity with that which had long remained buried near the Monte Citorio, and of which figures have been given by Zoega and others. The inscription was supposed, in the time of Pliny, to contain a compendium of the physical and philosophical learning of the Egyptians; but, in order to make this opinion credible, it would be necessary to admit that the princes of earlier days entertained very different ideas from those which have since been prevalent, respecting the comparative importance of the abstract sciences, and of national prosperity, and martial glory. If Sesostris was the son of Amenophis, he cannot have been the reigning king mentioned in this obelisc: but it may safely be attributed to *Pheron* the son of *Sesostris*, who, according to Herodotus, erected two obeliscs; and the occurrence of the name of Sesostris, as the father, may be considered as sufficiently conformable to the testimony of Pliny. The same names are found, with a slight variation, on a small statue of basalt, very highly finished, now standing in the British Museum; and Denon has copied them from an inscription in the Memnonium. (Pl. 118.)

44. *Nuncoreus*, according to Diodorus, was another son of Sesostris; his name occurs also in Pliny, and we may consider him as the son of Sesostris mentioned in Mr. Montagu's frizes. The name is also found at Philae, and, with a slight variation, on an altar of balsalt, figured by Caylus (Rec. I. Pl. 19), now in the king's library at Paris. The remains of the same name may also be observed on a block, apparently of white sandstone, in the British Museum, which is figured by Norden, in its old situation, as a part of the foundations of Pompey's Pillar at Alexandria, and it occurs on a fragment of a statue brought by Mr. Hamilton from Thebes.

45. The name of *Proteus*, or Certus, otherwise Ammenephthes, is only known as the predecessor of one of the kings named Ramesses, and we may safely employ it for the father of the Remesses of the frizes of Montague and Ficoroni, the whole of which are remarkable for the excellence of their workmanship.

46, 47. Until we obtain evidence of a more positive nature, we may give to the two kings mentioned on the sarcophagus of green breccia, the names of *Amænupthes* and *Anysis*, supposing them to have lived about the time of Amenephthes, or Amenophis the Fifth, and his sucessor Osochon. The father's name might, without difficulty, be read " Mænuphthah," supposing some titles to follow it. There are also two obeliscs of the same king, brought from Cairo, which stand near the sarcophagus in the British Museum, and the style of the workmanship somewhat resembles that of the times of Sesostris, and his immediate successors. It has been observed, that neither of the names can well be Alexander's, since that of the father is repeated much more frequently than that of the son, which could not have happened if it had been meant for Philip; and Alexander had no son who could have been mentioned in his sarcophagus. Nor is it at all probable, that Alexander should have erected any obeliscs at Memphis or in its neighbourhood. The god Ammon is no where mentioned among the titles of the king, and holds only an inferior rank among the innumerable deities represented in the tablets. We find both the names, without any addition, on a dovetail of copper, engraved in Lord Valentia's *Travels*, which was found at Behbeit, the Atarbechis or Aphroditopolis of the ancients, situated on the branch of the Nile that runs to Damietta.

48—50. We learn from Pliny, that the *Flaminian* obelisc, now standing near the Porta del Popolo at Rome, which was the smaller of the two formerly in the Circus Maximus, placed there by Augustus, and used as the gnomon of a dial, was the work of Senneserteus or Semnesyrtaeus, who reigned in Egypt at the time that Pythagoras visited it. This king seems to have been the same with Psammuthis or PSAMMIS; and the authority of the evidence is so much the stronger, as the period in question is not extremely remote. The father of Psammis, according to Herodotus, was Necos or NECHAO. The two names occur on all the middle lines of the obelisc; and that of the father on the pillar of a colossal Isis in the Supplement of Montfaucon: the *Sallustian* obelisc, which seems to have been partly copied from the Flaminian, has them both.

51, 52. Among the most common of all the names of the kings of Egypt, on a great variety of monuments, are those which were mistaken by Kircher for a sort of amulets or charms, which he denominated the Mophthomendesian tablets. They occur alone on three small obeliscs only, the *Medicean*, the *Mahutean*, and the *Monticælian*, of Kircher; but they are found in the external lines of the Alexandrian, the two at Luxor, the Flaminian, and the Sallustian, while none are ever found exterior to them. They must, therefore, necessarily be attributed to one of the latest kings of Egypt; and there is none so likely to have made such a display as AMASIS, a man of considerable magnificence, and at the same time of a cautious and artful character: indeed, we have no alternative left but to choose between him and some of the kings who revolted against the Persians, and who do not appear so likely to have had leisure or finances for public works of splendour. His father's name, like that of Nechao, contains the character denoting Vulcan, and it may be called *Maenuphthes*; but he was not the son of a king. Both the names are found in one of the middle lines of the Flaminian obelisc; and on that side the king is represented in the tablet as doing homage to his predecessor, who occupies the place of honour on the other sides.

56. There can be no doubt whatever respecting the signification of the name of PTOLEMY, as it occurs on the stone of Rosetta; but it is not quite so easy to determine its identity in some other cases, where it may possibly have been modified by contraction, mutilation, or combination. In this and a few other proper names, it is extremely interesting to trace some of the steps by which alphabetical writing seems to have arisen out of hieroglyphical; a process which may indeed be in some measure illustrated by the manner in which the modern Chinese express a foreign combination of sounds, the characters being rendered simply "phonetic" by an appropriate mark, instead of retaining their natural signification; and this mark, in some modern printed books, approaching very near to the ring surrounding the hieroglyphic names. The enchorial name of Ptolemy appears at first sight to be extremely different from the hieroglyphical; and it would have been impossible to deduce the one from the other, without a knowledge of the epistolographic forms of the separate characters, as ascertained by a comparison of the manuscripts. The beginning and end are obviously parts of the ring, which, in the sacred character, surrounds every proper name, except those of the deities. The square block and the semicircle answer invariably in all the manuscripts to characters resembling the P and T of Akerblad, which are found at the beginning of the enchorial name. The next character, which seems to be a kind of knot, is not essentially necessary, being often omitted in the sacred characters, and always in the enchorial. The lion corresponds to the LO of Akerblad; a lion being always expressed by a similar character in the manuscripts; an oblique line crossed standing for the body, and an

erect line for the tail; this was probably read not LO but OLE; although, in more modern Coptic, OILI is translated a ram; we have also EIUL, a stag; and the figure of the stag becomes, in the running hand, nearly like this of the lion. The next character is known to have some reference to "place," in Coptic MA; and it seems to have been read either MA, or simply M; and this character is always expressed in the running hand by the M of Akerblad's alphabet. The two feathers, whatever their natural meaning may have been, answer to the three parallel lines of the enchorial text, and they seem in more than in one instance to have been read I or E; the bent line probably signified great, and was read OSH or OS; for the Coptic SHEI seems to have been nearly equivalent to the Greek SIGMA. Putting all these elements together we have precisely PTOLEMAIOS, the Greek name; or perhaps PTOLEMEOS, as it would more naturally be called in Coptic. The slight variations of the word in different parts of the enchorial text may be considered as expressing something like aspirations or accentuations.

57. The appellation SOTERES, as a dual, is well marked in the inscription of Rosetta, and the character, thus determined, explains a long name in the temple at Edfou, which must mean " the two saviour gods," with various titles of honour, such as " the agents of Phthah, the emblems of triumph, the approved of Phre, the favoured of the Nile, the venerable consorts in empire."

58. The wife of Ptolemy Soter, and mother of Philadelphus, was BERENICE, whose name is found on a ceiling at Karnak, in the phrase, " Ptolemy and.. Berenice, the saviour gods." In this name we appear to have another specimen of syllabic and alphabetical writing combined, in a manner not extremely unlike the ludicrous mixtures of words and things with which children are sometimes amused; for however Warburton's indignation might be excited by such a comparison, it is perfectly true that, occasionally, " the sublime differs from the ridiculous by a single step only." The first character of the hieroglyphical name is precisely of the same form with a basket represented at Byban El Molouk, and called, in the description, "panier à anses:" and a basket, in Coptic, is BIR. The oval, which resembles an eye without the pupil, means elsewhere " to," which in Coptic is E; the waved line is " of," and must be rendered N; the feathers I; the little footstool seems to be superfluous;

the goose is KE, or KEN; Kircher gives us KEENSOÜ for a goose; but the ESOÜ means gregarious, probably in contradistinction to the Egyptian sheldrake; and the simple etymon approaches to the name of a goose in many other languages. We have, therefore, literally BIRENICE; or, if the N must be inserted, the accusative BIRENICEN, which may easily have been confounded by the Egyptians with the nominative. The final characters are merely the feminine termination. The enchorial text affords us a remarkable instance of the diversity which was allowed in the mode of representing the same name. The first character has not the least resemblance to the basket; but the first and second together are very commonly used in the manuscripts, as a coarse representation of a boat, which was called BARI, or possibly BERE, for it is doubtful whether Kircher had any other authority than that of Diodorus for BARI; and the word BEREZOUTS is used for another vehicle. The enchorial N may possibly have been derived from a horizontal line, turned up at one end; we have then the three dashes for the I, and the two angles seem to have answered to the KE, for a bird is not uncommonly scribbled in some such manner; so that we have either BARINICE or BERENICE, by a combination somewhat different from the former.

59—65. The temple at Ombos was dedicated, as we find from the Greek inscription copied by Mr. Hamilton, " in the name of the divine Ptolemy Philometor and Cleopatra, and their children, to Arueris Apollo, and the other gods of the temple, by the infantry and cavalry of the nome." We may, therefore, expect to find in it the names of these sovereigns, together with those of some or all of the earlier Ptolemies, and, accordingly, we are able to determine, without difficulty, some epithets which seem to be characteristic of this and the two preceding reigns; but, hitherto, nothing has been observed that can be considered as so clearly denoting either Philadelphus and his queen Arsinoe, or Euergetes and his Berenice, although some assistance might have been derived, in identifying them, from the enchorial text of Rosetta. We have, however, in the same temple, a name, evidently compound, in which a basilisc is followed by two feathers and a bent line; and to judge from a comparison of the enchorial text with the manuscripts, a basilisc ought to be the emblem of EUERGETES; the part of the name preceding it is, however, not Berenice, and must, therefore, in all probability, be ARSINOE, the daughter of

Euergetes. But it seems impossible to attempt to compare the characters employed with the sounds; since they sometimes occur in an inverted order, which the sounds could not do. Indeed the name seems to be very often repeated in situations where its most essential parts seem to be a quadrant of a circle, two feathers, and a bent or broken line; in other places, as at Dendera, the bird, the hand, and the oval, are added; and it is not impossible that the quadrant may have been meant as a representation of a lentil, which in Coptic is ARSHIN, and which alone may have been sufficient to identify the name. It occurs in the celebrated zodiac at Dendera, and very frequently at Philae, and it may possibly, hereafter, lead us very readily to discover the hieroglyphical name of *Philadelphus.* That of PHILOPATOR is satisfactorily ascertained by the assistance of the character employed for "father" in the Rosetta stone, though that character is much mutilated, and could not have been positively determined without this coincidence. The name is found in the *great* temple at Edfou still more distinctly than at Ombos, and it occurs several times at Karnak. EPIPHANES is never distinguished in any other inscription by the characters appropriated to him in that of Rosetta (N. 121); but we continually find a synonymous emblem, which is employed in the Rosetta stone to signify "enlightening," where the Greek translation has EPIPHANES; and this character, placed between two hatchets facing each other, can only have meant the "illustrious deity," or deities. In this form, the name occurs very frequently at Philae, and in the great temple at Edfou, where it seems to be the latest name. For the PHILOMETORES, we have a character which occurs in some other monuments, and means apparently "mother," the name containing it being found several times in the temple at Ombos. At Kous, or Apollinopolis Parva, there is another Greek inscription of the Philometores and their children; but in the hieroglyphics copied by Denon, the names of the sovereigns seem to be wanting, and that of a young prince only remains, a colossal statue of whom is figured by Montfaucon in his *Supplement,* having the same name in the belt, with the addition of " the son of King Ptolemy ;" it will, therefore, be justifiable to distinguish this personage by calling him *Cleopatrides.* The divine honours which are so often attributed in these inscriptions to the reigning sovereigns, afford us an explanation of the Greek inscriptions to the "Synthronous gods of Egypt," which repeatedly occur; and of the description

"Fraternal gods," as, indeed, Philadelphus and his queen are called in the Greek inscription of Rosetta.

D. ANIMALS.

73. A figure sitting on the ground, and stretching out one hand, seems to imply simply a MAN or person; which is certainly the sense of the enchorial character that commonly answers to it in the manuscripts; but in composition the figure often appears to lose this sense.

74. The horned snake, creeping along, is clearly meant, in some parts of the inscription of Rosetta, for HIM or IT; although it has other senses in composition. It is very remarkable, that the enchorial character, and that of the manuscripts, resembling a *y*, approaches extremely near to the Coptic F, which also means "him;" and HOF, or HFO, is the Coptic term for a snake; so that this coincidence seems to afford us another trace of the origin of the alphabet.

75—78. The BULLOCK, the RAM, the ANTELOPE, and the TORTOISE, are proved to be sometimes representations of the things which they resemble, by their occurrence in inscriptions accompanied by tablets; though some of them have probably, elsewhere, a metaphorical sense. The ram is often represented with two pairs of horns; the one natural, the other imaginary.

78*. The CROCODILE is identified by a very distinct drawing in a manuscript sent home by Mr. Bankes, and is repeatedly designated in the text by a figure representing it. The deity with a crocodile's head is a separate personage, and is denoted by a figure of the same animal with the tail turned under it.

79. The asp or BASILISC is so coarsely represented in the stone of Rosetta, that the object intended by it could not have been conjectured without a comparison with other inscriptions; the context was, however, sufficient to determine its meaning from the examination of this monument alone.

E. INANIMATE OBJECTS.

80. The essential parts of the name of EGYPT seem to be the square and the wheel, signifying "splendid land." In addition to these, or their

rudiments, the enchorial word has at the beginning a character which generally answers to an arm holding a feather, or to the flame of a lamp, an emblem which seems also to relate to Egypt in one of the lines of the inscription of Rosetta. A flame and a heart are mentioned by Horapollo and by Plutarch, as employed in the name of Egypt; but a word occurring so frequently is very likely to have been expressed in a variety of ways. The exact combination of characters generally used on the stone has not been observed in any other inscription.

81. The name of MEMPHIS cannot be determined without some uncertainty; the line of hieroglyphics, in which it is contained, being in several respects obscure.

84. The ladder is well marked as meaning COUNTRY; it may perhaps be intended to represent a field with its divisions; but it is uncertain whether or no it is the same symbol that enters into one of the names of Arueris (N. 13), the sculptures of the Rosetta stone being by no means highly finished.

85. It is remarkable, that the wheel signifying LAND, had been noticed by the Jesuits, as resembling the old Chinese character for the word *field*; but this is the only one, of a multitude of similar conjectures, that has been justified by more complete evidence. (*Phil. Trans.* 1769. Pl. 28.)

86. The star is shown to relate to a real STAR, by inscriptions accompanying the zodiacs. It has also elsewhere a figurative sense, meaning an attendant or *ministering spirit*.

87. The open square is found in both the combinations of characters, which are most commonly used for expressing a TEMPLE; the feather signifies ornament or consecration; the oblong figure, either the sacred inclosure or a sacred seat, the character for a god being sometimes placed within it. The feather is occasionally converted into an inclined oval, the square being at the same time a little altered; a difference which may be observed in other inscriptions, as well as in the Rosetta stone.

88. The character representing a SHRINE so much resembles the object which it denotes, that it was the most readily identified of all that are found on the stone of Rosetta. The character signifying a priest was the second; and the combination of both afforded a full confirmation of the truth of the explanation. The enchorial character for a shrine is derived from the sitting statue which always accompanies it.

89. The open square, occurring in HABITATION as well as in temple, must probably have meant *house* or building; or possibly stone only.

90. The THRONE, or chair of state, occurs in a great variety of tablets. It evidently bears its most natural signification in the character denoting statue, n. 102, and in some other instances; but it appears to bear, in some inscriptions, the metaphorical sense of a residence or habitation...

92. The characters denoting a DIADEM [that is a line over an oval,] are sufficiently determined by the first inscription of the stone; and they so much resemble the corresponding passages of the enchorial text, that we can scarcely hesitate to admit the intimate connexion of the two modes of writing, without seeking for any further proofs.

93. The sacred ORNAMENTS are expressed by three feathers, fixed to a bar, which appears to be held by two arms. The remaining part of the character occurs very frequently as a sort of termination, and seems to answer to —*ments*.

94—99. The boat or SHIP, the SPEAR, the BOW, the ARROW, the CENSER, and the BIER, are sufficiently identified, by the comparison of various tablets with their inscriptions. The ship occurs frequently as denoting the sacred boats, in which the deities are conveyed; though they are not always accompanied by water. But it has been observed, that the Egyptians attributed ships rather than chariots to the sun and moon, as gliding smoothly through the skies. The first part of the enchorial word, which has been supposed to be a B, is evidently identical with the character always found in the manuscripts written in the running hieroglyphics, as the first part of the delineation of a ship.

100. The TEAR, in some of its representations, is very clearly expressive of the thing intended; and this resemblance, together with its frequent attendance on a corpse and a bier, is sufficient to explain its sense. It occurs also sometimes within a border, as a peculiar deity; but it seems to be much more commonly emblematical of Osiris, of Apis, or of Mneuis. It is not unfrequently found as a detached figure, in a kind of pottery, with a green glazing; and may perhaps have been worn, instead of a mourning ring, as a memorial of a departed friend. It has most commonly been called the *equi sectio*, and supposed to represent a horse's head, or the rostrum of a ship, while the ingenious Kircher has made it a

phallus oculatus. Among the antiquities collected by Lord Mountnorris in Egypt, is an eye seen in front, and apparently shedding a tear.

101. The character for an IMAGE seems to mean *a wrought man;* the hands, connected with an eye, appear to be holding an oar, as an emblem of *labour.* The same character, with a slight variation in the form of the eye, means a rower, (n. 136.)

102. The sitting STATUE has no character to imply wrought; but it is followed by a bent line, which seems to be a term of respect, and may possibly answer to OSH, " great." The same bent line occurs on the great sarcophagus of green breccia, as a personification of one of the qualities of Osiris, probably his *magnificence.* It is often exchanged in the manuscripts for the divided staff; and both are represented in the running hand by a figure like a 9 or a 4. In the enchorial text this character seems sometimes to be expressed by a single line, either straight, or bent sideways into an angle, like part of a K.

103. LETTERS are denoted by a character which seems to represent some of the materials employed in writing; and which is indeed not extremely unlike an inkstand figured in Caylus's Recueil, and consisting of two parallel tubes at some distance from each other, with a cover connected by a chain instead of a hinge. Besides the very well marked passage in the Rosetta stone, the character occurs in many manuscripts near the representation of a Thoth employed in writing; and the enchorial character, corresponding to it, is also found in the term *sacred scribes* at the beginning of the inscription.

F. ATTRIBUTES AND ACTIONS.

108. The *crux ansata,* sometimes called the Key of the Nile, is usually employed as a symbol of divinity; but its correct meaning is LIFE, as Lacroze rightly conjectured, although his opinion respecting the origin of the character is inconsistent with the form of its oldest and most accurate delineations; and there is no one instance in which it is so represented as to stand in any relation to a sluice or a watercock. According to Socrates and Rufinus, the Egyptian priests declared to their Christian conquerors under Theodosius, who were going to destroy the Serapeum at Alexandria,

that the cross, so often sculptured on their temples, was an emblem of the life to come. This passage has been understood by some authors as relating rather to the cross without a handle, which is observable in some rare instances, and indeed twice on the stone of Rosetta; but this symbol appears rather to denote a protecting power, than an immortal existence. It happens, perhaps altogether accidentally, that one of the contractions for the word *God*, which are commonly used in Coptic, approaches very near to this character, except that the arms of the cross are within the circle.

109. ETERNITY is represented simply by a serpent rising in an oblique arch, and without horns: the serpent devouring its tail, and making a ring, is never found as an Egyptian emblem. Horapollo says that eternity was denoted by a serpent having its tail hidden under its body; and that such serpents were called URAEI, meaning in Greek BASILISCs, which agrees very well with the sense of the Coptic URO, "king;" but this description answers better to the *asp* of the inscription of Rosetta, which has also some relation to the representations of the deities, though it does not exactly mean immortality.

110. The cross with the serpent is a very common epithet, in the sense of everliving, or IMMORTAL, AENOBIUS: the waved line is in general a preposition, or a termination, meaning *of, to*, or *for;* and it appears to be synonymous with the hat (n. 177.) Almost all authors have very hastily taken for granted, that this character must relate immediately to water, wherever it occurs, although we find it repeatedly in every line of the inscription of Rosetta, where water is not once mentioned. The fact, however, is, that its prototype seems to have been a stream of water or of any other liquid, flowing *from* a vessel, and poured *on* some other object; and that the idea of the liquid was completely dropped in the general employment of the character; while that of the *connexion* only was retained; and the hat or cap being also similarly forgotten, while its connexion with the head of the wearer only was suggested by its figure. In this compound character, we have two particles nearly alike, the semicircle and the line; for that they cannot be very different is shown by the occasional substitution of two semicircles for the combination. One of them seems to serve for the connexion between life and eternity, "life *for*

ever;" and the other to make the new compound an adjective, "liv*ing* for ever."

111. The triangle or pyramid occurs very commonly among other emblems of prosperity and happiness; and it is found in the frize of Montague and Ficoroni, in the decided sense of an offering or a present in general, while, in another place, it is made an offering in its own form; so that we can only interpret it as signifying JOY, or pleasure, or prosperity. (Hierogl. 7 Mqr, Uqu; 9 Re, Rl; 7 Uq, Urs.)

112. POWER appears to be indicated by a sceptre having the head of an animal, which is often placed in the hands of the deities, and often stands with the cross, the pyramid, and the altar, as an emblem of the blessings attendant on the favourites of the gods. It is seldom used in the text of inscriptions, but it occurs once in that of Rosetta.

113, 114. STABILITY is denoted, on the Rosetta stone, and elsewhere, by the altar, which seems to have been fixed in the ground as a column. When repeated, it makes the verb ESTABLISH; but it often occurs singly, and not uncommonly as an unconnected emblem, accompanied by other characters of similar import; and it is sometimes found as a detached figure, formed of glazed porcelain. The two altars are very conspicuous objects in some of the epistolographic manuscripts, and are very useful in comparing them with the hieratic; but the word employed in the enchorial inscription of Rosetta seems to be derived from a different origin.

116. The bullock and the arm, which generally occur at the beginning of the inscriptions on the obeliscs, agree very well with the epithet MIGHTY in the translation of Hermapion. The arm is, in many other instances, used in compound characters.

117. VICTORY is denoted by a branch, perhaps a palm branch, with a semicircle and a circle, sometimes preceded by the waved line.

118. The character signifying FORTUNE somewhat resembles that which denotes "gold" (n. 105), but, instead of the arch, we have an angular line, which seems to be intended for a pair of arms grasping the vase. The whole assemblage approaches, also, a little to the form of a pocket, or purse, as it is frequently delineated.

119. The open square, bent inwards, clearly means SPLENDOUR or

glory, though it is uncertain what object it is intended to represent. In some cases, a crescent seems to be substituted for it, as if it bore some relation to the sun, and the moon afforded a parallel sense.

120, 121. ILLUSTRIOUS is expressed, in the inscription of Rosetta, by the open square, for "splendour," the oval, which signifies addition, or respect, making it a kind of superlative, and the pair of legs, which very naturally convey the idea of BEARING, or possessing; so that the whole makes the epithet EPIPHANES. This assemblage is, in some of the manuscripts, very commonly followed by a bird, or its equivalent, a half arch, apparently serving as an intensitive.

125. The eye, either with or without the pupil, and either preceded or followed by the undulated line, has a sense somewhat similar to all these, and is often employed at the beginning of the honorary inscriptions. On the Rosetta stone it means distinctly RITE, or adoration. The enchorial character, corresponding to it, expresses also simply *doing;* as in Greek the same word signifies to "do" and to "sacrifice."

129. The frequent occurrence of the Egyptian goose, or sheldrake, with a circle over it, between two proper names, sufficiently points out the meaning of these characters, which can only relate to the connexion between them, and which must naturally mean SON; the circle may perhaps be intended for an egg; but in the painted sculptures the disc is red, and the circumference light. The enchorial character nearly resembles the form in which some kinds of birds are usually expressed in the manuscripts. Mr. Bailey has also observed the occurrence of the bird between two proper names, and has identified it with the CHENALOPEX mentioned by Horapollo, as employed to signify son, on account of its courage in defending its offspring. This quality might rather have been expected to lead to its adoption as a symbol for a parent; but its existence in the bird in question is confirmed by the observations of modern naturalists respecting the sheldrake, the *tadorne* of Buffon, which has generally been considered as the chenalopex, and resembles very accurately the best of the hieroglyphic delineations of the bird, although the colours, as exhibited in the *Déscription de l'Egypte,* are not correctly natural.

133. A CHILD, or *infant,* is represented by a figure bent as if sitting, and putting his finger on his lip. This is sufficiently established by the

triple inscription: but it is still further confirmed by a plate of the *Description de l'Egypte* (Antiq. II. pl. 86, f. 1); in which a figure of this kind is represented as immediately derived from the father, who seems to be inspired by a beetle entering his mouth. The manuscripts afford us here some valuable steps, by which the enchorial character is connected with the distinct hieroglyphics. Another figure, which is elsewhere used as corresponding to a beetle, is also found in the enchorial text in the sense of son or offspring.

134, 135. A circle, with an arm holding an angular line, means a DIRECTOR; the angular line is intended for part of a rudder; and the same character, with the addition of the figure of a boat, denotes the pilot or HELMSMAN, as is obvious from many parts of the green sarcophagus. The circle and arm are also found in the character denoting *dedicate*.

136. A pair of arms holding an oar, and connected by a sort of sector, signifies a ROWER; and possibly also a labourer, or workman in general, as in *image*.

137. A stem of a plant, perhaps a reed, followed by an insect like a wasp or ichneumon, but probably intended for a bee, and by two semi-circles, is the complete emblem for a KING; but the reed is often used alone in the same sense, and the insect sometimes occurs without the reed. Plutarch says, that a king was denoted by a leaf, THRION; and Horapollo tells us, that a bee signified a people obedient to a king; hence this symbol might be interpreted *king of men*. Ammianus Marcellinus, however, asserts, more simply, that a king was denoted by a bee. It appears from the manuscripts, that the beginning of the enchorial character, which Mr. Akerblad reads PHU, is derived from the elementary traces representing the reed, the semicircle, a waved line, and a sitting deity, meaning *the divine king*, an assemblage which often occurs on the green sarcophagus, and elsewhere, as applied to a royal person. The remainder of the enchorial character seems to represent a termination consisting of a semicircle and a vessel, which is often added to a name, apparently as a demonstration of respect, like the vessel and the spiral in the case of the god Nilus.

138. CONDITION, or subjection, is denoted by a character which somewhat resembles an altar with an offering of flowers; but which

might also be intended for the cup of a flower, with an insect hovering over it.

139. In the term KINGDOM, the crown is figuratively employed for its wearer; a metaphor common in many modern languages.

140. The character denoting a LIBATION is very indistinctly traced in the sacred inscription of Rosetta, so that it would have been impossible to explain its original form without the assistance of other hieroglyphical monuments. The long water jar, out of which the kneeling figure is pouring a divided stream, somewhat resembles those which a modern Egyptian woman is seen carrying, in a plate of Mr. Legh's second edition.

141, 142. The vase with the stream, which frequently occurs in the character for PRIEST, is sometimes found alone, and must therefore probably relate to some particular CEREMONY performed by the priests, approaching to the nature of a libation. On the stone of Rosetta, the line is a simple curve, not waved; nor is the vase more distinctly represented. Instead of the sitting figure, a foot is sometimes substituted, as in the word *attendant:* and the enchorical character is a more tolerable approximation to this form than to the complete figure.

143. PRIESTHOOD is simply the *condition* of a *priest;* the character prefixed answering to the Coptic prefix MET, and to the Greek termination EIA.

144. The ornaments of the head are very generally used as indicating the person by whom they are worn; and flowers, probably those of the lotus, are frequently found on the heads of the priests, as well as in the inscriptions which accompany them. In the inscription of Rosetta, the sense SACERDOTAL agrees very well with the context, where this character occurs; though it cannot be deduced with absolute certainty from the comparison with the Greek.

145. It is by no means easy to explain why the figure like a buckle should clearly mean an ASSEMBLY: perhaps, however, the upper part may originally have been a crescent, implying monthly; and the scale or basin below is occasionally found supporting some offerings, which are set upright in it; so that the whole may have meant *a monthly exhibition.*

146. The character *god* is made an adjective by the addition of the waved line, and of the long drop, which seem simply to convert it into the

term SACRED; or, if the drop has any other meaning, it can only relate to worshipping or honouring; as the character prefixed in the enchorial text, which is equivalent to the scale or basin, is elsewhere employed to signify *honour* or *attention*. In some other instances, a circle and a waved line seem to be employed in a similar manner, for connecting one character with another like substantive and adjective.

147. An epithet implying CONSECRATED, or dedicated, is composed of a trident, or triple branch or root, followed by a bent line. It occurs very commonly near the beginning of inscriptions, on obeliscs, and elsewhere.

148. A little oblique cross, over an arm with a feather, seems to mean to GIVE, and perhaps to fight and to defend; as, in Coptic, the word TI has both these senses. It is often preceded by a circle and a semicircle.

149. The hand bearing the triangle or pyramid manifestly means, in the frize of Montagu and Ficoroni, to OFFER, as an oblation to a deity.

150. In the inscription of Rosetta, we find the word DEDICATE expressed by a bent line and a sitting figure, with the circle and the arm holding the rudder; the character already interpreted *consecrated* precedes, but it is not absolutely certain that it belongs to the same phrase.

151. The term LAWFUL is naturally enough derived from a deity in his judicial capacity; the figure is preceded by a bird, placed between two semicircles, which must here mean *according to*, answering to the termination *ful*. Sometimes a curved line, supported by a stem, is substituted as a synonym for the figure of the judge.

152—154. The character representing GOOD strongly resembles the figure of a lute, depicted in the chamber of the harps, among the catacombs, and may have alluded to the pleasing sound of music. The plural, with the scale or basin, which implies BESTOWING, makes the epithet EUCHARISTUS, which in Greek is somewhat ambiguous, meaning either grateful or MUNIFICENT; the latter, however, must be its sense in this inscription, because *good gifts* or *delights* may be plural, but *gratitude* not so easily. The lute is also found denoting good in other parts of the inscription. The enchorial character for the scale could scarcely have been suspected to be derived from it, without the assistance of the manuscripts, which constantly exhibit an intermediate form, intended, perhaps, to comprehend one of the lines supporting the scale.

155. The semicircle, with two oblique dashes, seems to mean GREAT in the name of Thoth, who is called in the Greek inscription of Rosetta, Hermes the *great and great:* while, in other places, this character seems almost always to convey the sense of a dual. The enchorial epithet of Thoth is a little like the crown with two semicircles, which is most frequently found among the titles of Osiris, especially when he sits in judgment.

155*. The two kinds of hats, worn by the different deities, seem to be intended by the characters of the Rosetta stone, which express the UPPER and LOWER regions or countries. These two characters are also found together in the green sarcophagus as the names of two goddesses; and they occur together in one or two passages of some of the manuscripts, and in an inscription at Philae; so that, although the representation is very indistinct in the particular case of the Rosetta stone, there is little doubt that the cap of Osiris meant, in this case, *superior*, and that of Hyperion and other personages *inferior*.

160. The ring, which implies a NAME, and which, elsewhere, distinguishes proper names, seems to be an imitation of the label, called a "phylactery" in the Greek inscription of Rosetta, on which the name of a figure was usually distinguished.

161. A disc, with rays descending from it, is one of the few characters in which the form gives us some assistance towards determining the sense, which is found to be ENLIGHTENING; though the Egyptians do not seem to have been very correct in their delineation of the motion of light, which they make to diverge in curved lines, like those described by a common projectile.

162. The square block, the semicircle, and the chain, are employed very clearly in the sense of LOVING or beloved; the Coptic MAI. In the enchorial character the square and semicircle seem to be sometimes transposed, and sometimes changed into an oval.

163. PRESERVER, or saviour, is represented by a sort of trefoil, with a long stem, which answers to a cross or obelisc in the enchorial text; but, in other passages, the character takes the form of a still simpler club: and, in others again, it has something like a bulbous root.

164, 165. A frame, like a ladder, supported by a stem, occurs sometimes as a part of a head dress, but it is difficult to say if it represents any other object. Followed by an arm, and a pair of legs, it signifies SET UP, and this combination of characters is of very frequent occurrence; sometimes also the bent line or divided shaft forms a part of it. In Coptic, *set up* is expressed by *set on foot*, which seems to retain the analogy of the hieroglyphical character. The substitution of a pair of feathers for the legs, however, does not appear materially to alter the sense; the context, where it occurs, requiring the word PREPARE or construct.

G. RELATIONS.

166. Two ovals, with a semicircle and an arm, very clearly signify IN ORDER THAT. The ovals seem to mean *to* or *for*, and the arm action or *doing*; as our own *that* seems to be allied to the German *that*, which means *deed*. The same combination of characters appears to denote, in another passage, *to add to*; and one of the ovals is sometimes omitted. The Coptic may be either HINA or ETHBE.

167. The symbols, employed in the sense WHEREVER, seem to mean separately, *at, in, one*, or *in, place, one*; and, transposing the two last, we may make a very good Coptic word E-U-MA.

168, 169. The arm and chain signify AND or ALSO; and the oval sometimes takes place of the arm, without much variation of the sense; this combination is also found in the sense of *with*, or *together with*. The elementary ideas seem to be *put, with*, or *add, with*. Between the names of Ptolemy and Berenice at Karnak, the arm and chain are separate.

170. The half arch, or the fork, which is perfectly equivalent to it, followed by two curls and two semicircles, means MOREOVER: the reduplication probably resembling that of many of the Coptic verbs, which generally imply a continued action.

171. The combination of the loop or sling, with two semicircles and three ovals, means very clearly LIKEWISE. The loop seems to represent a bucket, intended for one of a pair, to be carried on a pole, as they are frequently delineated in the tablets: so that it must mean a *companion*: and accordingly we find it in a very common epithet of a king, on obelises and elsewhere, with a circle and a bar, denoting *the companion of the sun*, or

simply *resembling the sun*. In the enchorial character for *likewise*, the symbols seem to be transposed, and the loop is doubled.

172. An owl, signifying IN, seems to be nearly synonymous with the half arch, which is also sometimes to be understood in the sense of *all*: both these characters occur also in many instances where they can only be considered as marks of respect, and not very essential to the sense; and in this they resemble the Coptic prefix M, which is a particle not very distinctly intelligible, nor capable of being translated; it is also not a little remarkable, that the M of Akerblad's alphabet is the enchorial character which answers to both of these symbols.

173, 174. A hare over two waved lines is employed, either alone, or together with a head, dash, circle, and dash, which have separately a similar sense for UPON, OVER, or *at*; and it is remarkable, that a similar relation exists in Coptic between EHREÏ, and EJO; JO or DCHO also meaning a head. The enchorial character, in some of its forms, is manifestly a coarse imitation of an animal. The head is always represented in the manuscripts, by a character nearly like a Greek Σ; and this may possibly have been the origin of the Coptic letter JANJIA, if it was derived from a hieroglyphic; but it is equally probable that it may have been intended for a combination of a *delta* and a *chi*. [An Armenian letter of a similar form has also the sound of G soft, or DZH.]

177. The hat, interposed between "an image" and "the king," can only mean OF or FOR; it is often substituted, in passages which are frequently repeated, for the waved line; each being probably equivalent to the Coptic NTE, or rather N; which also sometimes makes an adjective of a substantive, as NNUB, golden, from NUB, gold.

H. TIME.

178. A DAY seems to be very naturally expressed by *splendour* of the *sun*, or sunshine.

179. A crescent turned downwards, with a star and the sun, makes up the character signifying a MONTH; to which a semicircle and a scale or basin are sometimes added. Horapollo says, that a month is denoted by a palm branch, or by an inverted crescent; but the crescent is too indistinct on the stone of Rosetta, to have allowed us to recognise it, without the assistance of the collateral inscriptions.

180. A YEAR is denoted by a bent line with a little projection from the middle, which seems to represent a plant with an annual shoot or bud; it is commonly followed by a semicircle and a block or dash.

182, 183. The sixth month, MECHIR, is remarkable for having half as many crescents as the twelfth MESORE: this relation would without doubt be further illustrated, if we could discover any thing like a calendar, among the immense mass of Egyptian literature which is still in existence. The manuscript, which Montfaucon calls a calendar, merely because it is divided into twelve columns, has no just pretensions to the name.

I. NUMBERS.

186. UNITS are denoted by short lines, like the Roman I. Mr. Akerblad first noticed the first three numerals in the last line of the sacred characters of Rosetta, where the Greek text is deficient, and the words "first and second" only remain; and this observation alone was sufficient to prove that the hieroglyphical characters related to a real language, and were not simply ornamental decorations, as some persons have imagined.

187—196. The twisted line, distinguishing the ORDINAL NUMBERS, answers to the Coptic MAH; which is prefixed to the cardinals in the same sense; in the enchorial text the corresponding character follows the number. The THREE points are more commonly employed, when they follow a word, to make it plural; but when they signify a numeral, they are generally placed immediately above some other character; and, in the enchorial inscription, this numeral is distinguished by making the lines oblique and joining them.

197. For the number TEN we have a Greek *pi*, either square or rounded, not only in the inscription of Rosetta, but in many other places.

198. We find the number SEVENTEEN occurring twice, as a date, in the inscription of Rosetta; the Greek text, in another part, alluding to the same period, has 18; and the enchorial words are too indistinctly marked to allow us to judge of the identity or diversity of the two numbers; but the difference of a day is of no consequence, since the festival of the "assumption of the kingdom" may easily have begun on the 17th of

Mechir, and have continued to the next day, which is the date of the decree.

199, 200. The enchorial character for THIRTY, applied to years, seems to be the same as is elsewhere used in the sense of the *thirtieth day;* but the numbers are almost always confused in the running hand, and exhibit several deviations from the regular system of the sacred characters; the number FORTY, for example, in the remarkable passage relating to the 42 assessors of Osiris, seems to be denoted by a single line with a dash on it.

201—203. The curl, like the figure 9, meaning A HUNDRED, and the notched circle, supported by a cross, denoting A THOUSAND, occur, in several inscriptions, so combined with units and tens, as to leave no doubt respecting the numbers that they represent. This is particularly evident from the consideration of an inscription "believed to have been found at Karnak." *Déscr. de l'Egypte. Ant.* III. Pl. 38. F. 26—30.

204. PLURALS are distinguished by writing a character three times, or by putting three dashes after it; and sometimes, perhaps, though very rarely, before it: occasionally also by repeating a part of a collection of symbols once only. In the manuscripts, the three dashes are generally joined into a crooked stroke; which, in the enchorial inscription, sometimes both precedes and follows the word: while, in other cases, the second stroke is converted into a single vertical line, which serves to limit the extent of the characters meant to be made plural; the representation being so imperfect, that this assistance is more required than in the sacred characters: and it may be observed, that this second mark is never wanting in the enchorial inscription, as it must frequently have been, if the character had been alphabetical; since many of the Egyptian plurals end precisely as their singulars do; and even when they differ from them, it is not by the addition of any one uniform termination...

General Character and Subjects of the Egyptian Monuments.

By means of the knowledge of the hieroglyphic characters, which has been already obtained, we are fully competent to form a general idea of the nature of the inscriptions on the principal Egyptian monuments that are extant. Numerous as they are, there is scarcely one of them which we are not able to refer to the class either of sepulchral or of votive inscriptions; astronomical and chronological there seem to be none, since the numerical characters, which have been perfectly ascertained, have not yet been found to occur in such a form as they necessarily must have assumed in the records of this description: of a historical nature, we can only find the triumphal, which are often sufficiently distinguishable; but they may also always be referred to the votive; since whoever related his own exploits thought it wisest to attribute the glory of them to some deity, and whoever recorded those of another, was generally disposed to intermix divine honours with his panegyric. It has, indeed, been asserted, that the Egyptians were not in the habit of deifying any mortal persons; but the inscription of Rosetta is by no means the only one in which the sovereigns of Egypt are inserted in the number of its deities; the custom is observable in monuments of a much earlier age; indeed, in such a country, it might be considered as a kind of dilemma of degradation, whether it was most ridiculous to be made a divinity, or to be excluded from so plebeian an assemblage; but flattery is more prone to err by commission than by omission, and, consequently, we find the terms King and God very generally inseparable. The sepulchral inscriptions, from the attention that was paid in Egypt to the obsequies of the dead, appear, on the whole, to constitute the most considerable part of the Egyptian literature which remains, and they afford us, upon a comparative examination, some very remarkable peculiarities. The general tenor of all these inscriptions appears to be, as might be expected from the testimony of Herodotus, the identification of the deceased with the God Osiris, and probably, if a female, with Isis; and the subject of the most usual representations seems to be the reception of this new personage by the principal deities, to whom he now stands in a relation expressed in the respective inscriptions; the honour of an apotheosis, reserved by the ancient Romans for emperors, and by the modern for saints, having been apparently extended by the old Egyptians to private individuals of all descriptions. It required an extensive comparison of these inscriptions to recognise their precise nature, since they seldom contain a name surrounded by a ring in its usual form: sometimes, however, as on the green sarcophagus of the British Museum, a distinct name is very often repeated, and preceded by that of Osiris; while, in most other instances, there is a certain combination of characters, bearing evident relation to the personage delineated, which occurs, after the symbols of Osiris, instead of the name; so that either the ring was simply omitted on this occasion, or a new, and perhaps a mysterious name was employed, consisting frequently of the appellations of several distinct deities, and probably analogous to the real name. That the characteristic phrase, so repeated, must have had some relation to the deceased, is proved by its scarcely ever being alike, in any two monuments that have been compared, while almost every other part of the manuscripts and inscriptions are the same in many different instances, and some of them in almost all; and this same phrase may be observed in Lord Mountnorris's and Mr. Bankes's manuscripts, placed over the head of the person who is brought up between the two goddesses, to make his appearance before the true Osiris, in his own person, and in his judicial capacity, with his counsellors about him, and the balance of justice before him. (Hierogl. 5. E F G e f.) In this instance the phrase consists of the names "Hyperion" and the Sun, preceded by a block and an arm with an offering (Plate LXXVIII, O), and it may be interpreted, without any violence, " the votary of Hyperion and of Phre." In a small manuscript, engraved by Denon, the part, which resembles the characteristic phrase of other manuscripts, is followed by the name of a king which is nearly identical with that of the father of the Pseudomemnon in the British Museum; the one having the hieralpha laid flat, the other the traces of the pedestal, which is equivalent to it...

The coffins of the mummies, and the large sarcophagi of stone, are generally covered with representations extremely similar to some of those which are found in the manuscripts. The judicial tablet is frequently delineated on the middle of the coffins; above it are Isis and Nephthe, at the sides; and apparently Rhea in the middle, with outspread wings. The space below is chiefly occupied by figures of twenty or thirty of the principal deities, to whom the deceased, in his mystical character, is doing homage; each of them being probably designated by the relationship in which he stands to the new representative of Osiris. In the sculptures, the figures are generally less numerous; the same deities are commonly represented as on the painted coffins, but without the repetition of the suppliant, and in an order subject to some little variation. The large sarcophagus of granite, in the British Museum, brought from Cairo, and formerly called the Lover's Fountain, has the name of Apis, as a part of the characteristic denomination. This circumstance, at first sight, seemed to make it evident that it must have been intended to contain the mummy of an Apis, for which its magnitude renders it well calculated; but, when the symbols of other deities were found in the mystic names upon various other monuments, this inference could no longer be considered as absolutely conclusive...

We have a most valuable example of a dedicatory inscription, on a larger scale, in the decree preserved on the stone of Rosetta, which, besides its utility in affording the only existing clue for deciphering the hieroglyphic characters, gives us also a very complete idea of the general style of the records of the Egyptian hierarchy. Of the triumphal monuments, the most magnificent are the obeliscs, which are reported by Pliny to have been dedicated to the Sun; and there is every reason to suppose, that the translation of one of these inscriptions, preserved by Ammianus Marcellinus, after Hermapion, contains a true representation of a part of its contents, more especially as " the mighty Apollo" of Hermapion agrees completely with the hawk, the bull, and the arm, which usually occupy the beginning of each inscription. These symbols are generally followed by a number of pompous titles, not always very intimately connected with each other, and among them we often find that of " Lord of the asp bearing diadems," with some others, immediately preceding the name and parentage of the sovereign, who is the principal subject of the inscription.

REMARKS

ON

MR. BELZONI'S PLATES.

The Plates, which accompany Mr. Belzoni's work, afford us an excellent opportunity of illustrating and confirming some of the interpretations of the hieroglyphical characters which have been published in the Article Egypt of the Supplement of the Encyclopædia Britannica.

Plate I. The principal figure of the catacomb is represented sitting on a throne or chair of state: his belt or apron is marked with the name of King Psammis, N. 50 of the Article Egypt.

The square tablet suspended from the neck may either mean "*approved by the sun,*" or possibly "*distinguished by the erection of an obelisc:*" the wand or rather mace held in the hand has an inscription to this purpose. "*The good god, the giver of comforts to both the regions, the protector of religious rites, the King Osiris Psammis the son of Nechao, the companion of the Sun and of Osiris.*" The five columns of hieroglyphics over the altar contain a similar inscription, with the interposition of some additional epithets.

The vulture soaring over the king seems to represent some tutelary genius: it holds a ring, which in other cases serves for the support of plumes or other honorary trophies. The inscription between the vulture and the head implies "*The royal superintendent of both the regions, the joyful,* or *brilliant, the great, the living, the powerful.*" But to judge from other inscriptions, those in particular of Mr. Montague's frizes, this line belongs rather to the vulture than to the king. The vertical column behind the figure contains a number of similar epithets. "*The minister of the gods, the living, the established, the powerful, the great guardian of sacred rites, the possessor of riches, the adorner of the priesthood, the noble, like the Sun, everlasting, adding honour to his ancestors.*" There is not sufficient authority for all the terms here employed, but such of them, as are not probable translations of the symbols, are at least not improbable illustrations of them.

The altar before the figure is loaded with an offering of some substance cut into slices, and standing in a compact mass: whether of fruit or of cakes, or of any other nature: above it is written, "*The priests, attendant on the ceremonies of the good god, do him honour by these rites, the living, the mighty, the benefactor of the country.*" These characters face the former, and belong to figures supposed to be looking towards the king, whether they may be represented in any other part of the drawing or not.

Plate II. The tutelary vulture here expands both its wings, and holds in each foot a ring with a plume supported by a handle. Over the vulture's left wing we have "THE GOOD GOD THE GIVER OF COMFORTS TO BOTH REGIONS? PSAMMIS, THE BRILLIANT AND JOYFUL, THE LIVING;" over the right, "THE SON OF THE DISPENSER OF DELIGHTS? NECHAO THE COMPANION OF THE SUN." The lower part of the plate consists of two halves, which either are or ought to be the exact counterparts or reflections of each other, though a few of the characters are turned the wrong way. The vulture is represented holding the symbol of life and the ring in one claw, standing on a cushion or carpet, which has generally been taken for a bowl or basin, but which is here represented as a flat surface; below it stands the flowery head-dress of the priests, perhaps intended to imply the elevation and consecration of the objects above it; at least the vulture occupies the place of honour, and seems to be the object of the respect indicated by the characters of the three columns facing it, which together exhibit an inscription exactly resembling that which is almost universally found on the obeliscs. The hawk and globe are the symbols either of the sun, or of his son Arueris, and it is difficult to say which of these deities is here intended; he has a basilisc erected before him as a mark of honour, or of divinity. The bull and the arm together imply the *mighty*: the owl occurs so often that it scarcely seems to affect the sense, but it appears generally to denote some respect: it is followed by a character like the half of a composite flower, which, to judge from the passages in which it occurs, seems to mean *delight*; it is sometimes exchanged, for instance, with the lute, which means *good* or *graceful*: the sceptre, with its appended plume and drapery, is an emblem of *dominion*; the bent line means *great*, the flowering sceptres probably *flourishing*, the handled cross *living*. These symbols are always inclosed in a square with a fringe, as if they were intended for a banner, on which the hawk is standing, and they seem rather appropriate to an emblematical representation of that kind than intended to convey any precise sense expressible by distinct words: which however would be something like this: *The glorious sun, mighty, the source of delight, the great governor, flourishing in life and beauty, [has protected]*. The next column has " THE KING OSIRIS PSAMMIS, [*powerful and venerable*."] The third " THE SON OF *the warrior* NECHAO OSIRIS." In fact, Osiris seems to be little more than the MAKARIOS of the Greek inscriptions: but when Osiris appears in his individual capacity, as a judge or otherwise, his name is generally accompanied by some distinguishing epithets, such as are found in the fifth line of the first Plate.

Plate III. The names of Psammis and Nechao, having their phylacteries surmounted with globes and plumes, and suspended over what seem to be stools with a fringe of drapery hanging from them, are here placed in the middle of three figures in different situations, all of which seem to represent the tutelary winged goddess, frequently found on the coffins of mummies, and possibly meant for Rhea. The names are also found on each side of the upper figure with expanded wings, without any other addition than *King Osiris Psammis, the Son of Nechao*. Over the wings of the figure is " *Everlasting honour to the powerful goddess, the daughter of* the Good Genius, that attends on the commands of the Greatest of the Deities, *the directress* of the son of him who dispensed comforts to the upper and lower countries." A part of this inscription is repeated over each of the lower figures, which seems to be *The goddess daughter of the* Good Genius. The last character is different on the two sides, on one a trapezium only, on the other a bowl or carpet, a semicircle, and a bar with a prominent edge.

Plates IV, V. These are representations of Psammis doing homage to, or rather embracing, the figures of two singular deities, with their feet joined, who appear to be personifications of some of the qualities of Osiris. Over the king, in Plate IV, is his name, followed by the epithet Vulcanian, or devoted to Phthah. Over the deity, who holds the scourge, or flail, and the hook, we have " THE SON OF the powerful, the honourable and venerable deity, the preserver, the great judge: divine rites of the priesthood are offered." A beard case seems to be attached to the cap before the ear, as in many other instances. The deity of the Fifth Plate, is a personification of *Stability:* a pair of weeping eyes are inserted between the two lower plates or bust, and the hands hold the hook and flail. Over the king is KING OSIRIS DISPENSER of *comforts to the countries.* PSAMMIS the powerful.

Over the spreading horns of the deity we find THE GOD STABILITY, THE IMAGE of the *nature of divine things.* Behind the legs, *Divine rites to Stability the powerful: the great minister of sacred rites, the priesthood declares it:* LIKE TO THE SUN.

Plates VI, VII, and VIII. The three next plates exhibit the most remarkable feature of the whole embellishments of the catacomb: they contain a sort of procession, beginning with four red men, with white kirtles, followed by a hawk-headed divinity, then (Plate VII.) four white men, with thick black beards, and with a simple white fillet round their black hair, wearing striped and fringed kirtles: after these (Plate VIII.) are four negroes, with hair of different colours, wearing large circular ear-rings, having white petticoats supported by a belt over the shoulder: lastly, three white men, with smaller beards, and curled whiskers, bearing double spreading plumes in their heads, tattooed, and wearing robes or mantles spotted like the skins of wild beasts. Now Mr. Belzoni is disposed to consider the red men as Egyptians, the black bearded men as Jews, and the tattooed as Persians: and these conjectures seem to accord remarkably well with the history of the times concerned: for Necho, the father of Psammis, is known both from sacred history and from Herodotus, to have had wars with the Jews, and with the Babylonians; and Herodotus mentions his expedition against the Ethiopians. So that this procession may very naturally be considered as consisting of captives made in his wars, though they are not held by a cord, as we often find captives represented on other monuments, but, as it is said, are exhibited standing on the back of a long serpent, as if brought by some supernatural means into the power of the conqueror.

In the II Chronicles, xxxv. 20, we find this passage, "After all this, when Josiah had prepared the temple, Necho, King of Egypt, came up to fight against Carchemish by Euphrates: and Josiah went out against him. 21. But he sent ambassadors to him, saying, What have I to do with thee, thou King of Judah? I come not against thee this day, but against the house wherewith I have war: for God commanded me to make haste: forbear thee from meddling with God, who is with me, that he destroy thee not. 22. Nevertheless, Josiah would not turn his face from him, but disguised himself, that he might fight with him, and hearkened not unto the words of Necho from the mouth of God, and came to fight in the valley of Megiddo. 23. And the archers shot at King Josiah; and the King said to his servants, Have me away, for I am sore wounded. 24. His servants therefore took him out of that chariot, and put him in the second chariot that he had; and they brought him to Jerusalem, and he died, and was buried in one of the sepulchres of his fathers. And all Judah and Jerusalem mourned for Josiah." And again, Chap. xxxvi. 1. "Then the people of the land took Jehoahaz the son of Josiah, and made him king in his father's stead in Jerusalem. 2. Jehoahaz was twenty and three years old, when he began to reign, and he reigned three months in Jerusalem. 3. And the King of Egypt put him down at Jerusalem, and condemned the land in an hundred talents of silver, and a talent of gold. 4. And the King of Egypt made Eliakim his brother king over Judah and Jerusalem, and turned his name to Jehoiakim. *And Necho took Jehoahaz his brother, and carried him into Egypt.*" We are also informed in Jeremiah xxxvii. that in the time of Zedekiah the son of Josiah, who reigned instead of Coniah the son of Jehoiakim, the army of Pharaoh " was come forth out of Egypt: and when the Chaldeans that besieged Jerusalem heard tidings of them, they departed from Jerusalem:" soon after, however, Nebuchadnezzar brought back his Chaldeans, took the city, and carried Zedekiah, blinded, and in chains, to Babylon. The history related by Herodotus agrees, as accurately as could be expected, with several of these particulars. Book 2.

"Now Necos was the son of Psammetichus, and reigned over Egypt; it was he who began the canal leading to the Red Sea, which Darius the Persian afterwards completed: its length being four days' sail, and its breadth such that two galleys might manœuvre in it abreast of each other: the water being derived from the Nile. It begins a little above the city of Bubastis, and is carried near to Patumus, a city of Arabia, discharging itself into the Red Sea. The part first dug was that which lies in the plain of Egypt near to Arabia: along this plain the mountain in which the quarries are situated runs along towards Memphis; and the canal is carried for a considerable distance at its foot from west to east, and then turns south through a pass in the mountain towards the Arabian gulf. Now the shortest and most expeditious passage from the Northern Sea, or the Mediterranean, to the Southern, or Red Sea, beginning from mount Casius, which is the boundary of Egypt and Syria, is a distance of a thousand stadia: this is the shortest way, but the canal is much longer, its course being indirect. And in digging this canal, in the reign of King Necos, 120 thousand Egyptians lost their lives. After this the King gave up the attempt, having been stopped by an oracle, which declared that he was only labouring for the advantage of the barbarian, or foreigner: and he employed himself in warlike pursuits, building galleys both on the Mediterranean and on the Red Sea, the traces of his dockyards still existing: and these he used when he had occasion for them. *And Necos joined battle with the Syrians in* MAGDOLUS, *and conquered them, and after the battle he took* CADYTIS, *a large city of Syria.* The dress which he wore when he obtained these victories, he dedicated to Apollo, sending it to Branchis in Milesia. And having reigned in the whole sixteen years, he died, and left the throne to his son PSAMMIS. But PSAMMIS only reigned six years; and having made a warlike expedition into Ethiopia, he died, and was succeeded by his son APRIES, who was the most fortunate of the kings down to his time, except his great grandfather Psammetichus, and reigned twenty-five years."

The city Cadytis is again mentioned in the third book as "belonging to the Syrians of Palestine," and " as a city not much less than Sardes:" so that there is sufficient proof that it could only have meant Jerusalem, which was sometimes called *Kadesh*, or holy.

This agreement of sacred and profane history with so remarkable a representation, in this interesting catacomb, is too striking to allow us to abandon the explanation without a struggle. But it must be confessed that there are some difficulties in reconciling the name of Psammis with some other monuments, and in particular with a most important fragment of an enumeration of the kings of Egypt, discovered by Mr. Bankes, at Abydos. In this there are only two kings intervening between this Psammis and the Memnon of the ancients: so that if Pliny is right in his account of this obelisc, the popular tradition respecting the colossus, supposed to represent Memnon, must be erroneous. This indeed it would not be difficult to admit, as very likely to have happened in the case of any popular tradition; but there is a still greater difficulty in the inscription found by Mr. Bankes on the leg of the colossus at Ebsambul, in which Psammetichus is mentioned; and if this was the same Psammetichus, as appears in some respects to be the more probable, it would follow that the king who founded that temple was more ancient than Psammetichus. But it is abundantly certain that our Psammis was prior to the founder of that temple: so that either that Psammetichus must be of much later date, as the employment of the Greek Ψ in the inscription would indeed appear to indicate, or this catacomb was not constructed in honour of the son of Pharaoh Necho. It has also been observed by an accomplished scholar, who is much attached to the pursuit of Egyptian antiquities, that, according to the testimony of Herodotus, (II. 169) all the kings of this dynasty were buried at Saïs, and that we must either reject this evidence, or admit that neither Psammis nor Necho can be the personages here represented. We may however hope that future researches will furnish us with materials that will enable us to remove this and many other difficulties, which at present envelope the chronology of the kings of Egypt.

Plate XIII. The inscription being omitted, it is impossible to say to what goddess or queen the bullock is intended to be sacrificed.

Plate XIV. The female figure appears from the inscription, though it has been very hastily copied, to be the queen *mother* of the " AMASIS" of the Article Egypt.

Plate XV. The inscription would probably have determined if this bull is meant for Apis, or for any other animal of the species.

Plate XVI. This tablet is too imperfect to allow us to form any conjecture respecting the sense of the inscription. We have in it, " Minister of the Royal temple . . . Living God."

Plate XVII. The two female figures, and the three basiliscs, in this plate, seem to relate to one deity only, the same that is represented with outstretched wings in Plate III; and the inscriptions are all nearly of the same import: it is not uncommon to see a basilisc employed as a personification of a goddess, whose name is placed over it.

Plate XVIII. The goddess exhibited in this plate is the *Buto* of the Article Egypt. The most remarkable circumstance about the figure is the tight drapery, which is divided into irregular hexagons, without any regard to the alteration of their form by the projection: and this disproves the argument respecting the flatness of the carpet or basin, as inferred from the division of its surface into equal squares. Again, each perpendicular or oblique series of hexagons contains an inscription with the name and titles of the " *Good god Psammis, the son of Nechao :*" in compliment to whom the goddess is dressed in his livery. She holds the king's right hand with her left; and with her right she presents to him a breastplate which hangs round her neck, and which seems to be the *Alethia*, or *Truth* of Diodorus, who tells us that the president of the judges wore " a breastplate adorned with jewels, which was called Truth . . . . and delivered the sentence of his colleagues, by the form of *touching the successful party with the symbol of justice*, which he wore." Article Egypt, Sect. v.

The king has his name on his belt, and over his head, as in other cases, accompanied by a few of the usual epithets. The name of the goddess is also followed by her relation to the *Great God*, which is not very distinctly intelligible.

Plate XIX. Osiris is seated on his throne of state, supported by pillars or feet, in the very appropriate shape of the emblem of stability, with those of life and dominion interposed : he holds a hook in each hand, and in the left the flail also: the king, with his name on his belt, and over his head, is presented to him by *Arueris*, the son of the Sun, as appears from the inscription behind him. Osiris is styled king of the gods, and is attended by a goddess, whose name resembles that of Buto, with the addition of a frame or harrow, or perhaps a cage, which she also carries on her head, so that it is clearly intended as a characteristic distinction, and probably as denoting a different deity. Of Buto's attributes, we only know that she was the nurse of the children of Osiris and Isis, and that she is sometimes represented as a companion of Isis, generally with the horns, and sometimes perhaps with the head of a cow: but the harrow is not usually one of her emblems. The dress of Osiris here, and that of the personifications of his attributes in Plate V, is almost entirely white, which, according to Plutarch, was the usual dress of Osiris; though sometimes it was black. The whole tablet is surmounted by the winged globe, accompanied by the inscription which is scarcely ever wanting where this deity is introduced: the symbols constituting the name seem to be a bent bar and a hand: the following characters appear to mean the *sacred father of the protecting powers, living, unalterable, reigning, and ministering.*

Plate XXXV. *Sakiet;* perhaps derived from *Senskita,* the old name; as the inscription has the *Senskitic Isis.*

THE END.

LONDON:
PRINTED BY THOMAS DAVISON, WHITEFRIARS.

www.ingramcontent.com/pod-product-compliance
Lightning Source LLC
Chambersburg PA
CBHW070833230426
43667CB00011B/1780